OFFICIAL REPORT

OF THE

SEVENTEENTH INTERNATIONAL

CHRISTIAN ENDEAVOR CONVENTION

HELD IN THE

AUDITORIUM ENDEAVOR AND HALL WILLISTON,

CENTENNIAL PARK, AND IN THE GOSPEL

TABERNACLE AND MANY CHURCHES.

NASHVILLE, TENN., JULY 6 – 11, 1898.

First Fruits Press
Wilmore, Kentucky
c2015

First Fruits Press
The Academic Open Press of Asbury Theological Seminary
204 N. Lexington Ave., Wilmore, KY 40390
859-858-2236
first.fruits@asburyseminary.edu
asbury.to/firstfruits

THE COMMITTEE OF '98.

OFFICIAL REPORT

OF THE

SEVENTEENTH INTERNATIONAL

CHRISTIAN ENDEAVOR CONVENTION,

HELD IN THE

AUDITORIUM ENDEAVOR AND HALL WILLISTON, CENTENNIAL PARK, AND IN THE GOSPEL TABERNACLE AND MANY CHURCHES.

NASHVILLE, TENN., JULY 6–11, 1898.

Copyrighted. 1898, by U. S. C. E.

PUBLISHING DEPARTMENT,
UNITED SOCIETY OF CHRISTIAN ENDEAVOR,
646 WASHINGTON ST., BOSTON, MASS., U. S. A.
1898.

Committee of '98.

Headquarters: Room Endeavor, Hotel Tulane, Nashville, Tenn.

Motto of the Committee of '98.

I am only one; but I am one.
I cannot do everything;
But I can do something.
That I can do I ought to do,
And by the grace of God I will do.

CHAIRMAN	REV. IRA LANDRITH
VICE-CHAIRMAN, LOCAL EXCURSIONS	J. D. BLANTON
SECRETARY	B. G. ALEXANDER
FINANCE	EDGAR JONES
HALLS	M. B. PILCHER
RECEPTION	J. U. RUST
ENTERTAINMENT	PEYTON ROBERTSON
MUSIC	ERSKINE REED
REGISTRATION	JOEL O. CHEEK
PRESS	W. L. NOELL
USHERS	E. S. McFADDEN
PULPIT SUPPLY	T. A. REYNOLDS
DECORATIONS	MRS. M. C. DORRIS

Convention Musical Directors and Singers.

MR. E. O. EXCELL, CHICAGO, ILL.
MR. P. S. FOSTER, WASHINGTON, D. C.
MR. E. F. YARNELLE, ELKHART, IND.
MISS YARNELLE, ELKHART, IND.
MR. C. L. ESTEY, PHILADELPHIA, PENN.
JUBILEE CLUB OF FISK UNIVERSITY.
LEADER, MRS. G. W. MOORE.
KNOXVILLE QUARTETTE, KNOXVILLE, TENN.

CHRISTIAN ENDEAVOR AGLOW IN DIXIE.

A Second Siege of Nashville. — No Mason and Dixon's Line in Christian Endeavor. — The Opening Sessions of the Seventeenth International Convention.

THREE AND A HALF decades ago Nashville was for many a stirring time the focus of great forces. The week of July 6 to 11 the brigades of an army mightier than any that ever bore sword and gun, an army engaged in a war more momentous than all other struggles put together, centred in that beautiful Southern city. From the distant Pacific and the pine woods of the North, from the great prairie States and the hills pierced with mines, and from every corner of the pleasant Southland, the cars arrived, ringing with song, fragrant with prayer and joyful expectation.

As in former years, to those on official excursion-cars it was a Convention all the way. For example, Massachusetts began at Pittsfield, Mass., with its station filled with bright-faced Endeavorers met to speed the delegates on their journey. This route lay through Cincinnati, where prettily decorated depots, and earnest bodies of Endeavorers distributing their gay circles of cardboard, and lobbying committeemen buttonholing the leaders, all made it warmly evident that Cincinnati wanted the International Convention of 1899.

Louisville Endeavorers, too, gave hearty greeting, with streamers of Kentucky's purple and white, with refreshments in the railroad Young Men's Christian Association, and with a smiling Kentucky welcome.

Mammoth Cave afforded opportunity for a veritable subterranean Christian Endeavor convention. We never before realized the beauty and fulness of our Endeavor vocabulary of song. As the throngs of merry young Christians, charmingly and grotesquely masquerading in the weird cave costumes, in which some were frights and some piquantly pretty, wound along these stupendous galleries, they had a song ready for all occasions. After bending and twisting down through the Corkscrew, what more appropriate than, "I'm coming, I'm coming, for my head is bending low"? After sitting in the tangible darkness of the Star Chamber, what more fitting than "There's sunshine in my soul," "The light of my soul is Jesus," "Let a little sunshine in"? Then after the cockcrowing and the sunrise, which every visitor to the famous cave remembers, what better than "The morning light is breaking"?

They piled stones high upon the Christian Endeavor memorial heap. They sat in Jenny Lind's chair. They stood by the bridal canopy, but no one accepted the obliging offer of it for a ceremony. Possibly they feared the hornet's nest which came next. They prompted the guide when he failed to get off with sufficient promptness the traditional jokes. Reverently at the close they sang the doxology in the Methodist chapel, and so ended that delightful subterranean Christian Endeavor convention.

There were attached to the Massachusetts train two cars filled with Michigan troops on their way to Chickamauga, and with them was held another and far more characteristic convention. The long aisle was crowded with Endeavorers, and many a patriotic song was sung and many a hymn of the church militant. President Gardner, of Massachusetts, gave them a rousing talk, telling them about our Endeavorers that died on the *Maine* and those that fought at Manila. President McCrory, of Pennsylvania, talked to the boys in a manly and noble way, and told them that they could be all the better soldiers if they would be Christians.

The blue-shirted and slouch-hatted fellows listened respectfully, and many of them eagerly; for not a few of them were themselves Endeavorers. Hearty hand-shakes for all of them, and heartfelt "God bless you's," and some of the visitors' Bibles transferred to knapsacks, and this blessed railroad convention was at an end.

It was with just such journeys, happy and helpful, that the Endeavorers came up to Nashville.

They found a city gorgeous with the Convention's white and scarlet, and doubly bright with the flitting white caps of the reception committee. They found thousands of Southern homes offering splendid hospitality. They found a city full of beautiful wide-open churches.

They found, as soon as they could wash off the travel-stains, a most remarkable series of opening sessions crowding eleven large meeting places.

These eleven meetings were held in the following churches: Vine Street Christian, Rev. W. E. Ellis, pastor, presided; First Presbyterian, Prof. J. D. Blanton, Nashville, Tenn., presided; First Cumberland Presbyterian, Rev. I. D. Steele, pastor, presided; Tulip Street Methodist Episcopal South, Rev. A. P. McFerrin, pastor, presided; Arrington Street Cumberland Presbyterian, Rev. Charles Manton. Paris, Tex.. presided; Moore Memorial Presbyterian. Rev. Angus MacDonald, pastor, presided; Grace Cumberland Presbyterian, Rev. W. T. Rodgers, pastor, presided; Second Presbyterian, Rev. J. H. Morrison, D.D., pastor, presided; McKendree Methodist Episcopal, Rev. J. C. Morris, D.D., pastor, presided; First Baptist. Rev. J. B. Hawthorn, D.D., pastor, presided; Fisk University Chapel, Rev. James L. Hill, D.D , Salem, Mass., presided.

The general topic for all the meetings was "Enduement with Power." The following speakers delivered each a thirty-minute address. Rev. Ralph W. Brokaw, Utica, N.Y.; Rev. J. Z. Tyler, D.D., Cleveland, O.;

Rev. Wm. Patterson, Toronto, Ont.; Rev. Teunis S. Hamlin, D.D., Washington, D. C.; Rev. John H. Elliott, Rochester, N. Y.; Rev. J. Wilbur Chapman, D.D., Philadelphia, Pa.; Rev. Gilby C. Kelly, D.D., Birmingham, Ala.; Rev. W. I. Chamberlain, Madanapalle, India; Rev. M. Rhodes, D.D., St. Louis, Mo.; Rev. Chas. Manton, Paris, Tex.; Rev. Canon J. B. Richardson, London, Ont.; Rt. Rev. Samuel Fallows, D.D., LL.D., Chicago, Ill.; Rev. J. H. Garrison, LL.D., St. Louis, Mo.; Rev. David James Burrell, D.D., New York City; Rev. Floyd W. Tomkins, Jr., Providence, R. I.; Rev. John T. Beckley, D.D., New York City; Rev. I. N. McCash, LL.D., Des Moines, Ia.; Rev. Howard Agnew Johnston, D.D., Chicago, Ill.; Rev. I. J. Spencer, Lexington, Ky.; Rev. A. C. Dixon, D.D., Brooklyn, N. Y.; Bishop Alexander Walters, D.D., Jersey City, N. J.; Bishop B. W. Arnett, D.D., Wilberforce, O.

Each of these meetings, so blessed in deepening the spiritual life of all in attendance, was brought to a close by a short season of quiet communion with God. These closing moments were in charge of Rev. Ernest Bourner Allen. Lansing, Mich.; Mr. W. T. Ellis, Philadelphia, Pa.; Rev. Rufus W. Miller, Reading, Pa.; Rev. Thornton B. Penfield, Brooklyn, N. Y.; Rev. Chas. J. Palmer, Lanesboro, Mass.; Rev. J. F. Cowan, D.D., Boston, Mass.; Mr. Miles M Shand, Washington, D. C.; Rev. E. H. Pence, Janesville, Wis.

[NOTE.—It is regretted that all of the addresses were not reported in full, but herewith is given many of these opening addresses.—*Scribe*.]

Address by Rev. Teunis S. Hamlin, D.D.,
Washington, D. C.

SURRENDER OF THE WILL AS THE CONDITION OF RECEIVING THE HOLY SPIRIT.

We are living under the dispensation of the Holy Spirit. He takes the absent Saviour's place. Whatever Jesus did for his disciples during his earthly life the Spirit is now to do for us. If our Lord taught, counselled, guided, reproved, warned, comforted; if he was companion, friend, brother; if he so represented God as to be able to say, "He that hath seen me, hath seen the Father;" all this the Spirit now does and is — and even more. Such was Jesus' definite promise before he left the world. The truth that he had been obliged to leave untaught because of the inability of men to understand and appreciate it should be all disclosed by the Spirit. The comfort that he had so freely bestowed should not fail, but be ministered even more unstintedly by the other Comforter. Jesus came that men might "have life, and have it abundantly;" and the imparting, nurturing, and perfecting of that life is the Spirit's work. As the Saviour led a little band of men hither and thither about Galilee and Judea, so the Spirit will lead us through all the mazes, perplexities, and wanderings of our daily life. It is God who so loved us that he gave his Son. It is the Son who died for us, making the atonement on which rest all our hopes of pardon and eternal life. But it is of the Spirit that we are new-born; enlightened to perceive the love of God and the sacrifice of Jesus, the Christ; called and constrained to repentance; won to love for the God whom we had feared, and the Redeemer to whom we had been indifferent; drawn into the life of self-denial and devotion that we had dreaded; and led on to perfected Christian manhood, "to the measure of the stature of the fulness of Christ."

We are thus utterly dependent upon the Holy Spirit for salvation. From the first movings of desire to be followers of Jesus, through all the lifelong following, until we are safe forever in a sinless and glorious heaven, we gain all our inspiration and power from him. The entire divine part of religion is his work within us, while the human part of religion is receiving, and cherishing, and using the divine.

What, then, are the human conditions, within our control, of receiving the Holy Spirit? No question could be more important, since this is just asking, How are we to become and continue Christians?

Now the answer that we will give will turn upon our conception of where, within ourselves, the Christian life is centrally located. Some would say, "In the emotions." They make religion a matter of feelings. "Is not love the great thing?" they ask. "And is not love a matter of the feelings?" "Yes," to the first question, but a most emphatic "no" to the second. Love is the great thing; is the whole law of God; is evidence that one is divinely born anew. But just because love is so great it cannot be a matter of the feelings, which are superficial and variable. Jesus says all the "heart, soul, mind, and strength" are to be gathered up, and thrown without reserve into the act of loving. Moreover, the feelings have no independent existence, but are creatures of circumstances, coming and going, rising and falling, waxing and waning, as conditions vary from hour to hour. But love moves steadily and mightily onward, quite regardless of the feelings. Whether I am sick or well, happy or sorrowful, exultant or despondent, I love my child just the same. I may express more, or be more demonstrative, at one time than at another, but beneath a varying manner the stream of self-denying devotion flows with uniform current. This is the controlling principle of my life as a father; the source of all my feelings, happy or wretched, according as my child does well or ill.

So love toward God is the sum and substance of religion. It is not an emotion, but a principle; the most profound, solid, and enduring of which human nature is capable. It draws in its train emotions of great joy or great misery according as it is directed toward worthy or unworthy objects, God or self, holiness or sin. But these emotions are dependent upon love, as daylight is upon the rising of the sun. They have no self-originated and self-sustained existence.

Yet it is in the feelings that many would locate religion. When they feel well-disposed toward Jesus, feel contented and happy in religious observances, feel inclined to sing hymns, offer prayers, give money to missions, or bestow care upon the poor, or sick, or outcast, they regard themselves as followers of Christ. But when such exercises pall upon them, or when they find delight in other matters, they at once conclude that they have no religion. So they consider a state of exalted feeling the condition of their receiving the Holy Spirit. They believe that as soon as their emotions are ecstatic he will certainly work in and through them mightily. They accordingly associate his presence especially with what we call "revivals;" where there are unusual means of grace; exceptionally urgent appeals to the feelings; where fear and hope are greatly aroused; where the contact of a crowd stimulates the subtle excitement that flows from one to another, and sways all before they are aware what is transpiring. Hence they conclude that the thronging audience at church, or convention, or camp-meeting, offers the best opportunity for receiving the Holy Spirit. They yield to the emotions of the place and hour; spur their jaded feelings; sing more loudly; respond more vehemently; and when nature is fairly exhausted, believe that their end is gained.

But what will come on the morrow? Reaction, inevitably. The ecstasy of yesterday will seem a delusion. They will doubt the reality of this experience, and be strongly tempted to go on from that to doubt the reality of religion altogether. If it was only emotion, it was worthless. If, being chiefly emotion, it still had a basis of intelligent decision, it may have moved them onward a step, and a long step, toward the reception of the Holy Spirit. Just this is the legitimate and important work of the feelings, — to move men to action. They are not themselves action, but they may incite to it. For this purpose it is wise and right to avail of the contact of the crowd, of masterly eloquence, of soul-stirring song and prayer. But after all, the coming of God, the Holy Ghost, will not be in " wind, or earthquake, or fire," but in a " still, small voice."

Others locate religion centrally in the intellect. Education is their watchword. To know seems to them the vital thing. They point out that our Lord said that to know God and himself is life eternal. But everything turns on what we mean by "knowing." For instance, Jesus says, " Ye shall know the 'truth.'" But he instantly adds, " The truth shall make you free; " i. e., free from the dominion of evil. For purposes of religion the knowledge is nothing without the freedom. We often fail to discriminate between religious truth and all other truth, as to their purpose and use. The truth of science is an end in itself. When the geologist has ascertained the facts about the earth, his work is done. Art applies those facts to human uses; builds houses, constructs highways, organizes manufactures and commerce; transmutes the scientific truth into the industries and comforts of life. Theology is a science; religion is an art. When the theologian has ascertained the truth about God, man, sin, and salvation, his task is finished. But just here the Christian's task begins. How shall he use this truth for his personal redemption? It does not become religion until so used. Up to that moment it is as purely scientific as mathematics or botany.

Knowledge, then, is not in itself a preparation for receiving the Holy Spirit. The greatest theologian that ever lived, if he were only that, might not be at all a spiritual man. Indeed, it is a matter of special comment when such a man is notably spiritual. Our common instinct is to regard vast erudition as hostile to that humble and docile temper which is essential to spirituality. And the apostolic word confirms our instinct : " Knowledge puffeth up, but love buildeth up."

This is not at all to depreciate religious knowledge, but only to define its place and use. We are all solemnly bound to know every last fact that we can learn about God and ourselves. A more utterly false proverb was never formulated in ages of darkness and oppression than that "ignorance is the mother of 'devotion.'" It is the mother of superstition, bigotry, and cruelty. It makes men cringe in abject fear, as though the God of love were full of hate and revenge. It makes them hypocrites, assuming physical postures of reverence that the heart disavows, and uttering confessions of faith that the intellect pronounces irrational and absurd. Ignorance is to be dreaded and shunned as a fatal spiritual plague.

But one is not to turn from ignorance to knowledge alone, as though it were religion, or even religious. Not when we have committed many chapters of the Bible to memory, or perfectly learned some catechism, or mastered the historic confessions of faith, have we met the condition of the Holy Spirit's coming to us with power. These are good things to do. But we may do them all perfectly, and still be as cold and hard and unlovely as before. They may minister to pride instead of humility; may crowd us further and further from God, instead of drawing us into his presence. We are to get all the truth we can; but unless it emancipates us as we get it it is not religious. To know God is life eternal; but the knowing that is this only begins in the intellect, whence it moves mightily forward to subdue the will and revolutionize the life.

And now we have spoken the word that describes the citadel of religion, because it describes the citadel of personality. That word is the " will." Far below the emotions, and far back of the intellect, lies the will. We wonder at the majestic spectacle of armor and armament, towering above the waves, that make the battleship an object of faith to friends and terror to foes; but deep in the hold are the mighty engines that drove the *Oregon* over its seven thousand miles from the Pacific to the Atlantic, and without which the heaviest guns and the most expert gunners would be utterly useless. The will is the engine of this great and marvellous thing that we call a man. Whatever his endowment or equipment, however splendid his capabilities, no one can predict whether they will be used for good or for evil, against right or against wrong, until the will discloses itself. It may drive them headlong in rebellion against God, or carry them all most efficiently into his service against the kingdom of sin.

Now as religion is just the right attitude of the whole man toward God, and as the Holy Spirit's mission is to bring us into that attitude, it is evident that the vital work must be done at the centre and source of personality; viz., the will. The Spirit of God cannot come to us for illumination and cleansing and power until the will consents. However delightfully the emotions may be excited; however clearly the intellect may perceive the essential truth of God, sin, and salvation; whatever experiences of feeling we may have and testify to, or whatever confessions of faith we may make; — all are unavailing while in the depths of our nature the will quietly arrays itself against God. And, on the other hand, there may be little or no emotion; there may be a minimum of knowledge; but if the will cordially surrenders to God the man is carried; and truth, and joy in it, will follow in good time. We shall not have conquered Cuba until our flag flies over Havana, its capital. There may then still be outlying districts to subdue, but without waiting for such details of consummation we can then truthfully call the island our own. And when the will has bowed itself to God, with or without profound emotion, with or without clear and complete intellectual processes, the essential work of salvation is done, and we may unhesitatingly call ourselves children of God through faith in Jesus Christ.

Now, from whatever point we view personal religion, this truth will clearly appear. Is religion obedience to God? But the essence of obedience is surrender of the will, which leads in its train all duties of obedience? Is it love? But this, as we have already seen, is not an emotion, but an all-embracing principle which can lie nowhere else than in the will. Is it faith? But faith is not the assent of the intellect to truth scientifically known, but the commital of one's self, and centrally of one's will, to truth incarnate, to Jesus himself; so that, in the apostolic phrase, "faith is wrought through love." Is personal religion friendship with God or, to hold exactly to our theme, with the Holy Spirit? Let us not shrink from this form of words, though it sounds unfamiliar. Jesus called us "friends;" and whatever he did the Holy Spirit does. We are seeking the condition of receiving the Spirit for salvation and for power; let us say, reverently, it is the tender to him of our friendship, and the earnest purpose to make him our friend. And this is a matter of the will, as all friendship substantially is. It involves, of course, some knowledge or acquaintance. It naturally entails some pleasure. But the pivotal thing, if you and I are to be friends, is the consent of our wills. Only this can enable us to bear and forbear; make us patient with each other; keep love aflame in hours of separation, or doubt, or unfavorable appearances. If our friendship rests only upon pleasure in each other, upon similarity of tastes and mental pursuits, it will be short-lived. But if it springs from appreciation of such sterling traits of character as determine us to cultivate, cherish, and retain each other's friendship, it will survive all mutations of feeling. Only those value friendship aright who purpose to win and keep it; that is, who locate it in the will. And only thus can we gain the friendship of the divine Spirit. He waits and longs to bestow upon us that friendship, with all its priceless blessings; but the indispensable condition lies within our own power; it is the surrender of our wills to him.

The duty to which we are thus summoned at this hour is by no means the easiest possible. It is far pleasanter to be swayed by emotion, or to revel in mental gymnastics, than to take in hand that sturdy and often stubborn servant of our life, the will. We are not here, however, to find what is pleasant, but what is true and right. We seek the choicest gift that heaven can bestow, the permanent indwelling of the Holy Spirit for salvation and power. That gift is ready. It waits only upon our readiness to receive it. And that will be ours the moment we intelligently and heartily surrender our wills to God.

Address by Rev. M. Rhodes, D.D.,
St. Louis, Mo.
THE RELATION OF THE HOLY SPIRIT TO CHARACTER.

One of the most significant facts of our time, as well as one of the most inspiring prophecies which now lifts its light upon us, is the disposition to question the effectiveness of mere sentiment or emotion as a method for the recovery and highest development of our human life, and to put forward the one adequate process, so distinct in the revelation and purpose of God. It is not easy to eliminate human wisdom as a final force from our participation in God's processes, but it is very necessary. All evangelical faith and power depend not upon ignoring human gifts, but upon rigidly keeping them in their place. This growing sense of dependence, this yearning for the conscious presence of the divine within us, and of the operation of God through us, is the gratifying assurance that we are more and more discovering our correct position in God's kingdom, and the measure of our resources, not in things about us, but in the illimitable God. I think we are coming to wholesome surprise at our weakness in the higher realms of thought and service. We are beginning to see that there is a supreme need that God would grant to the Church "a spirit of wisdom and revelation." The answer to this fitting prayer means that we should "no longer be dazzled by the knowledge which relates to things seen and temporal; 'it would be outshone by the transcendent glory of things seen and eternal.'" A kind of modern practical atheism has been touching everything holy; but I am grateful in the conviction that it is going into bankruptcy, and that God's people are awaking to the fact that the Holy Spirit is the appointed administrator of the affairs of the Church on earth, and that our self-helplessness and dependence are not partial but complete.

In any continuous and specific utterance on the Holy Spirit we must guard against one mistake. The proportion of truth must be maintained. From the mediation of Christ and the Word the Spirit of God must not be isolated. The Spirit is not here to speak of himself, nor to operate upon the human mind and heart distinct and apart. Any effort which puts the "Lamb slain from the foundation of the world, and slain to its final judgment," in the background is plainly a departure from the truth as it is in Jesus, and a decided source of limitation both to Christian character and service, for which there is no remedy so sure and successful as the full apprehension and abiding contemplation of Jesus Christ in his work of ransom. Through the mediation of our Lord we have the gift of the Spirit; and by the illumination of the Spirit we are taught the full significance of our union with him, what Christ is to us in his propitiation, how he is with us by his promises, and that he is in us, which is the final mystery. It sounds well to hear one speak of God's nearness, but the enlightened, trusting soul has a large privilege in Christ.

> "To think of Him by our side
> Is almost as untrue
> As to remove His shrine beyond
> Those skies of starry blue.
>
> "For God is never so far off
> As even to be near.
> He is within. Our spirit is
> The home *He* holds most dear.
>
> "So all the while I thought myself
> Homeless, forlorn, and weary,
> Missing my joy, I walked the earth,
> Myself *God's sanctuary*."

What a wonderful revelation by the Spirit is this supreme fact to the soul! It is the girding of power and of comfort as well. "I can do all things through Christ which strengtheneth me." God's Spirit in this not only reveals the truth to the soul, but he fills the soul with the energy of his grace, "giving us summer when it is winter, light when it is darkness, tenderness and tremblings, joys and delights that are not of this world."

What I desire to make plain is that the Holy Spirit is always bringing the grace of Jesus to us, and that we can only realize the enduement of power by implicit trust in the sacrificial work of our Lord, whether for pardon or greater grace. Of these things of God we are taught in the school of the Spirit. It is not the preacher, not the theologian, but the Holy Ghost, who "interprets the meaning of the atonement; and through him we learn that the deep inward quickening spirit of religion reveals itself through Christ in his travail, in his agony, in his wounds."

Nothing is more noticeable in the disciples than their larger apprehension of Christ, and their increased devotion to him, after the promised power of the Spirit had come upon them. The revelation of the Spirit here is the very secret and source of the enduement with power.

Let us look now at the relation of this enduement of power to character. The work of the Spirit in behalf of a saved man is twofold. He is to develop a saint no less than to qualify for service. His graces are just as essential as his gifts. Maybe we are thinking just a little too much of the Spirit's qualification for service, and not enough of his need in personal spiritual development. What a man or woman attempts to do in the kingdom of God often fails on others because of what others fail to see of Christian excellence in them. The human temple the Spirit would fill must first be made clean and strong and beautiful by the Spirit. The consummation of character is "the mind of Christ." We must remember that with the coming of Christ and the Holy Spirit there has been an immense addition to Christian character. Our Lord set it before us in himself; we may attain to it by his grace and Spirit. As we should not be content with the character of the past, so we should realize that it would not suffice for the demands of the present. It belongs to the greater works which our Lord declares should be done after his going, to furnish such personal expression of his own character and life, such possibilities of grace and goodness, as were unknown to the world before. "Many prophets desired to see these things which we see and have not seen them," to count among themselves such a company of saints, and with Bishop Andrews to give God "thanks for their faith, their hope, their labors, their truth, their blood, their zeal, their diligence, their tears, their purity, their beauty." We should blush to be content with a righteousness that is limited to a bare legal obedience like that of the scribes and Pharisees, with no glint of God's love and pity, and without a touch of that gentleness and purity and self-sacrifice which have made Jesus supreme and illimitable in the ages.

What we need to impress upon the world to-day is a largeness, a charm of character, that reveals Christ incarnated in humanity. I hear men talking constantly of an inspired Bible. Ah! my friends, we can trust the Book. I wish we were as sure of some other things. What we need is inspired men and women. It is the living epistle that is most widely read, but the living epistle is the creation of the Holy Ghost. Oh the power of it when in seeing this you see Christ! Such a character involves our daily habit, temperament, home life, every relation to God and man. In a world like this, in a day like ours, it will cease to be commonplace; it will become peculiar; but the world will say, "The tabernacle of God is with men." Such character not only furnishes the sublimest history of the Church, but her strongest testimony as well. The varied test of centuries has proven it and it has not faltered; by many images of mercy, heroism, self-sacrifice, and unfailing devotion; by the splendid courage of the martyr and the patient, masterly endurance of the missionary; proved itself in many a patient and suffering life, in many a noble endeavor that challenged the completest self-abandonment, in many a peaceful and triumphant death, and last, but not least, in the beautiful peace and service and holiness of many homes. The simple faith, the utter self-forgetfulness, the high fortitude, unusual magnanimity, and kindness shining like stars in cloud-rifts under abuse and slight, the lowliness of mind which enables the great and famed to rise above all social prejudice and custom, to descend to men of low estate, that some ministry of Christ may be rendered,—this is the character God's

Spirit only can work within us, and this, I venture to say, must not only be one fruit of the enduement with power, but one of its sources.

We are wont to think much of Mr. Gladstone's intellect as we add our note to the diapason of praise which the good of all lands started at his death, and which still rolls on. Surely he was gifted beyond the average of men; but his highest culture, that which has made him greatest, and has impressed me most deeply, was his spiritual quality. What a superb, imperial character was his by the grace of God! There see the enduement of power in an eminent degree. How much of his Christ-mindedness now comes to view, as does the splendor of the bow on the retreating clouds! When he was Chancellor of the Exchequer he often met a poor crossing-sweeper on his way to church. He was careful to recognize him. Missing him one day, he learned he was ill, and obtaining his address, he went to see him. When the rector of the parish called he asked the sick man if any one had been to see him. "Yes; Mr. Gladstone." "What Mr. Gladstone?" said the surprised clergyman. "Why, Mr. Gladstone himself," said the poor man, wondering that any one should think that there was another. "He often speaks to me and gives me something at my crossing; and when I fell ill he came to see me and talked with me and read to me."

When the great man was wont to spend his vacation at Fasyne there had not as yet been established a post-office, and the mail was brought from a village near by by an old woman. She is described as a repulsive person given to cursing and never known to enter the house of God. All shunned her but he who was the peer of all. Mr. Gladstone was frequently seen through the open door of her humble cottage kneeling on the earthen floor in prayer for Mary Laing. In Parliament, the great and famed, the friend and foe, listened to him; but in these scenes which men are often disposed to count as commonplace heaven threw open its gates and he was a spectacle to the angels.

But the great Commoner not only showed what manner of man he was in the homes of the poor and of the lost, but everywhere. I may note one instance in which the excellence of his motive and the largeness of his manhood were splendidly illustrated.

Mr. Chamberlain, long his political friend, finally abandoned him for his own selfish ends, and marked his desertion with great personal abuse of his opponent. Mr. Gladstone made no reply, nor was there any chill in his usual kindness and courtesy. Later, a gifted son of Mr. Chamberlain entered Parliament. His entry was announced by a speech full of severest invective against the great man nearly four times his age. The father heard it. At its conclusion there was an intense anxiety to know what Mr. Gladstone would say. Though the house was wrought up to the highest pitch of excitement, Mr. Gladstone was entirely self-possessed, his great brow lifted above the fog of such littleness, splendid and radiant in the light of the conscious approval of God's favor. He spoke quietly of "the great promise of the young member," congratulated the father of such a brilliant son, and "expressed the deepest sympathy in the pride which his former colleague must feel in the eloquent effort to which they had just listened." The entire body, unused to anything like sentiment, was still and moved with emotion, save Mr. Gladstone, who proceeded with his speech, as if nothing extraordinary had happened. There was no cant nor affectation about Mr. Gladstone; his greatness was simply asserting itself. It was a sublime triumph of grace, an illustration of the character the Holy Ghost builds, quite as much an expression of the enduement with power as if he had stood up to preach a sermon. He was too large for any selfish motive or malign feeling. So was Christ formed within him. So was his love shed abroad in his heart by the Holy Ghost, so was he possessed and led by the Spirit, that all those fetters and limitations of character so common even among good men were set aside. He was a freeman made so by the truth; no longer the poor, hampered servant, but the privileged friend of the Lord Jesus. It is impossible to estimate his power anywhere without taking into account his relation to Jesus Christ, and to the Holy Ghost. I grant that as the ruder chisel and unskilled hand can do something with the block of marble, so education, and culture, and refined home manners can do something for character; but they can never make it live in the higher spheres of thought, and feeling, and service; they can never complete it. God alone can finish his own work. Saul of Tarsus was respectable in his time; but Paul gloried in tribulation, and in what he endured, as well as in what he said and did, revealed the mind of Christ. He lost no time, allowed no opportunity to slip away, weakened and defeated no good service in fret and worry, in hasty judgment, and in the waste and weakness of looking after wounded pride, in taking care of his character, or in the bluster of a hundred things which indicate a small and not a strong nature. He was composed, wise, well-adjusted, prompt, busy, kind, prayerful, and mighty through God to the pulling-down of strongholds. How many good men and women there are who are weak because of such defects as irritability, impatience, a hasty tongue, prejudice, unbelief, pride, envy, — a petty, hurtful brood that no gifts of learning or skill can compensate, but that must always prove to the Christian life what the ball and chain do to the prisoner's limbs. I know no way to burn up this dross but by the fire of the Spirit. There is no defect of character, no error that debilitates and enslaves the human mind, for which the Holy Spirit is not the effective remedy. Because he is here, character may be, and is in many instances, distinguished by such elements as wisdom, and reverence, and gentleness, and love; and these are elements of power. Dean Church points out that "after Christ, the soul of religion — I do not say the foundation, or necessary adjuncts, or organs, but the soul and energetic principle of religion — could be only love, love with its freedom, its inventiveness, its generosity, its joy. Obedience to God must take the shape of love. After such a self-sacrifice, self-sacrifice and self-devotion must become not an occasional heroism, but the natural and habitual mood of the religious soul."

And this is the mind of Christ wrought in men and women by the Holy Spirit. What the Spirit is here to do with and for human character, what we should seek daily to attain, and what I venture to say is one feature and result of the enduement of power not frequently dwelt upon, but most needful, is clearly set forth in the New Testament. Walk as Christ walked. Know his love, the fellowship of his sufferings, and the power of his resurrection. Paul is full and rapt in his descriptions, and most "suggestive of what is true and bright and happy and noble in character, breathing the profoundest peace, the strongest moral effort, the most joyful surrender to God, all that purity of thought and motive without which man cannot hope to see the face of God in the next world, or to live the life of God in this." Passing by that wonderful epic in the Corinthians on love, listen to this outburst, as if some hand had flung open a gate of heaven: —

"Put on, therefore, as God's elect holy beloved, a heart of compassion, kindness, humility, meekness, long-suffering; forbearing one another, and forgiving each other, if any have a complaint against any; even as the Lord forgave you, so also do ye; and above all these things put on love, which is the bond of perfectness. And let the peace of Christ rule in your hearts, to the which also ye were called in one body; and be ye thankful" (Col. 3: 12-15, R. V.). And as showing the illimitableness of personal excellence by the grace of the Spirit, and as if to transcend this splendid "summary of all that can make a man not only holy but great, not only a saint but a hero," he adds, "Finally, brethren, whatsoever things are true, whatsoever things are honorable, whatsoever things are just, whatsoever things are pure, whatsoever things are lovely, whatsoever things are of good report; if there be any virtue, if there be any praise, think on these things" (Phil 4: 8, R. V.). Then Peter comes to swell the great harmony in words as beautiful as the music is sweet: "Finally, be all like-minded, compassionate, loving as brethren, tender-hearted, humble-minded; not rendering evil for evil, or reviling for reviling; but contrarywise blessing; for hereunto were ye called that ye should inherit a blessing" (1 Peter 3: 8, 9, R. V.). It is all very beautiful and wholly possible, through Jesus Christ by the power of the Spirit. Much will be said in this city to-night about the enduement with power for service, and it is well; but I cannot get rid of the thought that we are more disposed to think of service, the objective thing, than of character, the subjective need. We shall be weak and limited in our service until the Spirit has wrought in us the mind of Christ. This is the source of power. What the Master was we must believe we can be, and we must seek to be, only surely by the Holy Ghost. Such there have been; such there are now. They are the witnesses of the King in all God's varied, wide kingdom. They are his co-laborers, helping, one here, another there, hastening the advancing conquest, until the holy city, new Jerusalem, descends out of heaven from God having the glory of God. Let our faces be turned to this great acquisition, the mind of Christ. This is the enduement with power.

"If there is, therefore, any comfort in Christ, if any consolation of love, if any fellowship of the Spirit," if these things are not the merest fancies and delusions, then in all you think, and say, and do, "have this mind in you, which was also in Christ Jesus; who being in the form of God, counted it not a prize to be on an equality with God, but emptied himself, taking the form of a servant being made in the likeness of men; and being found in fashion as a man, he humbled himself, becoming obedient even unto death, yea the death of the cross" (Phil. 2: 1, 5-8, R. V.).

Address by Rev. Chas. Manton,

Paris, Tex.

THE PROMISE OF THE FATHER.

There are many promises in the blessed Word, but of all, there is only one promise that is spoken of as *the* promise, exalting it above every other peculiar to the Christian,—a promise to be claimed, a gift to be received, and a command to be obeyed. Just what that promise is is learned from Acts 1: 4, "Wait for the promise of the Father, which, saith he, ye have heard of me," when coupled with Acts 1: 5, "But ye shall be baptized with the Holy Ghost not many days hence,"—a promise belonging to all of the children without respect of person, ever available, never variable in its fulfilment, only as we are variable in our service. The promise is one in perpetuity, in its bestowment, not once for all, but continuously repeated. There may be currents of greater power and breadth; they may flow now swift, now slow; of greater or lesser depths; but ever flowing, like the gulf stream, warm with power to kiss into beauty whatever it touches. The promise of the Father is rich indeed to those who wait. The power and the blessing of united waiting is what we need to learn.

How slow we are to wait for the Father! Our thoughts, our plans, our arrangements, rather than his.

Happy, indeed, are we, this Wednesday evening, to be found in multitude, waiting for the promise of the Father. This great Convention, well planned, devoutly prayed for, will be made the place of power as we tarry for the baptism of the Holy Spirit.

The history of this great movement has ever borne the impress of waiting hosts, and more than ever have we come to feel the need of divine wisdom; more than ever are we conscious that the only power for the redeemed life is the power of the Holy Spirit. The promise is, "Receive ye." This united waiting for the baptism of the Holy Spirit will equip us for service; this tarrying and emptying will fill our lives with his presence, and make conscious our acceptance, and qualify us with saving power.

This waiting is eclipsed by the divine waiting,—the waiting of a Father, that he may give himself to the waiting one.

What a marriage! For what? That the glory of the bridegroom may be revealed in the bride.

Waiting, waiting for divine equipment. The soldiers of our homes, the boys of the army, wait, for their equipments come to them piece by piece. The divine equipment is ready; the tarrying is with you. "Theirs not to reason why; theirs but to do and die," has come down to us to be repeated over and over. Gallant blunders are made to-day. It is ours, as soldiers of the cross, to learn obedience, remembering we have the promise, "Ye shall be baptized with the Holy Ghost," while the command comes to wait in fellowship with one another until hearts are so blended with oneness of purpose that the blessing will come upon all, here and now, in renunciation of self, of unfaithfulness and indifference, until we are able to go forth in the energy of the Spirit to win the world to Christ.

Waiting, united in voice, heart, and hope, for the descent of the Holy Spirit, the one supreme promise of Christ to his friends? "Behold, I send the promise of my Father upon you." He is the source. He is the beginning. All that is nearest to him cometh forth from him.

Upon that day when the Holy Spirit fell upon the assembled multitude it was a day to be remembered, in that each individual was made to experience the baptism, the worth and power of it intensified, because it was in the possession of each; no question arose as to its reality, and no doubting one, to question its conscious experience.

This day is memorable because of the gathering of the disciples of the Christ, in this nineteenth century, from the North, South, East, and West, to receive, day by day, spiritual enduement, knowing full well that the Father waits with the promise to clothe us with the power of his Word and the Spirit, in the full knowledge that it is not by might, nor by power, but by the Spirit, that God proposes to equip for service.

This enrobing is for the individual; it is to be the seal and assurance of the development of the Christ life, the investure of all true wisdom and holiness. Those to whom this blessing came possessed characters and fitness for the work that left much to be desired, but when endued with power from on high they were wonderfully equipped for, and adapted to, the noble mission for which they were appointed.

They stood in gentle but bold defiance before Jewish councils, and in the presence of Roman swords, only to become strong and to endure, rejoicing because they were counted worthy to suffer shame for Christ. They were strong in defence of the resurrection, strong to grasp the great truths of the mission of Christ. It was the promise of the Father that made these men strong in the midst of every obstacle, every opposition and persecution, opening their eyes to see the might and majesty of the kingdom of grace.

It is this we need; it is this that will make us strong; it is this, Christian Endeavorers, as workmen of the Lord, we need to strive for,—that power from the Holy One without which the most heroic efforts will fail; with it the youngest saint can be engaged, and his humblest endeavor will succeed.

What need we, then, with our youthful fire and energy, zeal and zest, but to realize the full meaning of the promise of the Father?

Remember, it is the illuminated man who becomes the centre of illumination. The rain and sunshine fall alike on all the beauty of the garden, but it becomes white to the lily, red to the rose; different and various, one thing to the tree, another to the vine, yet it is all to all. In itself it is rain and sunshine, but adapting itself to the nature of each, and as received, becomes appropriate to each.

So the promise of the Father is the coming of the Holy Spirit, one and undivided, distributing himself to every man as he will.

Wait! Tarry! Be still! for the promise of the Father "for ye shall receive power, after the Holy Ghost is come upon you."

Address by Rev. J. H. Garrison, LL. D.,
St. Louis, Mo.

SOME HINDRANCES TO SPIRITUAL ENDUEMENT.

The chief characteristic of the Christian dispensation as seen by the prophets, by the forerunner of Christ, and even by Christ himself, is the new and more copious outpouring of the Holy Spirit, and that, not upon a chosen few, but "upon all flesh." The universality of this gracious gift was no less a striking feature of the new dispensation than the peculiar forms of its manifestation. The Prophet Joel, as quoted by the Apostle Peter on the occasion of the beginning of the fulfilment of his prophecy, said: "And it shall be in the last days, saith God. I will pour forth of my Spirit upon all flesh: and your sons and your daughters shall prophesy. And your young men shall see visions. And your old men shall dream dreams: yea, and on my servants and on my hand-maidens in those days will I pour forth of my Spirit; and they shall prophesy."

It will be seen from this that the outpouring of the Spirit in the present dispensation is to be "upon all flesh." That is, no racial or national lines are to constitute a bar to this divine gift. Neither is it to be limited to sex, for "your sons and your daughters shall prophesy." It is wonderful how the Holy Spirit ignores our ecclesiastical rules and usages! Nor is it to be limited by age, for "your young men shall see visions, and your old men shall dream dreams." Nor are social conditions to stand in the way of the universality of this spiritual enduement, for "on my servants and on my hand-maidens in those days will I pour forth of my Spirit; and they shall prophesy." There is then no sectional line, no color line, no age line, no social line, in the realm of the Spirit. All may claim and enjoy the benefits of that fulness of spiritual blessing peculiar to the Christian age.

It is in harmony with this prophecy of Joel that John said of his own ministry, in contrast with that of Christ, "I indeed baptize you in water unto repentance: but he that cometh after me is mightier than I, whose shoes I am not worthy to bear: he shall baptize you in the Holy Spirit and in fire" (Matt. 3: 11). Again, the Apostle John attributes to Christ's forerunner the following language: "I have beheld the Spirit descending as a dove out of heaven; and it abode upon him. And I knew him not; but he that sent me to baptize in water, he said unto me, Upon whomsoever ye shall see the Spirit descending and abiding upon him, the same is he that baptizeth in the Holy Spirit" (John 1: 32, 33). Jesus himself said to his disciples, after his resurrection, when charging them to tarry at Jerusalem until they were endued with power from on high, "For John indeed baptized in water; but ye shall be baptized in the Holy Spirit, not many days hence" (Acts 1: 5). Since Christ is here designated as the one who ministers the Holy Spirit, we may infer from this fact the universality of the gift, since he is the Saviour of all men. It is safe to infer, also, that this gift of the Spirit which he confers is vitally related to the progress and triumph of his kingdom.

But all do not enjoy the illuminating, life-giving, and strength-imparting influence of the Holy Spirit. Not all Christians, even, have availed themselves of those gifts of the Spirit which it is their privilege to enjoy as followers of him whose special prerogative it is to administer the Holy Spirit in such measure as each one is fitted to receive. And this brings us to state some of the hindrances to the enjoyment of the fulness of the divine power which is the spiritual birthright of all Christians. First of all, let it be said with emphasis that the hindrances to the reception of the Holy Spirit in such measure as to fit each one to do the duty that is laid upon him are not upon the divine side, but upon the human. Jesus taught that his Father is more willing to give the Holy Spirit to them that ask him than earthly parents are to give good gifts to their children. Besides, we have just seen the universality of the divine purpose in bestowing the fulness of spiritual blessings upon men in this age. We must look, therefore, to human conditions to find the hindrances to the reception of the Holy Spirit. Of course, we encounter here the old problem of divine sovereignty and human freedom. But we waive it with the single remark that there is a reciprocity between the divine and human spirits, which the Scriptures everywhere recognize, and to which every man's consciousness testifies. God always and everywhere respects human volition, and moves upon the human spirit in harmony with the laws of man's mental and moral constitution. If this were not so, the salvation of men would be simply a question of the divine will, and that would be no question at all, for God wills the salvation of all men. But man's co-operation with God is no less necessary in the attainment of the highest spiritual blessing than in the matter of forgiveness or reconciliation with God.

It is plain that unbelief or disobedience would prove an effectual barrier against the reception of the Holy Spirit. The condition of soul out of which unbelief and disobedience arise is in such antagonism with the spirit of Christ that reciprocity is impossible. Faith and love are the lines which connect the human soul with the divine, and along which the divine life and power are conveyed to the human spirit. The stronger the faith and the love, the stronger will be the current of divine life that flows into the human soul.

When Peter told the convicted Pentecostians to "repent and be baptized every one of you in the name of Jesus Christ, unto the remission of sins, and ye shall receive the gift of the Holy Spirit," he was laying down a fundamental law in the kingdom of God; namely, that an utter turning away from the sins of the past, a complete about-face, and an absolute, unconditional surrender to Jesus Christ, as Lord of all, are conditions precedent to receiving, in its fulness, the gift of the Holy Spirit. Is it not probable that the lack of a thoroughgoing repentance that reaches to the very core of the moral being and reverses the moral judgments, and a lurking spirit of disobedience which hesitates to make a full and open surrender to Jesus Christ, are serious hindrances to the reception, on the part of many professed Christians, of the enduement of the Holy Spirit? The question at least deserves the serious consideration of every one who feels that his spiritual life is not what it ought to be, and that there are certain causes which hinder his progress in the divine life.

A wrong *motive* may vitiate our desire for the enduement with power from on high. Why do we desire the Holy Spirit? Is it that we may excel our brethren in this or that line of service which we have decided to enter upon, and thus acquire reputation and influence among our fellows? Simon Magus wished the Holy Spirit in order to promote his own glory and gain. God does not grant his Spirit for such unworthy purposes. Are we willing to serve God in any humble sphere where his providence may place us? And are we desirous of having such measure and such particular gift of the Holy Spirit as will fit us for service in that sphere? If so, we are in that condition of mind and heart which fits us to receive the spiritual gift which we need.

Perhaps we have a wrong *theory* or *understanding* of the Holy Spirit, which hinders our reception of him. It may be that we are looking for ecstasies and rhapsodies as the only sign of the presence of the Holy Spirit. Failing to receive this proof, and refusing to accept others, we may be unconsciously rejecting the Holy Spirit. Perhaps we have been expecting such an illumination of the Holy Spirit as will free us from the obligation of studying and being guided by the Holy Scriptures. We regret that there are those who claim such a measure of the Holy Spirit as to render them independent, in a measure, of the teaching of Christ and of his apostles. It is very safe to say that any impulse that leads one to treat lightly any command or doctrine of Christ and his divinely guided apostles is not from the Holy Spirit, but from an unholy spirit.

One of the most common hindrances, we think, to that enduement with power from on high which all Christian workers need in order to the highest efficiency is the lack of any high and worthy *ideal* of Christian life and Christian service. Too many of us are content with being nominal Christians, and living a poor, lean, spiritual life. There is no hungering and thirsting after righteousness. There is no exalted conception of what a Christian ought to be, and do, and suffer, for the sake of Christ, and the extension of his kingdom. About all that many of us aim at is to keep our lives sufficiently respectable to maintain fellowship with the Church. We have not planned any hard service for the Master, any work of self-denial and self-immolation. There is a lack of that heroism in our Christian life which was so prominent a characteristic of the disciples of Jesus in the first age of the Church. There are too few Hobsons in the Church, who are willing to sacrifice their own selfish ease and, if need be, *life itself*, on the altar of Christian service, in order to defeat the enemies of Christ. Such a spirit of self-abandon in the service of God would invite and insure such a measure of divine power as would qualify us for success in every righteous undertaking. If we would undertake larger things for God, and *harder* things, and things which require and anticipate the co-operation of Omnipotence to bring them to a successful issue, we might well expect larger measures of divine power to accompany our efforts. God dealeth with us as with sons. What father is there among you who, if his son, for the honor, protection, and welfare of the family, engage in some hard and difficult undertaking, will not stand by him with whatever measure of support he is able to render him, until his task is accomplished? Not only so, but the father would feel proud that he had a son willing to engage in so difficult a task for the sake of the family, and capable, with his help, of bringing it to successful completion. Who can doubt but that it would delight the heart of our heavenly Father if his children here on earth, banking on his infinite resources, should engage in the largest and most difficult enterprises, looking to the extension of his kingdom in the world and the redemption of the race? Who believes that he would withhold the necessary enduement of power from those who would give themselves, unselfishly and for his glory, to enterprises that look to world-wide conquest in behalf of truth and righteousness?

After all, this is only saying that what the Church needs to-day, above everything else, is the utter consecration of itself and all its powers and energies to the speedy accomplishment of its divine mission in the world. If it would but lay itself out in earnest Christian endeavor to bring this world right speedily under the sway of Jesus Christ, and manifest a willingness to surrender everything in its life, in its teaching, or in its practice, that is a hindrance to the success of its holy mission, the very gates of heaven would be opened to pour out upon it a measure of divine power that would soon make the church militant the church triumphant. The promise of Christ, "Lo, I am with you alway, even unto the end of the world," is made to a church that is seeking to make his reign universal. What vast spiritual enterprises await the aggressive action of the Church! What mighty strongholds of Satan await the assault of the awakened and panoplied sons of light! Let the Church of God, like a mighty battleship, clear its decks for action, and bring all its powers to bear against the batteries of sin and unrighteousness, of ignorance and superstition, if she would realize, to the fullest extent, the promise of the divine presence, and experience that fulness of spiritual power and energy which God always grants to those who make themselves the agents for carrying out his beneficent purposes in the world.

It is well to hold on to the old Gospel and to be zealous for "the faith which was once for all delivered to the saints." But conservatism is a virtue which may easily degenerate into cowardice or timidity. We must take the old Gospel and apply it to the new conditions of our time. Nor must we be afraid to face the new problems which have grown out of the progress of Christianity in the world. We cannot do this, except as our minds and hearts are open to receive the new truths that God is revealing to us by his Spirit, in the enlarging experience of the Church, in the unfolding pages of human history, and in the light that is shining from every department of human knowledge and research. The Church must cut loose from everything but Christ and what Christ approves; and under his leadership, and unimpeded by the ecclesiastical and theological lumber of the past, go forth to face the new issues and fight the new battles of our time. The Church that expects to be Spirit-filled must be both progressive and aggressive.

May it not be that our divisions, our denominational rivalries and jealousies, our sectarian narrowness and party spirit, our excessive zeal in behalf of our denominational tenets and theories, have prevented the outpouring of the Holy Spirit in richer abundance upon the Church? Whatever may be said in justification of the origin of our denominationalism, and its inevitableness under the conditions which have existed, and the improbability that these denominations will cease to exist in our day, one thing, at least, is certain: the time has fully arrived, in this closing decade of the nineteenth century, when the Church of the living God must put away its sectarian strifes, its small controversies, its mutual jealousies, and close up its divided ranks for a united assault upon the strongholds of the enemy, if it is to hold the respect of thinking men, and win the approval of him who is its Founder and its living Head. We cannot be loyal to Christ and do less than this. Not until the Church, in spite of differences of opinion and of organization, has learned to co-operate fraternally for the advancement of the kingdom of God will it be worthy to be called the bride of Christ. Not until the sacramental hosts of God shall consent to stand shoulder to shoulder, arm to arm, and heart to heart, against the serried ranks of the enemy, and wage a united war against a common foe, will Christ's prayer for the unity of his disciples, breathed out under the shadow of the cross, be fulfilled. Not until this prayer of our divine Lord is fulfilled in a larger measure than it is to-day can the Church hope to receive the fulness of the divine Spirit to equip it for the conquest of the world.

This, then, is our message: God waits to be gracious to his Church. He is willing and anxious to pour out upon it the Holy Spirit in rich abundance, when it puts itself in condition to receive the blessing. But we must put away our unbelief and our disobedience before we are ready to receive the Holy Spirit. The man or the Church that says this or that *right* thing cannot be accomplished is guilty of unbelief. To doubt that the right will triumph over wrong is practical atheism. The Church must apprehend its true mission in the world, and undertake it in earnest, in order to receive the fulness of the divine blessing. It can expect God's co-operation with it only as it is doing God's work. It must cut itself loose from those theologies and theories of the past which hinder its progress, and must go forward, unhampered, to meet the new issues of our day. It must put away its alienations, its jealousies, its bitter controversies, and close up the gaps in its columns, and move forward as a united host under the leadership of King Jesus, if it is to conquer the strongholds of the enemy and win the world for Christ.

This will require faith and courage of a high order; but if we heed the voice of our great Leader we cannot hesitate as to our duty. How we were all thrilled by one of the reports of the night entrance of Commodore Dewey's fleet into Manila harbor! When the captain of the flag-ship, *Olympia*, signaled, "We are now nearing Manila Bay," the commodore signaled, "Steam ahead!" A little further on the captain again signaled, "We are now entering that part of the channel supposed to be mined." "Steam ahead!" was the commodore's response, and he signaled back to the fleet, "Follow me!" Soon there was a flash on the shore, and the boom of a cannon from one of the forts. "We are fired upon from one of the forts of the enemy," signaled one of the captains. "Steam ahead!" was signaled once more by the brave commodore. On went the fleet, in the darkness of the night, over submarine mines and under the frowning batteries of the enemy, until it reached the very centre of the harbor, where, when day dawned, the squadron stood in battle array, every ship floating the Stars and Stripes, and the band playing "The Star-Spangled Banner!" There before them stood the Spanish battleships and the belching batteries of Fort Cavite. Then came the onset, and the victory which has thrilled the world.

So the Church, as the old Gospel-clad ship of Zion, moves forward through the moral darkness of the world to accomplish her divine mission. Ever and anon the signal is given by some conservative leader, "There is danger ahead; we are leaving behind us the old theories, interpretations, and usages of the past." "Steam ahead!" is signaled back from our divine Commander. But another timid soul cries out, "The batteries of the enemy are opened upon us because we are threatening their strongholds. The Christian Endeavor army, in its war on political corruption and the liquor traffic, is drawing the fire of these powerful antagonists!" "Steam ahead!" comes back the response from our great Leader. "Had we not better be content with the progress we have made, and pause here and rest upon our laurels?" suggests some timid and cautious leader in the Church. "Steam ahead!" is the decisive signal waved back from our supreme Commander from the heavenly heights.

Some glad morning, not far distant let us hope, when the mists that now obscure the issues between the Church and her foes shall have cleared away, the whole ecclesiastical squadron shall appear in solid array, each vessel flying the banner of the cross, with the name of Christ inscribed thereon in letters of light, and all confronting the hosts of unrighteousness and the forts and batteries of Satan. Then shall come the great and decisive battle in the age-long conflict between right and wrong. Then shall righteousness triumph in the earth, and truth shall be crowned with everlasting victory!

Address by Rev. Ralph W. Brokaw,
Utica, N. Y.

THE SOURCE OF POWER.

After expressing his appreciation of the fitness of the general subject for these opening meetings, the discussion of which he compared with the reverent humble invocation at the beginning of a service of worship, Mr. Brokaw said that the word "power" in his topic was an attractive word, because power is an attractive thing.

All men are striving after power, — power over nature, over one another, power to win success. But in considering our part of the subject, — at the outset, — we should distinguish sharply between the *instruments* of power and the *quality* itself.

Material power, for example, is not in the saws and planes and chisels of a wood-working mill, not in the belting, not in the gearing and shafting, but in the engine — and even back of that, in the brain that devised it. So also is psychical power. In the spiritual world the same facts obtain. We must not mistake the display of power in our organizations for the power itself, which is behind and above them, — in the thought of the mighty God. This is the power that took the incoherent heterogeneous Parthians, Medes, Elamites, and Phrygians on the Day of Pentecost and fused them into a living, operating, unified force for the conversion of the world. Before that they were as ineffective as dough would be for cannon-balls. We have much to say about over-organization in our churches; but, as highly as we are organized, we have not yet reached the pentecost point of organization when Christians were all of *one* mind and worked harmoniously for the accomplishment of one supreme purpose. The Church is waiting now for a Christian statesman of broad view and large heart, who can lead the hosts of the Lord out of their captivity to sectarianism, so that our petty rivalries and wicked wasting of means and men shall cease, and, like a mighty army, the Church of God shall move on toward the establishment of the Kingdom of his dear Son.

The source of power then is *in Him* who made Pentecost memorable and historical, and I trust prophetic. "I believe in the Holy Ghost." So we confess, and so we *ought* to confess.

But what of *him?* Yes, of *him*, not "it." The Holy Spirit is one of the Holy Trinity, — a thinking, intelligent being, of whom, when we speak, we are not like persons treading in slippery places, if we say that the personal pronouns are applicable here.

His work is varied. He opens the windows of the mind to let in light for the discovery of truth. He is the interpreter of Christ; he is the comforter and guide of God's people. He convicts and converts men, making effective our human words and deeds. He produces upon different minds, and with them, results that vary as the products of vegetation vary that are moistened by the same rain and grow out of the same earth. He influences men in every walk of life, giving us our Spurgeons and Beechers and Clarks and Parkhursts and Moodys, giving us also our heroes from the ranks, the heroes of the engine-cab, the farm, the kitchen, and the shop. We should depend upon him. Without him— "*Nisi dominus frustra*" — as the Dutch coat-of-arms puts it. With him the many become one and the one wins.

If I turn the faucets in my house, and the pipes do not deliver water,

I do not conclude that the reservoir is empty, but that there is an obstruction somewhere. So to get power from on high we must remove the obstructions from out of the way of the Holy Spirit. Unbelief, selfishness, easily besetting sins, are among these, and then we must pray to and wait before God.

When we are empty then we shall be filled. The Holy Spirit is as free as the air, but as the air cannot get into a hermetically sealed vessel, no more can the Holy Spirit get into our life unless we want him and permit him to come in.

Then according to our equipment and moral earnestness shall be our success as Christians, and our success in Christian work. Without him we are as spent balls. With him we can do all things. He is our opportunity. Shall we neglect our opportunity? Often late at night, as I am about to leave my library, the books on their shelves seem to reproach me, saying, "You have not used us as much as you might have. You have not gotten all we have to give." And I feel reluctant to turn from them to my bed. Let us so draw upon our great source of spiritual power, that at the last Jesus will not reproach us for our inexcusable weakness.

Address by Rev. J. Z. Tyler, D.D.,
Cleveland, Ohio.

WHY SHOULD WE DESIRE ENDUEMENT WITH POWER?

There is a deepening desire, among professed Christians, for a fuller spiritual life. This desire manifests itself in the increased demand for the better class of devotional literature, in the prominence given to it in religious conferences, in the spread of the "Quiet Hour," and similar practical methods for spiritual growth among young people. The prominence given to the subject in such a great international and interdenominational gathering as the present is profoundly significant. He who is at all familiar with the present current of religious life is deeply impressed by this wide-spread desire for a fuller and more fruitful spiritual life.

It is one of the hopeful signs of our times. A need clearly recognized is in a fair way to be supplied. All progress is conditioned upon a desire to improve. Any person or any people satisfied with present attainment has already begun to retrograde.

But let us undertake to set before our minds, as definitely as possible, just what we mean by this "enduement with power." Let us distinguish between what it is and what it is not.

When Christ made promise, just before his ascension, saying to his apostles, "Ye shall be endued with power from on high," the promise contained something peculiar to them, as the chosen ambassadors of Christ. By his own appointment they were clothed with authority, and in the fulfilment of this promise they would be clothed with power to execute their new commission. Are we to suppose that we are to be endued with power in the same sense and to the same degree? Certainly not. The position of the apostles of Christ is a unique position. From the very nature of their work, and the position they occupy in the kingdom of heaven, they can have no successors.

Nor does this enduement of which I speak mean divine inspiration. God's will has been fully revealed in the gospel of Christ. The Holy Spirit led the apostles of Christ into all needed truth. God has no new message, nor is the world in need of a new gospel. The old Jerusalem gospel, preached in its fulness, is amply adequate to meet the world's deepest wants. I do not believe in the doctrine of continuous revelation, and so am not urging that we seek an enduement that will bring to us divine inspiration and new revelations.

Nor is this enduement a clothing with miracle-working power. The early churches, under the first preaching of the divine message, were granted this confirmation of the new faith. Various gifts were bestowed upon many of the first disciples of our Lord; but inspiration taught, at that time, that these gifts were to cease. Miracle stood around the growing Church like scaffold around a rising building; but as the scaffold is removed when the building has been erected, so was there a withdrawal from the Church of this miracle-working power. I am speaking of that which the gospel offers as a divine gift to every obedient believer. I am speaking of that divine help which every struggling soul feels that it needs. I am speaking of that divine power which comes to the living Church of the living God through the vital bond which makes them one in Christ. I am speaking of that which is needful to make the Church more harmonious in its fellowship and more fruitful in its service. I am speaking of that divine indwelling and fulness which makes the kingdom of God a conquering power among men. I am speaking of that which will fill us with love, and joy, and peace, and long-suffering, and gentleness.

The offer of the gospel is manifold. It comes to us under condemnation of personal sin, and offers us a full, and free, and divine pardon. But it offers more. It comes to us in our ignorance and blindness and offers us divine instruction and guidance. But it offers more. It comes to us as a marvelous message of exceeding great and precious promises sweeping through this earth life and rising to the fadeless glories of heaven. But it offers more.

It offers, here and now, to bring us into a living, personal, spiritual fellowship with God himself. It promises to fill us with an abiding guest,— even the Spirit of truth. It is of this divine fulness, made possible to man through Christ and to be expected according to the word of Christ, that I speak.

It was this divine life within the Church that moulded its elements into marvelous unity. It was this divine life that gave them songs in the night of their suffering. It was this divine life that made them victorious over the world. And it is more of this divine life that a divided Church needs to-day to harmonize its discords, and lead it to larger victories. It is more of this divine life that we need to mould us into the image of Christ and bring us to the fulness of the stature of Christ.

But in seeking this divine fulness it is well for us to scrutinize our motives. According to the divine standard, the motive is the measure of the man. And it is possible for men to seek even this divine enduement from motives not altogether worthy.

It may be sought for the delightful sensations supposed to attend its reception. You have, no doubt, attended services where this seemed to be the supreme desire. They sought a divine intoxication. They sought an exuberance of emotion. The value of the service was measured by ecstatic hallelujahs. As those who seek intoxication at the wine-cup, so these sought a spiritual intoxication, and regarded the gift as high wine. The moral quality of such a motive is unworthy.

Some seek it with the vague desire of being blessed, or of "getting a blessing," as they phrase it. This blessing is sought in a selfish spirit and for its own sake. Yet this is not the Bible idea. Saints seek blessings that they may themselves become blessings. The divine promise of blessing is bestowed to make us channels of divine blessing upon others. Abram, the father of the faithful, stands at the head of the list, because through him and his seed should all the nations of the earth be blessed. Divine blessings are not to be sought for selfish ends.

Nor should we seek this divine enduement to save us from the drudgery of service. We are not to become such instruments in God's hands that we shall cease to cultivate and to use all the personal powers with which he has endowed us. It may be beautiful and appropriate from one point of view to sigh for, and to sing, "Oh to be nothing," but it is more divine to seek for and to sing, "Oh to be something." There is an indolent spirit which seeks divine enduement simply to avoid personal struggle. Like the woman at the well in Samaria, they say, "Give me this water, that I thirst not, neither come hither to draw." All longings satisfied; henceforth, all labor needless.

I think the story of the Yankee deacon is to the point. An indolent young minister, who thought the promise of power precluded the need of personal preparation, came as a pulpit supply to the church of this deacon. In the opening prayer the young minister prayed vociferously and long to be clothed with power. "Grant unto thy servant power, O Lord, great power," he prayed. The sermon disclosed no special power, however, unless it was lung power. After the service the deacon, taking him by the lapel of his coat, said, with Yankee shrewdness and nasal twang, " My young brother, 'taint power you need; you need ideas."

The motives which should move us in seeking divine enduement are themselves divine in their character. They may be intensely personal without the taint of selfishness. The desire to be more like Christ, the desire for personal purity, the desire that the spiritual may dominate the carnal, the desire that every thought and imagination of the heart may be brought into captivity to Christ is a personal, yet an unselfish, desire. In our deepest experiences we all realize that what we need is not more light so much as more life. And so Jesus said that he came into the world that we might have life and have it more abundantly. That we may do what we ought, we must first be what we ought. This fuller life will lift us above littleness, and narrowness, and bigotry.

We should seek this enduement that we may be of more service to man. Power is granted to us that we may use it in blessing. We stand in the midst of ignorance and strife and wretchedness. We need a deeper insight into human wants, a more brotherly solicitude for struggling man, a diviner power to help. We need that the divine power shall come down upon us, but we may descend to the lowest depths of human experience with divine strength to uplift. Oh, there is need, there is deep need, that the Church of Jesus Christ should learn that it is in this world to continue from generation to generation the gracious ministry of Jesus Christ himself.

We should seek divine enduement, this fuller, deeper, spiritual life, that we may be brought into a more intimate fellowship with one another. The secret of Christian fellowship is to be found in this divine fellowship. That which hinders the cause of Christ to-day, that which wounds the heart of Christ, is the division and strife among those who are his professed followers. The time may never come when there will be more perfect unanimity in the intellectual conception of truth. The time may never come when there will be perfect agreement as to expedients and methods of spreading abroad a knowledge of Christ. But may we not hope that the time will come when all partisan spirit, all sectarian rivalry, all spiritual discord, shall pass away? May we not hope for the time when the question, "Who shall be greatest?" will lose its personal and party interest? These glorious results are to come chiefly through deeper, richer, fuller spiritual life.

When the tide is out the rocks and shoals manifest themselves, and stagnant pools stand here and there; but when the tide comes in, the full flood, these are swallowed up and disappear. So must the people of God rise above and lose sight of these ugly things by the incoming of a fuller tide of the divine life.

For such purposes as these, impelled by such motives, we should personally and persistently seek this enduement of divine life and power.

Address by Bishop Benjamin W. Arnett, D.D.,
Wilberforce, Ohio.

It affords me great pleasure to meet you in this historic spot, a place dedicated to the education of the human mind and the training of men and women to usefulness and good citizenship.

The author of our text needs no introduction to a Christian audience, for of all the great moral and religious teachers, there is none who has exercised a greater influence in the Church of God than the apostle to the Gentiles. In matters of human duties he is authority in all denominations, and is one of the greatest moral teachers the world has ever had. He has led more men to victory than any other moral hero, and throughout the centuries his commands have been obeyed. To the Ephesians he said, "Be strong in the Lord and in the power of his might."

"Be strong in the Lord and in the power of his might" are the final words of Paul the apostle to the church of the Ephesians. In the preceding chapter he has portrayed human duty and responsibility, laid down the rules for husband and wife, child and parent, and for master and servant. He also gives the apostles direction for Christian worship, and declares that it is first, pure; second, spiritual; third, that it is emotional; fourth, joyous; fifth, it is vocal; sixth, it is musical — it is congregational.

It is addressed to God in Christ and becomes the foundation for universal thanksgiving. He declares that Christianity consecrates and elevates the union of husband and wife, for it begets mutual sympathy, mutual confidence, mutual forbearance. When two are thus joined together, it is almost a prevention of a matrimonial wreck.

Paul, having laid the foundation of this church, was looked upon as a father as well as a teacher. He exercised a great influence not only over the members of his own congregation but over the citizens in general; his words were not a mere expression of counsel or advice, but it was to the people the wisdom of a father expressed, the command of a general, the voice of a representative of God; consequently his words were significant in that every one felt that he was under obligation to obey. Thus, when he said, "Be strong in the Lord and in the power of his might," each individual felt that there was no escape from his command — it was obey and live, disobey and die; for they had not forgotten the instruction of how to obtain heavenly strength, given in the third chapter and sixteenth verse. The central thought of his instruction to the members of his church was that they were to obtain this strength through Jesus Christ, that faith is the medium through which this strength is conveyed from the original source. Then each individual was to act in the machinery either as a belt or a wheel to convey this power from individual to individual and from family to family.

I will not be able to give a definition satisfactory to all persons present as to what is meant by strength and power, but I may by illustration give some idea of the importance of the command, and give the results of the obeying and disobeying of it.

Strength and power are not relative terms; they cannot be used interchangeably the one for the other.

I speak of A as being a strong man. I mean that he possesses physical strength. I speak of B as being a strong man — he is strong not spiritually but intellectually a strong man. I speak of C — he is a strong man; but I mean that he possesses moral strength, is able to obey the law, and walks between God's "shalls and shall nots." In speaking of D, another strong man in the church or community, we mean that he possesses what is known among Christians as spiritual strength, or he possesses more than an ordinary degree of spiritual influence. He walks and lives continually on the Mount of Transfiguration, and can hear, either by day or night, the voice of God saying, "This is my beloved son, in whom I am well pleased." We see the diversity of the illustration, consequently the difficulty in giving a definition; for each individual spoken of receives this strength from different sources. A, in order to perpetuate his physical strength and keep himself in harmony with the physical laws, must have bread, meat, and water. B increases and maintains his strength by observation, thought, reading, conversation, and by listening to others. C maintains his place as a moral hero by self-control, obedience to divine and human law; while D maintains his strength by faith and prayer, by union between himself and the Christ, consequently the presence of the Spirit. Again, we illustrate strength by several pieces of wood. We take the first piece and find that the particles are easily separated; that is pine wood. We take another and find that requires great exertion to separate a particle or break a piece; this we call oak wood. But we have another piece of wood that we use our utmost physical strength to break or to separate the particles. We pull to the right and to the left, but fail; we pull it up and down and still fail to break it; indeed, it is almost impossible to break a piece of wood known as hickory, so tenaciously do the particles adhere to each other. This is the ideal strength that Paul commends to the Christians of Ephesus, and this is the kind we recommend to-day. The affection that ought to exist between man and man, family and family, race and race, ought to be like unto the particles of the hickory.

The third illustration of what we mean by strength carries with it the idea of the ability to bear up, as a table or wagon; which is able to bear and to carry a load, as the elephant, or horse, or man.

The fourth idea lies in a rope or chain, which often depends upon the quality of the fibres, or at other times upon the number of fibres—strength, in this case, is more in quality than in quantity. We may put in this class the chain and the cable. The chain may be of iron or steel; in this case we must consider the quality of the material, rather than the bulk. So in all phases of human life one individual is finer in character than another; the other is equally strong, but possesses a greater quantity of material.

The apostle was philosophical in giving the command and making the distinction between strength and power. It is difficult, then, to draw the line between strength and power, whether physical, intellectual, moral, or spiritual; for at first sight it appears as though they were the same thing at different stages of development. That idea is true relatively but absolutely, it is incorrect. We will now give an illustration by one of the distinguished philosophers as to the place of strength and power in the economy of man and life.

Dr. J. W. Lee says, " It is impossible to understand the meaning of creation until we see dust standing erect in the form of a living man; and if there is mind in the universe, and if there is purpose in the order and movements of the earth, then man is the culmination of that purpose and with reference to him was the order constituted and the movements determined." Man is a compound being composed of matter and mind; he is connected with five kingdoms and two worlds, and is subject to physical and spiritual laws. He stands upon the earth, breathes air, drinks water, eats bread, and communes with his God. This world was made for man, it is his temporary home; it was made for him in a sense that it was not made for any other living creatures; for his connection with the mineral, vegetable, and animal kingdoms is so intimate that he must communicate with them three times a day, or his happiness and pleasure are very much disturbed.

By his superior power man is able to utilize the forces of nature to his own protection. The woods furnish material for his shelter, " the minerals and plants administer to his ills," and the world becomes his schoolhouse—nature, Providence, and revelation his text-books. As far back as science can carry us, at the beginning of the quarternary period, we find in man all the marks of intellectual and moral superiority, wearing for his royal vesture the skin of a wild beast, upholding in his right hand a roughly hewn flint as a sceptre which he uses as a means of defence and a tool of labor. He early built an altar to religion, to patriotism, and to education; these were, of course, built around the family altar, and from that day until now there has been a continual evolution of thought, life, and action, passing from naturism to animism and from that to spiritism. The high plain on which the human family now stands has been reached by three roads: the intuitive road, which starts from the lowest and most remote depths of the moral and intellectual condition of uncivilized man; while the road of reason begins with the semi-civilized and passes on up to the enlightened of many countries and nations; the revealed way had its beginning in God's promise to the uncrowned and dethroned monarch of Eden, and has been known through history as the High Way.

Preceding the reign of Jesus Christ the forces of nature and the natural forces of man were united and formed the power of the moral, religious, and intellectual progress of the races; but those of us who have the privilege of living on the high plane of our Christian civilization can, if we will, add to these natural forces the divine power that comes through faith in Jesus Christ and the Holy Ghost. And in order to utilize the powers that nature and God have put at our disposal, we must recognize the fact that man must make provision for his body, mind, soul, and spirit. " The provision for his physical nature is bread ; for his social life is power ; for his intellectual nature, truth ; for his moral nature, righteousness ; for his æsthetic nature, beauty ; and for his spiritual nature, love."

The original storehouse of these essentials of true happiness are so convenient in situation and so superabundant in supply that no man can plead poverty and be justified ; for Christianity has so organized the forces of religion and education that it supplies the demands at home, and through the missionaries supplies the wants of man to the uttermost parts of the earth. And what failure there may be in the regular forces of Christianity, it is supplied by the auxiliary forces, such as the Young Men's Christian Association, the Woman's Christian Temperance Union, and the subsidized forces,—printing-press, Sunday schools, etc. But after all these forces and powers have been united and concentrated upon some object they fall far short of the highest good to man, because they are human and finite and may fail ; but if we desire the utmost success we must have all our forces and powers marked with the divine stamp and energized by power from on high.

We have given you illustrations of strength and power and of the evolution of religious thought as seen in the history of the union of the natural forces, and now we call your attention to the union of spiritual strength and power. Come with me to a station or depot of some of the railroads of our country, and we will find a locomotive standing on the track, the baggage-car, the express-car, the passenger-car and the Pullman sleeper all connected by modern appliances and ready to start for some distant city. We examine the locomotive and cars and find that everything is perfect — the boiler is strong, the wheels of the locomotive are strong, the wheels and trucks of all the cars are strong, the body of the coaches are made of walnut and hickory wood, embellished, everything perfect ; and so far as strength is concerned there is nothing more to be desired. But strength will not move the train from where it stands though one hundred years pass away. We must have power — the fireman puts water in the boiler, and the fire in the boiler comes in contact with the water, the fire and the water generate steam-power, the power remains in the boiler, the strength of the steel confines the power within certain limits as long as the strength of the boiler is greater than the power of steam within ; but as soon as the power of the steam becomes greater than the strength of the boiler there is an explosion. The conductor cries, "All on board." The cars are all crowded with people on their way to the Christian Endeavor Convention at Nashville, July 6, 1898. They wait, but what for? For the application of power to the train. The engineer, at the command of the conductor, turns the throttle-valve and liberates the power in the steam chest ; it soon finds its way to the cylinders, and touches the head of the piston-rod, and hurries along to the driving-wheel under the locomotive ; and when the locomotive is full it passes through the couplings to the next car, and this is filled with power ; and so it continues until every car on the train is filled with power from the locomotive, and the train starts on its iron pathway at the rate of forty miles an hour because of the union of the strength of the cars and the power of the locomotive. Strength and power are essential to every train ; for if the train is weak it will soon fall to pieces, and without power it would not move. The safety of a train depends upon the strength of its parts ; but the speed of a train depends upon the perfectness of the road-bed, strength of rails, and amount of power. But after all some may say, "What has this to do with the subject or the endowment from on high?" In this we recognize the peculiar position of man, and recognize his complex nature. It requires a complete system of metes and bounds to control the physical and to put him under subjection. To obey divine laws requires more strength of will than man possesses ; to keep him in line of duty to his fellow man and to his God he needs the Holy Ghost.

The limited knowledge he possesses of his own mysterious body has often caused him great pain ; his limited knowledge of the origin of evil has caused him sorrow, sickness, and death to the soul ; his ignorance of the physical and spiritual laws about him has caused him to stumble and fall where it was his privilege to stand erect and become the ruler of the situation. Man finds himself surrounded by enemies without and within, and realizes that life is a battle-field from the cradle to the grave, and realizes his own weakness as the apostle indicated to the Ephesians. He is instructed how he may acquire strength which will enable him to meet his enemies and drive them from the field. With divine strength man can meet all his foes and bind them hand and foot to his chariot wheels. If there ever was a time when the Church needed to receive a baptism of power, it is at this time. When the Master was about to leave the infant Church, he called the Christian Endeavor Convention to meet in Jerusalem. They were bidden to tarry there until they received, not strength, but power from on high. They were like the train standing at the depot — they were ready to go, but had not the necessary power to drive the train; so the Master bade them tarry until they should receive power. So should every child of God remain at the altar of consecration until he receives wisdom and power from on high. It will be noticed that the disciples first separated themselves from the world and continued with one accord in prayer and supplication. With the women and Mary, the mother of Jesus Christ, and with his brethren, when the Day of Pentecost was fully come, they were with one accord in one place. (See Acts 2: 1–21.) The account of the meeting on the Day of Pentecost reads like the report of the Annual Meeting of the United Society of Christian Endeavor, especially the one we held in San Francisco, where the representatives of the nations, designated in the Acts of the Apostles, were present with us and joined with us in prayer and praise. We were truly all together in one place, were of different nationalities, languages, and customs, but we all understood the language of the soul. The Christian Endeavor movement is the Day of Pentecost in motion; in sixteen years it has encircled the globe, multiplied its numbers with greater rapidity than any other organization since the time Peter preached the Inaugural Sermon of Christianity and enlisted three regiments of soldiers. The whole Church was baptized on the Day of Pentecost with the Holy Ghost and with power. How can this power be obtained? And how can we utilize it for the glory of God? There is but one way to obtain it, and that is just as the apostles obtained it. As in the case of salvation, there is the originating cause, the meritorious cause, and receiving cause, which includes man, God, and faith; it requires self-abnegation on the part of man and faith in the Lord Jesus Christ to be justified as well as to be sanctified. The reception of this power is an individual act. the result may be the union of individual acts which may become crystallized in the efforts of an organization, but in order to obtain this blessing we must meet in one place with one accord, all touching and agreeing upon the thing needful; it must be an intellectual and spiritual meeting, not necessarily physical. We must have our meetings on the Mount of Transfiguration and build our altars where Peter, James, and John built their altars, — on the Ten Commandments and the Golden Rule; we must empty ourselves that we may be filled with the Holy Ghost and power, and with the language of the poet cry out: —

> Oh for a heart to praise my God,
> A heart from sin set free.
> A heart that always feels Thy blood,
> So freely spilt for me!
> A heart in every thought renewed,
> And full of love divine.
> Perfect, and right, and pure, and good,
> A copy, Lord, of Thine!

And with Charles Wesley we all must pray:

> I want a sober mind,
> A self-renouncing will,
> That tramples down and casts behind
> The baits of freezing ill;
> A soul inured to pain,
> To hardships, grief, and loss;
> Bold to take up, firm to sustain,
> The Consecrated Cross.

Having obtained peace in faith through Jesus Christ, and realizing if any man be in Christ Jesus he is a new creature, old things have passed away, and all things have become new; and each one of God's children henceforth can say with the Apostle Paul, "There is therefore now no condemnation to them which are in Christ Jesus, who walk not after the flesh, but after the spirit."

He said again, "For I reckon that the sufferings of this present time are not worthy to be compared with the glory that will be revealed in us."

He further testifieth that, "We know all things work together for good to them that love God. For I am persuaded that neither life, nor death, nor angels, nor principalities, nor powers, nor things present, nor things to come, nor height, nor depth, nor any other creature shall be able to separate us from the love of God which is in Christ Jesus our Lord."

The testimony of Peter, the great apostle, is very encouraging, for without the Holy Ghost he was weak, vacillating, followed the Master at a distance, denied him, but after he received power from on high he was as bold as a lion, and led the fight against the enemies of Christ. When assailed he said, "Ye men of Judea and all ye that dwell in Jerusalem, be this known unto you, that these are not drunk but it is the fulfilment of the prophecy of Joel." When the multitude heard the words of Peter, they cried out, "Men and brethren, what must we do?" Peter said, "Repent and be baptized every one of you in the name of Jesus Christ for the remission of sin, and ye shall receive the Holy Ghost." Multitudes from different parts of the world repented, and were baptized unto the doctrines of the apostles, and remained steadfast in the faith; and from that day until now God has never been without a witness, and the army of Christianity has continued its onward march, going from conquest to conquest, with the following record of their triumphs: "Who through faith subdued kingdoms, wrought righteousness, obtained promises, stopped the mouth of lions."

The institutions of Christianity have come to us from the past, each one hoary with age, pregnant with possibilities; each one a child of a century, each century an heir of its predecessor, and the last century is the heir of all its predecessors. Each moral and religious leader of each generation organized his army, fought the battles of his day, gained victories when possible, and retreated in good order when defeated, transmitted his unfinished work to his successor, and he in turn transmitted cause and army to those who follow after, exhorting each to be strong in the Lord and in his might. Man has been engaged in the battle of life ever since he came from the plastic hand of his Maker. Every man is a soldier in the army of human activity; he must fight or die; he must fight if he would reign, he must contend for the faith that was delivered unto the saints. His foes are the world, the flesh, the devil. and his own heart — foes without and foes within.

The apostle, realizing the importance of the warfare, gave direction to the soldiers of the cross. His first command was, "Fight the good fight of faith and lay hold on eternal life." He cautioned them to be sure they were in the right army, fighting under the banner of the Nazarine. If they were following the ensign of the cross they were certain to gain victory. Those who have fought the good fight in the past, as well as in the present, have been divided. Some have fought the battle of intelligence against ignorance; morality against immorality; freedom against slavery; the spirit against the flesh; social reforms against the customs and habits of a century.

We have the same conditions to-day as described by the apostle, and need the same remedy; we have the same weaknesses, and need the same power; we have to contend with a part of the same army, and need the same divine armor. The apostle gave his advice to his brethren, and his command to the Church. He said to them, You will have a spiritual warfare on earth, you will have to fight for truth, for right, for liberty, for your native land and for personal liberty; therefore you will need to be prepared to meet your foe, who is older than the Church and possesses an immense amount of resources, gained by observation and experience. He is crafty and he is cunning; he has the power of deception and can inject things into the minds of men and cause them to follow his council. In order to meet this foe it is necessary to have more than human power and human armor. Paul's advice to the Ephesians is, "Put on the whole armour of God that you may be able to stand against the wiles of the devil." It is as true to-day as it was two thousand years ago that the child of God need not expect to meet the devil in the open field; for he fights from ambush, he is a bush-whacker and will take the stragglers of the army prisoners, or will capture the ambulances which contain the sick, wounded, and dying, and will then claim a victory; but the sheep he can never devour unless he first divides.

Another reason why we need the divine armor is that we wrestle not against flesh and blood but against the principality, against the powers, and against the rulers of darkness; therefore, in order to meet the conqueror — this foe of God and man — we need to be indued with power from on high. An army of thousands of different denominations, of different creeds, have met together in this the capital city of the State of Tennessee with one accord to ask divine help to meet the common foe of man. Let us all be united in asking for the outpouring of the divine spirit upon the president and officers of this Convention, and may each speaker be a battleship, and each Christian a source of power and influence.

Address by Bishop Alexander Walters, D.D.,
Jersey City, N. J.

SPIRITUAL POWER — ITS SOURCE AND EFFECTS.

TEXT: But ye shall receive power, after that the Holy Ghost is come upon you.—Acts 1 : 8.

Some years ago, while I was pastor in New York City, a fine-looking white man — evidently of gentlemanly birth — called early one morning to see me. He was so drunk he could scarcely stand. Amid tears he informed me that he was an officer of one of the most prominent churches of that city, and, of course, not wishing his pastor to know of his condition, he had come asking my aid. He told me that he had tried again and again to overcome the drink habit, but had failed to do so. The words of the text came to me, which I read to him, " Ye shall receive power, after that the Holy Ghost is come upon you." He believed the word, and after a mighty struggle received the Holy Ghost and was saved.

I have used the same text in a number of cases of fallen women, with similar results.

First. The Source of Spiritual Strength Is the Holy Ghost. The Trinity is composed of the Father, Son, and Holy Ghost. Therefore, the Holy Ghost is God. 'T was he who gave the world its form and beauty. Milton, speaking of the work of the Holy Ghost, says: —

"O Spirit that dost prefer before all temples the upright heart and pure, instruct me, for thou know'st: thou from the first wast present, and, with mighty wings outspread, dovelike sat'st brooding on the vast abyss."

In harmony with the same idea Job says, "The Spirit of God hath made me and the breath of the Almighty hath given me life." In Hebrews we read: "How much more shall the blood of Christ, who through the Eternal Spirit offered himself without spot to God, purge your conscience from dead works to serve the living God."

The incarnation of Christ is ascribed to the Holy Ghost. Hear St. Luke: "And the angel answered and said unto her [Mary], The Holy Ghost shall come upon thee, and the power of the Highest shall overshadow thee; therefore, also that holy thing which shall be born of thee shall be called the Son of God."

David, speaking of him, says: "Whither shall I go from thy spirit? or whither shall I flee from thy presence? If I ascend up into heaven thou art there, if I make my bed in hell behold thou art there. If I take the wings of the morning and dwell in the uttermost parts of the sea; even there shall thy hand lead me and thy right hand shall hold me."

Second. The Power. We can develop the intellect without the Holy Ghost. Capacity and willingness on our part, efficient teachers and favorable opportunities, may enable us to be giants in intellect; proper food and training may enable us to be physical giants; self-denial may enable us to be moral giants; but it takes nothing less than the Holy Ghost to enable us to be spiritual giants. There can be no spiritual development without the Christ-life. I believe, however, that the surest and quickest way to the intellectual, physical, and moral developments is with the aid of the Holy Ghost.

Third. The Special Work of the Holy Ghost. (1) *To convince of sin.* John 16 : 8 we read: "When he [the Holy Ghost] is come, he will reprove the world of sin, and of righteousness, and of judgment." It is his work to present Christ to us.

(2) *The Holy Ghost renews and sanctifies us.* Hear the words of Jesus: "It is the spirit that quickeneth. Except a man be born of water and of the spirit he cannot enter into the kingdom of God. That which is born of the flesh is flesh and that which is born of the spirit is spirit. Marvel not that I said unto thee, Ye must be born again."

In Romans we read: "We are made acceptable being sanctified by the Holy Ghost."

(3) *The Holy Ghost is our Comforter, Guide, and Teacher.* Hear the Master: "But the Comforter, which is the Holy Ghost, whom the Father will send in my name, he shall teach you all things, and bring all things to your remembrance, whatsoever I have said unto you."

(4) *The Holy Ghost is the source of all spiritual power.* When the disciples who had been with Jesus for more than three years, and had witnessed his wonderful miracles, listened to his burning words of eloquence, and had been the recipients of his tender care, were anxious after his resurrection to go into the world and testify of him and his works, he informed them that they were unprepared to go, because of their lack of spiritual power. He commanded them to tarry at Jerusalem until they were endued with power from on high. By obeying the command they received the power. A like command comes to all who have not received the Holy Ghost. Will you obey the command? If power for service is needed, power to overcome temptation, power to fulfil your mission in life, it will be given when you receive the Holy Ghost.

Fourth. The Baptism of the Holy Ghost Subsequent to Conversion. In Ephesians 1 : 13 we read: "In whom ye also trusted after that ye heard the word of truth, the gospel of your salvation: in whom also after that ye believed ye were sealed with that Holy Spirit of promise." Before Peter received the baptism of the Holy Ghost he was a pretty wicked fellow. John, the beloved disciple, was not much better. When the Samaritans refused to entertain Jesus while passing through their country on his way to Jerusalem John considered it an insult, and in order to resent it wanted his Master to cause fire to come down from heaven and consume them. He was anything but the loving John that he was after he received the Holy Ghost. On the night that Christ was apprehended and carried before the high priest Peter with bitter curses denied having met or known Jesus. A little maid frightened him out of his wits, but after he received the Holy Ghost he was willing to die for his Lord. When he was commanded by the Jewish Sanhedrim to cease testifying concerning Christ and his works he answered, "We are to obey God rather than man." What a change! In one case a maid frightened him; in the other the whole Jewish Sanhedrim court was not able to intimidate him. This wonderful change was the result of the baptism of the Holy Ghost. The statement is often made that regeneration (change of heart) and the baptism of the Holy Ghost are synonymous — one and the same. This cannot be so; if it were true it would seem that Christ had pardoned and cleansed others while he left his disciples uncleansed. Surely he would not have pardoned others and left his disciples, who were to be his special messengers, unregenerated. Again we are told by other objectors that the Holy Ghost had not been given. This is true in a special but not in a general sense; the Holy Spirit had been in the world from the beginning. The baptism of the Holy Ghost after conversion is the teaching of the Scripture and the experience of all who have received it.

During the apostolic times, and for many years afterward, the burden of preaching was the necessity of the Holy Ghost. When Paul went to Ephesus he said to the young converts of that city, "Have ye received the Holy Ghost since ye believed?" They informed him that they had not so much as heard that there was a Holy Ghost. He, knowing the importance of the matter, laid his hands upon them and prayed and they received the Holy Ghost.

Fifth. The Way To Obtain the Holy Ghost. The first thing to do is to realize the necessity of this baptism. It is hardly possible one would put forth sufficient effort to obtain such a gift unless he realized the necessity of it. The necessity is evident when a lack of power to do effectual work for God and to overcome one's self is discovered. If we are being continually defeated in our efforts to live a godly life, if a lack of liberty in spirit, unction in prayer, singing, and preaching is apparent, it is an evidence that we are not in possession of the Holy Ghost.

We Obtain This Power by Surrender and Faith. The surrender necessary for this baptism is the surrender of powers already quickened by the Spirit. Hear St. Paul: "I beseech you therefore brethren, by the mercies of God that ye present your bodies a living sacrifice, holy, acceptable unto God, which is your reasonable service." An unconditional surrender is what God requires of every man who would have the baptismal power. When you make the sacrifice believe with all your heart that God accepts of it. Hear St. Peter in his memorable sermon on the Day of Pentecost: "Then Peter said unto them, Repent and be baptized every one of you in the name of Jesus Christ for the remission of sins, and ye shall receive the gift of the Holy Ghost."

Sixth. The Gracious Effects of the Baptism of the Holy Ghost. All of the men who have done great spiritual work for God were men endued with power from on high. The apostles, the most noted of the fathers, the reformers, such as Luther, Calvin, Knox, the Wesleys, Jonathan Edwards, Chas. Finney, Moody, and the founders of the colored Methodist churches, such as Varick, Allen, Spencer, and Miles, were all men endued with power from on high. The indispensable requisite of the Church for spiritual success is the power of the Holy Ghost. Without it all is barren and unfruitful. He is the strength that will enable us to overcome the world, the flesh, and the devil, and to stand entire at last.

I would have you remember that the baptism of the Holy Ghost does not free us from personal efforts after holiness. It is the power that puts the machinery into motion, but we must do the oiling, etc. It is the quickening of the spiritual graces after they have been wrought in the soul by the Holy Ghost. But it is our part to keep them in good order, and we can do this by diligent study of the Holy Scriptures, earnest and prevailing prayer, and by self-denial and watchfulness. I say prevailing prayer, because there are many who fail to have their prayers answered because they do not continue them long and earnestly enough. If our prayers are not answered at once, we should continue for hours in the spirit of prayer, and if necessary, days, weeks, and months, until the answer comes. The answer is sure to come if the prayer is according to His will; and we know it is according to his will if we are asking for preparation for service and holiness of heart. Again, if we hope to develop our Christian graces we must practise self-denial. The Master constantly urged upon his disciples self-denial. Said he, "If any man will come after me, let him deny himself and take up his cross, and follow me." The Holy Spirit will aid us in our efforts of self-denial, but will not do the self-denying. We must remember that the "ceasing to do evil and learning to do well" is our part. We must avoid, as far as possible, all the temptations; and no matter how pleasing a thing is to the appetites or the passions, with the aid of the Holy Spirit we must deny ourselves of it. If we would overcome the world and fill up our full measurement of work, we must have the baptism of the Holy Ghost. Do you ask again how to obtain this wonderful gift? I answer, First of all you must be pardoned of your sins; second, you must be regenerated by the Holy Spirit. Regeneration is the implanting of the Christian graces. Sanctification or holiness is the maturity of the Christian graces wrought in the soul by the Holy Ghost. Baptism of the Holy Ghost is the special qualification for some service. The Master needs you; will you even now consecrate yourself to his service? He cometh and calleth for you; will you answer the call? The power is at hand; will you have it now? The call to-day is for devoted Christians — men and women — who are pure in heart and pure in their life; so pure that they can touch the lives of the impure and make them like unto themselves, holy. "Ye shall receive power, after that the Holy Ghost is come upon you," etc.

> "Oh that it now from heaven might fall,
> And all our sins consume!
> Come, Holy Ghost, for Thee we call;
> Spirit of burning, come.
>
> " Refining fire, go through our hearts,
> Illuminate our souls,
> Scatter Thy life in every part,
> And sanctify the whole." Amen.

Address by Rev. John H. Elliott,

Rochester, N. Y.

THE HEART OF THE WHOLE MATTER.

I imagine there must have been a tender interest associated with the last promise of the Lord Jesus, as recorded in Acts 1 : 8: "But ye shall receive power, after that the Holy Ghost is come upon you : and ye shall be witnesses unto me, both in Jerusalem, and in all Judea, and in Samaria, and unto the uttermost part of the earth." I am very sure that the disciples must have attached a great deal of importance to these words, just as friends now treasure up and dwell upon the last words of departing ones. That the words made a deep impression upon them is evident from the fact that they at once acted upon them. And that is where so many of us fail in giving practical evidence of our appreciation of the words of Jesus Christ.

In the outset let me call your attention to the fact that this gift of power by the Spirit was to be for a special purpose. Not simply that they might feel happy, or have a good time emotionally; not even that they were to be more clear as to their acceptance with him or more sure of salvation through his grace, but for the special purpose of power in witnessing for him — this is the heart of the matter. He said. "Ye shall be witnesses unto me in Jerusalem, and in all Judea, and in Samaria, and unto the uttermost part of the earth." In other words, beginning at home and then reaching out into the circle outside of home, and then the widening circle beyond that, and then even to the uttermost part of the earth. Sometimes men feel that they could do a greater work if they were in some other State or community, or amid other surroundings. But unless one has power for witnessing at home, with all its difficulties and trials, I have no confidence in their being greatly used in the regions beyond.

Let me ask and answer a few practical questions : —

First. What is the Holy Spirit?

1. "He is the third person in the blessed Trinity " is the common answer. But I notice that many of us do not put the emphasis upon the right word. We need to emphasize the word " person."

2. He is a real person, not simply an influence emanating from God the Father or God the Son. In that discourse of our Lord to his disciples recorded in the 14th, 15th, and 16th chapters of John's Gospel he lays much emphasis upon this truth. In the 14th chapter and 16th verse he says, "I will pray the Father, and he shall give you another Comforter, that he may abide with you forever." Here he speaks of another Comforter whose personality is as real as his own, and uses the personal pronoun in referring to him. Then a little farther on, in the 26th verse, he says: "The Comforter, which is the Holy Ghost, whom the Father will send in my name, he shall teach you all things," etc., again using the personal pronoun. Then in the 15th chapter, 26th verse,

again speaking of the Comforter, he says, "The Spirit of truth which proceedeth from the Father, he shall testify of me." Here the very expression shows that in the mind of our Lord the Holy Spirit was a divine personality and equal with himself. Then in the 16th chapter, from the 7th to the 14th verses, he is careful to emphasize this truth in a most impressive way. Eleven times or over he uses the personal pronoun "he" rather than the impersonal pronoun "it." Suppose I repeat the 13th verse to you, using the word that sometimes Christian people without thought use in speaking of the Holy Ghost. "Howbeit when it, the Spirit of truth, shall come, it shall guide you into all truth: for it shall not speak of itself; but whatsoever it shall hear, that shall it speak: and it shall show you things to come. It shall glorify me: for it shall receive of mine, and show it unto you." Do you not see at once that I utterly undermine the force of the statement, destroy its dignity, and mar its force?

Second. What does the Holy Spirit do?

1. His work is divine and equal with the Father and Son, in creation, redemption, and by and by he will take his place with them in glory.

2. In reference to the unsaved, he is said, among other things, to strive with men, to convince of sin, and to regenerate.

3. In reference to the saved, he is said, among other things, to teach and remind, to guide into all truth, as in John, 15th and 16th chapters; to strengthen and help, as in Rom. 8: 26: "Who helpeth our infirmities," etc.; to give wisdom, as in 1 Cor. 12: 8: "For to one is given the word of wisdom," etc.; to give courage and liberty, as in 2 Cor. 3: 17: "Where the spirit of the Lord is, there is liberty;" to intercede for us, to seal us, to dwell in us, etc. Then, again, the Holy Spirit and his offices is most beautifully presented to us in the Scripture under significant symbols. For example: (1) The oil — Ps. 14: 7: "Hath anointed thee with the oil of gladness above thy fellows." (2) Water — Isa. 44: 3: "I will pour water on the thirsty ground," etc. Water is cleansing, fertilizing, refreshing. (3) The Dew — this is a most beautiful symbol, and wonderfully illustrates the Holy Spirit in his quiet coming and benign mission. (4) The Wind — as in John 3: 8, etc. What could be more expressive? In the western part of our country people have a very vivid realization of the mighty power of the wind; but to my mind the place and mission of the Holy Spirit is most beautifully illustrated in the action of the wind upon the trees, for, as you know, the same wind that shakes down the autumn leaves and prepares the trees for winter also awakens their dormant life in the spring, shaking off the last clinging encumbrance or hindrance, and assisting in the marvelous transformation brought about by the indwelling life. As the Lord Jesus said concerning the mysterious work of the Spirit in regeneration, "So is every one that is born of the Spirit," well might we say, So is every one that is "filled with the Spirit." (5) The Seal — as in Eph. 1: 13: "After ye believed ye were sealed," etc. Among men we know that the seal sets forth, among other things, a finished transaction, the idea of security, a sense of ownership, the attestation of genuineness, and it leaves a likeness. I wonder how many of us bear about in our bodies the mark of the Lord Jesus.

I remember at one of the meetings my friend John G. Woolly held in Minneapolis, after his wonderful conversion, when I asked him for his topic, he said, "I am going to take a text, and you will find it in Gal. 6: 17: 'From henceforth let no man trouble me; for I bear about in my body the marks of the Lord Jesus.'" I had occasion to know that there were men in that audience who did not wish him well, and would have been glad to have seen him fall again (as he had so many times before) from the stand that he had taken against strong drink. But I think not a single man who heard him ever doubted after that address that J. G. Woolly was a marked man. I believe above everything else the filling of the Holy Spirit marks a man. (6) The Earnest — as in 2 Cor. 22: "Has sealed us and given us the earnest of the spirit," etc. (7) The Dove — I may not dwell upon these symbols at this time, but I would like to commend to any one who might be interested a little book by Marsh, of England, of the "Emblems of the Holy Spirit," which is most suggestive and instructive.

In this dispensation of the Holy Spirit his work may be briefly summed up as (1) conveying the mind and will of God; (2) convicting of error; (3) converting to righteousness and consecrating to holiness. The question which Paul propounded to those Christians whom he met down in the city of Ephesus is still appropriate to a great many professing Christian people: " Have you received the Holy Ghost since ye believed?" or, " Did ye receive the Holy Ghost when ye believed?" as the Revised Version puts it. And I fear that in many cases, if the answer was given in as honest and as straightforward a way as in their case, it would be the same: "We have not so much as heard whether there be any Holy Ghost." I am quite sure that Scripture clearly teaches that one may be born of the Holy Spirit and yet not filled with the Holy Spirit, and that one may be indwelt of the Holy Spirit and yet not receive him fully, just as it is possible for one to dwell in a house and yet not occupy all the rooms. And yet, alas! that is what mars and hinders so many Christian lives. The figure of a house suggests an illustration of what I mean. If you rent a small room in your house to an outsider, it does not matter whether it be one of the smallest and meanest rooms in the house, away up under the roof, you will be obliged to give them the right of way to get to that room; even if it is necessary that they should go through the hall and sitting-room and into the best portions of the house to get there, you must give them the right of way. And so in many a Christian life a small part of the dwelling-place of the Holy Spirit is given over to the evil one, and he will trail his slimy length through every chamber of the soul in order to reach the part that belongs to him, and so utterly befoul and besmirch what otherwise might be the home of abiding peace.

If you will study the record you will find that the disciples before Pentecost "received the Holy Spirit," but at Pentecost they were "filled with the Holy Spirit." I imagine some one saying, Then you believe in the second blessing? Yes, I do. Why not? Call it what you will, such a thing seems to be set forth in the Scripture and experienced in Christian lives. I think the early Church not only had a second blessing, but a third, fourth, and fifth — indeed, a repeated blessing as they needed repeated power. Do you know such an experience? If not, then I fear you have not "tarried at Jerusalem."

Third. How shall his power be secured?

Let us consider Pentecost for an answer to the question. And to sum up very briefly the lessons learned from a careful meditation on this tremendous event in the history of the early Church, for myself I find I can put it in this way: —

1. Prayer preceding.
2. Promise pleading.
3. Pentecostal power following.

This describes at once the simple method and the blessed result.

Let us look in on that meeting and note some of its results. In the first place, it was evidently a meeting in which no one was nervous about the length of time employed. Nowadays many people get nervous if the meeting runs a few minutes over time. We have come to a place where we run things by the clock, and I think sometimes we miss a blessing as a result of it.

I can imagine on the first day of this meeting at Jerusalem that perhaps they prayed for their misguided brethren, the Jews, and for the heathen — indeed, spent pretty much all the day praying for other people. Perhaps on the next day they began to pray for themselves in a general way; and on the third day, to be a little more definite and personal in their petitions. Perhaps on the fourth day they gave up the time to thanksgiving for blessings already received, and then maybe recounted the success of the past, until at last they did nothing else but simply wait for the promise, as they were expressly commanded to do in the beginning. There they were waiting. I can see them now — a quiet but sure emptying process going on all the time. Five days have elapsed, no evidence whatever yet of the promise being fulfilled; six days, seven days, eight days, nine days. It was a wonderful meeting. And the record says on the tenth day, when the Day of Pentecost was fully come. "They were all with one accord in one place." In other words, they were all empty. I think it is true that we will never find any company of people entirely of one accord until they are entirely empty. In fact, a number of people, all empty, are very much alike and easily of one accord. Then there came to them a wonderful experience; I do not suppose that it has been or will be repeated in the same degree, and yet I think it is true that just as in special cases there were individuals who were filled with the Spirit in the early Church, so now there are persons who have their individual Pentecost and are filled with the Spirit.

I know of one meeting, however, that I believe partook more of the character of the first Pentecost than any other I have ever known about in my Christian life. It was following a convention of the Young Men's Christian Associations of Minnesota. Dr. Marquess, then of Fulton, Mo., had given an address on the Holy Spirit, which had awakened in the hearts of many a longing to know more of his power for service. Some of the young men from the Minneapolis Association, going home on the train on Monday morning, planned together for a quiet meeting at the close of the men's meeting that evening. I was detained and did not get into the first meeting until almost its close. The leader was about to dismiss the meeting, when a young fellow arose and said something like this: "I propose that those who are desirous of doing so should remain at the close of this meeting to wait on God for a special enduement of his Spirit." He continued: "I have not asked the officers of the Association for the use of the room, but suppose that without question it will be granted, and I have it in my heart to suggest that we have no definite human plan about the meeting. Let those remain who desire to do so, and every one will be at liberty to go out at any time, and no one will question their motive, or sit in judgment upon them for going. We will have no stated time for the meeting; we will not say that it will be an all-night meeting, nor will we promise when it shall close. I would also suggest that there be no leader, but that for once we let the Spirit of God have his own way in the matter."

To my great surprise twenty or thirty young men remained. It was a wonderful meeting. No one said, "Now, brethren, let no time go to waste." There was no difficulty in that direction. There seemed to be the utmost liberty and freedom. Prayers followed one after another without hesitation, and promises were quoted or silence intervened without any one apparently noticing it. I remember very well to have heard the clock strike ten, and then eleven, and I was conscious during that time that some went out of the room. I don't know who they were, for the spirit of the young man who had made the suggestion seemed to have taken hold of the entire company, and I don't think any one even turned his head to see who was going. After that I was not conscious of the lapse of time, but I was keenly alive to the fact of the presence and power of the Spirit of God. I believe that men were as certainly filled with the Spirit of God that night as were men at Pentecost. Perhaps not in the same measure, because not for the same service, but certainly and definitely filled. When I stepped on the street I looked at my watch and saw it was between two and three o'clock. I don't know how many remained in the room. I was conscious that I had left others behind. I don't know when the meeting adjourned; indeed, I think it has never been dismissed. Some one will ask, "Do you not think that was a very vivid emotional experience? Was not the meeting full of excitement?" And I would answer, "No; it was one of the quietest meetings that I ever attended." Some one else may ask, "But was it really a practical experience?" And again I answer, Yes, because I knew men who were present at that meeting whose after lives proved that they had received a power never before realized by them. To illustrate: A week or two later I met a prominent pastor in one of the streets of the city, and he stopped me with this question: "Tell me, what did you do to the two young men that went up to that Young Men's Christian Association Convention from my church?" And when I asked him why he put the question, in reply he gave this testimony. He said, "I asked the question because at our prayer-meeting the other night, in the early part of the meeting, one of the young men, who has been a very useful man in our church, but has never shown any remarkable spirituality, nor even taken any prominent part in church work, voluntarily led in prayer, and I was conscious of a warm wave of blessing going through the whole church.

"It was very noticeable at the time, but I presume would not have made so deep an impression upon me but for the fact that toward the close of the meeting, when I gave a few minutes for testimony, the other young man arose in his place to speak. Now he is extremely modest and bashful, and had scarcely ever taken any part in church work of any sort. But he spoke with a freedom that was noticeable. And I again experienced clearly the same result following his words as followed the prayer of the other young man to whom I referred, a warm wave of blessing passed through the whole company, and I am satisfied," said the Doctor, "that something has come into the lives of these men that they did not have before they went to that convention." Then I remembered to have seen both of these young men in the early part of that meeting in the little upper room. "But," says some one, "do you regard that as a practical blessing?" "Yes, for I happen to know that the last young man referred to by this pastor led twenty-seven men to Christ the following winter in his own church."

It is very profitable for one to study the practical results that followed Pentecost. It is clear that those who were then filled with the Spirit received:

First. A new and fuller conception of their risen and divine Lord. So it may be with us.

Second. An enlarged view of the power and possibilities of gospel preaching and testimony when three thousand were converted in a day.

Third. A clearer grip on the fundamental truth of God's word. Note Peter's sermon.

Fourth. Added power for service.

Fifth. An impulse which kept them constantly looking to Jesus Christ for help; and since the Holy Spirit is ever occupied with him, if we are filled with the Spirit he will keep Jesus Christ in all his fulness constantly before us.

In closing, let me answer two questions that I feel quite sure some of you have in mind: —

First. How can I for myself be filled with the Holy Spirit? And I answer unhesitatingly, Plead his promise and by faith appropriate the gift, and with or without emotion act upon it.

Second. Will this power remain with me?

No, not without continual coming to him; not without the exercise of faith in him for power in service through the Holy Spirit. As Mr. Moody says, we are leaky vessels, and soon will run dry if the supply for our need is not steadily claimed and appropriated. Keep close up under the faucet, and then, if the vessel is leaky, the inflow being greater than the outflow, we shall be always full, always overflowing, always fresh.

Address by Rev. Howard Agnew Johnston, D.D.,
Chicago, Ill.

THE ONLY WAY TO THE THRONE OF POWER.

TEXT: To sit on my right hand, and on my left, is not mine to give, but it shall be given to them for whom it is prepared of my Father.— Matt. 20 : 23.

We all dream our dreams of the coming years. And in those dreams we give place to something of that same desire which dominated the hearts of James and John as they came and asked their Lord to give them a place near his throne when he came into his glory. We, too, would fain be close to him then. But I imagine that we make the same mistake about the way to secure a place by the throne which those sons of Zebedee made. Doubtless they thought it would be quite possible for their Lord to give them the places they desired if he chose to do so. And so we often have the idea that God can give us anything we desire, if it be God's desire to do so. But this is by no means the case. It is as if you were to go to the President and ask him to make you his Secretary of State, although you had no discipline in diplomacy or in statesmanship. He would be compelled to say, "It is not mine to give secretaryships to any and every man. They can only be given to those who are ready to receive them."

James and John had no adequate conception of what it meant to have a place by the side of Christ. What pathos in his words: "Ye know not what ye ask." I imagine the mind of Christ looked forward to the day when he was in Gethsemane, when the multitude came with swords and staves to take him. There were James and John, one on his right side and one on his left, but they forsook him and fled. Then a little further on I think he saw three crosses on the summit of Calvary, and thought of the possibility of James and John being crucified one on either side of himself. That was what it meant for them. Christ did not deny their request; but he gave them to understand that if they would have a place near to his throne it could only be by climbing by his side through Gethsemane and up the side of Golgotha, bearing the cross with him, and knowing the fellowship of his suffering. This must be the precursor to the fellowship of his glory. So doubtless he sometimes says to us, as we come and ask for blessings without counting the cost, and without appreciating even the beginning of the discipline essential to the power: "Ye know not what ye ask."

The pathos of the situation is not lessened as we read that the ten were angry with James and John when they heard their request. They also desired the same thing, without realizing the character of the life which alone could secure it. And Jesus turned to them and gave them the secret of power. He talked of the self-centred life of those who seek earthly place and power, and contrasted his own life with such a spirit, saying, "The Son of man came not to be ministered unto, but to minister." This, then, is the law of progress into power: the readiness to serve. Here we face an old familiar truth, but the living of it is still new to most of us. The matter of growing into the power of God is not a matter of glittering generalities. It is a matter of clean-cut conditions, definite, positive, and clear. It is as impossible to develop power in spiritual living without definite methods as it is to succeed in anything else. We need to lay to heart the truth that we must meet the conditions of power if we ever have the power. The place by the throne waits. We must climb thither.

Let us mark, therefore, this readiness to serve as the condition of power. We see its workings on every side. Consider the realm of electricity. There is Edison, the prince of electricians. What is the secret of his power? It is the readiness to serve the laws of electricity. His one aim is to discover how he may the more fully serve those laws. Just so long as he does this electricity lays its power in his hands; but the moment he becomes unwilling to serve its law, that moment his power is gone. Equally true is it of the statesman. Let the people believe their representative is truly serving them and he may have office as long as he will. Note the advertisements in the daily papers. They simply mean that the merchant is anxious to persuade the people that he will serve them well, and so long as they believe it his business success is assured.

It is exactly this same law which obtains in the life of the followers of Jesus Christ. It is as certain as the passage of time that when a believing soul is ready to serve the law of God, the power of God is given to that soul. It is the mark of the man of power through all the years. The readiness to serve is the fundamental spring of action in the soul that would grow into the power of God. Many have a wrong conception about this matter. They pray for an outpouring of the Holy Spirit, and wish they had more of the power of God. They ask, "How may we have more of the Holy Spirit in our lives?" But that is not the key question to unlock the problem of power. That question is not, "How can we have more of the Holy Spirit?" Rather is it, "How can the Holy Spirit have more of us?" That is the way to put it, and that is what we can do. With this attitude of mind and heart we can get at the very next point to which our attention should be given. Let us make it personal now. Could you put your finger down on the weak spot, or the sore spot, or the black spot in your life which needs to be changed? Could you be definite to-night in the conviction as to the next thing you need to do in order to grow in power as a follower of Christ? If so, then that is the place you must begin to build. What would you say of a general who has splendid fortifications in every point but one going about the strong points and laying the flattering unction to his soul that his stronghold is a splendid one? You would say the enemy would go around and come in at the one weak spot, and that the man was the victim of his folly. But no less surely must a soul that would develop strength be striving to develop symmetry. It is at the weak spot that we must build. It is by attempting the next thing to be done that will make us more efficient, that we will increase in power. There is no mystery about it. It is simply common sense. The readiness to serve is the spirit which attempts the next thing to be done.

But I desire to suggest the importance of cultivating this spirit which leads to power by giving place to a noble ambition. Nothing tells in the growth of a soul toward Christ more than a noble ambition to be a Christlike soul. The only ambition worthy of an immortal soul is the ambition to realize the purpose of God concerning us. That purpose we know is to have us become like Christ — to be conformed to the image of his Son. Now, I desire, if possible, to help you lay hold of this thought of God for us as immortal souls. Herbert Spencer tells us in his "Data of Ethics" that we count a thing a success or failure according as it accomplishes that which its form of construction shows that its maker intended it to be. For instance, it is evident from the form of the construction of a knife that it is intended to cut. Now whatever else it may serve to do, as an ornament, or in various ways, so long as it fails to cut we must say it is a failure as a knife. Likewise, an umbrella is intended to keep off the rain. It may serve for various other things, but if it should not keep off the rain it must be pronounced a failure as an umbrella.

Now, with this illustration in mind, consider man. Note how the very construction of the human constitution reveals what the Creator intended man to be. Evidently God intended us to realize the fullest development of our highest possibilities and powers. Therefore, whatever else a man may be or do, we must pronounce upon his life career as we measure him by this one standard. He may serve as a tailor's model. Some young men manage that much. He may develop splendid physical powers. Some men measure manhood by muscle. He may amass a vast fortune, securing enough gold to fill his grave. Some men measure manhood by money. He may unfold marvelous genius of intellect, and run the whole gamut of the world's thought with wonderful mastery. Some men measure manhood by mind. But if he shall do no more than this, though his name should be written high on the roll of fame, though the world should give him unstinted applause, yet you must write across his life record: He is a failure as an immortal soul. He did not rise into the realm of the spiritual man, where the soul can know God, where the moral quality unfolds, where character is builded as the exponent of the immortal man. The purpose of his God for him has not been realized in his life.

Ah, friends, as we think of it thus, must we not be roused to consider the ambitions which dominate our souls? If I were to go among you and ask what is your ambition to-night, you would tell me various things in reply. How many would say the absorbing ambition is to be like the Lord Jesus Christ? But surely we believe we cannot afford to be satisfied with anything less than this. We know that nothing less than likeness to Christ in increasing measure will make it possible for us to approach his right hand and his left when he comes into his glory. Would that we might each one see a vision yonder on our sky of the Christ-life which we are to strive to live! Christ the pith of every thought, Christ the wing of every word, Christ the spring of every action, Christ the pole of the heart, Christ the goal of the life, Christ all in all to the soul! Ah, to be dominated by an ambition like this will unfold in us and through us the very power of God in the blessed work in which we are laborers together with him.

It is to this life and this service that our Lord calls us to-day. In the Scottish Highlands there was a custom according to which a chieftain of a clan, when he desired to summon to his side suddenly his followers, would take a wooden cross and dip it in blood, and then hold it in a flame, thus giving it the name of the fiery cross. This he would give to a trusted henchman, who would hasten with swift feet to the nearest hamlet, announcing the summons and the place of rendezvous. The fiery cross would be taken by another, who would carry it swiftly to the next place of dwelling. Thus with great rapidity the message was sent to every inhabitant of the region. At the first summons the loyal members of the clan would immediately forego any task which occupied them and hasten with all possible speed to the appointed place of meeting. He who ignored that summons was branded thenceforth as a traitor. But, friends, our blessed Lord has taken his own cross and has dipped it into his own blood, and has given it to his trusted followers, saying: "Go! Hasten to the uttermost parts of the earth! Disciple every creature for whom I have died!" Shall we not do it? Shall we not rise to his call with a new consecration to his service? As we do we shall learn to climb the way to the throne and to the unspeakable joy of the redeemed.

Address by Rev. I. J. Spencer,
Lexington, Ky.
THE ENDUEMENT OF THE HOLY SPIRIT.

The thoughtful, earnest Christian desires to remove every obstacle in the way of receiving, as fully as possible, the Holy Spirit, God's greatest gift to man. Let us, then, seek to discover the hindrances. The Word of God is the sole standard of authority on the subject, and we accept its teachings with fullest confidence and satisfaction. The lack of hearty acceptance of God's revelation, of thorough reliance upon his promise and its conditions, or in other words, a lack of faith in what he has said, has kept back many from the possession of his spirit in any large measure. Moses lived "as seeing him who is invisible," and that secret made him suddenly good and great. It is our privilege to live as realizing the truth of God's word without a fleck of doubt that God will do everything he has promised, and that the conditions to be observed by us are both practicable and inviolable. In the second place, we learn that the reason any man fails to receive the Spirit of God is not that God is unwilling or unable to bestow, but that man is unwilling to receive. "The Lord's hand is not shortened that it cannot save, neither his ear heavy that it cannot hear. But your iniquities have separated between you and your God, and your sins have hid his face from you, that he will not hear."

Jesus declares that the Father is "much more" willing to give his Holy Spirit to them that ask him than any earthly father is willing to give "an egg," or "a fish," or "bread" to his hungry child. Certainly God's readiness to grant his Spirit could not be more explicitly affirmed. Men are not "straitened" in God, but only in themselves. The way to life is "narrow," but only on account of our sins. The greatest hindrance to the Holy Spirit is the unholy spirit, if indeed it be not the only one. Men may think the most formidable obstacle is lack of prayer, faith, or knowledge, but the Scriptures show it to be the presence of harbored sin. "If I regard iniquity in my heart the Lord will not hear me." Men may put away sin from their public actions and not be guilty of any conspicuous transgression, but God looketh upon the heart and maketh inquisitions among the thoughts. He declares that the pure in heart shall see God.

Israel shut up the windows of heaven by withholding from God's altar the best sacrifices and presenting instead "the torn and the lame and the sick." They robbed God of his own, and he said, in his mercy, "Bring ye all the tithes and I will pour you out such a blessing that there shall not be room enough to receive it." We are not our own, but God's. The whole heart and life must be surrendered to him before the ample blessing can be conveyed. Ananias and Sapphira kept back a part of their possessions while professing to render all, and perished under the signal displeasure of the Almighty. "A double-minded man is unstable in all his ways," and he that "wavereth" shall not receive anything of the Lord. "If the eye be single," if the fear or affection of the soul be fixed on Jesus only, then "the whole body shall be full of light."

"One must gain his full consent to serve God or else miss the full blessing." The unholy spirit, or, in other words, the worldly spirit, has various manifestations. The characterization of the world by Christ and his apostles strikes the student of their words with astonishment. Men generally do not realize that the world is such a malignant and malicious foe to godliness as the Lord represents it to be. By the world, speaking abstractly, is meant the spirit that rules in the ungodly; or, in the concrete, those controlled by that spirit. So pronounced is the opposition between the kingdom of God and the world that Jesus declares it impossible to serve God and mammon; that the world hated him and hated his disciples, and that it cannot receive God's Spirit. Paul says that only the cross crucified the world unto him and himself unto the world, that the God of this world seeks to blind believers to the light of the glorious gospel, and James announces that the friendship of the world is enmity and spiritual adultery in the sight of God, and that any friend of the world is God's enemy, and we know that God will not communicate his Spirit to an avowed enemy.

John says, "If any man love the world, the love of the Father is not in him," and that "whosoever is born of God overcometh the world." This hateful thing called the world, the characteristics of which are fully described in the New Testament, must be rejected and overcome by those who would receive the fulness of the Holy Spirit. It includes selfishness, covetousness, ambition, the fear of men, esteem of their praise, and the love of the lower, baser, and transient things of life.

When James and John asked to sit in regal worldly dignity on Jesus' left and right hand in his kingdom their ambition was worldly and needed crucifixion before they could reign indeed with Christ. Hence he prescribed his own cup of bitter suffering as their remedy, which they consented to drink. When Simon of Samaria saw that the apostles, by the laying on of hands, endowed believers with the Holy Spirit, he thought to purchase for a selfish, ambitious, or avaricious use the same ability to endow, but his heart was "not right," and seeing he was still in the gall of bitterness he begged Peter to pray that his wicked thought might be forgiven him.

Are there not to-day many who, like James and John, or like Simon, through worldly ambition or for selfish gain seek for God's holy enduement?

One of my children came to me with a request which I refused. Then the child said, "Papa, what does the Bible mean when it says, 'Ask and ye shall receive'?" I replied that the Bible also says: "Ye ask and receive not, because ye ask amiss, that ye may spend it in your pleasures." Is it possible that men ask selfishly for the Spirit of Christ?

Do persons ask the Lord for his Spirit chiefly for the sake of their own pleasure? Verily; but their request is not granted. They want "peace," "joy" and the spirit of "praise" and "gladness" in their hearts. They want to be "happy:" they want the Spirit of God as the Comforter, but not as the reprover of sin. I have learned that the Spirit brings not only love, joy, peace, and strength, but tribulation, temptation, and the refiner's fire as well. It comes not only with soothing, but with the piercing of the two-edged sword: it wounds as well as heals; it kills and makes alive. Jesus, being filled with the Spirit, was first led into the wilderness of temptation, and then out of it again into victory. The Spirit called Paul, not only to preach with marvelous utterances, but also to suffer great things for the name of Jesus. The Spirit, while making him willing to die at Jerusalem, also testified that in every city bonds and afflictions awaited him. Along with the sweet rose of Sharon in his heart there remained the bitter thorn in his flesh to pierce and subdue his pride. Stephen was full of the Holy Spirit, but suffered the world's scorn and crushing martyrdom, yet withal, the spirit of joy and strength in his heart made his face to glow like that of an angel.

So then, when we ask that the Spirit of the Lord Jesus may be born in us, we should not shrink from travail; when we ask for his sceptre of peace and the robe of righteousness, let us not recoil at the sight of the sword and of the "garment rolled in blood;" when we pray for comfort let us not rebel at tribulation that worketh patience; when we ask for coronation let us not refuse the proffered baptism of sorrow, for, says Paul, " I reckon that the suffering of this present time is not worthy to be compared with the glory that shall be revealed not only for us, nor over, nor about us, but in us."

If we would have the fellowship of his Spirit, we must also share the fellowship of his sufferings. We are joint heirs with Christ, "if so be that we suffer with him, that we may be also glorified together."

Yes, the bitter must mingle with the sweet, until, having come out of tribulation, God himself shall wipe away our tears and staunch our bitter griefs. The crystal river of peace is at the end, and not at the beginning of Revelation. At the beginning is the glorified Christ seeking admission into proud and lukewarm hearts, and charging his defective saint to repent, to be faithful, to endure, and overcome. Let no minister ask for the Spirit of Christ only that he may have larger congregations, a wider fame, a better salary, and more comfort in his parish.

Let no Christian pray for the Spirit of the Lord only to make his path pleasanter, his peace deeper, his praise louder, or his own feelings more joyful; but rather, to make his own life more abundantly lustrous or fruitful. " Herein is my Father glorified, that ye bear much fruit." But, while I point out the necessary sorrows and chastenings and urge a heroic readiness to endure hardness and suffering as a good soldier of Jesus Christ, I would not fail to emphasize the joy which the Spirit brings. Paul and Silas, scourged and dungeoned, were inspired to sing aloud for joy. Hannington, alone amid savages and hyenas in Africa and awaiting death, found the " perfect peace" promised to those whose minds are "stayed on God."

Albert Sturgis, on his way as a foreign missionary, wrote, " This is the happiest day of my life," and when his successful ministry among them was about to close he said he would gladly return from heaven, if it were possible, in order to serve his people. The Christian's experience, like exquisite tapestry, has only enough sombre to soften its brighter hues. God gives to his children only enough clouds to mellow the noontide and to gather up and shed forth the crimson glory of the setting sun. The fruit of the Spirit is not sorrow but joy, not warfare but peace, not weakness but strength, albeit joy ripens through sorrow and strength is made perfect in weakness.

> " The bud may have a bitter taste,
> But sweet will be the flower."

" The blackest soil grows the richest fruits, and the tallest trees spring heavenward among the rocks."

The next hindrance I notice is that men and women seek some special and favorite manifestation of the Spirit of God instead of asking for whatever gift the Lord may wish to confer, " dividing to every man severally as he will." We may not speak with foreign tongues, heal the sick, or raise the dead, but we may " covet earnestly the best gifts," asking God to grant whatever in his wisdom is best for us and our use in his service.

The "more excellent way " is that in which love is made the chief or sovereign thing, the way of love that " suffers long and is kind," not "puffed up," but humble, not "easily provoked," but bearing all things, thinking no evil, seeking not " her own," but others' weal, and rejoicing, evermore rejoicing, in the truth. He who is filled with the spirit of the thirteenth chapter of First Corinthians is full of the Holy Spirit of God, a vessel meet for the Master's use.

To be able to preach with power so that thousands fall under the sharp arrows of our King; to draw the multitude to repentance and baptism in the name of Christ, as Peter did at Pentecost,—this is the gift for which many pray and which few receive.

"Seekest thou great things for thyself? seek them not;" not thy will but thy Father's shall be done. Take the talent and use it as faithfully as though it were five talents.

God may grant you the power to love deeply in the home, in the school, in your own city or neighborhood, and thus reflect his glory. He may grant you the spirit of wisdom and foresight in business, so that, prospering, you may bring financial support consecrated to his kingdom. He may endow you with a chastened heart, and a voice of marvelous and melting sweetness to sing his praise. He may give to some lowly handmaiden such "beauty for ashes," such a "garment of praise for the spirit of heaviness," such compassion for sinners, such gentleness and kindness, that her coming is angelic and her presence brings salvation. He may grant to another the boon of heroic self-immolation, such as the loyal missionary exhibits, or many a Christian soldier exemplifies on the field of carnage, or many a sweet mother possesses,— a thorough self-abandon for others' welfare in the name of Christ, that sets the current of faith and hope to bounding where before it lay dying.

Through God's Spirit one's couch of pain may become his pulpit. The empty cradle, the vacant chair, yea, even the drunken son or prodigal daughter, may become the "door of hope" in the "valley of anchor," both to your soul and others.

Repentance, obedience, and prayer open the door to the incoming Lord. Then as waters issue from the fountain, as blossoms open and birds sing in spring-time, so the divine presence produces love, joy, peace, and all the priceless cluster of spiritual fruitage. He who surrenders himself to the inflowing tide of God's love need not trouble himself about the manner of its outflowing. It will make him a blessing in God's own time and in God's own way. God may work through the welcoming soul conspicuously as in the whirlwind or secretly as in the setting dew.

Men may "resist," the Holy Spirit by self-will, "grieve" by malice and ungentleness, and "quench" by selfishness. Resist not; i. e., grieve not, quench not, the Spirit, but be "filled with all the fulness of God" and "strengthened with might by his Spirit in the inner man."

The great pivotal passage in the Bible on this subject, the simplest, directest, and most joy-giving to the lukewarm who wish to be hot, to the deceived who desire illumination, to the poor who want to be rich, is that representing the glorified Lord as standing and waiting for admission at the door of the heart. Admit him by repentance, obedience, and prayer, and you need have no fear as to your own safety nor yet as to the manner in which he will endow you for service. As the fountain to the flood, as the sowing to the harvest, as the sun to the atmosphere and beauty of the day, so is the indwelling Lord to our own spiritual light, joy, and successful service to our neighbors.

O Lord, whether through pleasure or through pain, through love or fear, whether in prosperity's summer or adversity's winter, whether on the mount of crucifixion or transfiguration, help us to say, "I'll open the door and let the dear Saviour come in."

Address by Rev. Floyd W. Tomkins, Jr.,
Providence, R. I.
THE ENDUEMENT OF POWER.

1. Power may come from an inferior or from a superior. If from an inferior, then the man to be benefited must use and control the power. Food is an inferior power; to be strengthened by it I must select it, prepare it, take it, exercise and digest it. In other words, it only serves me as I command it.

If the power come from a superior then the man must submit in order to be benefited. He must be acted upon, and his state must simply be that of intelligent surrender. The power of the general endues the soldier only as the soldier acquiesces. The more superior the source of power the truer this becomes. And when that source is God the Holy Ghost, the submission of the human must be absolute if he would be blessed.

2. Hence there are certain conditions to be observed if we would be "filled with the Holy Ghost." The first is that of *absolute* submission. "Not my will, but thy will." "Fill me with thyself; empty me of myself." "O, to be nothing, nothing. Simply to rest at thy feet." In thus surrendering self there is nothing weak. It is the wisdom of a man who obeys the law of help.

3. The second condition is that of recognition. We must *know* the Holy Spirit. He must be to us *a Person, God*, loving, wise, ever and everywhere present.

4. We must expect great things. No doubting soul can be used by the Spirit. Faith in the Power must be real and strong and lasting.

5. We must consciously live all the time under the influence of this Spirit. It is not occasional brilliancy, but constant shining, that tells. When the apostles were first endued with power men thought they were drunk. Afterwards, when this Spirit's power became constant, men "took knowledge of them that they had been with Jesus."

6. The results of this enduement, this "being filled with the Holy Ghost," are natural and healthy. As in all life, so in the spiritual life, the effect of power is growth. A simple happiness, a clear trust, a sweet helpfulness, an unselfish service,—these speak the Spirit's indwelling and strength-giving. "Make me holy by the indwelling of Thy Holy Spirit." That little prayer speaks the whole truth.

Address by Rev. William Patterson,
Toronto, Ont.

SPIRITUAL LIFE; ITS MANIFESTATIONS AND DEVELOPMENT.

There is no contrast greater than that between life and death, whether it be in the physical world or the spiritual. But there are degrees of life ; namely, life, and life more abundant. A man may have physical life but at the same time possess so little of it that he is unconscious of his own existence, and his friends may be in doubt as to whether he is alive or dead. In like manner a man may have so little spiritual life that he will be without assurance of salvation, and his friends will be in doubt concerning his spiritual condition. Again there are those who are conscious of their existence, but who are so weak that they have to be fed and cared for by others. And in the Church there are many who have to be fed on the milk of the Word and who have to be taught and ministered unto. We come now to a higher stage in physical life, where a man has sufficient life to care for himself, but has none to spare, hence he is unable to work or to help others; and in the Church of Christ we have a great multitude who have enough spiritual life for themselves but have none to spare ; or, to change the figure, they are like wells which are full but have no overflow, and the world receives very little benefit from this class.

We now come to the highest degree of life, where we find it to be abundant; and in the physical world all great enterprises originate and are pushed forward by those who have an abundance of physical and mental life. It is also true in the Christian world that all the great movements for the helping of humanity and the spread of the gospel have been begun and are being carried on by those who have an abundance of spiritual life. Work is a toil to the man who has but little life, whilst it is a pleasure to the man who has an abundance of life. This is true whether you take it physically or spiritually. All people cannot have an abundance of physical life, but all Christians can have an abundance of spiritual life, and it is their own fault if they do not, for Jesus said, "I am come that they might have life, and that they might have it abundantly." But there are certain conditions which must be complied with and certain laws which must be obeyed if a man is to became strong either physically or spiritually. In the first place food is essential to development, and not only food, but the right kind of food. A man may exist on angel cake and lemon pie, but he will never become strong on that kind of diet. He must not only avoid things that are injurious, but he must partake of food that is nourishing if he is to develop physical strength. Even so must the Christian not only avoid poisonous literature, but must feed on the Word of God and literature which is helpful, stimulating, and strengthening. There is a great amount of religious literature in this age which is not harmful but contains very little spiritual nutriment, and one reason why so many young Christians have so little spiritual strength is because they live to such an extent on this spiritual pastry

Like children we turn away from the food that is nourishing to that which is more palatable, and physically or spiritually the results are disastrous.

The second essential to development is good atmosphere. What a contrast between those who work in poorly ventilated factories and those who work on the farm or in the open air! Now spiritual atmosphere is just as essential to spiritual development as pure atmosphere is to physical development. The question is not, can I be a Christian and continue to frequent the theatre, the ballroom, and such places? But the question is, can I continue to breathe the poisoned atmosphere of such places, and at the same time grow in grace and become strong spiritually? There was a great difference between the spiritual atmosphere which surrounded Abraham and that which surrounded his nephew in Sodom, and there was just as much difference in the men; for while the spiritual vision of Abraham was becoming clearer so that he could see the city of God with its foundations, and while his faith was becoming stronger so that he could take hold of the promises of God with a firmer grasp, the reverse was taking place in the case of Lot, until we behold that pitiable sight in the city of Zoar when the cities of the plains were in ruins. The history of these men is repeating itself in the lives of many Christians throughout the world.

A third requisite to the development of life is exercise. The faculty that is not used will ultimately become useless, but the more any faculty is used the stronger it becomes. In the same way that physical work develops the body, and mental work the mind, so spiritual work develops the spiritual nature of man. This exercise must be organized and directed in such a way that while life is being developed some good will also be accomplished. For example, a horse may put forth a great deal of energy while running in a field, but nothing is accomplished, whereas if he were harnessed and attached to a conveyance he would have the exercise, but work would also be done in proportion to the energy spent. In the spiritual sphere exercise and life should be so directed that while the Christian is being developed, the cause of God may also be advanced. Now if these conditions are complied with and these laws obeyed, Christian development and spiritual growth must follow. In every Christian Endeavor Society we have all these essentials to spiritual development. First we have the food, which is chiefly the Word of God read, sung, repeated, or expounded. Second, we have the Christian atmosphere in the meetings, which are distinctly religious, where there is Christian fellowship and communion with God. Third, there is the Christian exercise of taking part in the meetings and of carrying on Christian work both in and out of the society. Fourth, there is the girding and directing of this activity and energy by the different committees, each one of which has a definite aim in view and a definite work to do for Christ and the Church. I have not spoken of the absolute necessity of the Holy Spirit working in us in order that the spiritual life which he has imparted may be developed. I have taken it for granted that if we do our part he will do his, and if we are weak when we should be strong, it is not his fault, for he is more willing to give than we are to receive.

Address by Rt. Rev. Samuel Fallows, D.D., LL.D.,
Chicago, Ill.

THE INTELLECTUAL CONDITIONS FOR THE ENDUEMENT OF THE SPIRIT.

There is a philosophy that teaches that man is nothing but a material organism. The five or six senses or more are the sole avenues of knowledge. We live and move and have our being in the basement story of our existence. Mind is but a name for the resultant of a mere fortuitous concurrence of atoms.

This is not the philosophy of St. Paul when he avers, " Eye hath not seen, nor ear heard, neither have entered into the heart of man the things which God hath prepared for them that love him." But God hath revealed them unto us by his Spirit.

His philosophy rebels against this beggarly, limiting, materialistic, conception of human nature. It asserts that there is a spirit in man, and the inspiration of the Almighty giveth him understanding. There is an oversoul above our soul. We are in the midst of a supernatural world. The things of God are spiritually discerned; that is, they are discerned by the spirit assisted by the Spirit of God.

We must, however, be careful not to destroy in thought the unity of the real man in speaking of his powers or faculties. The mind — the comprehensive term which stands for man — is one.

We must distinguish between its capabilities, and not destructively divide them. Thus distinguishing, we may say that each faculty must do its appropriate work. With colors and sounds and odors, coming through the senses, the pure intellect may not of necessity have to do. The senses do not cognize the axioms of geometry. We do not solve a problem in Euclid by the affections. We do not fall in love by a process of reasoning. We do not fence in a field with bars of music, nor break it up with the fiery steeds of the imagination, nor sow it with ideas. Each faculty to its task. The faith faculty — the uppermost of our powers — lays hold on God and lays hold of it. The spiritual nature, evidenced by this faith-power, receives the direct impact of God's Spirit.

But the enlightening influences of the Holy Spirit must be accompanied by intellectual action. He is to take of the things of Christ and show them unto us. As the great agent of sanctification, he is to effect it through knowledge or the truth. With the reason we are to apprehend the truth. Not merely what I think or trow is the truth, for truth is objective as well as subjective, but until I think it, there is no truth for me.

The truths which are beyond the powers of reason to discover must still come to the bar of reason for approval or acceptance. Intelligence must ever be present for right thinking and acting. Love is the fulfilling of the law, but law to be fulfilled must be known. Knowledge apart from love is some " wild Pallas from the brain of demons, fiery, hot to burst all barriers in her onward race for power."

Love without knowledge may become fearfully irregular and fanatical.

The command of Christ was not merely to preach, to announce or declare the truth, but to *teach*. His promise is to be with them that thus instruct and guide. In the teaching there must be the impartation of knowledge, with unwearied patience and perseverance, with tact and discrimination, with specific individual application.

The enduement of the Spirit, whether considered as the original birthright of the Christian believer at his conversion, or first conscious acceptance of the Saviour, or as a special baptism of the Holy Ghost, is not for "mere ecstatic emotion," but for ethical results.

The promise of Christ is that when he, the Spirit, shall come, he shall lead us into all truth,— primarily, the truth of his word: spiritual truth, the truth of redemption, of salvation, of conscious acceptance with God. But there are some who wish to limit the " all" of Christ to what we term religious truth; but the declaration must be taken without any qualification, even as he gave it without restriction. " All truth is of God; " the universe, with all the truth it implicitly and explicitly contains, sprang from the everlasting word. The elder script of nature and the Book of books are from the same divine hand. They are confirmatory and complementary of each other.

The Christian's purpose is to do God's will; but to do it he must know it. The kingdom cannot come until his will be done. But the kingdom includes, every interest of man in all his multiplied relations to nature, to his fellow-men and to God. Man must know to do, and he must do to know.

Prayer can be made, and should be made, for the *constant coming* of the Holy Ghost, for his continual cleansing, strengthening, illuminating, and inspiring influence. He is to help in making the desire to know the truth and to do the truth the supreme motive of the soul; to assist in keeping the eye ever single, that the whole nature may be full of light.

This is the very essence of the prayer for the enduement of the Spirit, think of it as we may and phrase it as we will. It is the prayer that " the eyes of our understanding may be opened, that we may both perceive and know what things we ought to do, and also have grace and power faithfully to fulfil the same."

It is a prayer that the Divine Spirit may lead us out of all narrowness and bigotry, may purge our lips of all vitriolic speech, our hearts of unjust and unholy thoughts, and prepare our hands for every beneficent and Christ like act.

This enduement of the Spirit is, of course, the meeting and the blending, of the supernatural with the natural. It is the coming of God into his temple — the very effluence of his innermost being into the innermost holy of-holies of the human heart.

Lift up your heads, O ye gates, and be ye lifted up ye everlasting doors of the soul, and the King of Glory shall come in!

He enters. Then comes the ever unsolved, but gloriously felt mystery, the oneness of the believer with the Saviour, through the indwelling of the Holy Ghost. " It is not I that live, but Christ that liveth in me."

Address by Rev. I. N. McCash, LL.D.,
Des Moines, Io.
THE PLACE AND FRUIT OF THE SPIRIT.

The place of the Holy Spirit in Christian doctrine is a large one. The fruit of the Holy Spirit is varied by the law of sowing and reaping. Its recognition in the Bible distinguishes that book from the sacred books of the ethnic religions of the world. Vedas and Alcoran do not lift the veil and reveal the Shekinah to the soul. There is a distinct doctrine traceable through the Old and New Testaments.

In the creation of the material world, when chaos reigned, the Spirit brooded, as a great bird, over the faces of night and disorder. Out of the darkness was called our earth to represent, through its multiform products and surrounding firmament, the character, attributes, and feelings of God, himself Spirit. These could not express the tender emotions and concern for men. They awoke feelings of awe and sublimity, but love and gratitude slept.

Upon the earth a creature made in the likeness of God, made of material world, into which was breathed life from the Spirit, God, and in miniature was combined the earthly and spiritual world. To acquaint the creature with his creator's desires, God must manifest himself more fully than in majestic mountains, attrition of waves, beauty of flowers, songs of birds, and lambency of stars — a third creation, a new man, begotten by the Holy Spirit, the union of flesh and the Spirit in the person of Jesus Christ, the Divine Son, revealing the Father. The primal cause and factor in these three creations was the Spirit. " In the beginning was the word, and the word was with God, and the word was God, and the same was in the beginning with God . . . and the word was made flesh and dwelt among us, and we beheld his glory, the glory as of the only begotten of the Father, full of grace and truth." Again, " He that hath seen me hath seen the Father." God is Spirit and the source of all life.

So we have, then, Spirit in the creation of the universe, Spirit in creation and life of man, Divine Spirit begetting the Son in bodily shape of a man, uniting us in a fellowship with the Almighty, — Spirit, Spirit, Spirit. In the New Testament emphasis makes prominent its place. The Master at his baptism is identified by the descent of the Holy Spirit in bodily shape as a dove, when the voice proclaimed, " This is my beloved Son, in whom I am well pleased."

By the same Spirit he is driven out into the wilderness for preparation for his ministry. By it was he comforted in trial, and by it angels ministered to him when the trials were passed.

At the close of his earthly ministration the burden of Christ's last talk and prayer with his disciples was, "It is expedient for you that I go away, and if I go not away the Comforter (which is the Holy Ghost, John 14: 26) will not come unto you; but if I depart I will send him unto you." "When the Comforter is come, whom I shall send unto you from the Father, even the Spirit of Truth, which proceedeth from the Father, he shall testify of me." "And I will pray the Father, and he shall give you another Comforter, that he may abide with you forever; even the Spirit of truth whom the world can not receive because it seeth him not, neither knoweth him: but ye know him, for he dwelleth with you, and shall be in you." "He shall teach you all things and bring to your remembrance all things whatsoever I have said unto you."

A new kingdom was to be established. The kingdoms old were to be cast in another mold. A new dispensation, a new moral world, was being created out of the chaos of moral abysms, boiling iniquity, unrest, and spirit gloom, the kingdom of heaven, with all its order, light, function, authority, and aims. Pentecost is to be the beginning of a new regime, the genesis of a new earth. The first world was the earth, earthy; the second world is the kingdom from heaven. The things which "Jesus began both to do and to teach, until the day in which he was taken up, after that he through the Holy Ghost had given commandment unto the apostles whom he had chosen . . to wait for the promise of the Father . . Ye shall receive power, after that the Holy Ghost is come upon you: and ye shall be witnesses of me both in Jerusalem and in Judea and unto the uttermost parts of the earth." "But tarry ye in Jerusalem until ye be endued with power from on high."

The twelve men whom he had trained three and a half years were to proclaim the condition of salvation. Though they had his personal instruction, they still were unprepared to go before the world and herald with inerrancy the facts, principles, truths, and laws upon which the kingdom was to be founded and by which governed. The great facts the apostles knew, but they must be guided into all truth, into intellectual accuracy in stating the requirements of Christianity which were to be the constitution of a permanent government, in which Jesus of Nazareth has all authority, both in heaven and in earth. The Spirit was not given for moral cleansing; but to endue with power and bear witness of the truth. The Spirit came and confirmed the crowning in heaven of Jesus and the time of fulfilment of the prophecy: "It shall come to pass in the last days, saith God, I will pour forth of my Spirit upon all flesh; and your sons and your daughters shall prophesy, and your young men shall see visions and your old men shall dream dreams: yea, and on my servants and on my handmaidens in those days will I pour out of my Spirit; and they shall prophesy."

Out of the mist, and above the turbulent confusion, dry land appeared. The Sun of Righteousness to suffuse hills and valleys with effulgent glory had arisen, the Church had swung open the door, and men were invited to enter. Fallow fields are now to be broken and the seed of the kingdom, the Word of God, is to be sown.

The Spirit's place is not only at the inauguration, but in the extension, of the kingdom of Christ as its agent. He uses the word as his sword in battle. He reproves by that word and "convicts the world of sin, of righteousness, and of judgment to come." He is the power in the truth which pure men speak "not in the words which man's wisdom teaches; but which the Holy Ghost teaches; comparing spiritual things with spiritual."

That Spirit respects the power of each soul to choose its companion. Every heart has its secret chamber. Into it no companion enters except on invitation. God does not intrude himself, and when invited will not remain an unwelcome guest. Jesus before that door stands and knocks for admittance; Satan goes in only when the door is open for evil, and the Spirit comes in when the truth is welcomed.

A new life is begotten, "not by corruptible seed, but by incorruptible, by the word of God which liveth and abideth forever." We appropriate Christ to be justified in him. We appropriate the Spirit as a comforter. Christ receives us as sinners; the Spirit, because we are sons, enters into our hearts, crying " Abba, Father." He leads and sustains in trials for the truth as a tempted Lord in the wilderness, and brings the gold out of the fire bearing the image of Christ.

" Out of the mine and the darkness, out of the damp and the mold,
Out of the fiery furnace cometh each grain of gold;
Crushed into atoms, and leveled down to the humblest dust,
With never a heart to pity, with never a hand to trust.

" Molten and hammered and beaten
Seemeth it ne'er to be done;
Oh, for such fiery trials
What hath the poor gold done?
Oh, 't were a mercy to leave it down in the damp and the mold.
If this is the glory of living, better be dross than gold.

" Under the press and the roller, into the jaws of the mint,
Stamped with the emblem of freedom without a flaw or a dint,
Oh, the joy of refining out of the damp and the mold,
Stamped with the glorious *image*, thou beautiful coin of gold."

The devout soul obedient to Christ, "beholding as in a glass the glory of God, is changed into the same image, from glory to glory, even as by the Spirit of the Lord."

The spirit, mentioned three times in the Old Testament, and ninety-four times in the New Testament varies in place from the broodings over creation to the inauguration of the spiritual Church; from the moving of holy men of old to the indwelling of the Comforter; from the inspiration above wisdom to the guide into all truth.

FRUIT OF THE SPIRIT.

By his fruit the Christian Endeavorer has the evidence of his acceptance and proof to the world that he is developing the new life in Christ. "By their fruits ye shall know them." The outward form may speak of godliness and inwardly deny the power thereof. The creed may be venerable, or ritual beautiful—but dead. The introduction of the tulip from the East into Europe in the seventeenth century, awakened the spirit of speculation. The flower was so admired that fabulous prices for rare varieties were paid. Among all the varied hues and tints no blue tulip was found. A wealthy horticulturist offered two thousand dollars for a bulb and its flower of blue. A Chinese, understanding prismatic colors of light, arranged a prism so the blue ray fell constantly upon a forming bud. When it matured and opened it was the coveted color. With bulb and blossom the Chinese claimed and received his reward. When the bulb from the plant was planted next year the original color was produced. The life had not been changed. Forms and rituals, confessions and disciplines, may be followed, but without the Spirit they are a sky without stars, a valley without verdure, and a lake without life. The fruit of the Spirit is shown in moods as well as methods, in motives as well as motion.

Meditation is a mood that nourishes and mellows luscious fruit. Reflection on some truth, accompanied by desire to understand, that future conduct shall be shaped by it, will show new resolutions. David could say, " I meditate upon thy works, O God; I stretch forth my hands to thee."

The soul may seek to be alone with God; but it will not seek him in the cell and cloister, but in stretching the helpful hand to him in prison, when thirsty, when naked, when hungry, among the least of the earth.

The people of the village of Oberammergau represent in drama a passion play of the whole life of Jesus. Every tenth year that simple people choose men and women among themselves who best represent the temperaments of the characters who were with Christ. There is one man whose meditations upon Christ have so transformed his personal habits and appearance that in him one sees a living picture of some master painter of Jesus.

Meditation cultivates the soul. Wild berries may be found on hillsides and in caves of the mountains, but regular food must be gathered from tilled fields, trained vines, and pruned orchards. Virtues may be found pure here and there in human life; but graces most cultivated are richest in foliage and fruit.

The apostle to the Gentiles named nine varieties of fruit of the Spirit; viz., love, joy, peace, long-suffering, gentleness, goodness, faith, meekness, temperance.

LOVE.— What is it? It is the tenderest and richest emotion of the soul; the glory and depth of our life; the most powerful and most dangerous of human attributes — unfathomed and unfathomable passion. God is love, and affection for him is of the Spirit.

JOY.—What is joy? It is the Spirit praising, rejoicing, exulting. It is expressing satisfaction over effort which is made in serving God.

PEACE.—It is the Spirit in quiet waiting, robbed of anxiety, resting in the assurance that a supreme power and unfailing ruler will pilot through the storm and anchor in the fair haven.

LONG-SUFFERING.—Forbearing with those who are weak or persecuting, short-sighted and contentious. It is abiding the day in hope that the erring shall see eye to eye, and the mistakes and persecutions will be acknowledged faults, and reconciliation will be effected.

GENTLENESS.—It is the Spirit mingling with men. It is the Endeavorer's manner in business, on the street, at social gatherings. It is the attitude of the strong toward the weak, and the consideration of the needy and helpless.

GOODNESS.—It is the Spirit at work, the extended hand to lift up the fallen, the breaking of bread to the hungry, the pouring in of oil to the wounded. Goodness is Howard improving prisons in Europe, Mother Bickerdyke in the army hospital; it is Clara Barton in downtrodden Armenia and feeding starving Cubans.

MEEKNESS. — It is spirit taking lessons. Over strings the fingers are directed by the Teacher of teachers, till the notes are touched that awaken ecstasy in the living lyre. It is the teachable mind learning of the Master.

FAITH. — It is the truth in action. It is the Spirit at war with all that opposes truth and righteousness. It is Noah warning his wicked neighbors of impending danger. It is Gideon cutting down the groves and driving away the enemies of Israel. It is John the Baptist rebuking sin in high places. It is Martin Luther nailing his theses to the door of the church at Wittenberg. It is the American army and navy, led by Dewey, Sampson, Schley, and Shafter, driving into the sea a tyrannous nation that feeble hands and emaciated bodies may enjoy peace in a free government.

TEMPERANCE. — The Spirit controlling the body, the intellect, appetites, and passions. It is the "bringing of all imagination and every high thing that exalts itself against the knowledge of God into captivity to Christ."

Such fruit born in the life of the Endeavorer will be gathered by the Husbandman. The power to live such a life will touch the springs of common humanity and will apply the principles of Jesus to human life. It is the power of an endless life, — a force raised to the highest power and utilized in the practical affairs of men.

INTERIOR AUDITORIUM ENDEAVOR.

THE OPENING SESSION IN AUDITORIUM ENDEAVOR.

Centennial Park.

NASHVILLE has enjoyed the very best Christian Endeavor Convention yet held in the world. In every particular except numbers, — and numbers are not considered an essential particular, — the Convention surpassed its splendid predecessors. It was more practically helpful. It was more spiritually uplifting. It will exert a more profound influence in more directions. It was more magnificently patriotic, more strikingly fraternal, more thoughtful, more expressive, more cordial, more lovable.

The very setting of the Convention was most fortunate. The heat that so many feared did not trouble us. Not a few Northern cities were hotter than Nashville at the warmest, and more than half the Convention days were cool and perfect. The beautiful Tennessee White City furnished auditoriums more commodious than any we have heretofore enjoyed. And beauty was everywhere in that lovely Southern city, delighting the eye as the Convention addresses delighted the mind.

The influence of our scholarly surroundings was felt. Fisk University, with its noble story of elevation for the black man, and Vanderbilt University, which also threw open its royal halls to the Convention, and Ward Seminary, another famous Convention home, besides the seventy additional institutions of learning, seemed to give greater dignity and solidity to our gatherings.

Never before, it should be added, has the Convention singing been more enjoyable or better managed. Jovial Excell, ingenious Foster, uplifting Estey, the stirring male quartette, the entrancing duets of the Yarnelles; above all, that human grand organ, the Fisk Jubilee Singers, set all our hearts to singing.

The opening session of the Convention, held in Auditorium Endeavor on Thursday afternoon, was in every way a magnificent success.

A delightful surprise came before the Convention was called to order. It was the presentation of a gavel made by a Kentucky prison Endeavorer — beautifully made, after working-hours, with penknife and file, from Kentucky wood. It was adorned with silver bands, too, and its mate made for Hall Williston was finely inlaid. These gavels worthily succeeded the Carey hammer, which was so great an inspiration to the San Francisco Convention. They were typical of what Christian Endeavor has done for the rough, gnarly timber of so many shackled lives.

Remarks by Rev. S. N. Vail,
Hopkinsville, Ky.

Mr. President: I deem it a great honor and privilege to present to this Convention a gavel, fashioned and made by a convict, serving in the stripes and chains of Eddyville Prison. He made this gavel with a penknife and a little file, in his cell, after his day's work, and in the light of a candle or lamp furnished by friends outside of the prison walls.

This brother was led to his Saviour by the Endeavor Society, and the polish and taste he has given to the otherwise rough material in this gavel are emblematic of the change effected by the Gospel in that prison; for instead of cruelty, it has brought into those wards sweet sympathy, converted the bare ground of the prison-yard into a greensward, studded with beautiful flowers, whose daily mission (in the light of an open Bible) is to teach those unhappy inmates the great lesson of trust in God; and it has filled the cells and workshops of that institution with the benevolent atmosphere of the Sun of Righteousness, while a number of its convicts are rejoicing in the forgiveness of sin and the hope of eternal life through Jesus Christ.

The earnest prayer accompanying this gavel when officially received is that it may not only be wielded for order in this Convention, but that its taps may be the voice of God, summoning this great army of workers to go and plant the Christian Endeavor banner in all the prisons of the land, of the nations, and of the world; for we believe that what the Gospel of Jesus has done already in the prisons of Kentucky, and even more, it can do in all of them. Let me remind you that over eighteen hundred years ago, our King placed his approval on, and made his provision for, the prosecution of this work in the promise: "Come, ye blessed of my Father, inherit the kingdom prepared for you. For I was in prison, and ye came unto me." And then proceeded to make his will so plain that the youngest Endeavorer might understand when he was doing it, by saying, "Inasmuch as ye have done it unto one of the least of these my brethren ye have done it unto me." Permit me therefore to present through you to this Convention, this gavel from the Christian Endeavor Society of Eddyville Penitentiary.

President Clark received the gavel with words of heartiest appreciation. Profound emotion was aroused by the reading of President McKinley's noble summons to the churches, calling for thanksgiving for victory and prayers for peace. The Convention sent to the President a suitable reply to this message; and its request was heeded at the opening devotional exercises, conducted by Rev. W. S. Jacobs, of Columbus, Miss. President McKinley's personal message to the Convention was also received with much enthusiasm.

President McKinley's Greeting and the Reply.

I take great pleasure in extending to the Convention cordial greetings and best wishes. Before the Christian Endeavor Society lie magnificent possibilities, and in congratulating the society on its splendid achievements in the past, I would bid it Godspeed to even grander and nobler success in the future.

WILLIAM McKINLEY.

President William McKinley, Washington, D. C. — The Christian Endeavorers of the United States, assembled at Nashville, Tenn., in the seventeenth international convention of the societies, and representing more than 2,500,000 young men and women of the United States alone, wish to thank you for your greeting, and express their heartiest sympathy with their Christian President, William McKinley, in his suggestion for a service of praise and thanksgiving to Almighty God. They have read the proclamation at their opening service, and have united as he desired in prayer for a speedy peace. FRANCIS E. CLARK, President.
JOHN WILLIS BAER, Secretary.

No one has worked more magnificently for the Convention than that great specimen of manhood, Ira D. Landrith, chairman of the Convention Committee, who was given a superb greeting as he came forward to welcome the delegates. In spite of the attendance, smaller than was hoped for, he was jubilant. "This Convention," he wisely urged, " is what God wanted it to be. With this smaller attendance he is going to do more than omnipotence itself could have done with forty thousand, since the main purpose of the Convention is to show the South what Christian Endeavor is; and now the citizens of Nashville and Tennessee can receive the full benefit of the gathering."

Address by Rev. Ira Landrith,
Chairman Committee of '98.

You are very, very welcome; and we are very, very tired and happy. What need I say more? If it be indeed true that "actions speak louder than words," then surely we have already proclaimed our pleasure in tones stentorian; and no word I may add can strengthen the chorus of welcome uttered in deeds by the Committee of '98 — welcome to all we have and are throughout this blessed Pentecostal week. Pentecostal? Yes; for the suggestion now assumes the dignity of a prophecy, and the prophecy is as certain of fulfilment as that God answers prayer. We have prayed daily — and the petition was fervently repeated around the world — that whatever good thing this Convention might be or do, it should be first of all, and above it all, and through it all, Spirit-full, and Lord-led and Christ-centred. The prayer has already been answered, and the answer will be day by day more and more abundant and rich.

Welcome to Nashville! Welcome to Tennessee! Welcome to Dixie! Read our welcome in the numberless pages of o'ertrue tales told about the Convention by the Press Committee; hear it glad and prolonged in the hammer strokes of the Committee on Halls; glance at the joyous word fashioned by our Decorations Committee in your glowing red and white, emblems at once of the blood-earnestness of our love and the stainless purity of your purposes; listen while the Music Committee converts the always sweet word into more beautiful melody. Welcome! Has not the Reception Committee expressed the sentiment in hearty hand-grasps and cheery greeting? Three thousand open doors of as many of Nashville's best homes bid you welcome to-day in the name of the Entertainment Committee; and every evangelical pulpit in this city of churches silently testifies to the welcome the Pulpit Supply Committee extends. Two hundred and fifty young men on duty in the various places of meeting beam their welcomes as they smilingly lead you each to the best seat in the hall. The Registration Committee has already recorded your name high upon the roll of the guests they are happiest to have with them. And, finally, the Committee on Finance whispers a welcome in the rustle of crisp, new bills, or rattles it in free silver dollars, and clinks it in the gold standard whenever the secretary draws the internal-revenue-stamped check which the chairman solemnly certifies. Yes, fellow Christian Endeavorers, you are welcome.

This Convention came to Nashville, we believe, because God had said to Christian Endeavorers, "I have a Southland which I will give thee for an inheritance," and because the divine finger pointed two years ago straight to Nashville as the gateway to Endeavor's land of promise. The Committee of '98 believed, when Washington, '96, made possible Nashville, '98, that the Board of Trustees were but instrumentally casting the Lord's own ballot; we believe it to-day. At every step of what at first seemed a march difficult, if not dangerous, we have seen walls crumbling, and mountains melting to the plain, and seas dividing to the right hand and to the left hand, and all to make easy our otherwise impossible progress; and these things are not of men's doing, but alone of Jehovah's will. Conscious as we have been that the work was Heaven-sent, we have tried to do it worthily and well. And now that it is done, however imperfectly, and now that the day for which we have eagerly labored and waited is here, we are supremely happy in expected blessings gloriously realized.

We asked for this Convention because we needed to have it come to our city and section. To be misinformed is ever a more dangerous and distressing thing than to be uninformed; and the time had come when a typical city of the South should learn exactly what Christian Endeavor is and does. To do this the schoolmaster abroad, an International Convention, was necessary. During these convention days we will unlearn much and learn more about this marvelous movement; and when the gavel falls upon your final meeting Christian Endeavor will be able to shout to its friends the world over, "By the grace of God, I came, I saw, I conquered." And the victory will be over misinformation, as wonderful a triumph as heroic armies ever won.

But we asked for this Convention for many another reason. We needed its spiritual power, its beautiful lessons of Christian fellowship, its influence in making us more zealous and intelligent as workers together with Christ, and the wider vision which we shall enjoy in our labor for the Master after we have mingled with you, the worthy representatives of many Churches, and States, and nations.

We Christian Endeavorers of the South need the opportunity we now have, of proving to the Christian Endeavorers of the North that whatever our fathers thought a generation ago — and your fathers will tell you that ours were as sincere as yours and as brave — both they and we, their sons and daughters, now love our reunited country next to God and to God alone, and recent stirring events have but made our desire the more intense to show to our English and Canadian kindred, in this very heart, the most American part of America, how much thicker is blood than water, and how happy we all are that the fratricidal Anglo-Saxon bitternesses of the past are dead now and buried in a grave fast growing green. We were anxious too, and are still, that in this Convention every tribe and nation, every race, and color, and clime, might learn that we count them brethren as worthy as are we to know and praise our Saviour, without whom both they and we would be worse than worthless.

Such are some of the blessings the Committee of '98 expected this Convention to bring, and it will. But if it had never come at all, or if, now that it is here, it should disappoint us in all these things, we are yet content in the consciousness that we have already been amply repaid for everything we have been able to do through these busy months of preparation. Have we not learned anew how sweet is sincere service? And do we not know as never before how blessed it is for brethren to dwell together in unity? And is not our city, and are not our churches, more nearly united in Christian effort than ever before? Ah, we know now that the bountiful Benefactor above always gives more than we know how to ask or think.

My delightful duty will be done when I repeat once more the welcome which fills the hearts, not alone of my associates and myself, whose names are known as the Committee of '98, but of the two thousand others who have been willing to labor unheralded and unknown, but faithfully and tirelessly, nevertheless, that Nashville, '98, might always be to you a pleasant memory for the hospitality it extended and for the unmixed blessing it brought into your life. God grant that it may be so!

Committee of '98.

The following is a complete list of the committee whose faithful work made possible Nashville, '98:—

REV. IRA LANDRITH, *Chairman.*
J. D. BLANTON, *Vice-Chairman, Local Excursions.*
B. G. ALEXANDER, *Secretary.*
EDGAR JONES, *Finance.*
M. B. PILCHER, *Halls.*
J. U. RUST, *Reception.*
PEYTON ROBERTSON, *Entertainment.*
ERSKINE REED, *Music.*
JOEL O. CHEEK, *Registration.*
W. L. NOELL, *Press.*
E. S. MCFADDEN, *Ushers.*
T. A. REYNOLDS, *Pulpit Supply.*
MRS. M. C. DORRIS, *Decorations.*

Address by Rev. James I. Vance, D.D.

Tall and slender, with a thin, eloquent face, Dr. Vance, of Nashville's First Presbyterian Church, is a most effective orator, and for the city's pastors gave us a cordial welcome. "The South," he declared, "has never opened wider gates to goodlier guests." He carried the Convention with him in his prayer that the gathering might put to utter rout the last ghost of sectionalism, those animosities which the war with Spain is quenching in the tide of a new patriotism. It was he who baptized the Convention with a name that will stick, "The Convention of Brotherly Love."

Pastors' Welcome by Rev. James I. Vance, D. D., Pastor of the First Presbyterian Church, Nashville, Tenn.

Fellow Christian Endeavorers: — All hail! In the name of one hundred pastors, with thirty-five thousand church-members at our back, and a city of one hundred thousand people enthusiastically in sympathy with our greeting, we speak the gladdest, strongest, warmest, truest Christian welcome to this great gathering of the sacramental chivalry of the Lord's anointed.

The clock is striking the hour for which our hearts have been waiting and listening these many months.

Come into our city; it is ready for you. Come into our homes; they are waving welcomes from every door and window and gate ajar. Come into our churches; they are your churches, too. Come into our hearts; you are there already.

Nashville has never opened wider gates to goodlier guests. The South has never held beneath its sky an army whose mission beat truer to all that is sacred and dear to both South and North, to both East and West, than this vast host which gathers to signalize the current year with the Seventeenth International Convention of Christian Endeavor.

We would make vocal every pulpit and pew; we would station a watchman in every church spire, and a messenger at every church door; we would put a tongue in every flower and tree, and give speech to all that is dumb, that the air may be filled with the music of a great chorus singing, "Welcome."

"Y. P. S. C. E" is the sesame at whose magic utterance all barriers disappear, all doors open, all hearts rejoice. All things are yours, for ye are Christ's. A thousand Christian welcomes!

We welcome you because our Lord welcomes you. We welcome you because you come in the name of the churches we love, and serve, and represent, because your march keeps step to the music of a united and conquering Christendom. We welcome you, for around this hour gathers a halo of answered prayer, and into these convention days will come the cheer of Christian comradeship and the blessing of deepened consecration. As we sit together here in heavenly places in Christ Jesus, we shall renew our vows, and looking into each other's faces, with the vision of a common faith we shall find once more that the things which unite us are greater than those which divide us, until with closed ranks and cheered spirits we shall press forward, stronger for the work of rescue.

Fellow Endeavorers, for the first time in its history the Convention meets on the soil of Dixie Land. While the Endeavor movement has grown less rapidly in the South than in some other sections, let me assure you that this has not been owing to any lack of loyalty to the great cause which Christian Endeavor represents. You will soon discover that you are meeting in an atmosphere thoroughly congenial to all that is championed by the evangelical faith. In the South, we still believe in the sanctity of a Sabbath that lasts twenty-four hours each week. We have no war to make on the old Bible. It has stood too long, and vindicated itself too often, to go down before the wind batteries of modern rationalistic criticism. We have no fault to find with the old Gospel; it was good enough for our fathers, and it is good enough for us.

We believe in a Christianity whose central fact is the all-sufficient atoning merit of Jesus Christ, whose sole source of growth and power is the indwelling Holy Ghost, and whose simple and sublime mission is to go into all the world and preach the Gospel to every creature.

Christian Endeavor stands on the same platform and subscribes to the same creed. It masses the youth of Christendom for Christ and the Church, and represents the Lord's latest, upward, onward step in the conquest of the world and in the establishment of his kingdom of grace. Nevertheless, it cherishes the old faith, clings to the old Bible, and preaches the old Gospel. It is the step of youth walking with vigor and alacrity in the "old paths," and singing with glad, victorious voices the music of the old songs.

All hail, Endeavorers! you are

> " A glorious company,
> The flower of men, to prove
> A model for the mighty world,
> And to be the fair beginning of a time."

We are expecting great things of you. We are looking and longing for a rich blessing on ourselves, our churches, and our city. Whatever else you do or fail to do, we want you to impress Nashville and Tennessee, and all this southern land, with the fact that Christian Endeavor stands for a deep and genuine Christian life, a consecration that glorifies itself with sacrifice, a faith that goes beyond all things to the living, personal Lord, and a Christianity that rises above the littleness of sect and section, and greets with brotherly salute all those who love the Lord.

Dr. Clark, officers and members of the Board of Trustees, and Christian Endeavorers of all sections and nations and colors and churches, in the name of the pastors of Nashville I welcome you to the best we have. We believe you have a great message for us and our people.

As we see the godly youth of the land mustered by the thousands in this great Convention, and think of the millions of young people they represent, all banded together for the glory of God and the good of man, we shall get a fresh vision of the hopefulness of Christianity. As we look into your happy faces, and listen to your inspiring songs, and catch the melody of your joy, we shall have a fresh vision of the gladness of the gospel. As we see you meeting in your church rallies and planning there for greater usefulness and efficiency in the dear home church, we shall have a fresh vision of denominational loyalty. As we see you stretching hands, warm with the pulses of Christian love, across denominational walls, and confederating this great company into a common host of believers,

> " Whose fears, whose hopes, whose aims, are one,
> Whose comforts and whose cares,"

we shall catch a fresh vision of the glory of that love which makes God's people one.

It is not accidental, but providential, that the Convention of ninety-eight meets in the South. It will put to utter rout the last ghost of sectionalism. The war with Spain is quenching old animosities in the tide of a new patriotism. As the sons of the soldiers who wore the blue and the sons of the soldiers who wore the gray march side by side under the same flag to make war upon a common foe, sectional boundaries fade out and disappear.

We are not Northerners nor Southerners nor Easterners nor Westerners, but Americans all, whose citizenship is the dowry of manhood rather than of locality and color.

> " Oh, east is east, and west is west, and never twain shall meet.
> Till earth and sky stand presently at God's great judgment-seat.
> But there is neither east nor west, border, nor breed, nor birth,
> When two strong men stand face to face, tho' they come from the ends of the earth."

While patriotism, with the sword of war, drives sectionalism out of the nation, shall not faith, with the sword of the Spirit, drive sectionalism out of the Church? I speak to-day for a Christianity that does not regard the points of the compass. Christian Endeavorers, be it ours to sweep the line of sectionalism from end to end with a brush dipped in the golden light of love, and blot it out forever.

> "Fold the banners,
> Smelt the guns.
> Love rules;
> Her gentle purpose runs."

Let this Convention be memorable in the future for its spirit of Christian fellowship. Let it be known in history as the " Convention of Brotherly Love." And as we wait here "with one accord in one place," may our Lord vouchsafe to us the glory of that other and pentecostal baptism of Holy Ghost power. Amen.

Christian Endeavor Conventions have often been welcomed by noble governors of States,—Francis of Missouri, Greenhalge and Wolcott of Massachusetts, McKinley of Ohio,— and the brilliant and deservedly popular Governor Taylor of Tennessee is now added to the list. He caught the audience with his first sentence: " As the flowers welcome the light of the morning, as the green earth smiles welcome to the summer sunshine and shower, as the possum welcomes the ripe persimmon and the old-time darky welcomes the possum, so Nashville gives welcome unto you." He held his audience spellbound through his witty, wise, and most Christian address, with its ardent love for our united land and its beautiful close in " Coronation." It is not every State governor that knows how to start a hymn.

Address by Gov. Robt. L. Taylor.

Mr. Chairman, Ladies, and Gentlemen : — As the flowers welcome the light of the morning, as the green earth smiles welcome to the summer sunshine and shower, as the possum welcomes the ripe persimmon and the old-time darky welcomes the possum, so Nashville gives welcome unto you.

This is a glorious meeting. The North and the South are united here in a glorious cause. I trust your deliberations will be harmonious as when Uncle Rastus held Aunt Dinah's hand in his and asked, "Who's sweet?" and Aunt Dinah dropped her head on his shoulder and answered, " Bofe of us."

It is my delightful privilege to greet you in the name of Nashville and the State. Through my lips two million souls within the borders of Tennessee give welcome to every son and daughter of every other State and country assembled here to join in the great endeavor to strengthen the Church and benefit mankind. We welcome you because we were looking for you and because we are glad you have come. We welcome you because we love you, and we love you because you are the apostles of love and the evangels of peace on earth and good-will to men.

There is no nobler endeavor in this world than Christian endeavor. It embraces all that is pure and good on earth, and it is our only shield from eternal death.

Whoever dries a tear, whoever heals a wound, whoever drops a kind word into an aching heart, or a coin into the shrivelled hand of poverty, whoever helps the helpless, whoever befriends the friendless, whoever illustrates the gospel of mercy by showing mercy, whoever scatters blessings in a wretched home and makes the flowers of peace and joy bloom at its door, whoever loves his fellow man and fears his God, is eligible to be mustered into the great army of Christian Endeavor. This mighty army with shout and song is marching on to the conquest of the world. Its banner is the cross of Christ and its watchword the brotherhood of man.

The nineteenth century is dying, and in the same grave with it, thank God, will be buried many of the prejudices and vicious superstitions which have confronted the Church in the past and which have blocked the progress of our civilization, and stood in the way of a united Christian endeavor. The dawn of the new century will usher in a new era in the history of mankind. It will usher in a more perfect organization of Christian thought and Christian effort without regard to creed or nationality. The hearts of nations will be fused in one great throbbing heart of love, and the spirit of tolerance and liberality will be diffused among them like the light of a glorious day.

The exultant forces of Christian Endeavor will present a solid front to the foe, and the devil and his angels will fall back in confusion before the armies of the Lord.

I think the twentieth century will be an age of liberty. The guns of Dewey are thundering liberty at Manila, liberty is booming from the guns of Sampson and Schley, and soon liberty will gleam on the bayonets and leap from the muzzles of 100,000 rifles when our volunteer armies close in upon Havana to drive tyranny into the sea. This war is only opening the way for the triumphal march of the Prince of Peace, and the battle-cry is "Liberty." Peace is the child of liberty, and liberty is the offspring of a just and holy war.

The Christian religion can only reign supreme in a land where peace and liberty dwell. Then let our invincible armies march, let our navies hover around the oppressors' camp; for it is the decree of God that the shedding of blood is the price of liberty and peace, and even the salvation of our souls, — the blood of heroes for liberty and peace, and the blood of Christ for salvation.

Sometimes in our Christian endeavor to rebuke sin we are compelled to use artillery. A little grape and canister now and then are splendid sermons, and there are hallelujahs in the rattle of musketry; for when the smoke of the conflict has cleared away churches will spring up and bloom like roses in the track of war, the music of the harvest song will follow the bugle-call, and happy homes will nestle among the hills where hostile armies once met and revelled in the carnival of death.

Not long ago I stood under the folds of the American flag in the midst of a great throng of American citizens. Behind me stood a line of old Confederate veterans wearing the worn and faded gray. In front of me stood a line of volunteers dressed in blue. The two lines confronted each other, not in war, but in peace; not in anger, but in love. The old captain in gray stood face to face with his son, a captain in blue; and in the name of the old heroes whose heads had grown gray in sympathy with the uniforms they wore, I presented a sword to the young captain in blue from the old captain in gray, and a shout went up from a thousand throats when the youthful commander proudly said, in acknowledgment of the gift, "All I can promise is that I will try to be as good a soldier as my father has been." The old flag flouted the air with joy above the blending of the blue and the gray. It was the covenant of eternal brotherhood between the two sections of our country through all the years to come. It was the symbol of our national unity. It was the pledge of the South's loyalty to the National Union.

As I looked upon the impressive scene I saw sectional prejudice and sectional animosity buried forever beneath the common hopes, common fears, and common destiny of a reunited people; and I saw in it the prophecy that our common country shall lead the world in the struggle for liberty for every nation, and for the elevation and happiness of our common humanity, and for the Christian civilization of mankind.

I saw in it a lesson which at last, thank God, the churches are beginning to learn, — the lesson that in the unity and harmony of Christian Endeavor lies the strength and power of the cause of Christ in this world.

Let us all rejoice that this great idea of union has dawned upon the Church as well as the State. Let us all rejoice that this glorious organization of Christian Endeavorers, delegated from the Protestant organizations of every Christian land, is the blossoming of a new and brighter hope for greater victories than were ever won before by the soldiers of the Cross.

Ladies and gentlemen, again I bid you welcome, and hope that your labors will bear fruits of hope and happiness for our fallen race.

The triumphs of your great organization must be the triumphs, not of war, but of peace and love. It is the mission of our armies and navies to break the chains of slavery from the bodies of men; it is yours to break the shackles that bind their souls.

God speed the day when Christian Endeavor shall girdle the globe, and when the song shall go up to heaven from every clime and every kith and kin: —

> "All hail the power of Jesus' name,
> Let angels prostrate fall;
> Bring forth the royal diadem,
> And crown Him Lord of all.
>
> "Let every kindred, every tribe,
> On this terrestrial ball
> To Him all majesty ascribe,
> And crown Him Lord of all.
>
> "Oh that with yonder sacred throng
> We at His feet may fall!
> We'll join the everlasting song
> And crown Him Lord of all."

The Fisk Jubilee Singers from the University then sung for us once and again, for the throng of people were fascinated with their quaint and delightful melody.

California was to have joined in the responses to the welcomes, but Mr. Merrill was unavoidably detained. However, the far East spoke well, through President Metcalf, of Rhode Island; Canada through Mr. Fergusson, chairman of the Canadian Christian Endeavor Council; and the South through President Grotthouse, of Texas. We all sung "God Save the Queen," in honor of Canada, and Texas added the last note, " Blest Be the Tie that Binds."

Response to the Addresses of Welcome, by Mr. E. P. Metcalf,

Providence, R. I.

In the behalf of those of the great Christian Endeavor family who reside in the eastern part of our country I want to express thanks for these kind words, although we have been receiving a Tennessee welcome ever since we reached your pleasant city. And while we are somewhat cold and conservative in the East, yet I assure you in this case we appreciate your warm welcome. We have looked forward to this Convention with very pleasant anticipations. Your bright *Sunshine*, which has been a frequent visitor in our homes for the past few months, has given us some idea of what we might expect, and from the present outlook our highest expectations will be realized.

For various reasons our delegation from the eastern part of the country is smaller than we could have wished, but we trust we may make up in quality what we lack in quantity. We haven't come here simply and solely to get what good we can for ourselves, but we have come with the purpose of bringing something to help and encourage those with whom we come in contact from the different parts of our land. We believe that the way to get is to give. And so, while the East has been privileged, under God, to give to the world this great society of Christian Endeavor, at the same time we received numberless blessings ourselves. We trust this will hold good through this Convention, and that those who give kind and helpful words may receive the comfort and satisfaction that comes to those who try to do what Christ would have them do. So we come here bringing what God has given us, praying that he will take our gifts and use them for the glory and for the honor of his name. We accept these welcomes in the kindly spirit in which they are tendered, and we trust that our coming here may be a help and an inspiration to all.

Response to the Addresses of Welcome, by Mr. G. Tower Fergusson,
Toronto, Ont.

Canada greets the South, and thanks you for your kind welcome. Although serving under a different flag, a flag which we dearly love, we nevertheless in Christian Endeavor work have learned to feel at home under the Stars and Stripes.

Latterly feelings of good-will and amity between the two great Anglo-Saxon nations have been common in the public press.

Hon. Joseph Chamberlain has voiced the sentiments of many British hearts when he said, in speaking of closer alliances, "I do not know what arrangements may be possible with us, but this I know and feel, — that the closer, the more cordial, the fuller and more definite, these arrangements are, the better it will be for both of us and for the world."

This we do know, that International Conventions have been a factor — a powerful factor — in fostering such a feeling between these two peoples as alone will make such an alliance effective. Those representing hundreds of thousands of young people have met. We know now how much in common we have. History has taught us our common ancestry. This accounts for similar traits, not the least of which is love for liberty.

You sing "Sweet Land of Liberty." We re-echo "Britons Never Shall Be Slaves." Nor is this mere sentiment. England has given her best sons and has spent millions of sterling in the cause of liberty. To-day your government is in a hand-to-hand struggle in the same cause. Your sons are on foreign soil for the cause of the downtrodden, and with the determination that the "oppressed shall go free."

Whatever may come in the way of closer relations between the United States and Britain, let us not forget the part, the important part, such conventions as these have played in making such alliances possible or effective.

I again thank you in the name of Canada.

Response to Addresses of Welcome, by Mr. H. H. Grotthouse,
Dallas, Tex.

And what now is there to be said? Some things cannot be said. Dixie has spoken her welcome to the great Endeavor band. It is as complete as it is genuine.

> "From the Northern climes we 've come,
> From the West and from the East;
> Thrice ten thousand hearts a Southern welcome share."

Dixie had the first note, and Dixie has the last note. And what shall it be? There is only one. If you agree with me, then sing it with me: —

> "Blest be the tie that binds
> Our hearts in Christian love;
> The fellowship of kindred minds
> Is like to that above."

Secretary Baer's report then came next.

It was he, too, that made the eagerly expected announcement of next year's meeting-place. "Since we have so recently visited Ohio, and since Philadelphia has already received an International Convention, the unanimous choice of the United Society has fallen upon Detroit." This decision was received with the heartiest applause, and Philadelphia and Cincinnati, through their representatives, promised Detroit the largest delegations they have sent to an International Convention. Then "Blest Be the Tie" was sung again.

Secretary John Willis Baer's Annual Statistical Report.

In its native land Christian Endeavor still moves forward. There are now, within the borders of the United States, 41,222 societies. Pennsylvania, with 3,679 societies; New York, with 3,117; Ohio, with 2,450; Illinois, with 2,072; Indiana, with 1,414; Iowa, with 1,358; and Michigan, with 1,072, are the States at the head of the procession, and in the order named. These figures do not include the Junior, Intermediate, and other societies.

So far as we know, Russia is the only country in the world without its Christian Endeavor society. England has 4,647; Canada, 3,456; Australia, 2,284; Scotland, 535; India, 433; Wales, 331; Ireland, 213; China, 139; Africa, 110. The list is too long to be reported fully here and at this time. The total enrolment from without the United States is 11,775 societies. The increase in South Africa, India, China, Germany, and throughout Great Britain has been large.

The Constitution for local Christian Endeavor societies has been translated and printed in thirty-seven different languages.

The total enrolment of world-wide Christian Endeavor is 54,191 societies, with an individual membership of more than three and one-quarter millions.

The Junior societies continue to increase rapidly. There are now nearly fourteen thousand societies in the world. One thousand of these are to be found in foreign lands.

Of those in the United States we mention Pennsylvania's, 1,535; New York's, 1,391; Illinois's, 1.046; Ohio's, 992; Indiana's, 590; California's and Iowa's, 552; Massachusetts's, 525, as being in the list of States each with an enrolment of more than five hundred Junior societies.

Last year we reported 366 Intermediate societies. This year the total has more than doubled; we have now 759 Intermediate societies. California leads the States, having 92; Pennsylvania has 86; Ohio, 63; Illinois, 56; New York, 49; Indiana, 39; Michigan and Massachusetts each, 36. The growth of the Intermediate societies bids fair to rival the thrifty life and progress of the Junior societies.

You will be interested to know that there are 77 Mothers' societies, 45 Senior or Graduate societies, 17 societies in the United States Army and in Volunteers' camps, 119 societies in the United States Navy and on board merchant ships. Christian Endeavor thrives in out-of-the-way and unexpected places. There are societies in prisons, schools of reform, workhouses, almshouses, asylums, institutions for the blind and for the deaf, schools and colleges, among car-drivers, policemen, travelling-men, life-savers on the coast, lighthouse employees, in large factories, etc., to the number of nearly two hundred.

In England, the Baptists stand first in Christian Endeavor; in Australia, the Wesleyan Methodists; and in Canada, the Methodists.

In the United States the Presbyterians lead, with 5,605 Young People's societies and 3,109 Junior; the Congregationalists are next, with 4,165 Young People's societies and 2,469 Junior; then follow the Disciples of Christ, with 3,268 Young People's societies and 1,483 Junior; the Baptists, 2,629 Young People's societies and 1,130 Junior; the Methodist Protestants, 1,095 Young People's societies and 364 Junior; the Cumberland Presbyterians, 889 Young People's societies and 414 Junior; the Lutherans, 891 Young People's societies and 355 Junior; and so on until more than thirty different evangelical denominations have been listed.

As you well know, it has been customary at our annual Conventions to recognize the States or countries having excelled in numerical strength during the year by presenting them with banners made of the ribbon badges of local societies. Notwithstanding the splendid record made by India, China, Germany, and Sweden, South Africa is entitled to the banner for the greatest proportionate increase in number of societies.

The banner for the largest absolute gain in number of societies has been in England's possession for four years. England has this year increased her roll by more than 700 societies. It has been decided, however, and we are confident with England's approval, that hereafter this banner will be retained for competition exclusively by the States in America, as it is hardly fair to put all England's record alongside of the growth of one State. Pennsylvania is entitled to this banner, having made the remarkable advance of 424 societies during the last year.

The Junior badge banner for the largest gain in Junior societies, taken last year by Ohio from Pennsylvania, will this year be returned to Pennsylvania. New York was not far behind Pennsylvania, and another year may make it exceedingly interesting for the Keystone State.

The Junior badge banner for the greatest proportionate increase in Junior societies is to be awarded to India.

Nine thousand societies in making their annual reports mention the money that they have sent directly to their own denominational missionary boards, and the amount is $198,000. These same nine thousand societies have given for other benevolences $225,000, making a total for these societies of $423,000. The Clarendon Street Baptist Christian Endeavor Society of Boston has for three years reported the largest amount given by any one society, and this year it again heads the list, with $1,519.77. The society in the Madison Avenue Reformed Church, New York City, is second, with $1,097.69.

The Tenth Legion has enlisted many thousands during the year. Started as it was but three months before the last Convention, it now has an enrolment of 10,300. It was the New York City Union that first conceived the Tenth Legion, thus crystallizing in a very practical and attractive method the old principle of giving not less than one-tenth of one's income to God.

You remember that the glory of Cæsar's Tenth Legion lay in the unfaltering loyalty with which, in each emergency, they were ready to dare or suffer at his word. The United Society's Tenth Legion believes to-day is a time of crisis for Christ's army; the missionary advance has been checked at home and abroad. Our Leader calls for larger self-sacrifice and braver service, and so we have emblazoned on our banner, not " Render unto Cæsar the things that are Cæsar's," but " unto God the things that are God's."

Application for enrolment can be made of the United Society of Christian Endeavor, Boston, and a certificate of membership will be mailed in return.

The Comrades of the Quiet Hour, an enrolment of individuals started this last year by President Clark, has now its nearly ten thousand members. Each comrade sets apart religiously at least fifteen minutes a day for communion with God. " Remember the morning watch " has for years been the practice of many, and hence this brotherhood of the Quiet Hour, already numbering its thousands, promises a larger increase in the coming year.

Any Christian will be enrolled if he will send his name to the United Society of Christian Endeavor, Boston; and a covenant-card will be sent in response to the application. The following is the covenant of the comrades of the Quiet Hour: " Trusting in the Lord Jesus Christ for strength, I will make it the rule of my life to set apart at least fifteen minutes every day, if possible in the early morning, for quiet meditation and direct communion with God."

At San Francisco last year Indianapolis carried away the banner for the best work done in the interests of Christian citizenship. This year the Christian-citizenship banner has been awarded to Kansas City, Mo. Omaha, Syracuse, and Minneapolis are entitled to honorable mention.

The banner for the largest number of those giving not less than one-tenth of their income to God is again returned to New York City. Cleveland and Brooklyn, in the order named, are not very far behind in this blessed work.

Philadelphia has a firm grasp upon the fellowship banner. Its extension of our fellowship again heads the list. Chicago comes next in this line.

During the last year the by-laws of the United Society of Christian Endeavor have been reorganized. Let me briefly mention some of the changes.

First. Any past or present member of a Christian Endeavor society may become a *life* member of the corporation upon election by a two-thirds vote of the members present at any legal meeting, and the payment of one dollar to the treasurer. Heretofore, life members paid twenty dollars, sustaining members five, and others one dollar annually.

Second. The corporation shall hold an annual meeting in the month of June or July in each year, at such place as the executive committee of the board of trustees shall appoint, for the election of officers and trustees and the transaction of other appropriate business. Heretofore the annual business meeting has been held in Massachusetts. It can now be held at the same time and place as the annual Convention. This will ensure a large attendance at the business meetings.

Third. The business affairs of the corporation shall be managed by a board of not less than one hundred, nor more than one hundred and fifty, trustees, who shall be chosen by ballot at the annual business meeting.

To secure full representation, a provision in the new by-laws calls for the appointment of a nominating committee to nominate trustees and officers for the ensuing year, this committee to report at the annual meeting. To ensure the widest geographical representation on the board of trustees, the nominating committee is instructed to nominate the president of each State, Territorial, and Provincial Christian Endeavor union in the United States and Canada as a candidate for election to the board of trustees. The suggestion is also made that the nominating committee carefully consider any names issuing from an authorized source that may be presented by any evangelical denomination entitled to representation on the board. Each evangelical denomination shall be represented on the board by at least one trustee for every thousand societies of Christian Endeavor in such denomination.

The societies were asked to state, in short sentences, the best thing that had been accomplished this last year. Here are some of the "best things," and they have been selected with a view to showing the great range of Christian Endeavor activity. We give them without comment of any kind; they speak for themselves:—

"Paid part of our church debt." "Purchased hymn-books, library books, and church furniture." "Paid part of our pastor's salary." "Sent money to educate children in schools in foreign lands." "Assisted our pastor in the evening service." "Supporting home and foreign missionaries." "Held cottage and tent prayer meetings." "Organized Sunday schools in country places." "Visiting and holding services in prisons, almhouses, hospitals, car-stations, and fire-engine houses, in parks and at steamboat landings." "Flower mission and 'fresh-air' fund work." "Organized chorus choir for Sunday evening services." "The study of missions and missionaries' biographies." "Formation of classes for systematic Bible study." "Special contributions for the sufferers in India and in Cuba." "Evangelistic work among the soldiers." "Distribution of good literature." "Warfare against Sunday baseball and Sunday excursions, whether by bicycle, train, or boat." "Well-planned Christian-citizenship victories won at the primaries." "Organized no-license campaign against the saloon." "Support of a missionary's family in Alaska." "Six hundred mothers and children taken from Boston to a near-by suburb for an afternoon's outing." "Home department of the Sunday school organized." "Opened a reading-room in our church." "Shut up a candy-store that was tempting Sunday-school scholars on Sundays." "Christmas dinners for the poor." "In charge of evening services during illness of our pastor." "Invitations to our church left at hotels Saturday nights." "Helped to close the doors of a gambling-den." "Increased amount given to missions per member from twenty cents to $2.50." "Forty of our members gave their hearts to Christ" (from the society in the Albany (N. Y.) penitentiary). "Sustained a good-literature exchange." "A picnic for fifty-four Chicago waifs." "Closed barber-shop upon Sunday." "Paying for a church pew for strangers." "Christmas box given to each inmate of the county poorhouse." "Made bandages and comfort-bags for the sailors and soldiers." "Paid our church coal bills." "Members delegated to escort two blind girls to our meetings." "Three hundred people fed in Philadelphia's slums upon Thanksgiving Day." "Furnished a bed in a hospital." "Furnished Testaments to soldiers." "Cared for four families (twenty persons) all winter." "Special missionary prayer meeting sustained weekly." "Support native preacher in Burmah."

There are many other splendid achievements of hundreds of societies we would gladly mention at this time, but lack of time prevents.

I have reserved for the last the best of my statistics.

Listen to the following testimony to God's blessing, and proof, too, of fidelity to his Church. During the past year 27,686 Juniors have become members of the Church. From the Intermediate societies 1,518 have joined their home churches, and 196,550 from the Young People's societies, making a total reinforcement of church-membership during the year amounting to 225,754.

The opening session closed with Dr. Clark's annual address. It is the strongest and most important of all his long series of annual messages, and the cordial applause that gave approval to his suggestions for graduation, for helping the Church, for larger and deeper activities, will bear rich fruit all over the land.

Annual Address by Rev. Francis E. Clark, D. D.,
President of the United Society of Christian Endeavor.

MORE FRUIT.

The one and only purpose of the Young People's Society of Christian Endeavor is to bear fruit. The divine commission to a Christian organization is the same as to the individual Christian. Let us hear *our* divine commission, fellow laborers, — "*I chose you and appointed you, that ye should go and bear fruit.*"

The doom of the unfruitful society is the same that awaits the unfruitful Christian. It is fit for the rubbish-heap and the fire. The test of one is the same as of the other, — " By their fruits ye shall know them."

Christian Endeavor stands or falls by this test. It realizes how searching and severe it is, but it can ask no other, for there is no other. Every church, every religious movement within the church, every individual, must in the same way be judged.

It is best, whatever heart-searchings it may cause, to bring ourselves each year, at this, our great annual feast, to this rigid test. Is the society of Christian Endeavor a fruit-bearer? Is it bearing much fruit? Are we still listening to the Master when, in this year of grace 1898, he tells us to go and bring forth *more* fruit?

The seed, the soil, but especially the fruit, may well engage our attention to-day.

The seed is the Christian Endeavor idea, — small, indeed, at first, and insignificant as a grain of mustard-seed, but potent because in it was the life of God.

The soil is the Church, or, in a broader way, the religious life, in which the society is established. And, oh, friends of youth, — fathers, mothers, pastors, elders, — let me speak an earnest word concerning the soil of Christian Endeavor. A seed, however good, will not flourish in barren soil.

The first Endeavor seed was planted in revival soil. In evangelical and evangelistic ground only has it since thriven at its best.

Does any elder in Israel say, " Our Endeavor Society is not what it should be"? Before you blame the seed or curse the fruit, consider the soil in which that society grows? Is it warm, sunny, evangelical, evangelistic? Then we may well be surprised if the fruit is not large and fair. Is the soil of the Church and religious community worldly, cold, sour, critical, formal? The Christian Endeavor fruit will be niggardly in quantity and gnarly in quality.

Let the soil of the Church be enriched by divine grace, and the fruit that the Young People's society bears will at once be sweeter, and fairer, and more abundant. In the poorest soil it will bear some fruit, but you cannot expect the best fruit except in the best soil.

TWELVE MANNER OF FRUITS.

But our chief concern to-day is with the fruit actually borne by Christian Endeavor, and especially with the new crop of 1898. It is no parody of Scripture to say that the society within these seventeen years has borne twelve manner of fruit. Count the varieties on these well-laden boughs: —

1. A revived prayer meeting.
2. A new sense of consecration.
3. A renewal of the covenant idea.
4. A new range of work by young people, for the Church, by our committees.
5. A new love and loyalty for the Church of God.
6. An aroused patriotism and sense of Christian citizenship.
7. A new type of interdenominational brotherhood.
8. A new type of international brotherhood.
9. A quickened missionary zeal, including a quickened love for the prisoners and the outcasts at home, as well as for the heathen abroad.
10. A new interest in the sailor and soldier, and the brave life-saver on our coast.
11. Systematic and proportionate giving to God.
12. The practice of communion with God in the Quiet Hour.

These twelve manner of fruits has the tree of Christian Endeavor borne. More luscious, more abundant, of greater variety, each year has the fruit become. I say this for our encouragement, and not by way of boasting.

NOT CONTENT.

But, even though we stop for a moment to enumerate the fruits, we are not content, for God is not content. Every year we hear the great Husbandman say, as he views his vineyard, "*Much fruit, more fruit*, MORE FRUIT."

What, let us ask it reverently and with heart-searching, does he expect in the coming year of service? What more fruit does God expect of Christian Endeavor in 1898? If we can but answer this question at this, our great annual feast, and meet his demand in the year to come, the Convention of 1898 will be memorable with all its memorable predecessors.

God himself helps us to answer our own question by the relations in which he has placed us. For a moment consider the chief of these relations. Every Christian Endeavor society has peculiar relations.

First. To all the young people who compose it.
Second. To the church of which it is a part.
Third. To the country to which its members owe allegiance.
Fourth. To the world, for the movement has now found a footing and welcome in almost every land beneath the sun.

If, then, I have interpreted aright God's demand for "more fruit" by a study of these relations, God is saying:

"More fruit from every member of every society in 1898."
"More fruit for the Church in 1898."
"More fruit for the nation in 1898."
"More fruit for the world in 1898."

I. More Fruit from Every Endeavorer.

"I am the vine; ye are the branches." Christ is the vine. Every society is a limb of the true vine. Every member should be a fruit-bearing branch. On this vine are over 54,000 Christian Endeavor branches, and three millions and a quarter of branchlets. Every one of them may be, should be, a fruit-bearing branchlet. O what a glorious vintage to the glory of God would that mean! Let this be our ambition for 1898: —

Every youngest member a fruit-bearer.
Every Junior a fruit-bearer.
Every inconspicuous member a fruit-bearer.
Every bashful and backward member a fruit-bearer.

It is not too large an ambition, for it is God's ambition for us. Grapes, remember, are borne only on the branches; and not only that, but only on the little branches. The ripened clusters do not hang from the trunk, nor from the great limbs of the spreading vine, but from the little, frail, insignificant twigs. The society as an organization does not bear fruit apart from those who compose it. The individual members must do the fruit-bearing, and it is only as each weak and tiny branchlet bears its part that the Master's demand for more fruit is met. Then let it be our recognized, strenuous purpose this year, as never before, to develop the fruit-bearing of every twig on all the vine.

Set yourself seriously to the task, fellow Endeavorers, to get service, and much service, and ever more service, from the younger and the backward. Let there be no dead wood on your vine.

How shall this be done? In many churches where it is not already found a Junior society would promote fruit-bearing, and would repay the labors of a faithful superintendent a thousand-fold. In some large churches an Intermediate society is needed for more fruit-bearing. In other places an alphabetical or other division of an overgrown society into two, three, or more sections, so that participation, prayer, testimony, service, responsibility, shall come to every one.

THE GRADUATE DEPARTMENT.

Still more universally, I believe, should graduate departments be formed, into which should pass, sooner or later, every older Endeavorer who has received the training of the society.

This plan I would most seriously urge upon your consideration as one of the great forward movements of the coming year. This forward movement will say to all Endeavorers, "Move on, move on from higher to higher; from much fruit to more fruit; from the Junior to the Intermediate, to the Young People's, to the Graduate Department of Christian Endeavor, where the full tide of your trained strength and tempered activity shall be poured into the channels of the Church."

This advance step provides exactly for this. The weekly church meeting becomes the Graduate Endeavor meeting, in which each will take some part aside from singing.

The numberless activities of the Church, the Sunday-school, the missionary society, become the Graduates' committees for service, while occasionally they will meet with their younger brethren to renew their consecration vows together. Thus will come to these younger and inexperienced ones the inestimable blessings of responsibility, of service, of fruit-bearing, and to us who are older the blessing of more fruit-bearing. Thus will the links in our chain be complete that bind the youngest Junior to the fullest activities of the Church.

SAVING BY LOSING.

Thus will the leakage between the younger and older Endeavorers and between the older Endeavorers and the largest activities of church life be stopped.

Thus, however old we grow, and however experienced, there will be no unnatural wrench from Endeavor service and Endeavor principles which have grown dear to us; for "once an Endeavorer, always an Endeavorer," will be true of us in precept and practice.

Does any one say: "Such a procedure would wreck our society; the younger ones need our constant guidance and supervision"? Ah! remember that in thus trying to save your society you may be losing it. If you are bearing the fruit that some smaller branch on the vine should bear you are robbing that branch of its birthright, and the Master of the more fruit that he demands of you.

One word of caution. *Do not graduate until you have trained your successors, and until you are ready to graduate into other church activities.*

By this plan the time of graduating is regulated, not by age or any arbitrary rule, but by willingness to enter upon other and perhaps larger service. It would be nothing less than a calamity if the Endeavorer *stopped* without graduating into something else; if he left his old work and took up no new work.

Let no active Endeavorer leave your society except through the door of graduation into other service of the Church.

Most strenuously do I commend this idea, especially to every large Endeavor society where are any inactive members, any fruitless branchlets. Most earnestly do I ask pastors to prepare the way for this graduation. Most urgently do I pray the churches to receive these graduates, these trained recruits, and make the most of their strength.

Look into this matter carefully, prayerfully, I beseech you, my brethren, young and old. There are in it untold possibilities of blessing. In this plan, I believe, is the largest degree of fruit-bearing, for it would ensure, if carried out, a bunch of the grapes of Eshcol on every smallest as well as every largest twig of the Endeavor branch of the true vine, from the first day of membership to the last day of life.

"More fruit-bearers for 1898." Shall not this be our rallying-cry? If we adopt it, this inevitably means, "*More fruit for the Church in 1898.*"

II. More Fruit for the Church.

Need I reassert for any doubting soul our time-worn, but never time-worn-out, principle that Christian Endeavor exists, not for itself, but for the Church? We have always proudly borne upon our banner, "For the Church!" Amid derision, and criticism, and cynicism, we have not lowered this standard. Every true Endeavorer sings: —

> "I love Thy kingdom, Lord;
> The house of Thine abode;
> The church our blest Redeemer saved
> With His own precious blood.
>   .   .   .   .
> "For her my tears shall fall
> For her my prayers ascend,
> For her my cares and toils be given,
> Till toils and cares shall end."

With almost passionate love he cries,

> "O mother dear, Jerusalem,"

and his "mother dear, Jerusalem," is his own loved Church. Then every year we will pray with increased earnestness, "More fruit for thy Church, O God; more fruit for thy Church."

In emphasizing the Graduate Department, I believe I have already suggested the greatest blessing that can come to many a church.

But to be more specific. By what particular service to the Church can we make the coming twelvemonth memorable? Let me answer: *In many churches by throwing our energies more fully into the Sunday evening and midweek services.* It is not enough to say that statistics frequently gathered in all denominations and in all parts of North America show that in proportion to their numbers nearly twice as many Endeavorers are habitually present at these services as of all church-members, old and young. We will not allow the good to be the enemy of the best. Remember, the Master is looking not only for fruit, but for more fruit; not for the last year's grapes, but for a fresh crop this year, larger and finer than the last.

ENDURE HARDNESS.

Do you say, "This is a difficult task, to infuse new life into the Sunday-evening service and the midweek meeting of the church"? Do you say, "It is a problem which many churches have given up as too hard to solve"? Christian Endeavor has never sought the easiest tasks. Nay, its glory is that it cultivates the heroic element; that it is willing to crucify ease and self in doing the hard work of the kingdom. It has spoken to many a young man and woman, as Paul spoke to the young Timothy, saying, "Endure hardness as a good soldier."

Let us make this problem ours. Let us feel that these services are peculiarly ours to sustain and foster by presence and prayer, and many a discouraged pastor will rise up to call you blessed.

I cannot go into particulars in this address. The Graduate Department will greatly help in this matter. The pastor's cabinet, composed of the heads of committees in the society, consulting with a sympathetic pastor, can often fully solve the problem. But however it is done, in some way, in all ways, let Christian Endeavor stand for the strengthening of these services, as it has come to stand for outspoken confession, for personal work, for proportionate giving, and for individual communion with God. Here is our hand, pastors, beloved, in a firmer clasp than ever for the evening service and the midweek prayer meeting.

By our vigorous local and State unions, too, as well as by our individual societies, I believe still more fruit can be borne for the Church, and I rejoice in the new emphasis that is being laid upon this all-important matter by some of our largest city unions.

It is still true, and always will be, that the business of a Christian Endeavor union is not to support this, that, or the other enterprise which some enthusiast considers good, not to sharpen the tools of the great army of axe-grinders who besiege every large movement, but to build up the Christian Endeavor cause, because, as we believe, it is the cause of Christ. This it can best do by planting and fostering new Endeavor societies, and by making sure that all existing societies within its circle are true to our cardinal and fundamental principles of loyalty to their own churches, their own denominations, and their own missionary work. To secure this end in the work of our unions, I would urge that every union have an advisory board of pastors of the different denominations, whose wisdom will help it in settling any difficult questions that may arise.

III. More Fruit for the Nation.

But Christian Endeavor is in the State as well as in the Church. "It is the largest patriotic society of young people in the world," as well as the largest church society. Then from this very relationship in which God has put us, we argue that there must be more fruit to bear for the national life of which we are a part.

What a splendid exhibition of latent patriotism suddenly aroused to action did the outbreak of the war with Spain afford! North and South clasped hands! East and West drew together! The old soldiers of '61 forgot which wore the blue and which the gray, for there was a common enemy against whom to turn all their guns. Silver and gold were forgotten issues. Republicans, Democrats, Populists, all were Americans in an instant.

This is the auspicious moment for another reunion of the young Christian forces of America, South and North, for their country's weal. Let the first Christian Endeavor Convention held in the sunny Southland mark the day of the obliteration of all sectional prejudice. There have never been any geographical lines in Christian Endeavor. There never can be. One God-given mission of this movement is to abolish sectionalism. Let us rise to our opportunity.

In the presence of the moral enemies of our nation's life let us unite as blue and gray have united against Spain. Are we Methodists, Disciples, Baptists, Presbyterians, Congregationalists, Lutherans? Are we Arminians, Calvinists? Do you live North or South of Mason and Dixon's line? I cannot tell from your looks. But I do know this: you are Christians. You are Christian Endeavorers. You are patriots. The enemies of your country are your enemies, and Spain is not her fiercest foe.

NORTH AND SOUTH TOGETHER.

A Society like ours is a wonderful healer of former breaches, as the presence of these thousands of Yankee men and maidens in old Dixie indicates. In Christian Endeavor God has brought us together in order that we may march together, and fight together against the enemies of our fatherland,— rum, impurity, and Sabbath-breaking, and corrupt politics, and national unrighteousness of every kind.

I am speaking to thousands of young men who, if called, would shoulder a musket to-morrow and start for Cuba. Many of you doubtless are grieved that your brothers will have the honor of fighting for a cause for which you as gladly would shed your blood. Ah! Militant Endeavorers, North and South, united by a common covenant, known by a common name, as you have come together in this Convention from every section, so come together to fight the moral enemies of your country. They are stronger than the Spaniards, more to be dreaded than any hostile coalition; they ravage our cities, inland and coast alike, as a thousand fleets of Cervera could not do. Endeavorers, as patriots hear the Master's call, not only to bring forth the peaceable fruits of righteousness, but to destroy the unfruitful works of darkness.

May I suggest that this coming year we should unitedly as never before stand for the sanctity of the Lord's Day against the constant encroachments of the enemy? The distractions and excitements of war, the loosening of moral restraints which are inevitable at such a time, the demoralization of camp and field, demand that we fight the enemy in the rear, as well as the foe in the field; and one of the foes that young Christian America will have to fight as never before will be the enemy that would degrade and secularize the Lord's Day, and with it dim the lustre of all spiritual things.

IV. More Fruit for the World.

More fruit from all Endeavorers, more fruit for the Church, more fruit for the nation, *more fruit for the world.* I have not forgotten while speaking to you that in the widest, and not in the narrow, sense this is an American Convention, that Canada is here as well as the United States, that the Union Jack is lovingly entwined with the Stars and Stripes. That is a symbol of our international mission: that Christian Endeavor has fruit to bear for all the world.

I have just returned from a magnificent British Convention of Christian Endeavor in Glasgow. There the same subjects were discussed, the same covenant pledge adopted, the same methods pursued, the same enthusiasm displayed; and there I heard three rousing British cheers for the coming British-American alliance. Those cheers are echoing in my heart to-day.

Go to Australia, and you will find Christian Endeavor strong and vigorous, and great conventions like this in the land of the Southern Cross. In South Africa, too, are thousands of Christian Endeavorers, and in British India. What does all this mean except that God is in part by Christian Endeavor affecting the union of English-speaking races? There is no other such tie binding their young people together. While our politicians have been *talking* about an alliance, we have been forming one, and within the last few months, thank God, the politicians seem to have come to our way of thinking.

AN ALLIANCE.

For arbitration as against war between all lands wherever peace with honor can be preserved thereby, we will always stand; and for an alliance of love and service with our own kith and kin on this side of the sea, and beyond the sea, let us not hesitate to declare ourselves. When in 1900 we go to London thousands strong, we will sign, seal, and deliver our treaty of alliance, and we will welcome all in every land who love our Lord. Is this fruit too large and fair for the Christian Endeavor vine to carry? O ye of little faith! let it not be thought a thing incredible with you that God can do this, for our alliance will be not to promote selfish schemes of selfish men, not to enthrone one and dethrone another, but to enthrone and crown the Lord Christ King of kings and Lord of lords in all the world.

Think for a moment of the young people of the Christian world united to win the non-Christian world to its rightful Ruler. That is the meaning of an alliance in Christian Endeavor, — a missionary alliance of the missionary races.

Every extension of our fellowship on both sides of the sea, every accession to our strength in the United States and Canada, in Great Britain and Ireland, in Australasia and South Africa, in Europe and Asia, means the union of forces that bring nearer the coming of the King in his glory. Let us, then, realize the wideness of our fellowship, the vastness of our mission, as one of God's world-cementing forces. Let us rejoice in this era of good feeling, and resolve that we will do our best to turn these united forces of Christendom against the strongholds of heathenism.

AN ADVANCE MOVEMENT IN MISSIONS.

In this connection let me earnestly urge the advance movement in missions so cordially approved of late by our mission boards, whereby an individual or society or group of societies may support its own missionary or native worker, or even its own mission station, on the field at home or abroad. I know of no more important advance step that has been taken for many a day by our mission boards, and I trust that every Endeavor society will soon have its personal representative in the home and foreign field of its own denomination.

There are many features of our work to which I would like to turn your attention if time allowed. Foremost among them is the Tenth Legion, already so productive, and sure to bear far more fruit in the future. More than ten thousand young men and women in the ranks of Christian Endeavor have already dedicated a tenth of all their present income and all their future earnings to Christ's cause and kingdom. And this is only the advance guard of a legion a thousand times ten thousand strong; a legion mightier than Cæsar ever led to victory.

I should like to speak especially of the Floating societies, consecrated by the death of the three Endeavorers of the *Maine*, and of the new and most important work for the soldier in the camp and field. I should like to dwell upon our wonderful prison societies, which contain in their fettered ranks so many of Christ's freemen. But time forbids even the barest mention of all this ripening fruit on the Christian Endeavor vine.

THE ONE CONDITION.

I cannot close, however, without reminding you of the one and only condition of fruit-bearing. It is *abiding*, abiding in Christ. "Without me ye can do nothing." These are Christ's words to you, fruit-bearer. Are you abiding in him? Are you letting Christ work in you? Do you realize that it is not through might, or power, or organization, or numbers, but through Christ's abiding presence that all this fruit is born for church and nation and world? Some of you have come to see this the past year as never before. In the Quiet Hour we have heard our Lord's voice. In the Morning Watch he has spoken to us words of blessed, quiet, absolute assurance. There is no abiding without meditation and communion. For this reason I plead for the Quiet Hour. It is the secret of abiding, and abiding is the secret of fruit-bearing. Oh, listen, Endeavorers! The closing words of this address shall not be mine, but the Lord Christ's: —

"As the branch cannot bear fruit of itself, except it abide in the vine; no more can ye, except ye abide in me. I am the vine, ye are the branches. He that abideth in me, and I in him, the same bringeth forth much fruit."

Bishop B. W. Clinton, D.D., of Nashville, Tenn., pronounced the benediction. Thus closed the best opening session of all the international Christian Endeavor conventions.

The Bible-Study Conference.

This came in Auditorium Endeavor, Thursday afternoon immediately at the close of the opening session. Its leader was Rev. J. F. Cowan, D.D., one of the editors of *The Christian Endeavor World*, who said it was just a mouthful to whet the appetite, not an elaborated system of Bible-study in forty-five minutes.

The book of Psalms furnished an Old Testament illustration of study by books. The little boy's statement that there are three books of Psalms in the Bible, " 1 Sam., 2 Sam., and Sams," was quoted as an introduction to a suggested harmony of those three books, by which the history which called forth the Davidic psalms might be studied together with them.

The Gospel of John furnished the New Testament sample. The key was hunted for, and found in John 20 : 30, 31. " Testimony," " belief," and " life " are a chain of words which give a clew.

The audience was disposed to question quite freely ; and had there been an hour, not all the quizzing of workers anxious for better equipment for work could have been answered. Bibles ? They were brought in plenty. Rapid turning and ready text-reading proved that Endeavorers believe in the solid spiritual growth which feeding on the Word alone can give.

THURSDAY EVENING.

Auditorium Endeavor.

IT was a sea of upturned faces which greeted President Clark at Auditorium Endeavor when he stepped forward to call the meeting to order. Badges, which adorned practically everybody, showed that the audience was drawn from every State in the Union.

The meeting was opened with a hearty song service, conducted by Mr. Percy S. Foster. Devotional exercises were conducted by Rev. C. W. Sweet, of Des Moines, Io.

President Clark said, in introducing the first speaker of the evening, that Mr. Washington held a most honored and unique place in the country. " I cannot think of a more honored place for the representative of one race than to be its spokesman and always to be gladly heard by the representatives of the other race. Principal Washington, I believe, stands in just such a position — one who is always gladly heard for the message that he brings, and one who is doing more to bring the two great races of America together, perhaps, than any other man."

During the progress of the address the electric lights flickered for a moment, and then the audience was in absolute darkness. The speaker happily remarked, " We are now all of the same color." While darkness reigned some one started, " Let a Little Sunshine In," which was sung heartily. In a few minutes the lights were again burning and the address was resumed.

Address by Principal Booker T. Washington,
Tuskegee, Ala.

At the close of our present war we are likely to find ourselves a very much mixed nation; so much so that I fear it may be a little difficult for the white man to find and identify himself. In fact, I feel rather anxious about the white man in this respect. There is no difficulty with the negro in this regard. He never gets lost in the mixture of colors and races. We have a great advantage over the white man in this respect. You see the instant it is proven that an individual has even one per cent of African blood in his veins he falls to our pile every time in the count of races. The ninety-nine per cent of Anglo-Saxon blood counts for nothing. We claim the man for our race, and we usually get him. It is a great satisfaction to belong to a race just now, when white Americans are likely to find themselves intermingled with the Mongolian and the Malay from the far East, and the Latin races from the South — I say that under such circumstances it is a supreme satisfaction to belong to a race that has such potential drawing-power as is true of my race.

At the present moment God is teaching the Spanish nation a terrible lesson. What is that lesson? Simply this: that no nation can disregard the interests of any part of its members without that nation growing weak and corrupt. Though the penalty may have been long delayed, God is teaching Spain that for every one of her subjects that she has left in poverty, ignorance, and crime the price must be paid; if not with the very heart of the nation, it must be paid in the proudest and bluest blood of her sons, and in treasure that is beyond computation. From this spectacle which is now before the world let America learn a lesson — the most costly product that any State can grow is ignorance, poverty, and crime, and I pray God that every city and State in the South may take warning. Every white man in the South is dependent upon every black man in the South, and every black man in the South is dependent upon every white man in the South. There have been placed in the midst of the South eight million negroes, that in most of the elements of civilization are weak. Providence has placed them here not without a purpose. One object, in my opinion, is that the stronger race may imbibe a lesson from the negroes, — patience, forbearance, and childlike, yet supreme, trust in the God of the universe.

These eight millions of my people have been placed here that the white man may have a great opportunity to lift himself by lifting up this unfortunate race. The strongest individual is he who is most ready to lift up the weak. The most powerful state is that one which is most ready to make strong the weak. The white South will be intelligent in proportion as the negro is intelligent; it will be in darkness in proportion as the negro is in darkness. Not long ago, on the outer edges of a Southern city, I saw a white child who represented the wealth and culture of a white family surrounded by a group of negro children in the playground. What those black children are that white child will be in a large measure. If these black children use language which is ungrammatical and impure, the white child will do the same. If these black children learn crime, the white child will do the same. If disease invades the body of the black child, the same disease endangers the life of the white child. My white friends, there is no alternative; we cannot escape the inevitable. Through public schools, through churches and private benevolence, God means that you shall make the highest effort to lift us up, if you would make and keep your civilization pure and permanent. If the negro goes backward in this country he will take you with him.

Amidst the excitement, the glamour, the interests, the deeds of heroism, that cluster around our present war, let us not forget there is a condition in the southern part of our country that will demand on the part of every Northern man and every Southern man our deepest thought and most generous help for years to come.

Let us remember that an edict of war cannot blot out ignorance, crime, and poverty. At the present moment there is properly deep interest in the thousands of young men who are going forth from all parts of our country in defence of honor and humanity; but I beg of you to remember that out from our negro colleges, out from Fisk, Hampton, and Tuskegee, there are going forth each year thousands of young men and women into dark and secluded corners, into lonely log schoolhouses, amidst poverty and ignorance; and though when they go forth no drums beat, no banners fly, no friends cheer, they are fighting the battles of our country just as truly, bravely, and heroically as they who go forth to do battle against a foreign foe.

Within the last thirty years — and I might add, within the last three months — it has been proven by eminent authority that the negro is increasing in numbers so fast that it is only a question of a few years before he will far outnumber the white race in the South; and it has also been proven that the negro is fast dying out, and it is only a question of a few years before he will have completely disappeared. It has also been proven that crime among us is on the increase, and that crime is on the decrease; that education helps the negro, that education also hurts him; that he is fast leaving the South and taking up his residence in the North and West, and that the tendency of the negro is to drift toward the lowlands of the Mississippi bottoms. It has been proven that education unfits the negro for work, and that education also makes him more valuable as a laborer; that he is our greatest criminal, and that he is our most law-abiding citizen. In the midst of these opinions I hardly know whether I am myself or the other fellow. But in the midst of this confusion there are a few things of which I feel certain that furnish a basis for thought and action. I know that whether we are increasing or decreasing, whether we are growing better or worse, whether we are valuable or valueless, a few years ago fourteen of us were brought into this country, and now there are ten millions of us. I know that whether in slavery or in freedom we have always been loyal to the Stars and Stripes; that no schoolhouse has been opened for us which has not been filled; that the two million ballots which we have the right to cast are as potent for weal or woe as the ballots cast by the whitest and most influential man in America. I know that wherever your life touches ours you make us stronger or weaker.

The next on the programme was the presentation of a banner to the local city union that had reported the best progress during the last year in promoting Christian citizenship. The banner for the last year was held by the Indianapolis City Union. The banner was this year won by the Kansas City Union.

Presentation by Rev. Philip Y. Pendelton,
Norwood, O.

Friends and Endeavorers, our banners are divisible. The Union Jack is not the real standard of Great Britain, and the American ensign is not Old Glory, and the banner that we are to deliver to-night is not the whole banner of this great cause, but like these pieces of banners, it represents but one part of a banner that is the grandest and the greatest under the sun.

These banners have their day and their glory; but this banner, of which citizenship is a part, has no day, and its glory reaches into the eternity of God. I rejoice, friends, that our citizenship is in heaven; and glad am I, also, that we are finding it out; and that we are incarnating the flag. What does an incarnation mean? God incarnated the King of his kingdom in the person of Jesus Christ, and the kingdom began. Here in these latter days we are incarnating the standard of the kingdom, because the triumph of the kingdom is at hand. When Jesus was incarnated it was because the fulness of time had come, and the incarnation of the flag of God's kingdom in the world indicates that the fulness of time has come for the triumph of the gospel in the world; and I am glad that we have a good-citizenship banner that you can see, even if you cannot see it to-night. It is seeable somewhere, because it is incarnate. I am glad, also, that we are awaking to this great fact, — that our citizenship is in heaven, and that we are members of that kingdom.

That indicates that we are assuming in the world of to-day our rights as citizens, and as representatives of the kingdom of God on earth, and representatives of that first of all. That is a glorious thing. We have kept recording angels up there busy in these latter years keeping track of the different avenues of our citizenship. We have got a place up there where those who dedicate their votes to God have their votes recorded, and there the Almighty expects them to live up to it. That is what this banner represents. It represents those whose votes are God's votes. Oh, that is the way it wins its triumphs!

The battleships and the thirteen-inch guns of the Lord God Almighty are ballots, not battleships or gunpowder.

I will say that this city won this banner by votes, and it is going to keep it that way.

Response by Mr. Thomas Jones,
Kansas City, Mo.

Mr. Chairman and Christian Endeavor Friends: — This presentation of the banner stands for one phase of Christian Endeavor, and a phase that is important, it seems to me, in these trying times and days in our country. I hope that we will be able to go back to Kansas City, though it be with an invisible banner, with an aroused conception and a clear understanding of our duties as young men and women towards our country's interests. We are to stand firm for the cause of total abstinence and temperance in this country, and as Christian Endeavorers we are to stand firm for the cause of Sabbath preservation. I feel that you are presenting the banner to the right city at this time. We hold the strategic point, almost midway between the Northland and the Southland, the East and West. We are not either primarily Republicans, or Democrats, or Populists, as a people, but Christian Endeavor patriots and citizens. We place above our Republicanism and Democracy Christian Endeavor conscience and principles, although we might be nominally divided into Republicans and Democrats and Populists in the last campaign that we have had. In the past few years the lines have been broken, and I trust that in the next few years they will be broken more and more, so that we shall stand solidly as young men, the flower and chivalry of the Northland and the Southland, not as Democrats and Republicans, but as Christian Endeavor patriots, in our decision. And I trust, my friends, that this banner that I shall take with me shall be an inspiration to us, and that we shall plant it, figuratively speaking, upon the heights of Kansas City, so that it will not only inspire us, but will encourage us and all neighboring cities of Kansas to stand for the cause of Christian temperance. I thank you, ladies and gentlemen, and you, Mr. Chairman, for the gift you have given us.

No report can do justice to Dr. Burrell's masterly temperance address that closed this session. It was compact of scathing invective, moving pathos, brightest wit.

Address by Rev. David James Burrell, D.D.,
New York City.

OUR ENEMY: THE SALOON.

We all from up North are mighty glad to meet you all down South. I suppose you have heard that before. Everybody has been saying it. Strange that a harp of a thousand strings should play one tune so long; but we are so glad to come down from the North, and see, as Dr. Clark puts it, new glory in Old Glory, and see the old flag, and all the people everywhere, North and South, loyal to it — the old flag that is glorious, that don't run, and won't run!

We are thinking about good citizenship, and you cannot think about good citizenship without getting out your gun and going for the saloon!

You know the temperance reform is only an infant of days. It is not a century old yet. In the year 1825 our country awoke to the stupendous fact that we were drinking seven and a half gallons of spirituous liquors *per capita* — and you people down South were doing your full share of it. Seven and a half gallons of spirituous liquors *per capita!* People's eyes bulged out. Something must be done. This thing could not go on. And the phrase "moral suasion" was born. And another good word came in, "teetotaler." Down in Baltimore, one morning, before the daylight came, there were three or four topers who had been on a magnificent debauch, and had just got an early headache on, and who were sorry for their sins, and had just signed a pledge in which they promised that they would not from that time on drink any more than they could conveniently carry; and that was the beginning of the Washingtonian movement, and the great temperance reform. It had a small beginning and a somewhat contemptible one, but "neglect not nor despise the day of small things." God was looking on, and had measure of the business.

It was only a question of time when we should get a betterment of things, when the people were in earnest, and God standing by.

To-day, though we must take into consideration the introduction of malt liquors, the consumption of spirituous liquors in our country is less than two gallons *per capita*. The world moves! This old world of ours rolls around once every twenty-four hours, and every time it goes around it gets a little further into the light.

At this moment we are thinking of the relation of the Church and the saloon,— the two great, predominant powers on earth for good and evil of to-day. The problem has about resolved itself into the relation of the Church and the saloon. It is for the Church of Jesus Christ to say how long the saloon shall live, and when the saloon shall die.

Now, what is the Church? *Ecclesia, called out.* It is the body of Christian people called out from the world to help God Almighty set up his kingdom of truth and righteousness upon the earth. It is not a holy club. There are some people who think that the Church is an association of good people. You are one of them, and you know better. It is not a society of good people, but of people who want to be good. But I tell you this,— you people that are not in the Church, but are outside looking in,— the Pharisees are not all in the Church, mind you. We know we are not as good as we ought to be—that is why we are in the Church. We feel our weakness, and the need of the sustaining power of this great spiritual labor guild. We cannot get on without sympathy and mutual prayer; we must get into the Church or we cannot hold out. But you outside think you are good enough without it, and that you don't need it. We are not the good people — the people who profess to be good. We are like Baxter, I think it was, who said, "I am not what I ought to be, I am not what I mean to be, but by the grace of God I am what I am." It is not a company of truth-seekers. We are not seeking the truth. We have found it. It is in the Bible. We have taken the Bible to be our infallible rule of truth — it is there. We are not looking for truth. God Almighty has revealed it, and put it into our hands in black and white, and all we are looking for is what old John Robinson spoke of, "more light, and even more light, to burst out of that Word of God."

Nor is it a great ethical society. We are not casting about for a code of morals. We have a code of morals. The Bible is our ethical code: the decalogue, delivered to us out of the thunder of the mountain, and the sermon delivered to us as an exposition of that decalogue, from the grassy slope of Olivet, and in between the decalogue and the Sermon on the Mount, the two great moral manifestoes that no learned infidel or other man has ever been able enough to criticise since the foundation of the world — in between the decalogue and the Sermon on the Mount stands Jesus Christ, the only man who ever illustrated both; the only man who ever lived that was as good as the law. And all we are trying to do, so far as ethical systems go, is just to follow him.

But what is the Church? It is the great living organism thrilled through and through by the electric power of the spirit of the living God, by which he is working, through the co-operation of a great multitude of people whom he calls to be laborers together with himself, for the setting-up of a mighty kingdom of truth and righteousness and the deliverance of this old world from the curse, and the realization of the old Homeric dream that Tennyson echoed when he sang about binding this world again as with gold chains about the feet of God.

That is what the Church is. It is business, and it is God's business, and that is what we old people and young people are about every day. I was up at the Giant's Causeway a few years ago with a lot of Presbyterian ministers.

There were twenty of us or more, and two sweet Irish girls in the company, and we were going up into the Giant's Causeway, and we had a young Irish guide — almost as good a fellow as Patterson here — and talked just like him. He was from Tomduff, away up in the North, and when we got off the cars he said, "Gentlemen, fall into line, join hands and shut your eyes, and don't open them until I tell you." We joined our hands, and it so happened that right here was Dr. Matheson, blind from his birth, who had come up there to see the sights, and here was the Irish girl; and we went forward, stumbling over the gorse and sand and stones, and with the roar of the sea in our ears, and waiting to see what should come presently, for we were expecting mighty things, and went stumbling on; and Dr. Matheson said something to me presently, and I said, "Do you see any of it?" "Oh," he said, "I feel it; the roll of the old ocean is through me. I know there is something great coming to me pretty soon; I am sorry that I have not got my eyes, so that I can open them when you do, but after all, I know there is something grand, terrific, coming in a minute before you; I am sure that my blood will be as hot as yours is. But no matter what you see," said he, and he gripped my hands, and almost cracked the bones. Holding fast, he said, "No matter what you see, there is no glory in all nature under the sky that is so good as this good-fellowship of ours, is there?" And indeed there is not; and just then our guide called to us, "Now look!" and we stood still and opened our eyes. There it was all around us, the great basaltic cliffs thrown up into all sorts of grotesque and beautiful forms: the organ and the loom and the cathedral, and off yonder was the sea and the sails, and down below the billows rolling in and rolling out again in thunderous white masses of foam, and the sea-gulls screaming just here! Oh, it was wonderful. But there was n't anything there that day that was as wonderful as this: the fellowship of Christian minds in the Church, — the mighty labor guild of God, in which we come together as laborers together with God, with a sword in one hand and a trowel in the other, to make war upon the works of the devil, and build up the temple that rises like Solomon's magnificent house, day by day, in this sin-stricken world of ours.

Now that is the Church. I did not mean to say so much about the Church, because the saloon is a great subject to talk about.

That comes next. What is the saloon?

I want to set the saloon over against the Church until you will blush to the centre of your heart if you have ever said a kind thing about the dram-shop; until you will blush if you have not lifted both hands in all your prayers against it.

What is the saloon?

It is the most concrete universal manifestation of diabolism on earth to-day. That's what it is.

It is the enemy of man, that blots his visage; it reddens his eyes; it soddens his flesh; it makes his body, that God meant to be a temple for the indwelling of his spirit, a mere common sewer and cesspool; it destroys his will; it paralyzes his heart; it destroys his soul, for it sends him with God's breath in his nostrils, and the arithmetic of hell in his brain, warring, hiccoughing, down to death, out into the eternal night, from whence comes the awful word, "No drunkard shall inherit the kingdom of God."

It is the enemy of the home, that puts out the fire on the hearthstone; it empties the barrel and the cruse; it makes man who was called to be a husband a fiend incarnate, until it drives his wife out in rags and tatters, and his children to face the pointed finger of scorn, that ever awaits a drunkard's bairns.

It is the enemy of the State. At one of our recent elections I went down into the lower part of Manhattan Island, and made the round of the polling-places there. I tell you the dram-shop is the Gibraltar of evil politics; it is the market-place for the sale of the purchaseable vote. It is the last ditch of municipal misrule. What is the use of our talking about reform, in New York, or anywhere else, and then turning white-livered whenever the saloon is mentioned? There is no reform! There is no reform possible for these great growing metropolitan centres of life until we point our guns at the dram-shop.

We have 9,000 saloons in New York City. Put them in line and see what a bloody road down to Jericho they will make! Thirty miles of continuous saloons; not a church, nor a schoolhouse, nor a delightful home to break the sweet monotony for thirty miles on both sides of hell's thoroughfare! Thirty miles of dram-shops, with a barkeeper in every door, his sleeves rolled back, and the paste diamond in his shirt-front; sleek and unctuous, waiting for his prey; thirty miles of open doors with their red lights of hell shining through! How are we ever going to have municipal reform when these are the recruiting-places for all evil politics, and will be until God's people and all right-thinking people close them up!

If I had a night or two, or a day or two, I think I could draw up a considerable indictment against the saloon, and I could summon a great cloud of witnesses to certify to it. I would show you the procession coming out of those doors,— men who were once honest toilers, and some of them in the learned professions; every one of them once lay an innocent babe on his mother's breast. I would show you them an unbroken line, that is going this minute,— some of your friends are in the procession,— lock-step, quick-step, going fast out into that awful night where no soul can behold the face of God, and where the worm dieth not and the fire is not quenched. I would ask them whether these things are true or not. And then the wives and the children! O God, pity the poor sunken-eyed, hollow-cheeked wives of the drunkard, the children of the drunkard, in rags and shame! O the dullard, that dares to drink his wife and children into shame! If he wants to go to hell, he may go; God has given him the right, but who ever gave a man the right to drag his wife and children down that way?

And I would stand with you and find more witnesses, in the doorway of the brothel; and I would take some of you dear people who are talking about the social evil with me. You cannot reform the social evil,—I speak with reserve in this presence,—you cannot touch it, until you see her coming out of that doorway, the woman whose feet take hold on hell; and on her right side is the barkeeper, and on her left side is the gambler, and they are holding her up, and there they go, the three,— the three great living horrors of civilization, and all three of them under the awful curse of a just and holy God.

I would go and walk through the corridors of the prisons, and show you thieves and murderers and all sorts of malefactors and evil-doers, and there would not be one among them as worthy of imprisonment as the barkeeper, because he is the maker of them all. Nearly ninety per cent of all your criminals come out of those red mouths of the pit and enter the barred doors of the prison.

A little while ago a man came home on Saturday night, an honest workman who had spent his wages during the evening, a kind husband under ordinary circumstances, and a gracious father, whose wife had been waiting for him with her little children; far into the night he came. He had been putting an enemy into his mouth to steal away his brains; he came through the door, and at her welcome he grasped her with his two hands, and before her screaming children strangled her, and the officer of the law came and took him to jail. The next day he awoke in his cell, and he said, "Where am I?" And the guard said, "You are in jail." "What for?" "For murder." For a moment he was silent with horror, and then he said, "Does my wife know?" And the guard said, "It was your wife you killed," and he fell in a swoon; and the constable that arrested that man and took him to the prison was the man that owned the dram-shop, that whetted the knife, that nerved the arm; and the man in the corridor was a partner in the concern; and the judge that sentenced that man to a life penalty at hard labor had voted to license it.

Well, there is no use going on with the indictment. I must just hurry on to ask about the relation, now, of the Church and the saloon. They do have a very intimate relation. Not like that which was illustrated at Bristol, where there was a church up on top of a hill, and out of it a stairway leading down, and under the stairway a spirit-shop, as our English friends call it, and the church leased the spirit-shop, and some wag, who was full of the glory of God and the sound sense of real piety, wrote one day on the step:—

> "There is a spirit above and a spirit below;
> A spirit of love and a spirit of woe;
> The spirit below is the spirit of wine,
> And the spirit above is the spirit divine."

What union hath God with Belial? What is the Church going to do about the saloon? There are only three things it can do.

The first is, do nothing. Just stand aside, and say, "There is no use — it is a necessary evil; the saloon has come to stay." God save you, young men and young women, from such cowardly sophistry as that.

"Come to stay!" Suppose it has! So have snakes, and tigers, and cholera, and yellow fever, and theft, and adultery; but you are not obliged to be co-partners with these things, nor to tolerate them, nor to compromise with them.

But the saloon has *not* come to stay — only until God Almighty laughs and holds the dram-seller in derision; only until God's Church wakes up to some sense of decency and duty; not a minute beyond that.

The second thing the Church can do is to license it. The word is from "*licet*," which means "it is permitted." In the Latin, as all you young people know, the word is impersonal. "It is permitted." The minute you translate it, it becomes intensely personal; and when you go to the ballot-box, you young men, and vote for license, it means "I permit it," and God will hold you to account at the judgment-bar for doing it.

> Licensed for what?
> Licensed to make the strong man weak;
> To bring the brave man low;
> Licensed the wife's fond heart to break;
> To make children's tears to flow.
>
> Licensed like spider for a fly,
> To set thy net for man, thy prey;
> To mark his struggles, suck him dry,
> And fling his shattered hulk away.
> Licensed where peace and order dwell,
> To bring disease and strife and woe;
> Licensed to make this world a hell,
> And fit man for a hell below.

That is what you are voting for. I do not care how big you make your license-fee, as long as I have a conscience in my breast and can see the glory of God shining in the face of the Christ before me I cannot vote to permit it.

The only other thing is to antagonize it. That is all that is left for the Church to do: war to the knife, and the knife to the hilt! No quarter! No let-up! John Gough was asked if he was really a prohibitionist. "No, sir," said he, "I am an annihilationist!" That is what all God's people must be.

But now let me bring to bear on that the argument *ad hominum*. I want to talk to you young men who are going to vote, and going to measure up the moral life of our nation in the coming days, and the young women, too, who are going to stand behind the young men and see that they do the thing in the right way.

What are you, personally, going to do about the saloon? When you leave this great Convention what position are you going to assume toward this great concrete form of diabolism on earth, as a follower of the Lord Jesus Christ?

First, you are going to be a total abstainer.

You ask me if you have not the right to drink. Shame on the man that stands on his rights in the kingdom of God! If Jesus Christ had stood on his rights, where would we have been, you and I? If he had stood on his rights in the Kingdom of Glory, where would you and I have been? But he gave up all things for our sake, in order that he might save some. "If meat make my brother to offend, I will eat no meat while the world standeth, and I will drink no wine while the world standeth."

Oh blessed declaration of rights,— the right to put all rights under foot for the sweet privilege of saving the soul of a man!

The second thing you can do is to exercise your functions as a citizen at the polls. I have a friend in New York City who has a telephone down on Water Street. He is in business there, and he found his telephone a great convenience in communicating with business men, and he thought it would be very nice to have a telephone up in West Chester, where his family lived. There was a long and vexatious delay. But when the superintendent came to say it was all right it was a stormy day. He said, " It is all right; you can take up the telephone now and speak to your wife." He took up the telephone and called, " Sarah." There was no answer. The storm was raging outside. The third time he got up to his domestic tone, " Sarah." And just then the lightning struck the wire outside and tipped him up and rolled him over on the floor. He got up presently, all mussed up and troubled, and said to the superintendent, " That's all right, you can go, sir, it is working well; that's Sarah. I know Sarah."

I will tell you what to do in the Church.

This is what we want: we want young Christian men and old Christian men to let the people know, to let our politicians know, that we are at the other end of the wire, and it is a live wire. We are twenty odd million strong in America, and we have begun the movement; we have got the men, and we have got the money, too, and we can do as we please in the name of the living God about the saloon. And I close right here, with this word, The saloon will live as long as we Christian people say it shall live, and when we say the word it shall die the death.

" Roll swiftly round, ye wheels of time,
And bring the welcome day."

Hall Williston.

Mr. Excell swung the chorus and audience delightfully together with his accustomed bubbling good humor, and the exuberant good-nature in which he left them prepared them for swallowing sweetly their bitter disappointment at a telegram from the only and original Sam Jones, announcing illness that would prevent his speaking. The most of the remaining bitterness was extracted when it was announced that Dr. A. C. Dixon would be his substitute. The presiding officer was the Rev. Chas. B. Newnan, of Detroit, Mich. After Dr. Dixon had shot out a few of his flashing brilliants everything was forgotten but intent listening.

Address by Rev. A. C. Dixon, D.D.,
Brooklyn, N. Y.

My subject is one word which occurs nine times in the Sermon on the Mount, " Blessed." It means happiness without the hap, a state of joy that does not depend upon chance. It is the key, and the key-note, to the whole sermon,— the key that unlocks every sentence, the key-note with which every truth harmonizes. It is like the thread in the rock-candy, around which the crystals of truth cling.

First of all, the " blessed " life is in the present tense. Pope wrote a good many half-truths, but when he said, " Man never is but always to be blessed," he did not tell a tenth of the truth. " Blessed are the meek." " Blessed are the merciful." " Blessed are ye when men shall persecute you." We do not have to wait to go to heaven before heaven comes to us.

Again, the " blessed " life is a savory life. A man, to be really happy, must have a savory Christian character. " Ye are the salt of the earth, but if the salt has lost its savor, it is good for nothing." Did you ever see people just good for nothing? They do not seem to be good for prayer-meetings, nor church, nor revival, nor anything else, all because they have lost their savoriness. Their religion does not taste good. Salt makes things taste good. Your porridge did not taste good this morning because it lacked salt. It was simply insipid, unsavory. Christian man, does your religion taste good? Men have no use for salt when it has lost its savoriness; they cast it out and tread it under foot. And men have no use for religion that does not taste good. Let me illustrate what I mean. In a former pastorate there was a man in my congregation who could talk like Demosthenes or Cicero. He used excellent grammar, and seemed to know the Bible pretty well from Genesis to Revelation. He could quote Longfellow and Tennyson and Whittier, and a stranger would be charmed by his eloquent utterances. But when he rose to talk in a prayer-meeting the crowd began to wither; and when his talk was over the prayer-meeting was like a sweet-potato patch on a frosty morning, black and blue. The people knew that in his life there was something unsavory, that he would drink before the bar with worldly friends, and that he was not as honest as he might be. His good grammar and fluent utterances did not make amends for the unsavoriness of his character.

There was another man in that congregation who would sometimes come to prayer-meeting with a circle of coal-dust around his hair. He was a coal-cart driver, and he was now and then so hurried to get to the prayer-meeting that he did not make his toilet with as much care as he ought. But the people leaned over to listen when he talked. And why? Because they knew that he lived every day for God. He would pick up a tramp on the road, and give him a mile-ride on his cart that he might talk with him about Jesus. His religion tasted good. Good religion in bad grammar tastes better than bad religion in good grammar.

Jesus tells us, next, that the "blessed" life is distributive. "Ye are the light of the world." Salt has to be distributed. It is not the nature of salt to struggle to get anywhere. You must pick it up and bring it into contact with the substance before it will do its work. But not so with the light; it distributes itself. Put it under a bushel and it will struggle to get out; if there is a crack in the bushel it will shine through it. When light ceases to be distributive it ceases to be light. The moment it ceases to scatter there is darkness. It is not reflection. You cannot raise a crop by moonlight; reflected light is cold. "Ye are the light," not reflectors. Light is made by a process of combustion on the altar of God's service, consumed for his glory.

Jesus said, "Go ye into all the world, and preach the gospel to every creature." That word "go" is as big as the earth and as little as the space between you and the next man. "Follow me, and I will make you to become fishers of men." Every Christian is primarily a fisher, and secondarily, a feeder. His business is to catch men for God, and then feed the sheep. The fish lives in the lower realm of mud, and gravel, and grub, and darkness; the sheep lives in the higher realm of landscape, and sun, and star, and sky; and by the process of catching the fish, according to the gospel plan, it is transmuted into sheep. It is the sheep who are to be fed, while the fish are to be caught. It does not say feed the fish, nor cultivate fish, but catch fish. The work of feeding and cultivating men may be philanthropic, but it is not the basis of Christianity. First, there must be the transmutation of character wrought by the Spirit of God, and unless there is this transmutation of character there can be no development along truly Christian lines. "Ye must be born from above."

I was in the New York Aquarium, and greatly enjoyed it. There were all sorts of fish, big and little, ugly and pretty, and there were a thousand people studying fish. About fifty of them had their little books drawing pictures of fish and marking their habitat, but there was no one catching fish.

I went to a convention some time ago and it reminded me of my visit to the aquarium. There were scores of men there who had been studying fish. They could tell all about the gold-fish on Fifth Avenue and the mud-suckers and eels on the Bowery. But not one of them, so far as I could see, had been fishing. Not a minnow had been caught. Jesus did not say go and study men, nor write about men, but "become fishers of men."

I was talking to a deacon who is at the head of a great corporation. If you saw him in church you might think he would never unbend, but it was in the fishing season, and he had just bought a new rod. He forgot his rod as he talked about the pleasures of fishing. He said, "A five-pound bass at the end of that rod is Mozart and Beethoven and Shakespeare and Cicero all in one thrill." He had the fishing spirit, don't you see? He was a genuine fisherman. Would God that we Christians had the spirit of fishing for men like that! Our delight in it would excel all the pleasures of music and poetry and oratory.

And it is not mere pastime. Fishing for men is our business. Last summer I was at Lakeside, O., where there were five waterspouts seen in Lake Erie and a meeting of the Federation of Women's Clubs on one day. The waterspouts and the women's clubs were both great in their way, but what interested me most was the manœuvring of a United States life-saving crew. The lifeboat was brought out slowly, and the life-savers in their uniforms went about their work in the most deliberate sort of way. They seemed to be very careful lest their boat might be scratched a little. I said to a friend standing by, "I would not like to have to depend on those fellows to save me from drowning, for I would be at the bottom of the lake before they reached the water." "Last winter," he replied, "when a sky-rocket went up a mile from the shore and the cry of lost men and women was heard coming through the storm, in less time than I am taking to tell it that door was opened, the life-boat was out, and they were gone to the rescue." One scene was manœuvre, the other was business. The one was play, the other was work urged on by the cry of dying humanity. How is it with us? Is our work a sort of manœuvring? On Sunday morning do we preachers go before the church with a kind of gospel manœuvre? Do you go through song and sermon just because the time appointed for manœuvre has come? Do the people look on and say it is a pretty good effort? Oh, if we could hear the cry of lost humanity amid the storms and surges of sin in this lost world, our manœuvring would become business, and blood-earnestness would take the place of half-hearted service. Then sinners would be won to Christ by the thousands, and our joy would be equalled only by that of the angels in heaven.

Again, the "blessed" life goes beyond the law. The law says. "Thou shalt not kill." Jesus says, "Thou shalt not hate." The law says, "Thou shalt not commit adultery." Jesus says, "Thou shalt not lust." The law says, "Thou shalt not swear falsely." Jesus says, "Swear not at all." Let your word be your bond. Some people say they keep the spirit of the law when they break the letter of the law. I know an old man who never swears except when he gets mad; and the first time he swore after he joined the church was when a horse tramped on his foot; the second time was when his wife tramped on his temper. But he says, "I am not a profane swearer; I break the letter of the law, but I keep the spirit." He thinks that keeping the spirit of the law means to come short of the letter. He is mistaken. The gospel is keeping the law and going beyond. The spirit of the gospel refuses to desecrate the Sabbath, and more, fills it with worship. No one can be truly blessed who breaks the law, for sin is the transgression of the law, and sin is the mother of misery.

Once more, the "blessed" life involves right living, right giving, right praying, right fasting, and right hoarding. "When you do your righteousness," do it before God, not before men. Live before God. I preached two sermons once on living carefully before the people. I burnt them up. They burned well, for they were very dry. I never expect to preach them again. If you live right before God you may be careless as to how you live before any one else. So let giving be a personal transaction between you and God. "Let not your right hand know what your left hand does;" in other words, don't tell yourself about it. Sometimes we compliment ourselves upon what we have given and get swelled up with pride, and true blessedness can only go with humility. So with praying. Pray not to be heard of men, but God. So with fasting and hoarding. "Lay up for yourselves treasures in heaven." Hoard, but not here.

Work on earth, but have your bank-deposit in heaven. In proportion as a man has a good bank-account in glory he is rich, and in proportion as a man has a good bank-account here and not there he is a pauper. "Seek first the kingdom of God and his righteousness and all other things shall be added." Some men who have sought the other things think because they have gained all things else the kingdom will be added. By their industry and care they have grown rich, and therefore they expect the kingdom to be added. It is a delusion, and delusions will sooner or later bring unhappiness.

Finally, the "blessed" life is narrow. "Strait is the gate and narrow is the way that leadeth unto life." If you are ever happy in this world or the next, you must submit to the limitations of honesty and truthfulness and virtue and spirituality. There is no blessedness without narrowness. When a man says he is broad on the ten commandments, keep your hand on your pocket-book. If he is broad on the command, "Thou shalt not steal," he is a rogue; or broad on the command, "Thou shalt not lie," he is a liar; or broad on the command, "Thou shalt not commit adultery," he is an adulterer.

Jesus closes his sermon with two illustrations of the proposition that the "blessed" life is narrow. One is taken from botany and the other from architecture. First, we are fruit-trees. Christianity is an orchard, not a forest. The Christian is known not by his height or bigness, but by his fruit. "The fruit of the spirit is love, joy, peace, long-suffering, gentleness, goodness, faith, meekness, temperance." Unless we can stand this narrow test we are not Christians. "By their fruits ye shall know them."

The next illustration is from architecture. Two men build houses, one on the sand, the other on the rock. Because one was built on the sand it was washed away and destroyed. Because the other was built on the rock it remained steadfast. Building is a narrow process. When you go to build a house you narrow down the trees. No man would go to the forest and bring a whole tree to build into a house. He cuts off the roots and branches, removes the bark, and narrows it down. If you build a house with granite you do not try to put into it a mountain of rock. With drill and chisel you narrow the granite down to the proper size. If you build with brick you go to the great field of clay and sand and narrow them down, and when you have narrowed down clay and sand to brick size, and burnt them, they are ready for the walls, and not till then. So with building character for God. It is a narrow process. Unless you submit to the limitations of virtue you cannot build solid character. And without solid character there is no true blessedness.

One illustration, and I will close. A young man came to the city and fell in with two companions, one of them from his old home. They tried to induce him to go to the races. He said, "I will go, but I will not drink or gamble." On the train a lady sitting just behind them overheard their conversation. One of them, with a drunken swagger, said to him, "You are a milksop; you are tied to your mother's apron-strings; it is pitiful to see one so narrow and puritanical in his views." That young man, about eighteen years of age, with the freshness of a pure country home on his face, replied, "Yes, boys, I am willing to admit all you say, and somehow I feel if I were at my mother's apron-strings now I would be a trifle safer, and I am not going to the races, but will get off at the next station." When the station was reached he got up and quietly moved out while they followed, laughing and pesting. He said afterward, "As I stood on the platform there came before me a scene that took place two years ago. The open Bible was on the plain country dining-room table, and sitting by the side of it a form dearer to me than life. She bowed her gray hairs and read to me from the old book, then knelt down and commended her boy to God as he was about to go to the great city to seek his fortune; and I said, 'God helping me, I will try to be as narrow as my mother's virtue, and as honest as her Bible.'" That young man will be somebody, and he is happy. The other two fellows that would not submit to the limitations of honesty and sobriety and virtue are on the road to wreck and ruin, and the misery that follows. The man who is willing to be as narrow as his mother's chastity, and as honest as his mother's Bible, is building character that will bring with it a truly blessed life.

The Usher Committee.

Sweet and touching was the interlude which the singing of Mr. Yarnelle and his daughter furnished, and gladly would the audience have lengthened it. Mr. Shurtleff's fine poem was then listened to.

Convention Poem by Rev. Ernest Warburton Shurtleff,
Plymouth, Mass.

A CHARGE TO THE REPUBLIC.

When in creation's morning
  God hung the world in space,
And turned upon its darkness
  The glory of His face,
Not on the Orient flaming,
  Nor mountain's towering span,
He set His loftiest glory,
  But on the brow of man;
And when He crowned man lord of all
  That tread earth's vast domain,
He made a kingdom where the soul
  Should in His image reign.

And in that holy kingdom
  He fixed the just decree
That Right alone should sanction
  Man's earthly sovereignty:
That through the future ages,
  In valiant beauty strong,
The Right should ever triumph
  In conquest over Wrong.
The Wrong might for a while usurp
  Truth's everlasting throne,
But the Right should rise again and claim
  Earth's kingdom as its own.

And gloriously the ages
  Have witnessed to this law,
Since Moses from Mt. Pisgah
  The Land of Promise saw.
When Right hath ruled the nations,
  How proud their fame, how just!
When Wrong hath swayed their sceptres,
  How humbled in the dust!
So was it when Chaldæa's fall
  Mocked great Belshazzar's reign,
And Rome, beneath her Cæsar's rod,
  In ashes strewed the plain.

For not by pomp imperial
  Any earthly nation stands;
For, though its pride touched heaven,
  'T is only God commands;
And all man's selfish glory
  Is heraldry of doom,
A meteoric moment,
  A flash, and then the gloom.
Assyria, Egypt, Babylon,
  Imperial was their sway;
Then fell the shadow of God's hand,
  And darkness closed their day.

Nor Nero, nor Napoleon,
  Howe'er so vast their host,
Can take again the sceptre
  Of the honor that is lost;
But from them who in God's image
  The law of right obey
The rod of sceptred honor
  Shall never pass away.
And righteous nations, founded thus,
  Shall lift their splendor high,
Like mountains, throned upon the earth,
  But crowned in the starry sky.

My country! Oh my country!
  Thy brow with stars how bright!
Thy beauty and strength, how wedded
  In bridal of the right!
In calm or storm unshaken,
  In darkness or lightning's flame,
Thy mountain altars tower
  To God in Freedom's name;
Thy breaking waves on every strand
  Of Freedom's birthright roar,
As if ocean, filled with the Pilgrims' song,
  Would echo it evermore.

Within thy loved dominions
  Who doth not read God's plan,
That the glory of a republic
  Is the brotherhood of man;
Thy Southernland savannas,
  Thy Western mountains gray,
Thy Northern lakes, thy prairies,—
  They are one fair bourne for aye.
And into that beauteous fatherland
  Let only the loyal come,
Who love one flag, one government,
  One shrine — the nation's home.

But see! the storm has gathered.
  'T is an hour to try men's souls;
And over thy peaceful borders
  The thunder of battle rolls.
'T is not that the foe hath menaced
  Thy peace with his haughty word,
'T is not that against thy bosom
  He lifteth his ruthless sword —
Thou mightest have dwelt in quietude,
  A calm on thy hills and leas,
Thy navy at listless anchor moored,
  Thine army encamped at ease.

But a stifled moan of anguish
  Came from Cuba's alien shore;
Could America's heart be silent
  With the cry of the lost at her door?
Her courts, her schools, her temples,
  All sounding humanity's name,—
Could she harden her heart, unmindful,
  When the call for humanity came?
Nay, this fair land shall never cease

To answer the outcast's cry,
For this home of the free is humanity's land,
While the free sun lights yon sky.

And if now our cities echo
To the march of the marshalled throngs,
If now the noise of battle
Stills at home the hearthstone songs,
'T is not that direful vengeance
Hath fired the patriot's blood,
'T is humanity he remembers,
In the name of Right and God!
Long did our calm commander wait;
But when this end he saw
He said, "If peace wins not for peace,
So be it,—let there be war!"

Then forthwith swept our navy
Across the rushing tide,
And tossed our starry pennons
O'er waters crimson dyed;
And forthwith in Manila
Our cannon knelled the hour
Of dying despotism
And greed's inhuman power.
And long as after years record
A hero's conquest there,
The country's pride shall deepest be
That Right made Victory fair.

And in far Santiago,
By Morro's castled height,
Again a leader's conquest
Was won in the name of Right.
He dashed with his dauntless seven
Through the fire of the cannonade;
Though death itself had called him,
The hero had obeyed;
For death but brightens duty's cause
To him whose soul is brave;
'T is sweet to die when Honor lives
To smile above the grave.

But America! fame-lauded,
How art thou tested now,
While thousands bring their laurels
Of praise to deck thy brow?
They bid thee build thy navy
A hundred-fold as strong;
Equip thy coasts with castles,
Thy plains with armies throng;
Then reach abroad thy ponderous arm,
Like England's o'er the sea,
And seize the gems of ocean's isles,
Thy spoils of war to be.

They bid thee gird thy loins
In terrible array,
Control by fear the nations
That hate while they obey:
By dreaded power imperial

Sweep aloft thy flashing sword,
  While none shall dare affront thee
Who hear thy awful word.
But is it so, my country proud
  Thy glory shall increase?
And wouldst thou purchase by man's hate
  The benisons of peace?

They bid thee who in mercy
  Wast armed man's woe to share
Wage now a war for Mammon;
  Oh what a fall were there!
Nay, let the war continue
  As first heaven did subscribe,
Its spoils the wage of honor,
  And not the Republic's bribe.
Then woo we again the ways of peace,
  And if there are treasures lost,
There never was battle won for right
  That counted too great a cost.

Build if thou wilt a navy
  That shall spring from its open docks,
And wheel o'er the sea in squadrons
  As thick as the feathered flocks;
Call if thou wilt an army
  That shall compass the North and South,
Build fortresses and castles
  At every harbor's mouth;
But let erewhile that good increase
  Which is the nation's soul;
For what were all this armament
  Did Love not sway the whole?

Love! — strong as the sun that holdeth
  The starry worlds by its power,
And tender as light at morning
  That waketh the sleeping flower;
As keen as the fiery lances
  That pierce winter's ice and snow,
And fair as the brush of sunbeams
  That paints on the clouds its bow.
Love throned with Right, as light is throned
  With the blue serene of the sky —
These twain best make earth's kingdom strong
  As heaven's is strong on high.

For moral force, not armies,
  The Republic loudest pleads,
The wealth of righteous spirits,
  And chivalry of honest deeds.
Expand thy soul, my country,
  And thy foes shall bow in awe,
For the majesty of morals
  Is peerless in peace or war.
Though all the ocean's isles were thine,
  And thy navies on every sea,
Thou wert poor indeed unless thy soul
  Filled that immensity.

Then speed, victorious navy,
  Across the sounding flood,
By sun and star heav'n guided,
  As by God's flaming sword;
Before your prows the ocean
  Shall toss its flowers of foam,
As if the sea gave garlands
  Because Christ's fleet had come;
And the thundering waves, amid their roar,
  Shall shout their battle-song,
That deliverance comes to save the weak
  By the mercies of the strong.

By army and by navy
  Let God's just will be done,
And be there never a battle
  That is not in honor won.
America! This moment
  Demands events sublime!
The destiny of nations
  Is waiting on this time!
The searching eyes of all the earth
  Amid this darkness gleam;
Now let the fair Republic shine
  In righteousness supreme!

The next and last speaker of the evening was Rev. R. S. MacArthur, D.D., of New York City. His masterly address is given herewith.

Address by Rev. R. S. MacArthur, D.D.,
New York City.

GOD'S HAND IN THE NATION'S CONFLICT.

The unexpected, we might almost say the impossible, has happened: the American nation, after thirty years of peace, is again engaged in war. We have, however, reason to thank God that this is not a war between different sections of our own country, but that all parts of our beloved land are united against a common foe. We greatly deprecate the necessity of war. We had hoped that one of the brightest glories in the life of civilized nations, as we pass over into the twentieth century, would be the adoption of international arbitration for the settlement of all international disputes. But in this truly humanitarian and genuinely Christian hope we are disappointed. War is a relic of barbarism. War in itself considered is legalized assassination; war is scientific murder. War is barbarous immanity; it is feral madness. War is precisely what General Sherman in his blunt Saxon called it — "hell." It may for a brief time stimulate various industries; but it cannot wholesomely and permanently stimulate any industry. It is simply destruction; it is plague, epidemic, and evil of a thousand kinds. God can, and God often does, overrule war for good. He often causes the white horse of peace and prosperity to follow closely in the footsteps of the red horse of war and destruction. But Christian nations ought to be able to settle all disputes by a resort to arbitration, rather than by recourse to the arbitrament of the sword. But if there is any nation with which we can engage in war without compunction of conscience and with the approval of the highest Christian conviction, it is with cruel and tyrannous Spain, whose hands are red with innocent blood and whose heart is black with manifold crimes.

GOD'S PRESENCE IN CURRENT EVENTS.

We often fail rightly to recognize God's presence in the events of the hour.

We too frequently relegate him to distant countries and to remote centuries. We ought to remember that he is as truly in the world to-day as he was in any period recorded in Biblical history. His presence is as genuinely given to the great philanthropic and Christian movements of the world now as it was vouchsafed to Moses or Joshua, to David or Solomon, to Isaiah or Daniel, to Paul or any other apostle. If only we had spiritual ears sufficiently sensitive we might hear in reading the history of Gladstone, whose name is now enrolled among the immortals, the voice of God saying to him, at different stages in his eventful life, "As I was with Moses, so shall I be with thee, brave and triumphant Gladstone." If we listen well we shall hear above the booming of cannon, the sighs of the defeated, and the shouts of the victorious in Manila Bay, the voice of God saying, "As I was with Moses, so shall I be with thee, O heroic Commander Dewey. No Spanish ship shall long stand before thee, thou leader of victorious Americans, in this triumph of humanity, of liberty, and of true Christianity." It is not too much to say that no battle was ever fought between the Israelites and the Canaanites, or any other foes of Israel's God and God's Israel, whose history is recorded in the Bible, which gives more marked evidence of God's presence, power, and approval than the battle in Manila Bay.

If the record of that battle were found in the Bible, the account showing that all the enemy's ships were sunk or disabled, that hundreds of the enemy were killed and many hundreds more wounded, and that not an American ship was destroyed or seriously injured, and not an American life lost, every destructive critic of the Bible, and many critics who are esteemed orthodox, would promptly affirm that the story was absolutely incredible. They would declare, without qualification, that its statements were colored if not created by writers prejudiced in favor of Israel and of God; they would challenge contradiction in their declaration that the story was an interpolation, or at least an unpardonable exaggeration, and written long after the alleged occurrence of the events — and written when legend rather than sober history dominated the thought and directed the affirmation of the writer. This is not an overstatement of what would have occurred had the record of this battle been found in the Bible. We ought to remember that God has never abdicated the throne of the universe, and that the pierced hand of Jesus Christ is still upon the helm. From his watch-tower in the heavens he is directing all its movements. We lose much by separating unduly, and so unwisely and unrighteously, between what we call secular and sacred events and histories. To the truly devout soul there is no secular history, in the sense that it is a history apart from the immediate presence, power, and purpose of God. All life is sacred; all events are divine in their control; and all movements are beneficent in their ultimate purpose. It is eminently fitting, therefore, that we should recognize God's hand in the nation's conflict.

SEEN IN THE MOTIVES OF THE AMERICANS.

God's hand is seen, in the first place, in the motives which has led the American nation into its war with Spain. If ever there was a just war, our war against Spain is a just war. We waited long before aggressive measures were adopted; we used every argument to induce Spain to do justice to Cuba before we took the decisive step. Spain was deaf, not only to the cry of its starving and dying people in Cuba, but to all the entreaties of the United States, and to the promptings of humanity in all other noble people. We have not undertaken this war for the acquisition of territory; we are not earth-hungry as are many of the European nations; we are not like Russia, reaching out our hand in all directions for additional territories. In the providence of God, we may acquire great territorial areas before this war closes. We began it to give liberty to suffering Cubans, almost under the shadow of our own flag; but God has ordered the war so that the first victory was won practically on the other side of the globe, and the first blessing of peace may be enjoyed by the people of the Philippine Islands, whose condition was, in some respects, vastly worse than that of the Cubans.

This victory and its consequent responsibility are God's ordainment and not our choice. We dare not, however, shrink from the responsibility which this victory has unexpectedly laid upon the American people. The misgovernment of Spain in these islands almost surpasses belief. Many portions of the islands have never been explored; their great treasures have been neglected, and their people are sunk in ignorance and misery. Friars, recruited from the lowest, most ignorant, and most debased classes in Spain, are the virtual rulers over great portions of the Philippines; they practically combine the functions of civil tyrants. The character of the population and certain phases of the civilization on the islands are the results of their gross immoralities. There are Jesuit priests in the islands of a higher order who wage honorable ecclesiastical warfare with these vicious friars. We may be obliged, for a time at least, to retain possession of these islands. We must maintain order within their borders; this obligation we cannot set aside. We certainly cannot return these islands to Spain; to do so would defeat in great part the high and holy aims with which we have begun this war. We may not be able to give them to Great Britain, to Japan, or to any other nation; to give them to any nation would arouse the jealousy of all the nations with possessions in the Orient. Without doubt, we shall be obliged for a considerable time, possibly permanently, to retain possession of this territory thus providentially placed under our control. American control of these islands, even for half a century, would transform them into the garden of the world. In natural fertility, in variety of production, and in beauty of landscape, they would become, under our control, a second paradise; and the most beautiful product in this paradise when cultivated by American hands and hearts will be the tree of civil and religious liberty.

We have not engaged in this war for the gratification of personal or national revenge. Without doubt the slogan, "Remember the *Maine*," will quicken the step, nerve the arm, and fire the heart of many American soldiers, sailors, and marines. But that is not the dominant battle-cry as we engage in this war. Such a slogan is unworthy a people rejoicing in a Christian civilization; that war-cry is worthy of only a heathen and barbaric people. Our motive is vastly higher, nobler, and diviner. There is a righteous wrath, a holy indignation, a divine avengement, to which we cannot be indifferent, and whose inspiration we may rightly feel, as we sing with Milton:

> "Avenge, O Lord, thy slaughter'd saints, whose bones
> Lie scattered on the Alpine mountain cold."

But revenge as an imprecation, as an expression of mere human desire, must not be a controlling motive in this war. Indulgence in revenge would only make Americans as savage and cruel as are the most barbaric Spaniards themselves. Vengeance, in the sense of punishment in the full meaning, belongeth unto God alone. He can and he surely will repay; and to him we can and do refer the final arbitrament of the destruction of the *Maine*. Ours is a war for peace, for compassion, for humanity. This is a truly Christian sentiment. If Spain were to attack our coasts and capture many cities, the most ardent lovers of peace would in these circumstances indorse a war of self-defence. But if a war of self-defence be justifiable, a war for the defence of others who are unable to defend themselves is still more truly justifiable and Christian. Many say the Cubans are not worthy of the sacrifices we may have to make on their behalf. But their worthiness is not the dominating factor in our action. They are weak and we are strong: they are suffering and we can relieve that suffering. Our question is not, "What can we do for ourselves?" But it is chiefly, "What can we do to help others?" We are engaged in a crusade of brotherhood; in a holy war for humanity. We are striving to lift up the downtrodden. We are proving to the world that we are our brother's keeper. Our national policy is not and must not be a selfish one. The good we possess we must share. This motive is high and holy; but the appeal to the passion of revenge is utterly unmanly and un-Christian. We must never lose sight of the noble motive with which we have entered upon this war.

GOD'S HAND IN THE PRINCIPLES INVOLVED.

God's hand is clearly seen, in the second place, in the principles involved in this war. Few nations of Europe can appreciate either the motives which control our action in this war or the principles involved in the war itself. These nations do not engage in war except for national advantage; and they cannot understand how it is possible for the American people to have any other motive than national aggrandizement. They, therefore, suspect our motives and depreciate the importance of the issues involved. This is a war between widely differing civilizations. It is a war between ignorance, bigotry, and superstition on the one side and intelligence, liberty, and a true Christianity on the other side. Out of Spain's nearly 18,000,000 population, well-nigh 12,000,000 are illiterate. It is a war between Latinism and Anglo-Saxonism; it is a war between the most despicable civilization of modern times and the most Christianized civilization of all times; it is a war between the sixteenth and the twentieth centuries; and, in its ultimate issues, it is a war between Romanism and Protestantism. In Spain, Romanism has stood for illiteracy and bigotry, for the satanic inquisition of Torquemada, and the hadean tyranny of men like Alva and Weyler; and Protestantism, as involved in this war, stands for the opposite of these mediæval and tyrannous principles at every stage of their development and in every form of their manifestation. A sense of the solemnity of the issues involved is seen in the demeanor of all the troops as they march down our streets. There is no levity in their manner, and no hilarity in their speech; they move with a sense of high and holy duty as their controlling motive. The dignity of the hour and the providential duty to which they are called give to the movements of our soldiers a solemnity fitting the tragic drama and the humanitarian duty in which the nation is engaged.

This is a war for the triumph of nations which have the right to survive. Our blessed Lord formulated a universal and eternal principle when he said, "Unto every one that hath shall be given, and he shall have abundance; but from him that hath not shall be taken away even that which he hath." This statement is not true simply because our Lord made it, but he made it because it is eternally true. Whosoever rightly improves what he providentially possesses shall, in harmony with natural law, possess vastly more; but whosoever misimproves what is committed to him shall lose all that he has. This law is universal and eternal. Spain proved herself unworthy of her great possessions alike in the new world and in the old world. God has virtually placed the American people at the portal of the twentieth century, and has given them command, not only to refuse admission to the civilization of the sixteenth century, but to drive it utterly from this Western hemisphere. Scientific men have recognized this law and have described it as the "survival of the fittest." Darwin calls natural selection, by which he means the process in nature according to which plants and animals which are best fitted survive and propagate the "survival of the fittest." A similar law is fully illustrated among the nations of the earth. Lord Salisbury has recently appropriately described certain peoples as "dying nations." Each nation has its subtonic, its diapason, its pervasive, unitive, and concordant note. So has each century. The eighteenth century went out in revolution and blood; but out of that revolution came the sovereignty of the people, which under God is the chief glory of the nineteenth century. The nineteenth century will go out with the spirit of humanity, with the note of brotherhood, with the duty of altruism, as its diapason, as its inspiring slogan, as its divine bugle-call to the nations of the earth. In this spirit the fife sounds and the pibroch shakes the air as the nineteenth century closes and the twentieth century opens.

Spain has proved to be utterly unworthy of the great opportunity which Divine Providence placed before her. She must see all her colonial possessions taken from her cruel grasp. Her hands are slippery with blood, and they can no longer hold colonial possessions secured by tyranny and long retained by oppression. Whoever contrasts the glory of Spain at the time of the abdication of Charles V. with her present degradation will have a striking illustration of the operation of the law that only the fittest can survive. On the

25th of October, 1555, the eyes of the whole world rested on the scene in the hall of the great palace at Brussels when Charles V. abdicated his throne.

Brussels was then the gay capital of Brabant. Its gardens surrounded it with a sea of verdure; its streets rose on the sides of the hills like seats in an amphitheatre. In this historic hall were assembled warriors and knights resplendent in their robes, and famous for chivalry in battle and brilliancy in the court. Here was Egmont, the flower of Flemish chivalry; here was Horn, proud, sullen, and defiant. Behold the mighty Charles entering the hall leaning on the shoulder of William, the Prince of Orange. Charles is but fifty-five years old, but his grossly wicked life has made him a feeble old man. His shoulders are bowed and his legs are feeble. Never handsome, he is now positively ugly. His lower jaw so protrudes that his few remaining teeth make eating and speaking difficult. Near him is Philip, his son and successor. He has the enormous mouth and protruding jaw of his father, as well as that father's intense bigotry and inhuman intolerance. To Philip was given that day authority over the destinies of half the world, — over Spain, over great parts of America, and soon, through the conquest of Portugal, parts of the East Indies and Africa. Into his hands were placed the destinies of one hundred millions of people, and of many additional millions then unborn. He was utterly unfit to rule these mighty nations. He possessed all the intolerance and bigotry of his father and many vices to which his father was a stranger. Charles retired to the monastery of San Yuste, situated in a secluded region in the western part of Spain. While here he expressed the deepest regret that he did not burn Luther at Worms. He constantly urged Philip to use the utmost severity in dealing with heretics, conjuring him to cherish the "Holy Inquisition" and adding, "So shall you have my blessing, and the Lord shall prosper all your undertakings."

Prescott, doubtless, is right in affirming that Charles did more to fasten the yoke of superstition on the necks of the Spaniards than all other rulers. His example controlled the policy of the pitiless Philip II., and indirectly that of the imbecile Philip III. Philip's marriage with Mary Tudor made him king-consort of England. The mines of Mexico and Peru filled his coffers with steady streams of precious metals. He directed the creation of the so-called Invincible Armada, which attempted in 1588 the destruction of England. He intended to strike an absolutely decisive blow at Protestantism throughout the world. Pope Sixtus V. had made England over to him as his possession. His fleet consisted of 130 vessels, and was thus larger than had ever before been seen in Europe. The utmost consternation seized all ranks of people in England upon the news of the approach of this terrible Armada. All honor to Howard, Drake, Hawkins, and Frobisher! But all glory to God for the winds that blew and that sent so many of those ships to the bottom of the sea! Only fifty-three of the 130 ships returned to Spain. Well might Elizabeth strike a medal with the inscription: *Deus flavit, et dissipati sunt*, "God blew and they were scattered." In a room in the Escorial Philip died a death similar to that of Herod, as described in the Acts of the Apostles. Nothing could surpass the cruelties of which he was guilty in the interests of the Roman Church and the kingdom of Spain. The glorious battle just fought, and the superb victory won at Manila Bay, was but the continuation and conclusion of the battle begun by Elizabeth, and thus sublimely completed by the heroic Dewey.

With the death of Philip II. closed that splendid and cruel era of Spanish history which began with the capture of Granada and the discovery of the new world. The imbecile Philip III. was so great a slave to form that he exposed himself to the heat of a strong fire. the servant whose duty it was to remove his chair being absent and etiquette forbidding the king to do it for himself, and so his death was caused prematurely. But we may be well assured that this was but a preliminary roast later continued, and which his many and great crimes fully warranted. The Inquisition cast its dark shadow not only over the reign of Charles and Philip, but also over that of Ferdinand and Isabella. Isabella sincerely believed that the auto da fe, "act of faith," as the burning of the condemned was called, was rendering God good service. She said, " In the love of Christ and his Maid-Mother I have caused great misery. I have depopulated towns and districts, provinces and kingdoms." Llorente computes that during the eighteen years of Torquemada's ministry there were no fewer than 10,220 burnt, 6,860 condemned and burnt in effigy, as absent or dead, and 97,321 reconciled by various penances.

Under Philip III. more than half a million of the Moors, or Moriscoes, Jews, and Protestants, the most skilful and industrious inhabitants of the peninsula, were driven into exile. This act of bigotry was a fatal blow to many of the most prosperous provinces of Spain, and the empty dwellings and neglected fields of these districts bore sad and eloquent testimony to the folly and cruelty of such religious bigotry. No words can overstate the satanic crimes of Philip II. and Alva in the Netherlands, and these countries in 1609 virtually achieved their independence. In 1639 came the loss of Portugal. During the latter part of the seventeenth century Spain was involved in dangerous wars with France, and lost by various causes at least eight million of her population. Then came the revolt of her American colonies; then in 1819 her cession of Florida to the United States; and now with slippery grasp she is holding on to Cuba and a few islands, — all that remains of the once magnificent colonial possessions which filled her with unholy pride and gave her almost unlimited power throughout the world. Spain is unfit to rule, and by the inevitable law of God in nature and providence she must be deprived of her rule. God is making the American people the rod of his righteous wrath to chastise this guilty nation.

The law of the survival of the fittest was conclusively illustrated in the destruction of the Canaanites by the Israelites. This event is often considered one of the difficulties of Scripture, but if the facts were fully understood the difficulty would entirely disappear. The Canaanites were not fit to survive. They were guilty of crimes which were long punishable by death in Great Britain and all her colonies. God wished to introduce a higher civilization than that of the Canaanites. He might have destroyed them by earthquakes, by epidemic, or by ordinary operation of natural law; but by using the Israelites as the instruments of his just wrath he more fully showed his indignation against the sin of the Canaanites. The same law is revealed in the case of the American Indian. God wanted the American continent for the development of the greatest civilization of the modern world. In carrying out that plan the Indian must conform to civilization or be destroyed by civilization. This statement does not justify any cruelty on our part toward the Indian; but it emphasizes the universality of uniformity of God's great law in the management of the world. In harmony also with this law the aboriginal tribes of the Peninsula of India were driven out by the conquering Aryans; so were the Finns supplanted by the Aryan races in Europe and Asia; and so the Tartars the Russians, and the aborigines, as we have seen in North America, and as we may see in Australia and New Zealand, by the Anglo-Saxon race.

The whole history of Spain, the Iberian Peninsula, is an illustration of this law. In prehistoric times the Iberians had possession. Then came the Celts, and hence the Celt-Iberian; then the Phœnician, and successively the Greek, the Carthaginian, the Roman, the Goth, the Moor, and finally the present heterogeneous Spanish nation. The story of the conquest of Spain by the Moslems is one of the best historic examples of this law. Fifty years after the death of Mohammed his conquering standards were carried through Asia to the Hellespont, and through Africa to the Straits of Gibraltar. This great crescent lay along the southern shore of the Mediterranean, with one horn striving to push its way into Europe at the Hellespont and the other at Gibraltar. Thirty-six years after the death of Mohammed, or in the year 668, the Moslems laid siege to Constantinople; and for six years the siege continued with unflagging energy and heroic courage. But for the use of the bituminous compound called " Greek Fires," which were poured from the walls upon the scaling parties and carried to a distance by tipped arrows or blown through tubes, the Arabs might have conquered, and the banner of Islam might have waved over Europe and finally over America. But the fierce and uncontrollable flame of the Greek Fire was too much even for Moslem courage and zeal. But although they were repulsed at the eastern extremity of Europe they found its gates were opened by treachery at the western extremity; and it is said that Count Julian was the Judas who betrayed his country into the hands of the Moslems.

Roderic, the last Visigothic king of Spain, entrusted Julian with the command of the fortress of Ceuta, which guarded the Straits of Gibraltar; he surrendered his post to Musa, the Mohammedan Governor of Africa. In 711 Tarik effected an entrance into Europe, landing at a point which to this hour preserves his name in the word "Gibraltar," Gibelal-Tarik, meaning "Mount of Tarik." The Gothic people, who more than two centuries before had conquered Spain, had lost their bravery and had become assimilated to the Latin-speaking provincials of the Peninsula. Roderic entered upon battle wearing silken robes, crowned with a diadem, and borne in an ivory chariot drawn by white mules. Disaffection alienated his chiefs, and his army, after a battle of seven days. was partly overcome by the enemy, and the remainder of his troops abandoned the field in disgraceful flight. Roderic himself was drowned while crossing the Guadalquiver. Thus perished the last of the Gothic kings, and thus triumphed the Moors. Cordova, Toledo, and all of the chief cities were soon in their possession, and for nearly eight hundred years they were the rulers over a great part of Spain. The Visigoths were a dying race; they were unworthy to survive, and they therefore perished.

In the destruction of the Moors and the triumph of the Spaniards in 1432 the same law was again illustrated. In 1469 Ferdinand of Aragon was married to Isabella of Castile; in 1479 these two states were united into a single kingdom; and in 1492 came the conquest of Granada. The Mohammedan was at that time reduced to a limited dominion, but the province of Granada, by the skill of the Moors, was one of the richest districts of Spain. Besides Granada, its potent and opulent capital, the district embraced seventy walled towns. Terrific was the battle of Granada. The Moors were weakened by internal dissensions as were the Goths whom eight centuries before they had conquered. Glorious was the victory of Spain when Cardinal Mendoza, climbing one of the historic towers of the Alhambra, waved the banner of Spain and shouted, "Granada is taken. Granada is taken." We have already seen that almost immediately upon reaching the zenith of her power and glory Spain began the downward course which has now well nigh reached its nadir. The establishment of the Inquisition, the neglect of wholesome industries at home because of the exaggerated reports of Golcondas in newly discovered islands and continents. the loss of the youth of the country who in spirit of adventure went to the lands recently acquired, the banishment of the Protestants, Jews, and Moors who had not been cruelly put to death by the officers of the Inquisition,—all these things hastened the downfall of Spain, until her name has become a byword and hissing among the nations of the earth. No nation, no Church. no man, can escape the operation of this great and universal law as to the survival of the fittest. Only as by the observance of righteous law, human and divine. we prove our worth, can we expect to survive in the terrific competitions of the time and the fearful conflicts of the ambitious nations of the earth. The nation which will not obey the laws of the highest civilization of the time will by that very civilization be utterly destroyed.

GOD'S HAND SEEN IN THE RESULTS.

God's hand will be conspicuously seen in the results of this war. Many of the results, no doubt, will be sad. We cannot expect that the losses inseparable from war will be all on the side of Spain. There will be darkened American homes, broken American lives, and saddened American hearts. War is war for evermore. Much as we deprecate war. now that we have been forced into it it is a kindness even to Spain to press the war with the utmost vigor, and make it as short, sharp, decisive, and terrible as possible. One result of this war will be the destruction of the sectional spirit in America and the union of all parts of the country in loyalty to the flag. During the last presidential campaign a dangerous sectionalism revealed itself in different parts of the country. It is now gone and we hope it will never return. There is now no North and no South, no East and no West. There is one country united in love and loyalty for the glory of the flag and for the honor of the nation. Some of the bravest officers and soldiers who may invade Cuba are men who fought against the flag during the Civil War. Those who wore the gray and those who wore the blue will vie with one another in protecting every star and stripe in the beloved flag. We do not forget the passage of the Sixth Massachusetts Regiment through Baltimore in 1861; that occasion is historic in the annals of the Civil War. Then the hostility shown toward that regiment was bitter and deadly. A few days ago the same regiment passed through the same city, and it received unmeasured hospitality. The city was gaily decorated, and the soldiers were pelted with roses instead of stones as on the former occasion. This difference of treatment typifies the new epoch upon which we have entered. The North and the South are one. Baltimore and Boston are one. All the States are one, and shall be one and inseparable forever.

Another result of the war will be a virtual, if not a formal, Anglo-Saxon alliance. The recent speech of Mr. Chamberlain has made a sensation throughout the civilized world. He has made not only all the Latins but all the Teutons anxious as to their future. The best classes both in Great Britain and in the United States will hail with joy this sympathetic alliance. A few pulmonary Hibernian patriots, whose chief subject of oratory and means of sustenance are dissensions between the different branches of the Anglo-Saxon race, will oppose this union; but all true Britons and Americans will welcome it with patriotic enthusiasm. A new day is dawning for the great Anglo-Saxon race. The Queen's birthday awakens an enthusiasm in the United States second only to that evoked in Great Britain and her colonies. It was an American who spoke of "the womanliness of the Queen and the queenliness of the woman." It was an American who gave us the toast, "Victoria, Queen of Great Britain and Ireland, Empress of India, and woman of the world." In her pure and noble womanhood she is queen of all pure and noble hearts in all parts of the world. This Anglo-Saxon alliance will not be of the nature of the so-called Holy Alliance, the Kaiserbund, or the Dreibund. But it will be an alliance for peace and not for war; an alliance for liberty and not for tyranny; an alliance for all that is noblest in human government and divinest in human liberty and progress.

The Anglo-Saxon race is marching forward to the conquest of the world. Already the English tongue is spoken by 125,000,000, while but 90,000,000 speak Russian, 75,000,000 German, 55,000,000 French, 45,000,000 Spanish, and 35,000,000 Italian. Great Britain and the United States united can control the destinies of the human race. A triumphant Anglo-Saxondom can speak the masterful word on all continents and among all peoples. Such a union would contribute to the advancement of every interest of the human race. Had such a union been in existence a few years ago thousands of Armenians would have been saved from horrible deaths; and were this union really compacted there would be now religious liberty for our persecuted brethren and all other Christian believers in Russia. The Union Jack and the Stars and Stripes entwined in loving and inseparable friendship and fellowship, and waving over an Anglo-American alliance, will be the crowning glory of the closing century. It will be one of the great factors in the evangelization of the heathen, the humanization of all governments, and the divinization of all peoples. It will be a sight which will rejoice the hearts of saints and seraphs, of angels and archangels. When this alliance shall have been recognized then the eastern sky will be radiant with the crimson and gold of the millennial dawn.

Another result of this war will be that the American Republic will come up to its great place in the Congress of Nations. This nation has now reached its majority: it will never again go back to childhood. It must take its place in bearing the responsibilities and discharging the obligations of the leading nations of the world. We have too long striven to be an isolated people. George Washington was one of the greatest men of the human race, but he was not omniscient. We have often made his farewell address a sort of fetich. He spoke according to his light, as all men must speak; but he could not conceive of the greatness of the republic whose foundations he so nobly laid. In his day Liverpool was farther from Washington than is Calcutta or Bombay in our day. In his day Boston was farther from New York than is Liverpool or London in our day. He could not conceive of a time when railways, telegraphs, and telephones would unite continents and make a whispering gallery of the world. We do well, indeed, to avoid the entangling alliances which he feared; but we shall do ill if we shirk the solemn and sublime obligations which we must now assume. We have too much left Great Britain to fight alone the world's battles. Henceforth the beautiful daughter must nobly stand beside her queenly mother. Matthew Arnold set forth the thought that Great Britain is overburdened with the care of empire. He described her as a "weary Titan,"

> "Bearing on shoulders immense,
> Atlantean, the load,
> Well-nigh not to be borne.
> Of the too vast orb of her fate."

We shall respond to the call to share in bearing this burden, and in rejoicing in these honors. The Anglo-Saxon is the great colonizing race; it is also the great missionary race. Great Britain has been the most potent missionary nation in the world. Her rule in Egypt and India has brought with its acknowledged evils untold blessings to many tribes and peoples. Her colonies, compared with those of France, Germany, and Russia, are abodes of prosperity and peace. Wherever her flag has gone, there law, liberty, civilization, and Christianity are found. Her "far-flung battle-line" is the symbol of peaceful possession and prosperous enterprise. She is illuminating the dark places of the earth. We need not hesitate to take our place loyally by her side. The heroic days of the American Republic are still to come. Great problems are demanding solution; and we must not fear the task of bravely meeting these problems. Our young men sometimes think that the glorious days of the Republic were the times of Washington and of Lincoln; but greater questions than either Washington or Lincoln ever dreamed of are soon to be asked and answered by the American people. We want statesmen who can stand beside John Bright and Gladstone, the uncrowned king of the world. We want statesmen who shall take their place beside the noblest Americans whose names shall shine forever as stars in the firmament of our history. Never did we need such statesmen more than we shall need them in the near future. Perhaps we ought not to bring politics into religion in the technical sense of these terms: but it is certain that we must put religion into politics in the true meaning of both these terms.

We shall not shrink from the new and enlarged mission which the providence of God is opening to the thought and duty of the American people. We have a message to all the nations of the earth. Every stripe in our flag is a herald of human equality, and every star is an evangelist of civil and religious liberty round the globe. We must push out into the Pacific Ocean. History began its sublime achievements on the shores of the Mediterranean. It erected its enduring monuments later on the shores of the Atlantic, and it is now laying the foundations of its grandest triumphs on the shores of the Pacific. The Hawaiian Islands lie like a necklace of pearls on the bosom of that emerald sea; that necklace, by the alchemy of American patriotism and by the mercy of Divine Providence, will be transformed into a star in the American flag. And we may yet have other islands in the sea as set stepping-stones to our possessions in the far East. We must speak our word with reference to the dismemberment of China; we are entitled to all the commercial privileges that China grants to all other peoples. Our trade with China now amounts to $20,000,000 annually, and it will soon increase to $100,000,000 annually. We need a naval base in the Orient; and we may yet require a squadron in Eastern waters sufficiently strong to oblige all nations to respect our rights. Backed by Great Britain and Japan, we must utter our protest against the selfish schemes of France, Germany, and Russia in the Orient.

These new problems will develop new resources on the part of our people. They will lead us away from the schemes of petty politicians who are seeking simply place and power. They will tend to the development of a true civil-service reform, of a virile statesmanship, and of a world-wide Americanism. The golden age of our politics is thus in the future. Let those deride who will, but some of us dare believe that a new era has dawned, that new issues have come, that a larger place in the world's history is to be ours, and that a fuller American patriotism and a nobler American citizenship than we have ever known will soon be realized. If this be a romance of dreamers, it is a blessed romance; but it is rather the sober truth of sound reason and the forecast of true American patriotism and Christian enthusiasm. Americans can never, like the Chinese, allow themselves to become a stagnant people. The Chinese Empire has had peace for centuries, but it has been the peace of the cemetery. China has been a dead sea and even a stagnant ocean. Certain doctrinaires in America, if their voices are heeded, would give America a similar isolation and stagnation. We must not listen to this selfish philosophy and this degenerative religion. It is the language of lotus-eaters rather than of men whose spirits are fed by American patriotism, and whose souls are inspired by a Christian evangelism. Great racial movements mark the close of the nineteenth century. The first duty of the Anglo-Saxon people is union in all parts of the world. Perhaps there may yet be a conflict between the Slavic nations and the Anglo-Saxon peoples. Russia has already hypnotized and paralyzed great portions of Europe and Asia. The battle royal of the world will be fought when mighty Russia and mightier Britain meet in terrific shock in some Armageddon. If that day shall come, God grant that the beautiful American daughter may bravely stand beside her noble British mother.

Out of such a union will come civil and religious liberty in the Philippines, in Cuba, and, finally, in Spain and throughout the world. From the Calvary Church went a noble young man and his heroic young wife as missionaries to Cuba. The months passed, and she went down to the mysterious land of motherhood. The babe returned alone. This woman's crime was that she was a Protestant. Bigoted priestcraft was so united with civil authority that there was not a spot in any cemetery in which this broken-hearted man could bury his young wife. Every effort to secure for her appropriate burial was in vain. When burial somewhere became a necessity there was no place found but an ash-heap where the offal of the city was thrown; and there our brother, with grieving heart, buried his loving young wife until opportunity was found for removing her body where the Roman priesthood could not trample upon all the tenderest feelings of humanity and upon all the sacred principles of liberty. The great God is not dead. He cannot be indifferent to such crimes against humanity. Wrong shall not be forever upon the throne, and right forever upon the cross. There may be a baptism of blood on the hills and valleys of Cuba, but, as God lives, liberty, civil and religious, shall yet be proclaimed throughout the Gem of the Antilles. Then the glorious gospel of the Son of God shall be preached in every part of that island; then converts shall be multiplied; and then the song of liberty shall be sung to the music of the Southern sea breaking on the Cuban shores as its divine accompaniment. God hasten the day when the colporteurs and missionaries of every class shall scatter the Bible and other Christian literature, which shall be leaves for the healing of a down-trodden, misguided, and broken-hearted people. God grant that the flags of Britain and America may be entwined in loving fellowship as the symbol of true Christianity and of evangelical aggression and achievement, while over both is placed the banner of Immanuel as the symbol of all that is divinest in religion, noblest in humanity, and lovingest in Deity. And to God, Father, Son, and Holy Ghost shall go up unceasing praise from a world thus largely delivered from superstition, and thus gloriously inspired with the beatific vision of a fully redeemed earth and so a realized heaven!

The good-night word, "I've Been Redeemed," came from the wonderful Fisk Jubilee Singers in such entrancing melody as makes an audience clamor for more, and they got "Swing Low, Sweet Chariot."

FRIDAY MORNING.

Denominational Conferences.

SIXTEEN spirited denominational rallies were held.
"The best Cumberland Presbyterian rally ever held," as Mr. Landrith's opening words called it, had a packed house in the handsome audience-room of the First Church, which seats one thousand. Mr. Excell led the singing and Mr. Yarnelle contributed one of his fine solos. The Cumberland Presbyterian pulse beat high, and this Church, which has always been aggressive, will feel for many a day to come the reflex effect of the strong addresses made.

The Christian, Moravian, United Brethren, United Evangelical, and Methodist Protestant rallies made up in intensity what they may have lacked in extension. In other sections of the country these rallies would have been larger, but they could not have been more helpful.

The Southern Presbyterian rally was as large as all former ones put together, and the best as well. Twenty addresses were made, and the following significant resolution was adopted : " We hereby express our appreciation of the Society of Christian Endeavor, our testimony to its helpfulness in our churches, and our desire to see its extension in our beloved Southern Church."

The Baptists were proud of the distinguished sons of the Church who addressed their rally, led by Rev. Frederick M. Gardner, of Boston, — Drs. MacArthur, Beckley, Rust, Mr. Yarnelle, the singer, General Morgan, Miles M. Shand, and Percy S. Foster.

Dr. J. L. Hill led the Congregational rally. Of course the Fisk Jubilee Singers were there. Rev. C. H. Percival, pastor of the oldest Congregational Church in Indiana, was present, also Treasurer William Shaw, Miss Antoinette P. Jones, of Floating Society fame, Dr. W. G. Puddefoot, a field secretary of the Home Missionary Society, and Miss Margaret W. Leitch, of Ceylon. Three-minute talks in quick succession made a rapid-fire action very pleasing and effective.

"A rally of good fellowship" was that of the Methodists, Dr. Kelly being the leader. It was truly a social Methodist love-feast, in which every one took part and which every one enjoyed. Secretary Du Bose, of the Epworth League of the Southern Methodist Church, and Dr. W. H. Withrow, ex-secretary of the Canadian Epworth League of Christian Endeavor, took part.

Dr. J. T. McCrory, of Pittsburg, Penn., made the principal address at the United Presbyterian rally. The marked growth of the denomination gave a jubilant note to his speech and to the meeting.

A one with three ciphers at the right expresses the attendance at the Disciple rally. Six-minute speeches were the rule, and with such a wealth of ready speakers as Tyler, Pendleton, Power, Spencer,

Sweeney, McCash, Garrison, and others whose names are household words, all went as merry as a marriage-bell.

St. Ann's Church was well filled for the rally of the Episcopalian Endeavorers, who are growing in numbers yearly. Canon Richardson, of Canada, and Rev. Floyd W. Tomkins, Jr., a leading rector of Rhode Island and an author of note, graced the occasion.

At the Lutheran rally an organization was effected by electing Rev. M. F. Troxell, D.D., of Springfield, Ill., as president. Short talks were made by many able speakers.

The African Methodist Episcopal Church was fortunate in having one of its bishops to preside at its rally, Bishop Arnett, and the gratifying progress which this denomination has made in Christian Endeavor was received with enthusiasm that promises still better things for the future.

NOTE.— Following are reports received from the chairmen of the different rallies. It is regretted that *all* had not been received at the time of going to press.— *Scribe*.

The United Evangelical Church.
By Rev. U. F. Swengel, York, Penn.

The denominational rally of the United Evangelical Church was under the direction of Rev. U. F. Swengel, trustee of the United Society of Christian Endeavor for the denomination. The meeting was held in the Sunday-school room of the Central Baptist Church. Rev. C. A. Stephan, of Illinois, led the opening devotional exercises. Rev. J. G. Eller, of Illinois, was elected secretary. Bertram Bookman was appointed enrolling clerk. Provision was made for reporting the proceedings to the various papers of the denomination. Rev. Mr. Eller read a very thoughtful paper on "Our Opportunities." Mrs. U. F. Swengel addressed the meeting on "What May We Expect from General Conference?" The topic "K. L. C. E. and Missions" was discussed in a very earnest manner by nearly all present. One society reported that it was supporting a missionary in South America, while the Juniors are supporting a boy and a girl in school in Persia. An informal but helpful discussion on "How Can We Help Our People To Be Pledge-keepers?" was participated in by several persons. This was a delightful rally, and all present rejoiced in the privilege of being there and in contributing something to it.

The Methodist Protestant.
By Rev. T. M. Johnson, Greensboro, N. C.

Reports of societies in many cases showed increased spirituality; many of the members are observing the "Quiet Hour," and joining the Tenth Legion. Seventeen of the conferences have Junior organizations, and one hundred and seventy-five societies reported. Several of the societies are supporting students in Japan, and it was decided to have all the societies unite in supporting a missionary, to be known as the Christian Endeavor missionary.

Rev. J. F. Cowan, D.D., spoke on "Denominational Unity of Purpose," and Rev. George McManiman, the newly-elected trustee, on "The Tenth Legion, and How To Enlist Methodist Protestants."

The following officers were elected: President, Rev. L. R. Dyott, Newark, N. J.; Vice-President, Rev. T. M. Johnson, Greensboro, N. C.; Secretary and Treasurer, Miss Mary Moall, Greece, Monroe County, N. Y.; Junior Superintendent, Mrs. J. W. Zirckel, Pittsburg, Penn.; Executive Committee: Rev. W. D. Stultz, Bridgton, N. J., Miss Sallie Spence, Newark, N. J., Rev. J. W. Trout, Elizabeth, N. J.

MARY MOALL, *Secretary and Treasurer.*

The following is the complete programme: —

Devotional Exercise.
Roll-Call of Conference Unions, One-Minute Responses.
Report of President, ... Prof. O. L. Palmer
Report of Secretary and Treasurer, ... Miss Mary Moall
Report of Junior Superintendent, ... Mrs. J. W. Zirckel
Report of Nominating Committee, election of officers, transaction of other business.
"Principles and Polity of the M. P. Church," . . . . Rev. James McCord
"Denominational Unity of Purpose," . . . . . Rev. J. F. Cowan, D.D.
"What We as Endeavorers Can Accomplish," . . . . Miss Mary Moall
"The Junior Work in Our Church," . . . . . Mrs. J. W. Zirckel
"The Tenth Legion and How to Enlist M. P's," . . . Rev. G. E. McManiman
Woman's F. M. Society, ... (by appointment) Miss Mary Moall
"Our Work in Japan: the Need," . . . . . . Rev. V. E. Huffer
Open Meeting: "How May Our Denominational Union Be Made More Effective?"

The Baptist.
By Rev. Frederick M. Gardner, East Boston, Mass.

The Baptist rally was held in the First Baptist Church. Rev. Frederick M. Gardner, of Boston, Mass., presided. Devotional exercises were conducted by Rev. A. U. Boom, of Tennessee. The following-named speakers addressed the meeting: Rev. J. O. Rust, of Nashville, spoke words of welcome to the city. Gen. T. J. Morgan, LL.D., of New York, spoke of the opportunities and obligations for missionary activity. Rev. John T. Beckley, D.D., of New York, spoke of the "Sovereignty of God in Missions." Mr. Percy S. Foster, of Washington, D. C., took for his subject the place of "Music in Our Worship." Another layman from Washington, Mr. Miles M. Shand, of the Department of State at Washington, spoke of the influence of Baptists in our national life. The other speaker was Rev. R. S. MacArthur, D.D., of New York, who spoke of the "Noble Name 'Baptist.'" Mr. Foster and Mr. Yarnelle sang effective solos. The meeting closed with the greetings brought from the Congregational rally by Miss Elsie L. Travis, of Boston. The greetings of the Baptists had previously been sent to the Congregationalists, and Mr. H. N. Lathrop, of Boston, had been appointed to convey the same. All the speaking was of a high order.

Free Baptist.
By Mr. H. S. Myers.

According to previous arrangements, the General Baptists and Southern Free Will Baptists met with the Free Baptists. The rally was called to order by Harry S. Myers, of Hillsdale, Mich., general secretary of the United Society of Free Baptist Young People (a denominational union). Prayer was offered by Rev. J. E. Cox, assistant editor of *The Messenger*, published by the General Baptists, at Owensville, Ind.

The state of the young people's work among the Southern Free Will Baptists was introduced by Rev. G. W. Binkley, of Nashville, Tenn. The Endeavor work has never been successfully introduced among them. The few feeble attempts have failed.

The work among the General Baptists was presented by Prof. Mrs. Ella C. Wheatley, of Oakland City College, Ind. A loose denominational union has been formed, and a number of good societies are at work.

The work of the United Society of Free Baptist Young People was presented by Mr. E. P. Metcalf, of Providence, R. I. As president of this denominational union, Mr. Metcalf spoke of the organization of local societies in many churches. A general secretary is employed. The society is now supporting two missionaries in India and will send two more in September, 1898.

They have organized the Christian Givers' League to supplement the work of the Tenth Legion among those local societies in the denomination not C. E's. They hold an annual convention.

The question of more hearty co-operation among these denominations was discussed by nearly all present. Its need is felt, since our beliefs are nearly identical, and it is probable that such work will hereafter be done.

The valuable points of the local society were given by some of those present who have been in successful work. The rally was closed with prayer by Rev. J. E. Curtis, Nashville, Tenn.

The Endeavor work was made practical on Sunday by the organization of a society in the Free Will Baptist Church, Cofer's Chapel, North Nashville.

Reformed Church in United States and Reformed Church in America.

A joint rally of the Reformed Church in America and of the Reformed Church in the United States was held under the leadership of Rev. Jesse W. Brooks and Rev. Rufus W. Miller. Among the speakers were Rev. Dr. Cornelius Brett, president of New Jersey Union, and Rev. J. H. Bomberger, D.D., president of Ohio Union, and Rev. W. I. Chamberlain, president of a Christian Endeavor Union in India. Fellowship between the two Churches, missions, Bible study, and Junior Endeavor work were discussed. Representatives were present from eight States and from India.

Christian.

By Rev. C. A. Brown.

The Christian Church rally, conducted by Rev. C. A. Brown, of Lebanon Ind., was held in Westminster Presbyterian Church. After an inspiring song service Rev. D. B. Atkinson, of Muncie, Ind., spoke on " The Relation of the Endeavorer to the Christian Church." He said that the Christian Endeavor had a great and important field of work in the Church in purifying every phase of life.

W. D. Sterns, of Haverhill, Mass., spoke on " Missionary Work for Endeavorers."

"The Pledge as Helpful to Church Loyalty " was the subject of an interesting discourse by Rev. Clarence Defur, of Atwood, Ill. The true secret of loyalty, he argued, was individual work, and a great harmony necessarily exists between the principles of the Christian Endeavor and the Christian Church. Several States were represented.

Moravian.

The rally of the members of the Moravian Church was held in the Sunday-school room of the Second Presbyterian Church, on North College Street.

In the absence of the regular officers Eugene G. Regennas, of Hope, Ind., was elected chairman, and Mrs. F. I. Willis, of Indianapolis, Ind., secretary.

A communication from Rev. W. H. Vogler, of Indianapolis, Ind., was read, and the various subjects referred to freely discussed and acted on.

The officers for the ensuing year were elected, and, notwithstanding that the attendance was small, the time was spent in a most enjoyable and profitable manner.

United Brethren.

By Rev. H. F. Shupe.

The United Brethren rally was held in the Sunday-school room of the McKendree Methodist Church. In the absence of Rev. H. H. Fout the meeting was in charge of Rev. H. F. Shupe, editor of *The Watchword*. The attendance was not large, and the time was given to a pleasant social rally. Rev. A. P. Funkhouser, associate editor of *The Religious Telescope*, assisted in making the occasion a pleasant one.

The Northern Presbyterian and Canadian Presbyterian.

By Rev. Howard Agnew Johnston, D.D., Chicago.

This rally was held in the First Presbyterian Church, and was presided over by the Rev. Howard Agnew Johnston, D.D., of Chicago. Mr. Estey had charge of the singing. The attendance was excellent, and the enthusiasm steadily increased to the end of the programme. The opening prayer was offered by the Rev. J. S. Edinburn, of Hamilton, O. The first address was given by the Rev. Wilbur F. Crafts, D.D., of Washington, D. C. Dr. Crafts discussed the distinctive place the Presbyterian Church has held as the champion of the Sabbath day. He argued the supreme importance of not only being faithful to the Lord's Day as individual Endeavorers, but also the duty of an aggressive effort to secure larger recognition of the Sabbath day throughout our whole country.

The next speaker was the Rev. William Patterson, of Toronto, Canada. Dr. Patterson represented the Canadian Church in the international fellowship which marked this rally. He spoke of Presbyterianism in its history, its polity, and its doctrine. In a most stirring and impressive way he reviewed the part the Presbyterians of Scotland and Ireland had had in the historic campaign for civil and religious liberty whose blessed heritage the people of America have so greatly enjoyed. He spoke of the way that all the different branches of the Presbyterian Church in Canada had become united, and prophesied of the day when such union would mark the Presbyterian churches of this country. Dr. Patterson was followed by Mr. John Willis Baer, who, as the presiding officer remarked, represents our denomination at headquarters. Mr. Baer, in a brief but intensely earnest speech, urged Christian Endeavorers present to a true consecration to the high ideals of Christian living.

Mr. W. T. Ellis, of Philadelphia, president of the local union of that city, who has charge of the publications for young people, gave an address in which he discussed the importance of giving its full place to our board's literature. At this point in the programme, while the congregation joined in a song, Dr. Johnston asked all of the missionaries who were present either from the home or foreign fields to come to the platform. Some twelve or fifteen missionaries responded and were greeted with applause as they were presented to the congregation, their names and their field of labor being mentioned for each one in turn. The subject of home missions was then discussed by Miss Petrie, of the Home Board in New York City, who made a number of very helpful and practical suggestions concerning methods which could be adopted by the societies. It was interesting to see that many of those present were taking notes throughout the entire meeting, and that these helpful suggestions of Miss Petrie were written down to be reported in many societies throughout the country.

The climax of the morning's programme was reached in the magnificent address of Dr. John Henry Barrows, of Chicago, upon the subject of foreign missions. In most entertaining, impressive, and stirring words Dr. Barrows told of his recent journey around the world, of the magnificent labors of the faithful missionaries in India, China, and Japan whose work he had personally investigated, whose homes he had visited, and whose self-sacrificing fidelity had excited his boundless admiration. He pictured the duty of the Christian Church of America to give the Gospel to those nations in Eastern darkness. He thrilled his hearers with an impassioned plea for consecration to this divine path. He prophesied the future of greater America as the providence of God has brought to our door unexpectedly millions of souls inhabiting the islands of the Atlantic and the Pacific. Most graphically did he speak of the results that have followed the giving of the Bible to the nations that were without the Gospel, and closed with the triumphant and confident conviction that the only possible outcome of the work of the Church of Christ would be the redemption of the world.

At this point the presiding officer presented the following resolution : " As individual Presbyterians gathered in the denominational rally at Nashville, Tenn., we desire to express to the United Society of Christian Endeavor our pleasure in the selection of the following representative pastors to be trustees of the United Society : —

"Rev. J. Wilbur Chapman, D.D., Philadelphia, Penn.
Rev. John Henry Barrows, D D., Chicago. Ill.
Rev. Wilton Merle Smith, D.D., New York City, New York.
Rev. Ralph W. Brokaw, Utica, N. Y.

> Rev. Teunis S. Hamlin, D.D., Washington, D. C.
> Rev. Hugh K Walker, D.D., Los Angeles, Cal.
> Rev. Geo. B. Stewart, D.D., Harrisburg, Penn.
> Rev. J. Clement French, D.D.. Newark, N. J.
> Rev. Maltbie D. Babcock, D.D., Baltimore, Md."

This was adopted by a rising vote.

The closing address was given by one of the new trustees, the Rev. J. Wilbur Chapman, D. D., of Philadelphia. His theme was "Loyalty to the Church and to the Denomination." He emphasized the importance of giving hearty allegiance to the pastor in the local church, and of recognizing the fact that we cannot be true Endeavorers except as we place the general interests of the church above the local interest of the individual society. It was a most fitting and effective close to the inspiring programme of the morning. The audience arose and sang "America," and was dismissed with the benediction by Dr. Barrows.

Protestant Episcopal.

By Rev. C. J. Palmer.

The meeting was held in St. Ann's Church, and was opened with prayer by Rev. C. J. Palmer, of Lanesboro, Mass. Addresses explanatory of the work in the Episcopal Church and Church of England were given by Mr. Palmer, and Canon J. B. Richardson, of London, Ontario, and Rev. Floyd Tomkins, Jr., of Providence, R. I. At the close of the meeting a session for informal conferences on methods was held, and reports of work in Hawaii, China, New Zealand, Australia, Japan, and many parts of the United States were presented; also words of commendation from several of the bishops were read.

In the audience there were representatives present from Texas, Maryland, Tennessee, Rhode Island, Massachusetts, Quebec, and Ontario. The meeting was in every way profitable and inspiring.

FRIDAY AFTERNOON.

Hall Williston.

THE meeting at Hall Williston, presided over by Rev. John T. Beckley, D.D., of New York City, was opened by the audience singing, " Keep Step with the Master," " Where the Saviour Leads Me," " Count Your Blessings," and " Let the Sunshine In," under the leadership of Mr. Foster.

Devotional exercises were conducted by Rev. N. A. McAulay, of Wilton Junction.

"For the Church" was the theme for four valuable five-minute speeches on topics pertinent to church life.

Address by Rev. J. H. Bomberger,
Tiffin, O.

THE PASTOR'S CABINET.

One of the conundrums of my boyhood days was the familiar one, "What five names of the Bible, covering five hundred years of history, express this request: The mother asked the father to give the son a whipping?" The answer was, " Adam, Seth, Eve, Cain, Abel."

I am asked to perform a similar feat of condensation this afternoon. What is the pastor's cabinet? Here is the answer in a nutshell: a special deputation (the executive committee) from a dynamite cruiser (the Christian Endeavor society) waits upon the rear-admiral (the pastor), and asks permission to throw another charge of guncotton (consecrated youthful energy) into the enemy's forts, and inquires which particular fort he wishes demolished next.

This is the pastor's cabinet in operation. It is the executive committee consulting with the pastor as to the best point on which to train the stored-up energies of the society. The wise pastor will ever be on the lookout for new points of attack, and promptly avail himself of this volunteered service.

There are few congregations in which some such points may not be found. It may be a scantily attended Sunday evening service. It may be a listless mid-week prayer-meeting. It may be a lagging Sunday-school. It may be the prevalence of a cold-storage social atmosphere. It may be an uncomfortable tendency to shrinkage on the part of the finances. It may be a lack of inclination and fitness for soul-winning effort. It may be an epidemic of questionable amusements. It may be any or all of these.

Whatever it is, definitely locate the evil. Admit its existence, and then point it out to the executive committee, having invited them to your home for that purpose, and grant them the privilege, and lovingly lay upon them the responsibility, of co-operating with you for the overcoming of that obstacle to congregational progress. The pastor who gives sympathy to his young people will have no difficulty in getting work from them. Make suggestions as to methods, but do not bear the burden for them. Let them feel the weight of the responsibility resting upon them. Get them to concentrate their energies and prayers upon that one thing until it is accomplished, meeting with them in "cabinet session," to discuss ways and means as often as may be necessary.

When this particular end is accomplished, as it will be, stop long enough to take a full breath, and then order the guncotton of consecrated youthful energies thrown into some other hostile fort.

Let me list the results sure to follow a fair test of this plan: —
1. A pastor with a lightened burden.
2. A congregation with a new lease of life.
3. A group of young Christians made strong by self-sacrificing service, and — this is a paradox — all the more deeply attached to the pastor who makes them bear the heaviest burdens and perform the most difficult tasks.

I do not spin this theory from the threads of fancy. I have tested the plan repeatedly, and it has never failed me.

Then followed the address by Rev. Mr. Arrick, of Kentucky.

Address by Rev. A. J. Arrick,
Mt. Sterling, Ky.

GRADUATE ENDEAVOR.

The subject before us contemplates not a concluded but a progressive endeavor. It reaches from the cradle to eternity. It begins at the mother's knee and ends around the throne of God, while celestial orchestras render commencement music, and diplomas are presented by the chief Instructor in the University of God.

Graduate Endeavor is advancing to a greater degree of usefulness. The sweet lullabies of the Christian mother sung to her new-born babe are but the preparatory lessons by which its infant lips are taught to lisp the children's prayer,

"Now I lay me down to sleep."

As it learns of the love and care of God at mother's knee, it has taken a step in Christian Endeavor which is preparing for still greater usefulness in praising God with childish simplicity and in leading others, by implicit trust, to the God of love.

As the years pass, the child enters broader fields of development and service in the Sunday school and Junior society — another graduation, where he exerts a greater influence for good. Having been taught to love God, to be like Christ, like him he is found about his father's business; in the house of God; gathered with other children in united service for him; doing as well as learning, and showing love by striving.

Another step up this hill of Christian progress is the Intermediate society, where there is an expansion of Bible knowledge and Bible training; an increase in Christian exercise, enlarging opportunities and a fuller understanding of what service means; an easy course, with rapid development, until the Young People's Society is reached, with its vigorous practical training for Christian work.

Here also there is progression,— practising that which has been learned, gaining greater knowledge; advancing through committee work to more efficient service; passing from the verse-readers' class to join the class of those who are ready to present thoughts which have been gathered in the quiet hours of the closet, where the soul and God were alone together.

Graduate Endeavor is stepping to the front ranks in church service. Schooled for awhile in the ranks of the society, the members become ready and anxious for greater usefulness, and step forward to take their places in the active work of the church. All the energy, earnestness, and enthusiasm of Christian activity, the same zeal for souls and the building-up of the society, is transferred to the church services and the work of the Church through all its branches. Their training has been in vain, and Christian Endeavor has been a failure, unless this shall be the result. Forgetting the society? No, never! One does not forget his Alma Mater because he passes beyond its walls into active life where he can make practical use of what he has gathered. Each achievement enkindles new zeal for the school where he was trained. But he would be a dullard indeed if he could never get beyond the classroom. The child that does not develop becomes an object of pity. What of the Endeavorer who is contented to remain with the society when he ought to be at work in the church itself, growing and expanding?

Graduate Endeavor lifts above party prejudice and religious animosity and makes people realize their oneness in Christ Jesus though they may differ as to non-essentials. We have heard a good deal about sectional lines. There are none. I was reared where springs of pure water gush from the earth to flow southward, bearing Northern love to meet the warm embrace of Southern chivalry. In after-life I came South to find the same Christian fellowship and love for country that I had known in my childhood home. I searched in vain for that much-abused sectional line. Like the driftwood which is gathered by Northern and Southern streams alike, and swept by the floods of the Mississippi far out across the Atlantic, it has been caught by the streams of patriotism and love for humanity gushing from Southern and Northern hearts alike, and has been swept by the flood of Christian sympathy far out until it forms an eternal barrier between Spanish cruelty and suffering Cuba.

True Christian Endeavor moves in an ever-ascending scale. Like the poet's youth, there is inscribed upon its banner that inspiring motto " Higher," and it stays not for any allurements, until it is found far up the heights of the Eternal Hill, above the snow and ice of discouragement and temptation and inactivity, above the chilling blasts of sin, in the Palace of the King.

Christian Endeavor entered the school of Christ when its lips first lisped the name of Jesus. It advanced in knowledge and usefulness until at last the great commencement day has come; the final examinations have been held; the chief Instructor and President stands to deliver the diplomas. Hear him: "I was hungry, ye gave me meat; naked, ye clothed me; sick, ye ministered unto me; in prison, ye visited me; come, ye blessed of my Father, you have been faithful in that which is least, I will make you ruler of much. Inherit the kingdom prepared for you." And the diploma, signed and sealed by the blood of the Son of God, is given; a crown of glory shining with the bright jewels of the souls that have been won is placed upon the brow, and we take our places at the right hand of God, Endeavorers who have graduated from his service on earth to the eternal service above.

The mid-week prayer-meeting was the next important subject presented.

Address by Rev. E. H. Pence,
Janesville, Wis.
THE MID-WEEK PRAYER-MEETING.

He needs the mid-week prayer-meeting most who thinks he needs it least, or who least thinks of his need. It was the risen Lord whom Thomas missed by missing a prayer-meeting in the upper room. It needs him most who thinks most that he needs to be there. It was Anna, who was so long habituated to the Lord's temple, who recognized the presence of the temple's Lord when he came. Without the prayer-meeting the Lord might come and we know it not, for there is the holy place, where as the Lord spake to Zacharias so he speaks to us. There the Church's nerve-centre is exposed to God.

Let us emphasize two or three relations which the Christian Endeavorer sustains, or ought to sustain, to this meeting. We are called to be witness-bearers, and we often wonder how we may thus be faithful. Have you considered the peculiar sort of witness which we bear by our fidelity to this mid-week prayer-meeting?

Serious-minded men quickly see the practical bearings of Christian morals, and they feel the force of the Christian appeal to reason; still, they may honestly believe that they can be as good outside the church as in, and as really fulfil their obligations to God. And, if moral precepts and mere intellectual appeal afforded the sum-total of Christianity, the Church should have gone to pieces long since for lack of a magnetic personal centre.

But the essence and life of Christianity are spiritual. It may be a fad to go to church; custom drifts that way and men with it — men who find no attraction there other than an appeal to sense by an oratorical choir or a musical preacher.

Did we stop there and go no further, they might suppose that we agreed with them in the opinion which they hold: that religion consists in assent to some truths which only fools, moral or mental, ever think to deny.

There in the outer court of the Gentiles they tarry. But by your fidelity to the mid-week prayer-meeting you point the way into the holy place where that spirit which Job affirms to be in every man, and to which the inspiration of the Almighty giveth understanding, comes face to face with God. The prayer-meeting proclaims that Jesus has come that we might have life, — spiritual life, — and that we might have it more abundantly; that Jesus has given it to some, and that to them it is the heart of Christ and Christianity. The prayer-meeting must be spiritual or die. It is to the fascinations and power of spiritual life that you bear witness by your fidelity to the mid-week prayer-meeting.

Again, devotion to this mid-week prayer-meeting is a vital test of character. In heaven, when we have become "just men made perfect," it shall be always our inclination to be good and always to do the good things. That part of heaven is not realized this side of Jordan. Every circumstance tends to make it our easy inclination to be faithful to the Christian Endeavor prayer-meeting; the tides of interest, associations, custom, set that way.

But it is fatal to true piety to do only those things, however many they may be, which we feel inclined to do. Christians stop growing when they lose their relish for hard things to do. The radical test of Christian character is the ability and resolution to do those things which at the outset seem difficult and require determined effort. Thus the athlete is made strong; so the oak-tree braced to the four winds has contributed so incisive a word as "oaken" to our speech.

The young Christian who confesses that he attends the Christian Endeavor prayer-meeting because it is attractive and does *not* attend the mid-week prayer-meeting because it is not attractive has in those words confessed to a fatal failure in his Christian endeavor.

The ability to deny and sacrifice self to do a duty for Christ's sake is the first equipment of the spiritual soul. This is the enduement of power which makes each day a Pentecost for some Christians. Test the good your Christian Endeavor prayer-meeting does you by the stimulus and strength you there receive to be faithful at the mid-week meeting.

Finally, here is love's opportunity. Has experience failed to teach us that the best blessing is in being one? By presence and song, by the stillness with which you listen for God to speak to your hearts, or through the speech of others; by your speech, studied or spontaneous, always savored with scripture, you may in this mid-week meeting add joy and abounding hope to the last days of those to the bequests of whose love and fidelity we owe so much.

The last of the "five-minute guns" fired " for the Church" was by Rev. Mr. Zartman, of Michigan.

Address by Rev. Parley E. Zartman,
Three Rivers, Mich.

THE SUNDAY EVENING SERVICE.

There is a problem as to the Sunday evening service. It meets each pastor, and the solution of it depends upon the personal equation of pastor and people, with the variant of circumstances. Under varying conditions these are the questions that press for solution: "Shall we have a Sunday evening service? How can we make it most effective?"

Of course, different conditions demand different treatment. It would be unwise and useless to administer quinine in a case of toothache. But, granting local difficulties, certain facts are evident. The Sunday evening service is needed — needed for the sake of the Church and for the sake of the people : for the former, to increase her usefulness as one sent of God; for the latter, to increase their apprehension of spiritual power. The need of the hour is for more preaching of the gospel, for more religion, pure and undefiled. Pastors, insist upon the Sunday evening service. Your people need more of the Church. The intensity of modern life, the pressure of world-cares, the alertness and activity of sin, demand strong and constant opposition of righteousness, secured only by frequent waiting upon God. It is not enough for God's peop l to meet on Sunday morning, though that is all that is possible for some of them. For those who can go to the evening service, yet do not go, the disuse of the privilege weakens spirituality; and the very hour of the evening service often is used in ways that dissipate and destroy all benefits derived at the morning service. To abolish the evening service is to lose a most potent and practical missionary and evangelistic force.

How make the Sunday evening service a success? There are a number of general observations applicable. Given a minister and people who appreciate their duty and their opportunity and are ready to use to the full the talents given to them, and no question arises. In most of our churches increased participation by the congregation would revive and strengthen many. There are too many listless people in the average congregation. Let there be hearty congregational singing — paid choirs are not often a means of grace. Have variety in the service; do not hesitate to change the regular order; flee formality. Occasionally have a special song-service, securing the best possible local talent. Conduct a question-box on any subject connected with practical Christianity; this revives interest, brings people and pastor into closer touch, reveals their minds, and gives unusual opportunity to present a practical gospel. Have a church alive and active all the week; that will interest and attract saints and sinners to both the Sunday services. Let the minister do his best. preaching so as to reach the hearts of men; let the sermons be pointed, personal, practical. Add to these requirements brains, a conviction of the truth, and the baptism of the Holy Ghost.

And why not marshal the forces of your young people? If they are called in the right manner they will respond with readiness and earnestness. Urge upon them personal loyalty to Christ and the Church, calling to mind the terms of their allegiance to him. There is no place where they can do more work, and more practical, than for and in the evening service. Let them call on the unchurched, let them advertise the Church and her services by lip and life, let them pray for it and work in it. Always at it for Christ will bring rich results.

A word as to the service itself.

Be Brief. Avoid all prolixity and tediousness. Suppress your desire to preach a long sermon. Give your people the sincere milk of the word, but let it be condensed. No long prayers, no long chapters, no long songs. Preach a plain gospel in plain speech, and when done, quit. Condense, condense, condense.

Be Bright. Smiles and sunshine become the courts of our God. Let the blessed sunshine in. Preach and practise the gospel of good cheer. Use all legitimate methods to keep up interest throughout the service, but remember that sensationalism soon palls on the taste. Unload theological *impedimenta* at the morning service, if you must unload it. Do not hesitate to break in on the order of service rather than break up the meeting; better, do not have a regular order. Have plenty of good music, in which all can join. Tell good stories; they carry home and fasten many arrows of truth. Serve the Lord with gladness.

Be Brotherly. Make your church the best fraternal organization in town, to which all men and women may belong by accepting the terms of fraternity named by Jesus Christ. Have an intense interest in people, and meet them as they leave the church, being careful to get hold of the visitor and stranger. Look carefully to the temperature of your own members — let the block of ice melt down or stay away. Get the young people to fraternize. Make people feel at home, and want to come again.

Most of all, above all, and in all, magnify the Gospel of the Son of God. Lift up the cross of Jesus Christ. This is your opportunity to be a minister of reconciliation. Be in earnest for God. Have faith in God. He will honor such work, and will bless it too.

One of the most attractive features of the meeting was, "Answers to Ten Questions," by Treasurer William Shaw. The ten questions, with their answers, follow.

Ten Questions and Answers,
By Treasurer William Shaw.

What is the United Society of Christian Endeavor? What does it do? What does it not do? How is it supported?

It is a corporation organized under the laws of the State of Massachusetts to promote earnest Christianity among the young people, and make them more useful in the service of God. It accomplishes its object by organizing and fostering Societies of Christian Endeavor. It is an organization of individuals as the law requires. Any past or present active member of a society of Christian Endeavor may become a life member of the United Society by the payment of one dollar, with the approval of the society or Board of Trustees at any meeting.

It enrolls the local societies and is the link that binds us together in our world-wide fellowship. It arranges for the International Convention. It elects the officers and Board of Trustees. It prints and circulates hundreds of thousands of copies of Christian Endeavor leaflets, books, etc. It pays for the translation of literature in foreign lands, and assists in the formation of new societies in all parts of the world. Under its direction the number of societies has increased in thirteen years from 250 to more than 54,000. It fosters denominational loyalty and interdenominational fellowship.

It does not exercise any authority or control over the local societies. It does not levy any taxes or assessments, or receive any contributions from the local societies. It does not usurp the place of the denominational authorities in the direction or control of their young people.

It is supported by the receipts from the publishing department, which prints the literature and topic-cards, and manufactures the badges and other supplies. Its affairs are so economically managed that it costs only about $13,000 a year to carry on its world-wide work. This is made possible by the co-operation of the *Christian Endeavor World*, which provides for Dr. Clark's salary, thus enabling him to give his whole time to the work at no expense to the United Society. In other ways, too numerous to mention, the paper has assisted in the advancement of the movement free of cost to the society.

What is the mission of local unions and how can they help the churches?

The purposes of the local unions are instruction, inspiration, and fellowship. They ought to be schools where the societies are taught the best methods of work. Their meetings ought always to inspire for larger and better service, and make real the genuine spiritual fellowship of Christ's disciples. They can help the churches by considering such practical problems as the churches are trying to solve, and by revealing to the young people their part in the solution of these problems. The principal object of a union is not to engage in some general work, but to develop the local society to the highest point of efficiency.

How would you galvanize our local union?

Perhaps the trouble is that it is already galvanized. One definition of galvanize is " To plate." It is silver-plated instead of sterling silver. It is satisfied with show instead of substance. But the question probably refers to this definition, " To restore to consciousness by galvanic action, as from a state of suspended animation." Then turn on the divine electricity. Make your connection Godward and manward. To break either means no power. Wake up and shake up your meetings. If you should suddenly wake up in any one of them you would n't know whether it was the February, May, September, or December meeting, they are all so much alike. Have live topics discussed by live men, and then live out the suggestions between meetings.

How long should one remain in the Christian Endeavor Society?

Just as long as he can do more good there for the extension of Christ's kingdom than in some other department of the Church, and until his presence there prevents the younger members from assuming their full share of the responsibility; until he is prepared to take up advanced work for the Master. There is a good deal of sanctified selfishness lying around loose in many of our societies. When a careful examination shows that the older members ought to move on into the wider work of the Church, the time has come to go.

How can we get our committees to do better work?

By getting chairmen who will stop trying to do it all themselves. It may be easier, but it is not business, nor Christian Endeavor. Insist upon monthly written reports. Examine the report-blanks issued by the United Society. Have regular committee meetings. For a change, let the members take turns in entertaining the committee at their homes: have a simple little lunch, or "English tea," and then spend the evening in planning for the month's work. If your vestry is conveniently arranged, why not have a general committee tea there? Such gatherings would be inexpensive, but exceedingly helpful. Don't try to "make bricks without straw." Use the splendid helps for committees prepared by the United Society.

What would you do with officers and committee chairmen who will not attend to their duties?

Just what I would do with a clerk in my office who persistently neglected his work. Ask for his resignation, or discharge him. Surely the Master's business is as important as our own, and yet we allow one or two thoughtless young people to hinder the work of the whole society for six months for fear they will be offended if we speak to them. It is not a personal matter.; it is the Father's business which we must not let suffer. The executive committee should take kindly but definite action at once.

What would you say to officers of local societies and Endeavor unions who do not find time to keep in touch with the work?

I would say to some of them, Let your bicycle rest at least one evening in the week; and to all, Take time if you cannot find it to see what the young people of the world are saying and doing. Nearly all of the criticism of the past has been due to lack of information regarding our real principles and work, either on the part of the critics or the one he was criticising. Read the *Christian Endeavor World*, get into touch with the world-wide movement, see how intensely spiritual and practical are the ideals that are there held up before the young people, and you will say with tens of thousands of others, I cannot afford to get out of touch with the movement.

How can the pastor make larger use of his Endeavorers?

By getting his arm around them — embracing his opportunities, as it were. We admire a statue; we love a man. Loving leadership inspires personal loyalty. By coming into closer touch with them in their work, by more definiteness of suggestion, and systematic preparation for the work to be done. By the organization of the Pastor's Cabinet, to consist of the officers and chairmen of committees of the Endeavor society, with regular monthly meetings, where, after the general conference, some practical topic in connection with the church work shall be discussed. Such a meeting would be of great educational value.

How can we get hold of the young men?

Get within reaching-distance of them. The devil gets close to them, and whispers "Come." We stand up in our meetings and say "Come," but they are not there to hear. How many of us in the past year have given one earnest manly (or womanly) invitation to a young man when we were near enough so that he could see the light in our eyes and feel the warmth of our hand-grasp? Have we something to invite the young men to that is worth while, or are we simply marking time? Young men like the "get-there" spirit. Do they see it in your society?

How can we make a prayer-meeting go?

Get some "go" in yourself, and then put yourself back of the meeting and push. Too many of us come to the meeting cold and dead, expecting to get warmed and quickened there. We ought and can come from such communion with God as will make the meeting go and glow from the start. No mechanical methods will take the place of spiritual fervor. But He who made the brain has use for it in his service. Cultivate variety, and create a homelike atmosphere. Conversation dies and interest flags in the chilly atmosphere of a tomb, but revives in the sunlight, or by the cosy hearthstone. Let the heart express itself as well as the mind. Don't think yourself wiser than everybody else. Use the best helps you can get.

"Christian Endeavor Reaching Out" was the next theme then taken up, and four addresses were made on subjects along the lines toward which Christian Endeavorers are working.

"To Sailors and Soldiers," the opening topic, was discussed by Rev. James L. Hill, D.D., of Salem, Mass. Just as Dr. Hill was stepping forward to speak a half-dozen soldier-boys of the Second Kentucky Regiment were escorted to the platform amidst tremendous applause by the audience.

Dr. Hill's address was overflowing with patriotism, and was heartily cheered by the audience.

He said that when the *Oregon* was chasing the Spanish warships she had thirty Endeavorers on board. On Dewey's flagship there was a society of Christian Endeavorers. On the torpedo-boat *Winslow* there was a Christian Endeavorer who died with a prayer on his lips and a smile on his face. One of the first things for the Christian Endeavorer to do in the army is to blot out the God-hated canteen.

Dr. Hill explained the difference between a soldier's canteen and an army canteen thus: "The first the soldier slings on his back; the second slings the soldier on his back." He made a strong plea for the active interference of Endeavorers to secure the passage of the bill now before Congress for the abolition of canteens.

At the close of the address the speaker introduced the soldiers on the platform, each one of whom was enthusiastically greeted with the "Chautauqua salute." Among the soldiers in the party were Private Caldwell, president of a Christian Endeavor Society in the army; Sergeant Storr, and the president and secretary of a Christian Endeavor society in the Second Kentucky Regiment. When the fact that one of the boys was a Pennsylvanian was made known, some one shouted, "The war is over now; Pennsylvania and Kentucky are going shoulder to shoulder in defence or our country." "Blessed Be the Tie that Binds" and "My Old Kentucky Home" were sung by the audience.

A Christian Endeavor banner belonging to the society in Camp Sam Houston was exhibited from the platform.

The next speaker took up the topic of work among railroad men and street-car men.

Address by Rev. George J. Burns,
Philadelphia, Penn.

CHRISTIAN ENDEAVOR REACHING OUT TO RAILROAD MEN AND STREET-CAR MEN.

A canal-boat was going along in New York State. Some men on deck in an enclosure were engaged in conversation. The lookout who sat at the front of the boat always announced the approach of a bridge. In the company there was a Frenchman who did not very well understand our language. As they approached a bridge the man at the bow of the boat cried, "Look out." The Frenchman stuck his head out to see what was coming, and receiving a blow, pulled his head in and said, "What funny people you Americans are! When you tell a man to look out you mean that he shall look in."

While riding along on the railroad we often see the sign, "Look out for the engine." As Christian Endeavorers, I think we should look out for the engineer, trainmen, and street-car men as well. There is something fascinating about a locomotive. Nothing perhaps shows the ingenuity, skill, and colossal power of our modern civilization as the railroad train—a solitary man holding the lever which controls this tremendous mass of wood and metal with its freight and passengers rushing past us at the rate of a mile a minute.

Through infinite grace a heavenly railroad has been constructed by a man of Nazareth, the carpenter's son, and we should endeavor to have all these trainmen come on board. On this heavenly railroad there are no free passes every one must pay his fare, but it is a broad guage. and whoever will may come On this road there are no collisions. for the trains all run in one direction. There are no smoking-cars nor palace-cars, no sleepers nor specials; all have the same accommodations. Here we do not have the sign and signal language of the whistle, flag, and lantern, but the spirit answers to the blood and tells me I am born of God. How shall the Christian Endeavor reach out to the railroad men and street-car men?

The first Christian convert of Africa was converted on wheels. Long before the modern railroad was thought of Philip saw a man riding along in a chariot, and under the direction of the Holy Spirit he ran and jumped aboard the chariot, and preached Jesus to the stranger, whose heart was hungry for a knowledge of God. The result was one more soul for Jesus; the stranger went on his way rejoicing.

But dead saints can never catch live sinners. We must be on the move or we cannot keep up to the train. Some Christian workers are like wheelbarrows, they move out into the highways and hedges only when they are pushed. If we would win the world to Christ we must follow the gospel plan and take men one by one. Preaching the glorious gospel to crowded audiences may be inspiring to the speaker, but it is face-to-face and hand-to-hand work that reaches the heart and saves the soul.

For many years the Young Men's Christian Association has been at work along the railroads, establishing reading-rooms and homelike comforts for the trainmen, and in this way great good has been accomplished and they would welcome the spiritual enthusiasm characteristic of the Christian Endeavor society. The street-car men in many places to a great extent have been neglected, and so have said, No man careth for my soul.

Here is a promising field for evangelistic work. The Philadelphia Union for two or three years has been sowing precious seed and now is reaping a blessed harvest. At one place the conductors and motormen were organized into a Christian Endeavor society of their own, and this is regularly enrolled in the union.

The meetings are held on Tuesdays, at 11 A. M., in the different car-barns. Each week a different minister is invited to speak.

An organ is furnished, for good music and lively singing is an inspiration to the meeting.

Tracts, Testaments, and religious papers are distributed, and these are appreciated by the men, not alone for their intrinsic value, but because of the interest manifested in their moral and spiritual condition. Thus getting in touch with the men and showing an unselfish spirit, their hard lot can be made easier.

As they are deprived of the Sabbath services and the precious influences of the gospel, let us carry the message of salvation to them.

We may help them by our deportment on the cars. It has been said that Christian Endeavorers can be told by the way they pay their fare.

In California they pride themselves upon using nickels and dimes where the people of the East and South use pennies. During the Convention last year in San Francisco a Christian Endeavorer gave a trolley conductor five pennies.

He looked at the pennies, then looked at her, and said, "No one but a woman would do a thing like that." Whereupon she replied, "The people in California have no sense."

Another way of helping them is to keep off the cars on the Lord's Day. To be effectual we must practise what we preach. One act is worth a ton of words. The mightiest agent for good on earth is a consistent Christian. How many souls have been turned to God by the charm of a good example! Sunday excursions and trolley parties on the Sabbath are a crying shame. Let no Christian Endeavorer be found in this multitude of evil-doers.

The topic for an address by E. C. Gilbert, of Oakland, Cal., was "To Commercial Travellers." Many valuable suggestions as to how commercial travellers could best be reached were offered. The experiences of the Christian Endeavorers of San Diego, Cal., were related.

That city has done a great deal for the commercial travellers, and the plans upon which they work are very simple, though very effective.

Address by Mr. E. C. Gilbert,
Oakland, Cal.
REACHING OUT TO COMMERCIAL TRAVELLERS.

There is probably no commercial traveller, able to appreciate the social privileges and pleasures of a home, who does not leave his home with a pang of regret. Of course, by constant absence some accustom themselves to that which was at first so irksome, but most of us long for the time to come when we may turn over our sample-bags to others and go "on the road" no more. How much greater is the sacrifice made by those who have experienced the pleasure and profit springing from Christian fellowship and Christian service! Would it not be well for such to inquire whether we cannot enjoy the same privileges while upon the road?

We fear that many are not aware that at the open rooms of our churches may be found Christian men who desire especially to meet strangers or transient visitors to their towns, and cordially extend to them the right hand of Christian fellowship. We wish to bring this fact to the attention of our fellow-travellers, hoping to enlist their active co-operation with these institutions, which are peculiarly adapted to meet the spiritual and social wants of a Christian man absent from the associations of his home. Most of us who are commercial travellers excuse ourselves from work for others because we cannot keep engagements with that regularity which is usually essential.

And many who are in sympathy with the work of the Young People's Society of Christian Endeavor have not identified themselves with it because absent from home so often, not having discovered that the peculiar nature of our business affords us unequal opportunities for usefulness. Why should we enlist in service for our fellow-travellers who are not Christians? To this we reply:

First. Because they are absent from the restraining influences of home and of friends, the loss of whose companionship often leads them to accept a substitute in society which is not only far from helpful, but even ruinous.

Second. Because of our opportunities for making their acquaintance.

Third. Because our experience as travelling salesmen peculiarly qualifies us to study the character of others and exert a personal influence upon them.

Fourth. Because we know Christ and believe that he is ready to bless others through us.

We would suggest that you can strengthen yourself and help others:

First. By extending your acquaintance with other Christians, especially commercial travellers. An excellent way to do this is by enrolling yourself as a member of the Commercial Travellers' Committee of the Christian Endeavor society in your church or city union.

Second. Co-operate with them in extending to your fellow-travellers invitations to church meetings and services, to the rooms of the Young Men's Christian Associations, and other moral and religious privileges. If you can accompany them, the possible personal sacrifice will doubtless be fully rewarded.

Third. Endeavor to arrange for the holding of a meeting for the study of the Scriptures and prayer, with other Christian travellers, in a private room at your hotel, on the Sabbath, or perhaps on other days. Have social singing in the parlors of the hotel; music hath charms even for the commercial traveller.

Fourth. Realizing that commercial travellers while upon the road are for the most part deprived of social pleasures and privileges they are accustomed to enjoy at home, desire that they should avail themselves of the advantages which the Christian Endeavor can provide for young men — through popular lectures, concerts, entertainments, and social receptions. As a medium of introduction and a convenience to commercial travellers, a uniform card of introduction is adopted by the State Union as follows: —

> This will introduce John Smith, a commercial traveller, who is an active (or associate) member of the First Presbyterian Christian Endeavor, of San Francisco. Any favors shown him will be greatly appreciated by this Christian Endeavor society.
> [Signed]   JAMES WILLIAMS,
> *Chairman Commercial Travellers' Committee.*

On the back of the ticket is the following: "This ticket will be honored by all Christian Endeavor societies connected with the California State Christian Endeavor Union, entitling the holder to free admission to concerts, lectures, entertainments, and social receptions which may be in progress during the holder's stay in your city."

What has been said so far in this paper has been addressed to the Christian commercial traveller — his duty to his fellows. Now for a few words to Endeavorers of societies who may not even have one commercial traveller member and desire to reach the stranger who is in your city on the Sabbath. First of all add a new committee to your list, which shall be known as the Commercial Travellers' Committee, or the Hotel Committee.

Let them meet every Saturday night in the church parlor or at the home of one of the members. After a few short prayers for guidance, go out and visit all the hotels in the neighborhood. Consult the hotel registers and thus secure the names of those who will be in town on the Lord's Day.

After securing these names, return to the meeting-place, and write your invitations with pen and ink, signing your own name as a member of the Hotel Committee, like the following, which is used by the Endeavor society of the First Baptist Church of San Francisco: —

> Come thou with us and we will do thee good.— Num. 10: 29.
>
> **Young People's Society of Christian Endeavor,**
> **First Baptist Church,**
> **320 Eddy Street.**
>   SAN FRANCISCO.
>
> *Dear Friend:* — Since it is your fortune to spend Sunday in our city we desire to make it as pleasant for you as possible, and hereby extend to you a most cordial invitation to the services of our church to-day, especially to our Young People's meeting at 6.30 this evening, held in the lecture-room. Our preaching services are at 11 A.M. and 7.30 P.M. Sunday-school at 12.30 P.M. Come and hear our pastor, meet our young people, and enjoy the hospitality of our church home to-day. Hoping to have the pleasure of welcoming you, we are,
>   Yours most cordially,
>   PETER JONES,
>   *For Hotel Committee.*

Early Sabbath morning take this written invitation, with a small button-hole bouquet made by the young ladies on the committee. This is given to the hotel clerk, who places it upon the table alongside of the plate, so that the stranger when he comes down to breakfast, finds this unique invitation awaiting him. Who could resist an invitation like this? He naturally thinks that some one is interested in him and has gone to some trouble to invite him to their church services, and wherever this work has been systematically followed up the efforts of Endeavorers have been crowned with success.

First. Seek them out as Christ would.
Second. Invite them to come as Christ would.
Third. Welcome them as Christ would.
Fourth. Entertain them as Christ would.
Fifth. Seek to do them a lasting good; find out what cities they are going to visit and give them letters of introduction to different societies, or a card like the following, which is used by the First Presbyterian society of San Diego: —

Young People's Society of Christian Endeavor,
First Presbyterian Church,
San Diego, Cal.

Will you not come to one or more of our services? We meet every Sunday at 6.15 P.M. We will welcome you and try to make you feel at home and that you are with friends.

This little card the writer received in a Christian Endeavor society over three hundred miles from San Diego. What this society is doing others can do. If you cannot get a commercial traveller to sign the Endeavor pledge you may succeed in getting him to sign the following simple pledge, which will be the beginning of better things: —

Commercial Traveller's Pledge.

I will attend church services in the city or town where I may be on the Sabbath, also the Endeavor meeting in the evening.

Signed...

I also promise to abstain from the use of alcoholic drinks as a beverage.

Signed...

The American Church at Berlin, Germany, is doing some excellent work among the strangers visiting that city. Every Sunday the different hotels of that place are visited by the young people and a cordial invitation given to all the English-speaking people to visit their church and worship with them on the Lord's Day.

A man away from home stopping at a hotel is more apt to take notice of everything hanging upon the walls of the office, parlor, or sitting-room than those people who are passing in and out every day. To the commercial traveller Sunday is a long day. If a Church or Endeavor Society are alive to their opportunities they will have hanging upon the walls of the hotels, post-offices, express offices, and railroad depots, neat and attractive photographs of their churches, framed, with an invitation to their church services printed neatly upon it. If it is pretty and attractive it will catch the eye at once and draw them to us. Why should the devil have all the beautiful and artistic signs? Haven't we just as good right to them?

The Howard Street Methodist Church at San Francisco has printed 5,000 calendars and scattered them broadcast over the city. We commend them for their energy and zeal in trying to reach the thousands of strangers in San Fran-

VIEWS IN STATE HEADQUARTERS.

cisco. The down-town churches of all our large cities should do their very best to draw the great multitude of people into our churches who are now aimlessly walking up and down our main thoroughfares.

Why leave all the street work for the Salvation Army? We are glad to record that a few societies (we trust there are more) have been doing this kind of work, going into the byways and hedges, as it were, and bringing them into the fold. Bethany Congregational, in the mission, and Calvary Presbyterian, of San Francisco, have been doing this street work; i. e., each Sunday night, for ten or fifteen minutes preceding the regular Christian Endeavor prayer-meeting, a short praise service is held on the street in front of the church, which attracts sometimes a large number, and when the invitation is given to come in it is gratifying to see the strangers following. As a result of this work several conversions have been reported. In a late number of the *Christian Endeavor World* it was with pleasure I noted the monthly reports of the street work of the West Side Christian Endeavor society of Chicago, with marvelous results. At each and every one of their meetings they had from two to a half-dozen conversions and many more asking for an interest in their prayers. On one of these occasions a drummer representing a large New York firm, stopping at the Palmer House, stopped to listen to their street meeting and was converted.

Every city should have a church directory containing the name and location and hours of meetings of each evangelical church within its borders. We are glad to say that many have such directories hung up in the hotels, depots, on the ferries, Young Men's Christian Associations, and many other public places. In addition to these directories my attention has been called to some very pretty combinations of photographic art and the sign-writer. Large cities could hold at least twice a year a service in one of the central churches, especially for the commercial travellers and railroad men, having them attend in a body, the pastor preparing his sermon particularly for them; let the platform be decorated with the national colors. Have travelling-bags placed here and there, filled with choice flowers. Every Christian Endeavor society, from the largest to the smallest, can do something for the travelling-man. During the past year it has been my pleasure to visit one hundred and fifty Young Peoples societies, from Shasta to San Diego, and I find those societies which are growing both in numbers and usefulness are those who are anxious to help save others. It may need only a little word of invitation to bring the stranger to Christ.

During the year I have spoken in regard to this work, and for railway men, at three conventions, to six city and district union meetings, and fifteen business meetings of executive committees of cities and counties, doing what I could to interest the young people in special work for commercial travellers and railroad men. I have rendered aid to one hundred and fifty societies. I have travelled over 4.717 miles by railroad, steamers, sailing-vessels, stages, and last but not least, "the silent steed," my bicycle; have written letters and sent out papers and leaflets, to the number of 5,120, to all parts of the Pacific coast.

In finishing this part of my paper, permit me to say a few words in conclusion: —

First. That we must use specific means to reach the commercial traveller.

Second. That the possibilities of this department of the work are greater than anything we have yet seen or perhaps imagined.

Third. That there are 75,000 to 100.000 travelling-men in our country, and that your town, although it may be small, is very likely to have a few.

Fourth. That there is no Endeavor society but can do *something* for this class of men.

Fifth. That you are not asked to give more, but the same attention as to other departments.

Sixth. That the commercial traveller has but little knowledge of the workings of the Young People's Society of Christian Endeavor.

Seventh. That the impression he forms of a man is almost instantaneous;

that it is carried the length and breadth of our land; be frank and courteous, but don't overdo it.

Eighth. And lastly, that results will be slow, but that to succeed we need simply honest, persistent effort on the part of an organized committee.

Mr. Frederick A. Wallis, of Louisville, spoke on the topic "To Prisoners" as follows:—

Address by Mr. Frederick A. Wallis,
Louisville, Ky.
REACHING OUT TO PRISONERS.

Christian Endeavor is not only reaching out, but is reaching in. Particularly is this the case in our prison work, the success of which in three years has been so marvelous as to be almost miraculous! It is reaching out in the sense that the prisoners are actually writing to our committee for literature and printed pledge to send back to their homes from whence they came, that Christian Endeavor societies may be organized there. It is reaching in in the sense that it has penetrated the darkness of prison-cells and sounded the glad signal-note of pardon, and sin-bound men can be heard crying out in the midnight of despair, as did the Philippian jailor, "What must I do to be saved?"

I come, therefore, to-day, bearing my greetings warm and heartfelt from our Christian Endeavorers confined within prison walls. Never before in an International Convention has there been greetings from the thief, the murderer, the blasphemer, the criminal; and while to-day it may sound strange and entirely new to most of you, yet how beautiful is such a message! There are in Kentucky about two thousand men and boys wearing the stripes as marks of retribution for sin and crime, while the inward lives of many of these men are pure and white, bearing no longer the stains and stripes of sin, for "with His stripes are they healed." I am rejoiced at this auspicious moment to bring you such tidings of great joy, for many prisoners have been made free indeed through the glorious gospel of the Son of God.

Listen to the greetings I hold in my hand, written by one of the prisoners of the Eddyville Penitentiary:—

To the International Convention of Christian Endeavor, Nashville, Tenn.:

Dear Endeavorers:—We appreciate the opportunity of addressing you in convention assembled, and send by this letter our heartiest greetings. Christian Endeavor is working a wonderful reformation in the Eddyville Prison. Many men whose lives were blackened by sin and crime are now serving God zealously on Christian Endeavor committees to bring their fellow-prisoners into this sweet and blessed pardon. Remarkable as it may seem, not a single released prisoner who was active in the prison Endeavor has been brought back for the second term. Only eternity can reveal the wonderful workings of Christian Endeavor here. God help you to plant a Christian Endeavor society in every prison in the land.

(Signed.) YOUR CHRISTIAN ENDEAVOR COMRADES
OF THE EDDYVILLE PRISON.

Again, here is a message from the Frankfort Penitentiary, written by a prisoner also:—

To the International Convention of Christian Endeavor, Nashville, Tenn.:

Dear Endeavor Friends:—We beg the privilege of joining the world to-day, congratulating you upon the grand success of Christian Endeavor throughout civilization. We beg the privilege, while we cannot be with you in person, of being with you in spirit during your meeting.

In this great day of Prison Reform Movement, when "Reclamation" should be the tendency and watchword, there is no organization which can be instituted in a prison so potent in bringing good results, so conducive to good de-

portment and the reformation of men as the Christian Endeavor work — it is a work peculiarly adapted to prisons. Thousands of unfortunate men in the States to-day are starving for the very succor that Christian Endeavor can supply. We trust that before another year rolls around you may be able to organize a C. E. society in every prison and reformatory in the world.
(Signed.) Fraternally yours,
THE CHRISTIAN ENDEAVOR SOCIETY
OF KENTUCKY PENITENTIARY.

Time and words would fail me should I so much as attempt to tell you what Christian Endeavor has accomplished in prison life in the short space of three years. I believe the theme of many a song in the land of the redeemed will be our blessed society and its work. In the Kentucky Prison societies we have 405 members holding regular Christian Endeavor prayer-meetings every Sunday; they have active working committees, and are bound by the same solemn pledge, and are doing a noble work among their comrades. When the secretary of the International '98 Committee requested names of those in Kentucky who would join the Prayer Chain for this Convention almost the entire prison membership responded.

Oh that I might tell you some of our experiences, that I might say something to push aside the iron bars of your prejudice, and let you look for a moment upon some of the saddest scenes of life!

I could point you to faces which tell of separation and unrest, broken peace and unsatisfied longings, and deep heart-yearnings. Sometimes it is fear that writes its lines on the pale, trembling cheek; sometimes it is perplexity which darkens the features; most generally guilt of sin, and the hungering for pardon; but worst of all, the awful thought that they are lost and forgotten. Oh, is there not enough gentle Christlike sympathy among this great Convention to prompt you to make an effort to inaugurate this glorious work in your own State? It is remarkable how easily these men can be reached and won. Some day these souls, snatched as brands from the burning, will shine as the most brilliant stars in the heavenly crown of those who respond to this work. In the name of Christ, for the sake of humanity, we call for united hearts and hands. We beg your prayers, your sympathy, your co-operation in some way. Then shall you hear the glad welcome, " Come, thou blessed of my Father, for when I was in prison ye came unto me."

" Where stern Justice stands aloof,
In pity draw thou near."

The meeting was closed by the audience singing " Throw Out the Life-Line," and the benediction by Dr. James T. McCrory, D.D., of Pennsylvania.

Auditorium Endeavor.

When the exercises began in Auditorium Endeavor at 3 o'clock the body of the hall was completely filled. President Francis E. Clark presided.

The devotional exercises were conducted by Rev. George W. Moore, of Nashville.

The praise service was entered into heartily by the audience. E. O. Excell conducted the singing.

The first address was on the theme, " Advisory Board of Pastors," by W. T. Ellis, of Philadelphia. He said that the Christian Endeavorers always saluted when the pastors passed by, just as soldiers salute their colors. It would be a sad day for Endeavorers when they failed to consult the pastors. The word of the pastors is law. Do what they say do; do not do what they say do not do. Every union should have some means of bringing its pastors together and consulting with them.

A new Christian Endeavor society has been formed in the First Pennsylvania Regiment in camp, and three of its soldier members were introduced to the Convention by Mr. Ellis, two privates and a sergeant, one being the society's president. Their reception was one of the most enthusiastic moments of the entire Convention; and their tent, pitched before the Parthenon, was thereafter thronged with visitors.

The next speaker was Mr. Miles M. Shand, of Washington, D. C., and his subject was "Practical Topics for Union Meetings."

Address by Mr. Miles M. Shand,
Washington, D. C.
PRACTICAL TOPICS FOR UNION MEETINGS.

It may be set down as a fundamental fact that if a Christian Endeavor union be true to its reason for being there flows from it a constant stream of inspiration, in whose current the members are borne on to better living and serving.

This inspiration flows in two great channels, — the channel of intelligence imparted concerning things pertaining to the kingdom, and the channel of Christian fellowship.

In order that the stream may serve its good purpose it is of prime importance that practical topics, and practical topics only, should be presented at the public meetings of our unions.

Practical! The word means capable of being turned to use or account. The topic and the speech which do not possess this quality had better be omitted from the programme.

In these days of rush, busy Christians have little time for or patience with the topic that is not practical. I believe there is a lessening desire for speeches that are merely flowery, and a growing demand for topics and talks that arrest the thought and impel to action along the highest lines of living.

The number of causes which commend themselves to the Christian in this period of numerous and various activities is legion — the mere mention of them would consume more time than is now at my disposal.

There are topics of first importance, and topics of secondary concern; and it seems wise, since a choice is necessary, that it should fall upon those of the first class, which includes all essential Christianity.

Topics which treat of great principles of life in the home, the Church, and the State always command the serious attention of the Christian world.

We do not need topics of life in some other world than this, fascinating as these may be, nor do we need topics of the "I want to be an angel" sort. The need is for themes concerning life here and now, of life filled with noble ideals, with high and holy purposes; life whose greatest longing is to be like the Master and to please him perfectly. This is the kind of mortal life which alone fits for the immortal.

Since it is to develop, under the divine guidance and blessing, such living that our unions have their being, it must be clearly seen and appreciated that the necessity is on us to meet the need, so far as lies within our power.

Is the standard suggested too high? The kind of life so often called impracticable, because it is unselfish and loving, the life which in action exemplifies the Golden Rule, is after all possible, aye imperative, if the Christian is "to follow on to know the Lord."

Doubtless it is often said that the subjects to be treated are old and trite, and that is true. It is also true that the home, that "dearest spot on earth," the Church redeemed by the blood of the Lamb and to be glorified, the country and flag to which we owe allegiance, require of us old-fashioned duties and call for old-fashioned service such as Jesus himself rendered nearly two thousand years ago. It is "the old, old story of Jesus and his love" which is to-day the hope of the world and the panacea for all its ills.

The topics may be presented, indeed they should be given, in an attractive form, without being sensational. Let me give you a single illustration, a topic concerning Scriptural Giving, a subject which is now receiving more serious attention than ever before. "Plenty of Money for Things We Like" was the topic which aroused great interest — and some opposition. The subject was handled in a most sensible and practical manner and could not fail to do good.

When one feels the needs of the great throbbing life of our young people, and the opportunities presented to lead that life into higher walks of thought and action, topics press upon him in abundance.

Let us, therefore, in this important part of our union work, make it fit the needs and fire the souls of our members, being assured that so we shall all be helped in our daily duties, inspired to walk the common paths of life in the fear of God and for his glory, made brave in trial, cheerful in trouble, courageous in adversity, strong to endure, willing to serve — hearing the plaudit at last, "Well done."

The next speaker was the president of the Brooklyn, New York, Christian Endeavor Union.

Address by Rev. Thornton B. Penfield,
Brooklyn, N. Y.

LOCAL UNION LIMITATIONS.

The Christian Endeavor local union stands in the centre of a great circle of influence, a circle which, like the one caused by the stone thrown into the pond, keeps growing wider and wider.

Because of the power and influence generated as the natural result of the joining of forces such as are brought together in the local union, there has been in recent years a tendency among many Endeavor workers to regard the union's field of usefulness as limitless; and to assert that the union should step out into a broader field of religious activity, and conduct missions, relieve the poor, support missionaries abroad, and attempt temperance and other reform crusades. Measured by the standard so wisely set by the United Society, such movements, helpful as they may be and necessary as they often are, should not be a part of the local union work. There are other organizations to do these things. That which is the legitimate work of the Churches and denominations, or that which is being already done by any organized effort, such as the Young Men's Christian Association, or any enterprise that will require salaried officers to carry it out, is not the work of the local union. Nor is the union organized to save souls. That is the work of each individual Christian.

The local union exists for two purposes and only two purposes; namely, for inspiration and for fellowship. Measured by this standard, the scope of the local union work does not include the raising of a regiment of volunteer soldiers, for instance, as was attempted in the Greater New York unions this year by well-meaning but misguided friends of Christian Endeavor; nor the running of a lecture-bureau to provide concerts, lectures, and entertainments for Christian Endeavor societies, and incidentally, to raise money to feed homeless wanderers, as was proposed in Brooklyn this last year. These are merely samples of what many people expect of the local union.

Dr. Clark has well said: "The local union is not a catch-all for every sort of religious enterprise, nor a dumping-ground for all kinds of philanthropic, or benevolent, or literary, or musical, or semi-professional organizations. The great object of every local union should be to fit the young people who belong to the societies composing it to do better work in and for their own Church."

Some one is asking, "Why not let the union take up a wider work, even though the churches and missions are attempting to meet these needs?" There is one reason, if no other could be given, and that is because each worker who would be required to manage these movements, if put in operation, ought to be so busy in his own church that he would have no time for this outside service. It is not my place to speak of what the union can do, or ought to do. The part assigned to me is to say, "Thus far shalt thou go and no farther;" but if you would see an example of ideal union management, I would point you to Philadelphia or New York. Let any local union president who is in doubt as to the policy his union should pursue place himself in correspondence with either President Kinports, of New York, or President Ellis, of Philadelphia, and he will not go far astray in his judgment.

The next speaker was the Rev. Jacob W. Kapp, D.D., of Richmond, Ind., president of the Indiana Christian Endeavor Union.

Address by Rev. Jacob W. Kapp, D.D.,
Richmond, Ind.
POSSIBILITIES OF LOCAL UNIONS.

Aggressive work and Christian Endeavor stand for the same thing. Christian Endeavor lives and flourishes so long as it does things. The different societies in our towns and cities have organized themselves in the local union in order to help themselves and unite their forces for general work. It is felt that what one would do in a timid and feeble way a number of societies united would do in a bold and positive way.

Association means encouragement, sympathy, help, and wise methods. Because Christian people can be helpful to each other, and because "the fields are white already to the harvest," therefore a great work awaits the united forces of Christian young people. There is a great work possible to the local union in developing Christian fellowship and the spirit of union among Christian people. Infinitely more can be done to destroy the spirit of sectarianism in the co-operation of Christian people than in seeking intellectual grounds for settlement of our differences. The various plans for union of denominations, good and praiseworthy as they are, are all open to serious objections, and probably can never be made to satisfy all persons. Bishop Huntington has lately written an article to show the hopelessness of the task of forming a basis for union. But co-operation in Christian work leads to Christian love, and Christian love leads to broad-mindedness and charity, and is the death of bigotry and denominational jealousy.

There is a story told of a slaveholder who had committed the care of one of his teams to a faithful slave for some years; at last one of the horses sickened and died. While the slave was burying the faithful animal the other horse came across the field and stood by watching the operation as a silent mourner. The master said to the slave, "I believe Dick loved Billy." Instantly the slave replied, "'Course he did, massa; why, they pulled together for twenty years!"

It is the pulling together of the various Christian forces in our cities against the common enemy and for a common cause that will unite the hearts of the followers of the Master and bring us into the realization of the prayer "That they all may be one." The Christian love engendered by co-operation in Christian service will lead us to understand each other better, and means the death of the chief obstacles in the way of Christian efforts by Christian people of different denominations. Christian workers who sit together in the committee-room planning for the extension of the cause of the Master, and who kneel together to tell the Christ of the desire of their hearts, will soon forget the differences that have held them apart, and the union so essential for the success of the cause of our Lord will be effected. There is also a great field for the local union work in securing better municipal government, and I need not discuss the bad government of many of our cities. Everybody knows that it is so. The fact that with few exceptions our city governments have fallen into the hands of unprincipled men and they hold their places by the sufferance, not of the saloon element of the cities alone, but also because many respectable and upright citizens voted for the same candidate for whom the saloon element worked and voted, makes it necessary that there should be a united effort in order to defeat men of that character and clean things up.

Our Christian citizenship campaign does not mean simply to talk about our duty and denounce the enemy. If we are going to wage war we will make ourselves ridiculous if we only shoot words at the enemy. Shooting indictment and convicting testimony and convictions and penalties for law-breakers and ballots on election-day against the unworthy, is the only kind of warfare that will count in this campaign. The very fact that there are many persons in every city indifferent and unconcerned about the municipal affairs, and that there are many who, though they are fully aware of the evils, are afraid to lift their hands against them, makes the work of educating and arousing the ignorant and slumbering by the local union imperative. The field of work here for the local union consists in part, it is true, in educating and awakening public sentiment, but it does not consist in that alone, but also in the face-to-face work with law-breakers. The local union must meet the enemy in his stronghold, assault and overcome him. Of course it means hard work, of course it means to be reviled, of course it means bitter and determined resistance; but if you came into the kingdom of Christ looking for an easy job, you made application at the wrong establishment. "The disciple is not above his Lord. If they have persecuted me they will persecute you also." The united force of Christian workers is needed for this work, and the local union will find a field waiting for its energy there. Allied to this is the missionary work. We are not only to fight evil; we are also to prevent evil. Much as we are interested in foreign missions, we must not neglect nor forget the need of the gospel at our door. Indeed, he who is consistently interested in foreign missions will also be aglow with interest in the home work, and the converse is also true. For development of interest in foreign missions the local union can find a large field. The old adage, "A stitch in time saves nine," is applicable with tremendous force in our missionary work, and it is to be remembered that if it comes to the time that the nine stitches are required, the rent is sure to show more or less all the life. Let the local union not fail to give its heartiest and most devoted efforts to save the boys and girls for Christ. Do all to foster and nourish and care for the Junior societies with the utmost diligence.

The wise husbandman cares for the tender plant with the full knowledge that it is only thus that he will get the strong stock. In every city there are Mission Schools, Homes for the Friendless, Rescue Homes, Doors of Hope, and kindred institutions. Many of these are in need of helpers and will welcome a band of earnest Christian people who can take charge of a service. Every local union also ought to be a school of methods. It is true that the great power of our society lies in the consecration of its members to Christ; but we must not neglect our duty in doing our utmost in the use of the means God has given us. Many societies do little, not because they are not willing to work, but because they do not know how to do the work. Others fall into ruts and do not know how to get out of them, and so monotony comes and the interest lags and gradually the work loses its zest and vim. Since the Christian Endeavor society is an organization for work by means of various committees, it becomes a matter of the highest importance that methods be studied. Aid should be given upon the part of one society to another in reporting methods that have been tried and found helpful; thus it is that every local union meeting should become the means of infusing new life into every society represented. New methods, better methods, more consecrated work, and larger plans, courage, and enthusiasm,— all of this should be the blessing that comes to the individual society from co-operation in the local union.

Two beautiful songs by the Jubilee Singers, who were always obliged to respond to encores, and then "The Christian Endeavor Bugbear" was introduced by Mr. Wells, put together, and finally put to death.

The speaker used a large image of a black bear, to which, as he proceeded in his address, he fastened the parts mentioned, closing with the literal overthrow of the " bugbear " by thrusts of a sword.

Address by Prof. Amos R. Wells,
Boston, Mass.

THE CHRISTIAN ENDEAVOR BUGBEAR.

In old English the word "bug" meant "terror." There is a "bug Bible." It is so named because the passage, "Thou shalt not be afraid for the terror by night," is translated, " Thou shalt not be afraid for the bug." So a bugbear is a terrible bear, a bugaboo.

I have brought with me a specimen of a Christian Endeavor bugbear. He is not even distantly related to Secretary Baer. The bugbear fell to pieces on the way hither. That is something bugbears are in the habit of doing. I must put him together again before I introduce him.

In the first place, his eyes fell out. Here they are. They are bold enough, but you can't trust a bugbear's looks. Try them. Suggest some little service of Christ, say to lead a prayer-meeting. The modest eyelids droop down in an instant. The terrified bugbear shrieks, "Oh, there are so many looking at me!" There's many a young man who will gleefully bang his hair and pad his knees and sew a big red letter on his sweater and parade up and down before the grand-stand at the foot-ball game, and the more people that look at him the better he likes it. There's many a young woman who will dress herself — if the term may be used — with low neck and no sleeves, and simper under the red light of a tableau for five hundred eyes to gaze at her. But ask the young man or young woman to stand properly clothed before sixty people in a prayer-meeting, and — down go the bugbear's timid eyelids: "Oh, there will be so many looking at me!" There are some eyes looking at them that they have left out of account — God's.

Here are the bugbear's ears. They are large like a donkey's, because the bugbear is very much of a donkey. They stick straight up, to gather in all uncomplimentary remarks. Those ears heard a snicker once at a Christian Endeavor meeting. "There's some one laughing at my testimony," said the bugbear. No more prayer-meeting testimony for two months. Those sharp ears once heard two people talking. "The flattest speech I ever listened to," said they. The bugbear was "just sure they meant him." Prayer-meeting silence for two months more. The bugbear's ears hear so much that is n't so that I'm afraid they will never hear God's "Well done."

Here is a part of the bugbear's anatomy you will be surprised to see, his brain. Did n't know he had one, did you? Well, he has, and he uses it vigorously; keeps it busy manufacturing excuses. You want something done in the Christian Endeavor society. "Oh, I'm not bright enough!" modestly declares the bugbear. It is marvelous how some brains shrink when exposed to religious weather. They must be all wool, sheepish. Girls that have brains enough to write a thirty-page letter about nothing are not bright enough to write a thirty-word testimony for the consecration meeting. Boys that are ready in their debating society to talk *ex tempore* on any question from seals to silver and from tariff to tiddledywinks, ask them to lead a prayer-meeting and they are not bright enough. In the stock market the bulls seek to toss prices higher and the bears seek to hug them down lower. The bugbear is always trying to depress the market for his own brains. He always quotes them below par.

And of course the Christian Endeavor bugbear has a mouth. Do you notice how melancholy it is, how down at the corners? And why, do you think? "They'll all laugh at me," whines the bugbear's mouth. People have told the bugbear that to be laughed at undeservedly is like sunshine to the squash-vine, which refuses to be squashed. People have reminded the bugbear that many a great man has floated to greatness on the very waves of ridicule that opposed him. People have told the bugbear that those who ridicule honest endeavors would ridicule dishonest cowardice, and with ten times more reason. But, alas! the bugbear would rather face God's frown than men's laughter, and so at every call for sacred service down go his mouth-corners and out comes his excuse, "They'll all be laughing at me." Poor thing!

Behold the bugbear's teeth! Did you ever see a set that looked more like a snarl? The snarl is there, and it often comes out. Whenever you ask for Christian work it comes out, and it always is, "People tear everything to pieces. People are so critical!" The bugbear fancies an army of sharp teeth around every prayer-meeting testimony, ready to rend it to atoms. People's teeth are hungry for truth, but the bugbear believes they are snapping for sarcasm. The bugbear's teeth are false teeth, and he thinks every one else wears false teeth. Ask him to bestir himself on any Christian errand and he quotes from the Bible, "There is a lion in the way, a lion is in the streets," the terrible lion of criticism, gnashing its fearful fangs.

What does the bugbear's tongue say? You have often heard it; this is what it stammers: "Others can talk so much better than I." "Won't you take part in the next prayer-meeting?" "Oh, excuse me! Others can talk so much better than I," says the modest bugbear tongue. No use suggesting that there is time also to hear from these wonderful others. No use hinting that if he talked more he might talk better. No use reminding him how mad he gets when others say of him what he says of himself. Argument is like wind to the windmill, and only sets his tongue to clattering with more voluble insistence, "Others can talk so much better than I, can talk, can talk, so much better than I."

Where is the heart of the Christian Endeavor bugbear? "Oh, my heart is in my throat!" he cries; and so it is. Well, what of it, bugbear? Your heart is still beating, isn't it? Nay, isn't it beating twice as fast as usual? If it has risen in the world, why should you care? If your heart is in your throat, that proves that it stands transference. Now put it into your work. "But no," says the bugbear, "I have no heart for your Christian endeavors. Don't you see my heart is in my throat?"

And the bugbear's lungs! They are weak lungs, as you can see. Indeed, the bugbear is always telling folks how weak his lungs are. "I really can't make myself heard," the bugbear says whenever he is asked to speak at a Christian Endeavor meeting. "And besides," continues the bugbear, "I stammer and hesitate so, you know." One is reminded of the case of Susie Silly. Her voice is a foghorn at the socials, but has quick consumption at the prayer-meetings. One is reminded of Dick Donothing. He imitated a rattling auctioneer at the last party, but he gets the lockjaw at the prayer-meetings. Why, when would souls be converted if it wasn't for the stammerers? Smooth, glib oratory slips like oil from the heart; it's the timid pitter-patter of the rain that sinks in. A poor, bashful voice God magnifies with that same speaking-trumpet which pulled down the walls of Jericho. But still our weak-lunged bugbear keeps on wheezing, "I really can't make myself heard. And, besides, I stammer and hesitate so, you know."

What say the front paws of the Christian Endeavor bugbear? See them, dolorously drooping! "I can't hold out," they say, and they look as if they meant it. These front paws can't hug anything, except a delusion; and the delusion they are hugging is that it takes more strength to hold out than to start out. Why, the starting out is ours, but the holding out is God's. "I will sustain thee," says God; whereupon we treasonably quaver, "I can't hold out." Plant a seed in the earth, and God will hold out nutriment to it, hold out water and air and sunshine to it, stretch out its rootlets and its first tender leaves, build up its great trunk, and hold out its spreading branches. Not yours is the holding out of the branches; yours is the planting of the seed. And yet when one would have you inaugurate some noble endeavor, lo, the front paws of the bugbear droop and waver, and the whine is, "I can't hold out!"

What say the back paws of the Christian Endeavor bugbear? "I'm shaking in my shoes," says one foot; "I'm scared out of my boots," says the other.

And so the bugbear, like "my son John," has "one shoe off and one shoe on." Ah, bugbear, does it make any difference whether you are scared out of your boots or in them? What boots it? Let your feet shake, so they hold you up; let your voice shake, so it shakes out God's truth. God's music sounds sweetest along the quivering strings, the vocal chords that stammer, the heart-strings that falter. Fright is no license for flight. Some of the bravest of battles have been fought by the worst-scared men. God does n't promise you confidence; he promises you conquest. But the bugbear does n't remember this. He thinks that shaking in one's shoes gives one the right to run away in them.

Some way, the bugbear still looks incomplete. What has been forgotten? Oh, the bugbear's watch. A Christian Endeavor bugbear could n't get along without a timepiece. And it is the loudest ticking watch in Christendom. What does the watch tick? "I have n't time." "Will you lead the next meeting?" Ticks the bugbear's watch, "I have n't time." "Will you serve on the lookout committee?" "I have n't time," screams the watch. To be sure, when one asks, "Will you go to my party?" or "Will you read this interesting novel?" the watch stops short and does n't even tick, but probably that is because it is horror-stricken. One might say, "You have just as much time as the hardest working Christian in the world." One might say, "Where there's a will, there's an hour." One might say, "God, who lends you time, has a right at least to your interest." But a bugbear never pays interest of time. As the slang saying is, he is running "on tick," and the tick, the tiresome, lying tick, constantly is, "I have n't time. No time! No time!"

And last of the bugbear's anatomy, the most ridiculous and contemptible and useless part of all, comes the tail. And this stump of a tail knows how to wag, and with every wag it says, "That is n't my forte." "Will you lead your friends in public prayer?" "That is n't my forte," wags the tail. "Will you tell your friends about your joy in Christ?" "That's not my forte," wags the tail. "That ability was not entailed upon me." Ah, bugbear, who said you had any ability? God will furnish the powder, if you will furnish a rifle. God will give the water, if you will give the pipe. All God wants is a willing emptiness, that he may fill it with power. "This Christian work is n't your forte?" That is fortunate; for it is God's forte, and maybe you will give him a chance to carry it on through you without interfering with him. But no; but no; the bugbear's tail slips between his legs and whimpers still. "It is n't my forte."

But now to complete the Christian Endeavor bugbear, we must breathe into it in some way the breath of life. And the breath of its life is lies, for it is the child of the father of lies. Here is the bellows that gives it life,—the inky bellows of falsehood. See, as I shoot in the black air, how it issues forth again as lies. Hear the brain saying, "I 'm not bright enough; " and the ears saying, "I heard them talking about me; " and the eyes saying, "There are so many looking at me; " and the mouth saying, "They 'll all be laughing at me; " and the teeth saying, "The critics tear everything to pieces; " and the tongue saying, "Others talk so much better than I ; " and the heart saying, "I 'm up in the throat; " and the lungs saying, "I stammer and hesitate so; " and the watch saying, "I have n't time; " and the front paws saying, "I can't hold out; " and the back paws saying, "I 'm shaking in my shoes, I 'm scared out of my boots; " and the tail saying, "It is n't my forte." Twelve different terrors in the Christian Endeavor bugbear, and every one of them a lie.

But now the bugbear is alive, and we must kill it some way. It would never do to let a bugbear loose in a Christian Endeavor convention. Let's shoot it. Here is the old blunderbuss of self-confidence. "I am as smart as the rest of them. I can give them as good as they send. I 'll not back down before anybody. I 'm not afraid of the whole crowd of them. I — I — I —." But the blunderbuss is too rusty. It won't go off. Probably it is n't loaded.

Here is the modern revolver. It is called philosophy. Doubtless it will kill the bugbear. "I am not afraid of John Smith, or Peter Brown, or Jack Robinson. Why should I be afraid of a crowd when I am not afraid of the separate individuals that make it up? Life is short. In a hundred years how I will laugh over my present fears! Why should one man be afraid of others any more than an ant of other ants? Why — why — why —." But neither will the revolver go off.

Ah, here is the weapon! The sword of the Word! the sword of the Spirit! the sword of the Lord and of Gideon! To close quarters with the bugbear! "So many looking at me?" "I will guide thee with mine eye!" "People talking about me?" "Christ made himself of no reputation!" "I 'm not bright enough?" "I will give you in that hour what ye shall say!" "They are laughing at me?" "The Lord shall have them in derision!" "Their criticism will tear me to pieces?" "Woe unto you, when all men shall speak well of you!" "Others can talk so much better than I?" "Who hath made man's mouth?" "My heart is in my throat?" "The heart is in the hand of the Lord!" "I stammer so?" "The tongue of the stammerers shall speak plainly!" "I can't hold out?" "The Lord will hold thy right hand!" "I 'm shaking in my shoes?" "Thy shoes shall be iron and brass, and as thy days, so shall thy strength be!" "I have n't time?" "There is a time to every purpose!" "It is n't my forte?" "I can do all things through Christ who strengtheneth me!" All things through Christ! All things! All things! All things! The bugbear is dead!

Three "betters" were urged by as many Christian Endeavor leaders,—" Better Socials," by President Clippinger, of Missouri; "Better Committee Work," by President Brett, of New Jersey; and "Better Prayer-Meetings," by Rev. Sherman H. Doyle, Ph. D., whose comments on the Christian Endeavor topics, published so widely by the American Press Association, are read by more millions than any other writings except those of Dr. Talmage.

Address by Rev. E. W. Clippinger,
Warrensburg, Mo.
BETTER SOCIALS.

That there is a lack of character to many of our socials is a fact that must be admitted. That they are often without any high purpose, and are barren of lasting results, are facts which few close observers would not readily admit as true. That there are larger possibilities, in and from the social, than are ordinarily developed there goes without saying.

There is nothing great or noble that does not rest upon great and noble truths and aims. The social is a poor thing, at best, if it has no great end to attain. We must not lose sight of the fact that the social is not an end in and of itself, but is a means to an end. That end is not simply to find a place and manner in which we can while away an evening. It is not simply to have a good time; though, seemingly, in the minds of many this is the sum total of the social.

Neither is it an institution whose end is to make money. The pay-social is far from the ideal social. There are better ways of making money than by transforming the social into a financial scheme.

Neither is its purpose achieved by certain sets, or cliques, getting together at the social and leaving all others to themselves. Too often the selfish, clannish few spoil the evening for all but themselves, and thereby defeat the very purpose of the social.

Neither is the purpose of the social achieved when some sort of amusement has been found for all present. The aim of the social is not amusement.

But first, last, and always the social should be a means to an end, and that end is *Christ*. The next time you give a social give it in the name of and for the sake of Christ. Talk with and impress upon the minds of the members of your society that hereafter this is the idea of your socials and the reason why you give them.

A noble motive makes the most commonplace deed or event noble. With

Christ as the first thought in your socials they will be nobler in character and more fruitful in results. And this does not mean, either, that we shall have nothing but long-faced piety at our socials. Long, sour-faced piety would kill a church. It would kill almost anything. There is nothing inconsistent in a social for Christ's sake and yet have it the most joyous kind of a social. Only let the form of the social take such a course as is noble, unselfish, for the good of all present, and Christ will add his blessing to it even as in the case of the wedding in Cana of Galilee.

It will be a better social if we take the spirit of the pledge of Christian Endeavor with us to the social. Why not be a Christian Endeavorer at a Christian Endeavor social? Be Christian Endeavorer enough to make a conscientious effort to induce some one to come; or go and bring some young friend who is not in the habit of attending Endeavor meetings to the social. Be Endeavorer enough to prove to strangers that there are no more pleasant or jovial gatherings of young people than a Christian Endeavor social. Be Endeavorer enough to use your social as a means by which you may draw strangers and outside friends toward the church, the Christian Endeavor meeting, and toward Christ.

It will be a better social if you will make an effort to look after the timid, those who seem not to be having a very enjoyable time and may never come again unless you do this. The social, mind you, is not primarily and always for ourselves. It is a means to an end, and that end is Christ. Therefore for Christ's sake look after those who have come and are your guests for the evening, and who otherwise may be disappointed, feel slighted, or wish they had remained at home.

ASK GOD'S BLESSING.

It will be a better social, it will have better and more lasting results, if you will make it a subject of prayer before you go and again after you leave. Is there anything inconsistent in asking God's blessing upon our joys, our pleasures? Can't one be as much in earnest at a social as at a prayer-meeting? Can't one laugh for Christ as well as sing for him? Can't a Christian Endeavorer pray over a social which is given for Christ's sake as well as over a prayer-meeting held in his name? If not, why not?

It will be a better social if you will not do your part in a perfunctory manner as a committeeman, but do all that you do simply as an Endeavorer. Never let it be felt that you have been appointed as a special committeeman to look after any detail of the social, but rather make every one feel that as an individual Endeavorer, moved by a spirit of helpfulness which has become a habit of your life, you talk, or work, or participate in any part of the social because of the pleasure you take in it.

It will be a better social if you will break down all that uncalled-for formality which invariably chills all about you. Make every one feel the warmth of a genial, generous nature within you. Break down that rigid formality in others by an exhibition of the opposite trait within yourself. Formality too often seems like the manifestation of a desire to have little to do with others. It always gives me the impression that there is something between us.

Smite quickly anything that looks like caste. Caste has no place at an Endeavor social. It is not Christlike, but is a generator of strife and ill-feeling.

In a word, carry into the social all the teachings of the Master, bathed in smiles and with a joyous nature.

Be social for Christ's sake, but do not forsake Christ at the social.

Have no selfish aim in your social, but make it first, last, and always, a means to an end and that end Jesus Christ.

Address by Rev. Cornelius Brett, D.D.,
Jersey City, N. J.

BETTER COMMITTEE WORK.

I thank you for this appointment in the absence of the honored gentleman from the West. My text has been given to me by the committee, and I will try to preach a purely extemporaneous sermon upon "Better Committee Work." I will treat it textually, as we preachers say, and divide it into three parts; for there are three words in it: Better, Committee, Work.

"Better" should be written upon everything that Christian Endeavor touches. If we are to have any motto after "For Christ and his Church," it should be "Excelsior!" the motto of the Empire State of New York — "Things Higher," forgetting the things that are behind, and reaching out unto the things that are before.

I find three kinds of Christian Endeavor societies. First, those that are pessimistic in regard to their own efforts. You have had an example in the Christian Endeavor Bugbear. We find whole societies that are controlled by this bugbear, — the society cannot do this, or cannot do that; our committees cannot work as other committees do. Now do get that out of your heads, friends, if you are members of such societies, and go back from this Convention saying, "What societies have done societies can do."

Then there is the perfectly self-satisfied society. "Don't you know what our committees are doing? It will be impossible to improve upon the record, to do more next year than we did last year. Just look at the report of committees and then the report of our secretary at the last annual meeting." It reminds me of a story they tell about the revival of 1857. When Mr. Beecher was making an address upon the platform of the old Burton Theatre, on Chambers Street, N. Y., and was speaking about the impossibility of reaching in this life a sinless existence, one old gentleman said, "Mr. Beecher, please except me; I haven't committed a sin in ten years." And the good man in his eloquence turned round and said, "Why, my dear brother, you ought to have been in heaven long ago!" Some of these self-satisfied societies are just ready to put on their ascension robes. But the average society, I think, is neither hopeless and despairing nor perfectly satisfied.

We are here in convention to-day ambitious for the future, wanting to do better, better work. We believe in "Excelsior." I wish that poem were repeated by the children of to-day as it was by the boys and girls with whom I grew up, where we had "Excelsior" at every exhibition, whether of day school or Sunday-school. Longfellow wrote that poem when he was a mere youth. I think if he had written another verse in maturer life, he would not have let that man stop (end) in the mountain and in the snow, where his voice cried through the startled air "Excelsior!" but he would have had the voice of the angels (take it up). It was the spirit of the young and ambitious man, who must fall some time in his ambition — fall for earth, but rise to heaven. He would have had another verse echoing through the skies higher than the monks of Saint Bernard. "Excelsior!" We want to keep on getting better, better.

Now, better committees. The committees are the spindles and the looms of Christian Endeavor. God gives us the power, but here is the workshop. I once went into a deserted factory at Leeds. It had belonged to the great Stewart estate, but when Stewart died the factory was closed. And there the water of the river poured on its way down from the Catskill Mountains toward the Hudson River and did nothing for that factory, because the spindles and looms were all out of order and the factory was closed. Do you want such a society as that, and the power of God flowing by you and not touching you and moving you? Your committees are to move in obedience to the power from on high, and each one must do its own work. Even if the power comes to you, remember that if the machinery is out of order the web and the threads will be tangled up and the material will come out with faults and flaws in it. You are to see to it, through the perfection of your machinery, that when the power comes down and touches you the work that comes out shall be approved unto heaven, and that you as workmen will be those that are not ashamed.

Now it is with all due respect to Christian Endeavor that I say it is not a modern institution. Paul knew all about it when he spoke about one spirit and diversities of gifts; when he spoke about one who was called to be a preacher, another a pastor, and another an evangelist. There were committees in the Church at Corinth, and Philippi, and the other churches with which Paul had anything to do. He organized committees just as soon as he organized churches, and we in these modern days have just revived old methods. Why, it is the principle of division of labor put into Christian work. I do not know whether any of you here are old enough to appreciate old farm-life in New England, or perhaps somewhere in the West, where everything you ate was raised on the farm, the clothing that you wore was raised on the farm, and the farmer and his wife did everything that was done. By and by civilization came, and it set up a division of labor. One boy found that he could be a carpenter, and another boy went to the city to make money in another way. So we divided up our labor, and in the greatest factories they have brought the division of labor down to the very finest point, so that in very many places one man spends his whole time just putting a little peg into a little bit of a hole.

Better work. Committees are organized for work and not for ornament. Will you take that home with you, you who are members of committees in your local societies? If there is no work for your committee to do, at the next meeting of your society ask for an amendment to your constitution: abolish your committee, and then find some committee for yourself that has something to do. Do not have a long list. They look very pretty on your programmes for the year, and in your annual reports, but oh! a lot of committees with nothing to do are a shame to any society. Now what kind of work are you going to do? Do your work, the work that is assigned to you and not assigned to anybody else, will you? Do not trench upon the authority of any other committee, but just do your work thoroughly, promptly; do not put off till to-morrow what can be done to-day. Do your work with all the heart and enthusiasm of a Christian Endeavorer; and when you get through make a written report. A written report, it is one of the most important things to good committee work. It inspires other committees to work. It puts on record what you have done.

In our legislative bodies, our ecclesiastical bodies, we won't take a verbal report. A man gets up and says. "I have done so and so," and the secretary or president will kindly say, "Where is your report, sir?" One of my good neighbors who has a very well-organized church found a young lady who failed to do her duty in this respect. She was a member of the guild. A part of her duty was to report to her pastor. He sent for her one day, and she asked, "Why have you sent for me, sir?" She knew him very well. "Why didn't you make your report to me?" "I didn't do anything." "Why didn't you say so, then? Now, you just sit down and write: 'My Dear Pastor, I am very sorry that I failed to make a report to you, and I will do better in the future.' Sign it and give me that." And that was her report. Write your report, even if you don't do anything. But see that you do something, thoroughly, well, promptly, just according to the line of work selected for your own committee, and then write about it in a very humble, concise manner, that it may go on the minutes of the society as part of your work in the line of glorious betterment.

Address by Rev. Sherman H. Doyle,
Philadelphia, Penn.

BETTER PRAYER-MEETINGS.

The Christian Endeavor Society has often been called the "Church at work," or the workshop of the Church. In the light of this comparison, the Christian Endeavor prayer-meeting may be likened to the engine-room of the workshop. The engine-room is the inspiration of the workshop. It transforms it from an agency of inactivity into one of tireless energy and industry. Abolish the engine-room and this characteristic of the workshop at once disappears. The prayer-meeting bears a similar relation to the Endeavor society. It is its inspiration. Properly conducted, the prayer-meeting generates the power, which, applied to the officers, committees, and members, produces through them the practical results desired. Do away with the prayer-meeting, and the Endeavor society might as well be done away with.

The first important factor in the engine-room is the engineer. He controls and directs the giant machine, and its success or failure depends largely upon him. The engineer of the Endeavor prayer-meeting is its leader, and the character and usefulness of the meeting are very largely determined by him. It is helpful or harmful, as he directs it. For better prayer-meetings, we should raise the standard of leadership. We want leaders who will thoroughly prepare themselves for their duties. An engineer is a skilled laborer. He is prepared for his position. It would be criminal to place an incompetent, unprepared engineer at the throttle of an engine, thereby endangering human life. Shall we less earnestly demand prepared leaders for our meetings, when the destiny of eternal lives may depend upon their work? The leader should see that there is variety in the meeting. The engineer does not keep his engine at the same temperature all the time. It constantly varies. So should the Endeavor prayer-meetings. No two meetings should be exactly alike. There should be system, but not sameness; order, but not the order of the graveyard, that is characteristic of death, but an order that speaks of intelligent life. The leader should *lead, direct*, not *be* the meeting. The engineer is not the engine; he directs it; but alas, too many of our Endeavor leaders think that they are the meeting, and thereby impair their usefulness and that of the meeting.

The second factor in the engine-room is fuel. The priceless value of fuel for engines is strikingly illustrated to-day, when the presence or absence of it in great battleships has been almost deciding the fate of nations. The fuel of the Endeavor prayer-meeting may be represented by the things upon which it depends for success, principally the Holy Spirit, prayer, and the topic. A successful prayer-meeting without the Holy Ghost is as impossible as a useful engine-room without coal. How could we have a successful prayer-meeting without him who " helpeth our infirmities, when we know not what to pray for as we ought "? What we most need to have better prayer-meetings is not more members in our societies, not more attendants at our prayer-meetings, but more of the Holy Ghost in those who do belong and who do attend; and God is more willing to supply this need than we are to seek it. Prayer is an indispensable element of fuel. Our need for better prayer-meetings is not more prayers, not longer prayers, but more faith and definiteness in prayer. Without faith, prayer is as " sounding brass and a tinkling cymbal." Would that, as Endeavorers, we had the faith of an Elijah in prayer. Elijah prayed for rain and then sent his servant out to see if the clouds were coming, and when they did not appear at first, sent him again and again till they did come. What a contrast to a congregation in one of our Western States, which assembled at the church in a time of need to pray for rain, and only one of them took an umbrella, and that one was a boy, most likely a Junior Endeavorer. He believed that God would answer their prayers and went prepared for the rain. A good wife told me once that her husband had been out of work for several years, and, after trying in every way to secure a position, had spent an entire week in prayer to God for work; that the next Monday morning a former employer sent for him to come and take his old position; and then she added, " Was n't that strange?" I at once concluded that it was the husband's faith and not the wife's that brought the answer, and yet perhaps if God answered some of our prayers so promptly we should think it wondrously strange. There is also a need of more definiteness in our prayers. In praying we are too often like the man who prayed that God would " send the gospel to all heathen lands and to the lands where the foot of man had never trod and which the eye of man had never seen;" or like a good old elder of whom I heard, who whenever, wherever, or for whatever he prayed began with Adam in the Garden of Eden and wound up with John in ecstatic vision on the Island of Patmos. Biblical prayers encourage definiteness in prayer. Elijah prayed for rain, and it rained. Hezekiah spread the ultimatum of Sennacherib before the Lord and prayed for one thing,—deliverance from the Assyrian army,—and the angel of the Lord destroyed the Assyrian hosts. The early Church prayed for the deliverance of the Apostle Peter, and their prayer was answered so promptly that some of them were frightened. Go up higher in prayer. Pray for what you want; want what you pray for, and believe that God will give it.

Another element of fuel is the topic. That our prayer-meetings may be better, I plead for a better scriptural discussion of the topic, a more thorough discussion of it, as based upon the topical references. Let some one be appointed to study and to explain each scriptural reference. For years I have written the comments on the topic for the American Press Association of New York from this standpoint, and I want to testify to the great carefulness with which these references are selected, and to their appropriateness, and helpfulness. They are the "Thus saith the Lord's" on the topic. They are God's opinion on the subject, and we need to know what God thinks about it. An intelligent biblical discussion of the topic will require previous research and thought, but this is just what we need to make our meetings better. An entire prayer-meeting is sometimes killed by unprepared rambling, meaningless remarks on the topic, introduced as follows: "I did not know until I came to the meeting what the topic was, but will make a few general remarks," and they usually are general. Study the topic in the light of God's Word before the meeting. Do not be satisfied with glittering generalities or extempore discussion. Glittering generalities will never take the place of a God-given gospel. Divine inspiration is infinitely better than human extemporization.

The last important factor of the engine-room that I will mention is the water. The peculiar thing about the water is that it must be transformed into steam before it is useful, and to be transformed it must be raised to a temperature of 212 F., or to the boiling-point. It may be warm or hot, but will not boil until it reaches 212, and is useless until it boils. The water may symbolize the members of the society in relation to the prayer-meeting. It is transformed water only that is useful in an engine-room. It is a transformed membership only that is useful in an Endeavor prayer-meeting,—one that is not only warm or hot in the service of Christ, but that has reached the boiling-point of entire consecration, of entire transformation, by the power of the Holy Ghost. A transformed membership will give us an ideal prayer-meeting. A transformed member will not always remain in the Christian Endeavor kindergarten of Bible verse-readers; a transformed member will never answer "Present" at the roll-call in the consecration service, or "Please sing two verses of hymn so and so." A transformed member will perfectly keep the pledge in relation to the prayer-meeting. Give us a transformed membership in our societies, and the question of better prayer-meetings will be solved forever.

An inspiring close to the session was the "quiet hour," led by Dr. Clark, with its eager testimonies from the hundreds of Comrades present. From all over the house came the words of gratitude. "I got more from my fifteen minutes' quiet with God than from five hours in my library." "I wish I had known it years ago." "It adds sweetness and beauty to every task of the day." "It opens my duty before me." "In it I lose sight of myself." So the glad words poured in, and the tide was still at its height when Rev. W. F. McCauley, of Ohio, pronounced the benediction.

Pastors in Conference.

In spite of its distance from the Convention halls and the lateness of the hour, the fine chapel of Vanderbilt University received a noble company of about two hundred Christian Endeavor pastors, who met to discuss some of the many problems pressing upon them in their guidance of their young folks.

It was fitting that the first Christian Endeavor pastor should direct the Conference. Dr. Clark first called upon Rev. Howard Agnew Johnston, D.D., of Chicago, to speak upon the pastor's relation to his Endeavor society. "If a society does not do good work," said he, "I ask first of all, 'What is the matter with the pastor?'" He punctured the plea of some pastors that they have n't time to attend the Christian Endeavor meetings. "What would you think," he asked, "of the superintendent of a great establishment who never entered one of its most important departments?"

Treasurer Shaw then told, from a layman's standpoint, how a pastor can win his Endeavorers. He declared that the reason why his own pastor of former days, Dr. Clark, had been so successful in drawing the young people was because he always trusted them.

The last part of the conference was spent in a very earnest discussion of the Graduate Department, following an address by Prof. Amos R. Wells, who also led the discussion. It is safe to say that in scores of churches this advance movement will be introduced as the result of that eager conference. Let our year's motto, pastors, be this: "Every young Christian trained, and every trained young Christian used."

CHRISTIAN CITIZENSHIP CONFERENCE.

This conference was held at the close of one of the most interesting meetings of the Convention and just after the testimony meeting of the "Comrades of the Quiet Hour." The meeting was well attended, and was opened by the chairman, Judge Anson S. Taylor, of Washington, D. C., stating that it seemed almost a pity to have to come down from the mount upon which we had been standing, but we should remember that Peter, James, and John had to come down from the Mount where they had been with Jesus, to attend to the affairs of life; so must we attend to the things that make for the advancement of his kingdom.

The principal topics discussed and emphasized in the conference were that of electing Christian men to office; that the saloon, "the greatest enemy of Christ and the Church" must go; that there could be no Christian citizenship in the person that makes, sells, or uses as a beverage alcoholic liquors; that politics should not be given over to the saloon element; that as Christians we should in all things seek to promote the reign of whatsoever things are true, honest, just, pure, lovely, and of good report.

FRIDAY EVENING.

Hall Williston.

THAT STORMY EVENING.

ON Friday evening came the expected storm, with its grateful coolness. The audience in Hall Williston enjoyed a very rich programme, in spite of clattering raindrops, sharp lightning, and the reverberations of thunder. Mr. Excell led the singing, and Rev. James Bond, of Nashville, conducted the opening devotional exercises. Dr. Clark added value to the badge banners by his reminiscences of their history. It has been decided not to be quite fair to pit our well-organized States against foreign lands with great room for the extension of Christian Endeavor, and so the banners for the greatest net increase in the number of societies are henceforth to be contested for only in the United States and Canada. England has held that for Young People's, and Ohio for Junior, societies. Pennsylvania, the banner-grabbing State, already the possessor of three banners, got both of these, and President McCrory received them most happily for his union. About seventy Endeavorers from the Keystone State stood before him while he spoke, Secretary Macdonald smiling at their head. "There's a royal banner given for display," they sung, and then an enterprising young man struck up "Home again, home again, from a foreign shore."

"Have n't you got more than belongs to you?" asked Dr. Clark, as Dr. McCrory marched proudly off with his booty. A search revealed the fact that the enterprising Pennsylvanian had carried off a third banner. "Oh, that's a little one," was Dr. McCrory's apology.

It was the banner for the greatest proportionate increase in societies, held last year by Ireland, and now handed over to South Africa, won by a growth in the year of from 22 to 110 societies,— four hundred per cent. The accredited delegate from Cape Colony could not reach the Convention in time. It would have done him good to see the show of hands by which we promised our prayers for the noble work in the antipodes.

Spain has held the banner for the greatest proportionate increase in Junior societies, and it required only a hint to draw out generous applause for our Spanish brothers and sisters in Christian Endeavor with their twelve Junior societies. India has won the banner by a growth of from 100 to 433 Junior societies in the year. Our delegates from India received it,— Miss Coleman from North India, and, from South India, Rev. W. I. Chamberlain, to whom the cause of Christian Endeavor in India is supremely indebted. The latter declared that if the United States expected to get the banner from India, it would not be Pennsylvania that would do it, but the Christian Endeavor Union of Hawaii or of the Philippines.

Two addresses of deep thought and profound eloquence closed the session. One was by that new trustee from the Disciples, Rev. F. D. Power, D.D., of Washington. He discussed the race problem, liquor problem, problems of missions, of reaching the masses, of Christian union, and found everywhere that the gospel is the key to all problems.

The other speaker was Dr. Barrows, from the beginning a staunch friend of Christian Endeavor, a man in whose well-deserved fame all Endeavorers rejoice. No man on earth could more appropriately treat the theme on which he spoke, "The Brotherhood of Nations." The fusillade of the storm finally got the better even of his clarion voice, and his address was broken in two, while Mr. Excell kept us all good-humoredly singing, and a brisk impromptu social went on. At length the storm abated somewhat, and the eloquent Chicagoan completed his brilliant oration, one of the finest ever presented to a Christian Endeavor convention.

Address by Rev. F. D. Power, D.D.,
Washington, D. C.
PRESENT-DAY PROBLEMS.

The gospel is the key to all the problems that confront our civilization. There are problems and problems. There is the question with so many curious souls, "Where did Cain get his wife?" and the still vaster inquiry, "How did sin come into the world?" Thousands of good people have time to worry over the problem of the beginning of the 20th century, whether January 1, 1900, or January 1, 1901.

Whatever be the solution of these questions, the 20th century will have some others of vastly greater practical import, which must be met. They are carried over from our time; they confront the Church to-day.

I. Here is the race problem. We have a land which is sought as an asylum by the oppressed of all nations. We have distinct races living side by side on American soil, with characteristics which arouse from time to time serious antagonism. We have anarchism and socialism, strikes and riots which sometimes threaten our social fabric with destruction. We have a diabolical gospel of hate preached in our great centres of population as well as a gospel of love and good-will. Questions arise here that demand for their solution all the patriotism, wisdom, and devotion of the Church of Christ. They will not be settled by legislation. Our Solons are not equal to it. Macaulay prophesied the overthrow of the American republic in the twentieth century because its Constitution had too much sail and too little ballast. Something must supply this want. The Gospel of Jesus Christ will satisfy all conditions of this race question. So we say of foreign populations, Let them come so long as they conform to our republican institutions and Christian civilization. America belongs not to us but to God. The immigrants of 1620 have no right to say to the immigrants of 1898," You shall not come." So we say of the Indian or Chinaman or negro, Give him a man's chance. Honor the manhood that is in him. "Except you guard the rights of the humblest serf that walks your shores, you cannot preserve the rights of England's proudest peer," said Burke in the English parliament. So we say of all classes and races, Treat them as God's creatures. Show them the Christ. Meet the stranger at Castle Garden with the gospel. "Honor all men." "God made of one blood all the nations of men." "The Gospel is the power of God unto salvation to every one that believeth, to the Jew first and also to the Greek."

II. Here is the social problem. All men are discussing social reform. Robert Louis Stevenson represents four tramps under a bramble-bush, propounding schemes to set the world right. They all agreed the world must be changed. "We must abolish property," said one. "We must abolish marriage," said the second. "We must abolish God," said the third. "I wish we could abolish work," said the fourth. "Do not let us get beyond practical politics," said the first. "The first thing is to reduce men to a common level." "The first thing," said the second, "is to give freedom to the sexes." "The first thing," said the third, "is to find out how to do it." "The first step," said the first, "is to abolish the Bible." "The first step," said the second, "is to abolish the laws." "The first step," said the third, "is to abolish mankind."

A new science, Christian Sociology, has come to the front. The Church is learning that it has to do with the bodies as well as the souls of men. Jesus fed the hungry, healed the sick, strengthened the infirm. He distributed food by miracle, to 5,000 at one time, and had baskets filled with what was left and taken to those not present. Out of 36 recorded miracles, 24 were for physical relief. He gives us the test in judgment, "I was an hungered, and ye gave me meat; I was thirsty, and ye gave me drink." "The Church in which the love of Jesus lives," said a German writer, "must see and relieve the humblest until Jesus is recognized again as king by the proletariat." Practical Christianity deals with human nature as a whole. To the Christian Church all that concerns man's material surroundings must be matters of vital concern. All questions of capital and labor, of pauperism and crime, of anarchism and communism, of sweatshops and slums, social discontent, violence, and revolution, are questions for our investigation and solution.

The Church is giving great attention to this problem to-day. It is reviving the lost office of the Good Samaritan, and while mindful of the temple service, has oil and wine, and a friendly inn for the fellow half-dead on the road from Jericho to Jerusalem. Christians are asking what Christ's attitude toward the aspiring, struggling, suffering masses would be if he were to appear among them; whether God or Mammon shall reign; whether equity and mercy, or selfishness and cupidity shall be dominant; whether the "earth is the Lord's and the fulness thereof," and as such is the common inheritance of all his children, or whether a few who want it shall claim it.

The trouble with us has been the idolatry of gold. The Englishman expressed it when in the chaste dialect of his little island he declared we were "too beastly prosperous." With the material power of wealth come gigantic speculations; monopolies, trusts, and combines, gambling with the daily bread of millions, great corporations that buy up government itself; the monstrous liquor traffic, blighting homes, breaking hearts, breeding crimes; extravagant display, awakening an envy that soon culminates in awful hate; misuse of means by Christian men and women in refusing to use it for God and humanity. "They that will be rich fall into temptation and a snare and many hurtful and foolish lusts which drown men in perdition."

What is the responsibility of the Church here? She must preach the gospel to every creature. She must go out into the highways and hedges and compel them to come in. She must teach the rich, "Take heed and beware of covetousness." She must be peacemaker, mediator between rich and poor, between capital and labor. She must see to it that the kingdom of heaven is as leaven that leaveneth the whole lump of human society. She must never, never, never suffer her mouth to be stopped by gags of gold. She must give her sympathy to flesh and blood, rather than dollars and cents. The solution of all the problems of sociology will come with the application of Christ's doctrine of human brotherhood, "the realization of the divine ideal in the affairs of men when it may be said, not only that an injury to one is the concern of all, but that the good of all is the constant concern of every one."

"The Golden Rule of Christ will bring the golden age of man." Then may we say with Browning: —

> "The year's at the Spring,
> And day's at the morn;
> Morning's at seven;
> The hillside's dew pearled:
> The lark's on the wing;
> The snail's on the thorn;
> God's in his Heaven —
> All's right with the world."

III. Here is the drink problem. We talk of hard times when it is estimated that Great Britain's drink bill is $700,000,000 a year, or an annual cost of $90 for every family, and Christian America spends $1,200,000,000, or $85 to every family, counting five persons to a home. Never was there a greater need for a prayerful consideration of this great living issue. Statesmen, philanthropists, Christians, economists, thinkers, and workers of every class must wrestle with this gigantic problem. Whether of the individual or of the nation we ask, "Who hath woe? who hath sorrow? who hath contention? who hath babblings? who hath wounds without a cause? who hath redness of eyes?" the answer comes, "They that tarry long at the wine. They that seek mixed wine."

The Bureau of Statistics of one of our first States — Massachusetts — made important and impartial investigations in 1869, and tells us of 3,320 paupers cared for during the year in State institutions, 65 per cent of the total number were addicted to the use of liquors. Of 26,672 convictions in the State for all crimes, 66 per cent were for drunkenness alone; in 22,000 out of the 26,000 drinking habits brought about the condition which led to the crime. In 1,836 cases of insanity, 36 per cent were users of liquors.

There is an awful leprosy upon us. There is a tyranny of one worse than the Turk, a slavery a hundred-fold more savage than that which bound the negro, fastened upon our body politic. We have licensed hell. We grant the devil, for a consideration, absolute freedom to produce misery and profligacy, cruelty and wickedness, disgrace and social demoralization; to transform the creatures of heaven into the felon, the harlot, the pauper, and the madman. We have permitted an organized satanic despotism to be reared in our midst, which has boundless resources, moves forward with gigantic strides, crushes millions of victims, inflames society with all the passions of the pit. It is the school of anarchy, the breeding-ground of criminals, the nursery of woe, the sworn foe of the Church. Economically, politically, religiously, this is the problem.

To meet it the conscience of the world must be awakened. Nothing will do but the total extinction of the saloon. We must smash the enemy.

You remember the battle of Manila Bay. It was in the black of night when Gridley, of the flagship *Olympia*, signalled to the admiral, "We are approaching the entrance."

"Steam ahead!" came the admiral's response.

Again the *Olympia* reports, "We are coming to the part of the entrance supposed to be mined."

"Steam ahead!" was the admiral's order.

Then a flash from the heights and a boom from a great gun. Again the signal: "The batteries of Cavite have opened fire."

"Steam ahead!" came the admiral's answer.

On the squadron went, under batteries, over mines, into the heart of the bay; and as the dawn broke, there stood the American fleet in battle array. flying the Stars and Stripes, facing the frowning forts and warships, the bands playing the "Star-Spangled Banner." Then came the conflict and the victory.

So must we crush the saloon, smother its guns, pulverize it. This is not the devil's world, and he must know it. "The hand pierced on Calvary is on the helm of the universe. The Church of the crowned Conqueror over death and the grave is moving on, conquering and to conquer, and all the foes of Jesus Christ must lie in sweet submission at his feet." The cross is the solution of this problem.

> "Still thy love, O Christ, arisen,
> Yearns to reach those souls in prison;
> Thro' all the depths of sin and loss,
> Sinks the plummet of thy cross.
> Never yet abyss was found
> Deeper than the cross could sound."

!IV. Here is the missionary problem. Millions of money in the hands of Christians, hundreds of thousands going for luxuries and amusements, and $5,000,000 a year set apart to carry the gospel to one billion of heathen people. "At no time during the half-century now closing," says Dr. Pierson, "have missions to the heathen been at greater peril of utter collapse." Two-thirds of the world's population are Moslems, Pagans, and Agnostics. Are Christian missions a failure? By no means. The world is an occupied field. Every race is being taught, and all nations hear in their own tongues the wonderful works of God. The gospel radiates from thousands of mission centres. Scores of boards, thousands of trained workers, with tens of thousands of native helpers, record hundreds of thousands of converts and millions of adherents. Mountains are dwindling, paths are straightening, gates are opening. The voice of the muezzin grows faint from his minaret; the triple Brahma trembles on his throne of caste; India, and China, and Japan, and even Africa, give promise of a Christian future. Missions a failure? No, and yes.

Our work is a failure in comparison to what it should be. Less than a tithe of the annual income of Protestant Christendom would carry the gospel within a year victoriously to the ends of the earth. Less than a tithe of the annual income of even American Protestants would have made before this the fruit of all lands to shake like Lebanon.

Jesus says, "Go ye into all the world and preach the gospel unto every creature." Is this the great commission or not? Does the great world lying beyond us need the gospel or not? Are we going to give all nations the blessings of the kingdom or not? We will never do it as we ought to do it, by doing it as we now seek to do it. Hear again the cross is the solution — the cross! the cross! The Church must learn at the feet of the Master. Labors, privations, sacrifices, perils, such as belonged to the first disciples, the Church must experience. The spirit of Gethsemane and of Calvary must come upon us. More of the cross must the twentieth century know, more than the nineteenth has ever known, if this great problem is ever to find solution.

V. Here is the problem of reaching the masses. That there are multitudes of our people who never enter our churches, yea, who are even hostile to our churches, none can deny. Sunday newspapers, Sunday excursions, Sunday wheeling, Sunday dissipations of every kind attract their thousands, and the gospel message fails to reach them.

What has been the trouble? We have built our churches in the fashionable quarter. We have forgotten the slums. We have not represented the Christ who declared his commission to be "to heal the broken-hearted, to give sight to the blind, to set at liberty the captive, and to preach the gospel to the poor." We have suppressed the laity. We have failed to utilize that mighty agency which means two-thirds of the force of the Church, — consecrated Christian womanhood. We have held the young in the leash. We have gotten away from that condition of the Church in Jerusalem when, scattered abroad, the disciples went everywhere preaching the word. We have reached out a gloved hand through the committee or the mission chapel. We have not gone personally to men and shown that sublime altruism which has led a wealthy, cultured, and mighty people of seventy millions to lay themselves at the feet of a few poor, miserable, starved, oppressed, down trodden Cubans and say, "You shall be free. If it costs our best blood and treasure, you shall be free!"

Thank God, we are learning. Our men, women, young people, and children as never before are coming to the help of the Lord, to the help of the Lord against the mighty. We have latent power enough in the Church, like the imprisoned sunlight in the beds of coal beneath the surface of the earth, which, freed, makes our steam and electricity and heat, to reach all humanity. We have only to let it out. A tart, dark-browed, rasping, close-fisted old brother was singing lustily, "There is sunshine in my soul to-day," and his wife heard him from the cellar, where she was splitting kindling, and called up to him, "Let some of it out, Silas!" We are letting a little sunshine out. By the masses we reach the masses. And who will deny to this great movement credit for the mighty impulse it has given to the work of the individual for the individual, the soul for the soul, the mass for the mass?

VI. Finally, here is the problem of Christian union. All other problems we may say will be solved with the solution of this one. United Christendom would mean the reconciliation of races, the harmony of society, the overthrow of rum, the conquest of the heathen world for Christ, the evangelization of the masses.

How is it to-day? To say nothing of the great Latin and Greek Churches, in Christian America we have 143 schools of Christians, divisions representing from 25 members to 6,000,000. One was excluded from the census because it numbered but 21 souls! It was to a united Church the grace of Pentecost was given. By a united Church the Roman Empire in three centuries was brought to the foot of the Cross. "I pray not for these alone," said Christ, "but for all them that believe on me through their word, that they all may be one, as thou, Father, art in me and I in thee, that they may be one in us, that the world may believe that thou hast sent me." "I beseech you, brethren, by the name of our Lord Jesus Christ, that you all speak the same thing, and that there be no divisions among you, but that ye be perfectly joined together in the same mind and in the same judgment."

Our divisions are strangling us. Our means are wasted, our power neutralized, by an unholy rivalry. The world can never be converted by a divided Church. A common Christendom with a common faith, practice, and aim would mean the fulfilment of the prayer, "Thy kingdom come!" The gospel can and will correct everything that needs correcting. Let men come to the common foundation laid in Zion and they will build up one Church, bright as the sun, fair as the moon, and terrible as an army with banners.

The twentieth century will solve these difficulties. Some one said to Capernicus, "If the world were constituted as you say, Venus would have phases like the moon." Capernicus answered, "God will be so good as that an answer to this difficulty will be found." And lo! Galileo came, turned his glass on the planet, and the phases of Venus were discovered.

Our divisions are another of our problems. They must be healed. The Church has been discordant. Her mighty harmonies have been unheard.

A boy six years old was sailing with his father down the Danube. All day long they had been sailing past crumbling ruins, frowning castles, cloisters hid away among the crags, towering cliffs, quiet villages nestled in sunny valleys, deep gorges that opened back from the gliding river. At night they stopped at a cloister, and the father took the boy into the chapel to see the organ. It was the first he had ever seen. His face lit up with delight, and every motion and attitude expressed a wonderful reverence.

"Father," said the boy, "let me play!"

The father complied. The boy pushed aside the stool; and, when his father had filled the bellows, stood upon the pedals. How the deep tones woke the sombre stillness of the old church! The organ seemed some great uncouth creature, roaring for very joy at the caresses of the marvelous child.

The monks eating their supper heard it, and dropped knives and forks in astonishment. The organist of the brotherhood was among them, but he had never played with such power. They listened; some crossed themselves; the prior arose and hastened into the chapel; the others followed; but when they looked into the organ-loft, lo! there was no organist to be seen, though the deep tones still massed themselves in new harmonies and made the stone arches thrill with their power.

"It is the devil!" cried one of the monks, drawing closer to his companions.

"It is a miracle!" said another.

When the boldest of them mounted to the organ-loft he stood lost in amazement; there was the tiny figure treading from pedal to pedal, clutching at the keys above with his little hands, gathering handfuls of those wonderful chords as if they were violets, and flinging them out behind him. He heard nothing, saw nothing, besides; his eyes beamed; his whole face lighted up with impassioned joy. Louder and fuller rose the harmonies, streaming forth in swelling billows, till at last they seemed to reach a sunny shore on which they broke. Then a whispering ripple of melody lingered a moment in the air like the last murmur of a wind harp and all was still. It was Mozart.

Who shall say that the touch of consecrated young Christian manhood and womanhood shall not under God bring out the full, rich, united harmony of the Church, and thus fill the world with his praise?

Address by Rev. John Henry Barrows, D.D.,
Chicago, Ill.
THE BROTHERHOOD OF NATIONS.

When Christ taught his people to say "Our Father" he laid down the abiding principle and announced the immortal fact of human brotherhood, and whenever and wherever Christ's finger, dipped as it were in his own blood, writes "Our Father" on the human heart he blots out the horror and heathenism of caste. Whenever we know Christ, in whom divine Fatherhood and human brotherhood have their proof and explanation, we know ourselves as members of a universal family, and all men as children with us of the same God.

I believe in the nation, and in the divinely appointed mission of every people. But nations are groups of families, of brethren, and the Christian attitude of people toward each other is fraternal. "Brotherhood" is a word falling lightly from our lips, sometimes with a failure on our part to realize that it is the greatest word in our modern life. It is the key that unlocks all our problems and solves all our difficulties. It expresses the attitude and sentiments which one man should hold to another; which classes and peoples should sustain to different classes and peoples. It is the solution of all our social and industrial difficulties. When the rich and the poor, the high and the lowly, recognize and realize brotherhood, underneath the firmament of God's fatherhood, then dawns the golden age; then breaks the millennial morning.

The brightest fact in our national life to-day is this: that at last our people, East and West, North and South, engaged in a righteous war, realize, and nowhere more gratefully realize than here, in this beautiful city and at this glorious Convention, that beneath our starry flag we are a united people and brothers all, the fellow-countrymen of Hobson and Dewey, of Fitzhugh Lee and President McKinley.

I love all influences that break down barriers of national exclusiveness and make human souls open-windowed and fraternal toward each other. Some things are great enough to do this — great literature, for example, and great art. There is a picture in Dresden which draws the feet of the children of all climes and continents across the threshold of the little room glorified by the Sistine Madonna. Great music works a similar miracle, and we listen with enchanted admiration to an orchestra playing on the same evening the music of Germany and France, of Russia and England, of Italy, Africa, and America. Heroism is not national and local in its power, and when a deed of chivalry is performed in the harbor of Santiago a responsive thrill goes through a hundred million hearts in a score of nationalities, and that brave Christian boy, Lieutenant Hobson, becomes a noble brother of the noblest spirits of all mankind. And so pre-eminently the great sacrifice on Calvary has become the moral lodestone of the race, and lifted on the Cross the Son of Man is drawing all men toward himself.

Now to me one of the supreme values of the Christian Endeavor society is its international character. This magnificent meeting is the gathering up of the threads of life and love, running out, not only to every State of America but to every province of Canada, and to every part of Great Britain, to the capitals of continental Europe, to the wide-reaching realms where Christendom comes into contact with Islam and the more ancient religions of Asia. The lines go out from this Christian centre to brethren in Australia and New Zealand, in southern Africa and in the isles of Japan. A composite photograph of the national representatives of Christian Endeavor would show us the races of mankind and womankind the world over. In a journey around the world I realized that the work which God inspired Francis E. Clark to begin and carry on with such wisdom and success is one of the grandest agencies of a true cosmopolitanism ever launched into history. In Cairo I attended a Christian Endeavor meeting where seven nationalities were represented. In Delhi, Lahore, and Madras I came to feel that Christian Endeavor is to have a large and splendid work in India, a land where no progress can be made until barriers are broken down,— barriers of caste and of race and of religion and of sectionalism, some of them centuries old and almost mountain high.

Right now, in the midst of our just war with Spain, I am willing to affirm that one of the chief needs of humanity is to feel the interdependence of peoples, and to realize their fraternal relations one to another. Steam and electricity are making this old planet, our common home, smaller and smaller. The sea no longer divides; it connects. Australia is nearer America to-day than the

Pacific coast to Boston sixty years ago. God says to us in his providence and by his Word, "Ye are members of one family. Love each other. Be not quarrelsome." But if one big brother continues for four centuries to cruelly oppress and brutally rob some of the weaker members of the household, if Cubans and Greeks and Armenians and Philippinos are trampled and crushed and fleeced and outraged by Turk and Spaniard, God, who works through agencies, may commission Great Britain and the United States to right these wrongs, and to overthrow the dominion of fraud and violence. Whatever virtues may have belonged to Spanish character, the spirit of humaneness toward the weak, of kindness and brotherhood, has not reached a conspicuous development, and will not until different ideals are lifted before the Spanish people and vastly better Christian agencies are at work among them. Lord Salisbury tells us that there are dying nations, and not all of them are pagan. You and I well know that if the influences which have made Great Britain and America what they are had prevailed for centuries in the Spanish peninsula there would be far less to deplore to-day in the spirit and conduct of our Spanish brothers. We are to love our enemies.

There was a time when the nations were in a chronic state of war, and each nation looked upon other nations as its foes. That time has passed, and to-day we are talking of alliances, we are holding international congresses, and are dreaming of a "parliament of man, a federation of the world." We are realizing that God is educating the race through the races. We are making world journeys, and some of us are trying to find out and appreciate the good qualities of other peoples. One of the advantages of extensive travel is that it teaches us to care for the changing life and fortunes, not only of Germany, Italy, and France, but also of suffering India, populous China, and progressive Japan. We Americans must be willing to admire things that are not American and familiar with our ways of thinking and doing. It is supposed to be characteristic of some of our countrymen abroad that they turn up their noses even at the Alps, because they are not so high as the Rockies; at the Rhine, because it is not so large as the Mississippi; at some of the finest buildings of Europe, because they are not so tall as some of the business-houses of New York and Chicago. They complain of Cologne Cathedral because it took so long to build it. And one man is said to have complained of St. Peter's that the people of Rome could fill it only once in a generation, whereas Niagara Falls would fill it in five minutes! Some Americans make themselves ridiculous by their obstreperous boastfulness, and succeed only in bringing reproach upon their own country. We were told in Calcutta by an Englishman that he travelled with an American of a very amusing sort, who always found fault with even the most stupendous things. They went together to the Pyramids, and the Englishman said, "You must acknowledge that these are wonderful monuments, vast, imposing relics of Egyptian antiquity, outlasting everything else which man has builded, looking out upon the Libyan sands, which have not succeeded in covering them, watching over the changing civilizations and rising and falling dynasties and peoples who have held the valley of the Nile." "Yes," said the American, "they are very great; but then you know there ain't no demand for pyramids."

My companion was not of that sort, and together we succeeded, during our fifteen months of absence from home, in finding a thousand things, both in art and nature and in human life, to kindle our enthusiasm and call forth wonder, affection, and delight.

I have discovered that the greatest of all empires is that of human kindness, and through my world-journey I have come to a new appreciation of the lovable qualities which exist in the various peoples of the earth. It is easy and common enough to criticize the sins and foibles of humanity, discoverable everywhere, in all cities, in all nations, and in all hearts. There is much of the untamed animal in man, and throughout Asia one feels that the struggle for existence, the effort to get food enough to barely sustain life, is the most serious of facts. But even in Asia, where tyranny, ignorance, superstition, idolatry, have wrought their most evil effects, there are at least superficial elements in human nature which are agreeable. A true heart must at least pity, if it cannot admire.

But I have found among the inferior races traits of character which I have wished to engraft upon the sturdier Anglo-Saxon manhood. Missionaries who have lived a score of years in China report to me that there is a splendid material in the rough-fibred race. Most travellers are charmed by the politeness of the Japanese. And I must say of the Hindus that their manners have a graciousness and a grace which are a rebuke to the domineering and abrupt ways too often found among Englishmen and Americans.

Some of the finest characters whom I have met, some of the souls most responsive to the claims of brotherhood, were among the better people in the French capital. It is not necessary to recount the noble traits which one easily discovers in the Germans, and I found the Irish and the Italians to be almost the most lovable of European peoples. Old Scotland won my heart, not only in Caledonia herself, but as she is represented by the grand Scotch missionaries whom I met in India. In travelling around the globe I met of course the various representatives of the British Isles, and gained a deep love for the genuineness and strength of the Englishman, whom I have found to be one of the most hospitable of men. The chief complaint which we Americans are apt to make of our European brethren is their ignorance of our own country. One English lady said to my daughters in Germany, " Are you from America? I am always getting Africa and Australia mixed up in my mind." A German lady said to them that she knew nothing of America except that we had snakes in our houses. A German student told me that the only knowledge he had of American children had come from reading " Helen's Babies " and " Peck's Bad Boy." Another German student said that he understood that in America the Fourth of July was celebrated only by the Republicans. One Englishman confessesed that he did not know what the Fourth of July celebration was about.

In going around the globe I have sailed beneath many flags, which I have come to love: the tri-color of France, the black, white, and red of Germany. I have seen the flags of some peoples who are not very dear: the star and crescent on the waters of the Bosphorus, the yellow banner of Spain on the Mediterranean, and the dragon-flag of China on the waters of the Yellow Sea. But I have rarely been out of sight of two flags that represent much of the future of mankind: the starry banner of America and the meteor flag of England. The great majority of those before me are of course Americans.

My heart is full, not only of Christian cosmopolitanism, but also of a deeper and truer patriotism, and I wish to remind you that it is the mission of America to promote brotherhood among the nations. And I wish to express my confidence, reborn out of what I have seen in the Orient and out of what I have seen in more than thirty thousand miles of travel in nearly all parts of our country, wherein during the last twelve months I have been able to touch the vital centres of American thought and character, — my confidence that this land, " to human nature dear," this land which is not unbeloved by God; that this country of ours, for which the ages have travailed in birth; that this republic, filled with God-fearing and man-loving people whose hearts respond to the calls of humanity and suffer " wherever Freedom lifts her cry of pain;" that this nation, proud and grateful for a history reaching from Plymouth Harbor to Manila Bay, is no longer to be treated as a foundling, to be nursed in a wilderness of solitude and isolation, but is the strongest and most chivalrous knight equipped for valiant service in the kingdom of God to be seen on the face of the earth. I have felt the pulse of national Christian conventions; I have had my Americanism re-fortified; I have entered the homes of men and women who pray to God for our country, — the home of many a Christian pastor East and West, and the home of the Christian President in Washington; I have talked with scholars, statesmen, far-sighted editors, university professors, devoted women whose hearts are aflame with the purest patriotism; I have faced many thousands of college students, and Christian ministers, and candidates for the ministry; I have conversed with the Grand Old Man of Andover. Professor Park, who has surveyed from his quiet watchtower on that sacred hill as much of the progress of mankind as has been seen by the Grand Old Man of Hawarden; I have stood by the graves of

Jonathan Edwards and others of the mighty American dead, as more than a year ago I stood by the graves of American missionaries in India, beneath the rustle of the palm-trees and the light of the Southern Cross; I have seen a puissant nation, rousing herself from sleep and shaking once more her invincible locks, and I wish to tell you that those timid and cautious teachers who are warning us to beware of our destiny and shrink back from it misconceive and underrate the mighty and noble spirit of the American people.

We have a mission, for we are a nation. Our destiny was wrapped up, De Tocqueville wrote, in the first Puritan that landed on our shores, a destiny vitally interwoven with Christian faith and the extension in all lands of the dominion of the Cross. The rightfulness of our separate existence is not questioned by us nor by many in Great Britain. The Fourth of July has been celebrated in London as well as here. It has long been celebrated in the Hawaiian and Caroline Islands. Some critics say that we ought to have remained a part of the British Empire, but I think that Providence was wiser. I cannot believe that this nation, representing, as Emerson has said, the sentiment and future of mankind; that this republic, the dome of whose capitol in Washington Castelar once called the "summit of the modern world;" that this land, whose unity and independence appear to have been engraven by God's almighty hand on the trend of the coast-lines and the courses of the hills and the paths of the rivers; that this continent, destined, as Mr. Gladstone has said, to contain 500,000,000 of people speaking the language of Milton and Burke, living beneath the institutions of Anglo-Saxon freedom, was ever meant to be the permanent dependency of that wondrous isle which Shakespeare saw and loved, set like a jewel in the silver circlet of the German Ocean. But I shall rejoice if, in the interests of peace, liberty, untrammelled commerce, and Biblical Christianity, there should be a league of heart, a moral alliance, the friendliest mutual understanding between the two peoples who dwell beneath the Stars and Stripes of America and the Union Jack of dear old England. The best service which you and I can render to mankind, my fellow-countrymen, is to make America as Christian as possible. The sight of other nations and other religions has brought me a deeper conviction than ever that Christianity, the religion of redemption and enlightenment, the religion which alone gives peace to the sin-sick soul and brightens with hope the future of individuals and peoples, is the best possession which America holds for herself and is commissioned to impart to others.

Before my faith the Christian religion looms up a glorious mountain of heaven. One morning, looking out from my room in Yokohama, I saw not only Mississippi Bay, and Treaty Point, and the ships of that harbor through which a half-century ago the regenerating forces of the Western world began to flow in upon Japan, but, looking forty miles away, I beheld the peerless beauty and majesty of the sacred mountain, cleaving the blue sky like a snowy wedge; and so Christianity rises before my imagination and my reason, as the bright and blessed mountain of God. About its feet are fertile farms and prosperous homes, such as are found only in the beneficent domain of Christian influence; in its heart are the treasures of all wisdom and all knowledge; down its sides flow the streams which have made European civilization possible, and which are yet to turn the moral wilderness of Asia into the garden of the Lord; about its summit play the golden splendors of millennial mornings, and it dominates all other systems, even as the snow-white and spotless cone of Fujiyama dominates the islands and the seas, the rice-covered plains, and the forest-crowned hills of beautiful Japan.

Auditorium Endeavor.

Opening the session in Auditorium Endeavor, the Fisk Jubilee Singers sang two pieces tandem, to save the time consumed by the inevitable encore. Then the male chorus rendered a splendid selection under Mr. Foster's leadership.

It was a real fraternal boon to have General Secretary Du Bose, of the Epworth League, to conduct the devotional exercises.

When Commander Booth-Tucker's tall form and scarlet waistcoat loomed up above the desk to speak on "Christian Heroism," the suggestion of Chairman J. Z. Tyler that he who was to speak was himself one of the best-living examples of heroic Christian service was responded to by the audience with generous applause.

Address by Commander F. DeL. Booth-Tucker,
New York City.

CHRISTIAN HEROISM.

Picture the scene, the wind-swept lake, the heaving waters, wave chasing wave, and each seeming eager to swallow the little craft in which the disciples were straining every nerve to reach the destination where with morning's break they expected to meet Jesus at his next great convention.

They could not tell how he would keep the appointment. But he had made it, and that was enough. They must be there on time, or they might find that he had come and gone. No palace steamer ploughed those waters. No Pullman sleepers hurried their pilgrim passengers from end to end of Palestine. The only boat available had been booked by the disciples themselves. But the meeting-place had been chosen, and they knew that Jesus would be there at the appointed hour.

"The wind was contrary." When has it not been contrary to the soul that sincerely seeks its Saviour? There may be differences in degree, but the world's currents of wind and tide are always in the opposite direction for those who start definitely and determinedly to meet Jesus at the Cross.

Doubtless you have come to this Convention with this object in view. If each Endeavorer could be asked the why and wherefore of his presence here on this occasion, from the president and secretary down to the last enrolled member, he would reply, "Sir, we would see Jesus!" We cherish in our hearts the hope that whoever else may be absent *he* will be *here*. We have seen him before. We desire to see him *again*, in a nearer and a clearer sense. Our souls hunger and thirst for a new and fuller revelation of his will.

On the rough surface of the storm-tossed lake, in the midst of their toil, during the darkness of the night, just when he was least expected but most sorely needed, Jesus flashed out upon the troubled waters of the Sea of Galilee. Swathed in electric beams that dazzled their eyes, allowing them a glimpse of the divinity that had shrouded itself behind his perfect humanity, he shone forth so unlike his ordinary self that they trembled and "cried out" at the revelation of his glory.

Have you ever had such an experience in your soul? Has Jesus flashed in upon you on the tidal wave of some great storm? You expected him at the end of your journey. Stroke after stroke you dipped your oars, it may be, into the raging waters of opposition and sorrow. But he met you half-way, long before you expected him, yet just when you needed him the most! Tell me, was not the vision of his glorious presence worth all the sorrow that had gone before? Were you not glad *then* that you had embarked when and where and how he constrained you to, though at the time it might have seemed so hard to flesh and blood — indeed, almost so unreasonable?

That little band of chosen heroes, what a thrill of holy happiness went through their hearts as the voice of Jesus sang in silvery tones above the storm-wind's blast! They were almost glad the tempest whistled and howled so loudly through the rigging, for did it not make them the more certain that none but the voice of Jesus could make itself heard above so fierce a storm? Like clarion call of Gabriel it flung its blessed assurances across the waves. They would rather be with Jesus on the raging sea, their garments drenched, their boat

Address by Commander F. DeL. Booth-Tucker.

on its beam ends, every muscle aching with the long night of toil, than be the owners of Herod's castle on the coast with its marble colonnades and Roman furniture.

Nearer and nearer the radiant form of Christ draws to the billow-beaten boat. Peter has given the order for the rowers to back water — the helm is hard aport; the crested waves sweep them nearer to Jesus. Soon he will be aboard. And yet, to at least one of those impatient souls each moment seems an hour. Why wait? Jesus has come half-way to meet them. Why not go the other half to meet him? See Peter balanced on the taffrail of the boat. One brawny hand grasps the rigging, the other is placed like a trumpet to his mouth. He is afraid the Lord may not hear. But the faintest whispers of a true heart are heard in heaven — heard before they are uttered, for are they not but the echoes of the voice of Calvary?

"If it be thou, bid me come," rings out across the waters. Should Jesus tread those waters and brave those dangers alone? No! No! Ten thousand times no! If Peter were the only one, he would be there. If he perished it should be at Jesus' side! Others desired, but only Peter dared!

Was it worth while? Anything is worth while that is dared and done for Jesus' sake. The very essence of Christian heroism is to do and dare what we might avoid. Peter might have remained in the boat with the rest of his comrades. There were a thousand arguments in favor of his doing so. It was not a question of his own salvation, that daring leap into the waters,— it was only a question of the *how much of his love!* Only! And yet it was one of his happiest and most triumphant experiences.

True, for a moment his faith faltered, and he began to sink. But the outstretched hand of Jesus lifted him above the crest of the highest wave and brought him safely to the boat.

Where are the water-walkers of this Convention? Christ calls you to walk, not over the crested waves of the Sea of Galilee, but over the heaving and storm-tossed waters of the ocean of humanity. See how they "cast up mire and dirt." The tempest rages, the winds are contrary. Through the long night of your Christian experience you have toiled in rowing and have gained but twenty or thirty furlongs in the direction where your soul desires to go. At times, it may be, it seems as though you had hardly made any progress at all. Of one thing you are satisfied: you do not belong to the five thousand listeners who merely wanted to crown Christ king in order that they might have an easy time of it and be saved the trouble of working for their daily bread — a type of Christian, alas, not yet extinct! At the command of Christ you have embarked in the boat *Salvation*. You have your hand upon the oar and are struggling to reach the appointed place.

But is there not something better still awaiting you to-day? Out of the boat of mere profession on to the tossing waters of sin, of poverty, of sorrow, of slumdom, of heathendom, he calls you to walk. You want to see Jesus, to feel his touch, to hear his voice, to realize his "Well done." It is *here* that he is to be met. It is these waters that he loves to tread. The extra risk of sacrifice are abundantly repaid, are they not, by the *extra smile?* Frederick the Great had a special Regiment of Guards into which none were admitted who were under six feet in height. Would you not like to be among the best, the most valued and most successful soldiers of the Cross, the six-footers of Calvary? "There were giants in the land in those days," the Bible tells us. Would you not love to be a spiritual giant, — one of the heroes of heaven?

Do not plead your natural timidity. Remember that what by *nature* you are *not*, by *grace* you can *become*. God has, it may be, purposely left these *gaps* in your natural disposition in order that you may turn to his grace to *fill them up*. Peter did not walk these waters by means of his stronger muscles, or his iron nerves. When he trusted to these he began to sink. But one touch of grace winged his feet and enabled him to promenade those waters just as if they had been the best asphalted boulevard of Nashville.

Heroes are manufactured, not out of natural heroes, but out of cowards by the magic alchemy of the Cross. As a rule, if you come close up to them, you will find that they are made out of the most commonplace people in the world. It does not want much *brain-power* to be *brave*. You need not be extraordinarily gifted. Your social position need not be high. Your education may be imperfect. You may be young and inexperienced — in fact a mere child. And yet in the highest sense of the word, *You*, — *You*, — *You*, — *Not somebody else, but you*, — may be a Hero of the Cross!

If you remain a coward you have no one to blame but yourself. The blood of Jesus and the fire of the Holy Ghost can make a hero out of you, not by a slow process of evolution, but by the same touch of appropriating faith as brought you into the enjoyment of Salvation.

Will you leap from the boat now and allow Christ to transform you into a water-walking Peter?

It seemed impossible that interest could reach a higher pitch, when Commander Booth-Tucker finished; but when Mr. Yarnelle threw his marvelously clear, sympathetic voice into the solo, "That Old, Old Story," hearts pulsed and swayed with a high tide of enthusiasm.

Dr. Tyler said he had never known a returned missionary who was not an enthusiast for missions, and Miss Margaret W. Leitch, of Ceylon, took but a minute to demonstrate that she was on fire with zeal for the great world fields of missions.

Address by Miss Margaret W. Leitch,
Ceylon.

THE FORWARD MOVEMENT IN MISSIONS.

Say not ye, There are yet four months and then cometh harvest? Behold I say unto you, Lift up your eyes and look on the fields, for they are white already to harvest. And he that reapeth receiveth wages, and gathereth fruit unto life eternal; that both he that soweth and he that reapeth may rejoice together. —JOHN 4: 35, 36.

This call of the Lord Jesus comes to each one of us to-day. Never were the harvest-fields so white as now; never was the need of reapers more urgent; never was the promised joy and reward more sure.

OPPORTUNITIES IN CEYLON.

When I went to Ceylon as a missionary the greatest surprise which came to me there, the thing which I found to be entirely different from what I had expected, was the wide-open doors. I had read about the poverty, the ignorance, the superstition, but I had no conception until I went there of the marvelous opportunities on every hand for Christian service. As a single example, look at the opening for work among the children. Ceylon is a great educational centre. There are, in connection with the five Protestant missionary societies working there, more than 1,200 mission schools, with a total attendance of 61,000 children who are under daily religious instruction.

I sometimes hear people in this country speak of foreign mission work with a kind of despair, saying, "It seems a hopeless task to reach those millions who are sunk in superstition." But are not those who say this forgetting the children? The children in heathen lands are not yet sunk in superstition. They do not yet know the depths of Satan. They have bright minds and eager hearts. What an opportunity to tell them of the Friend of little children; their hearts will open to his love as flowers to the sunshine. Surely the work among the children must be pleasing to him who "took up children in his arms and blessed them."

In Ceylon there are 16,000 native Christian communicants and 3,000 trained native workers. What an opportunity comes to a missionary, who is placed in the centre of a district of 50,000 or 100,000 people, to inspire the native Christians and the trained workers and direct their work!

Now look across from Ceylon to the great Empire of India. There is, at this time, a work of strategic importance to be done among the students and the educated class.

There are over six millions of students in government and mission schools, over half a million of whom are in English schools. There are five millions of English-speaking natives now in India. These, and those who are constantly increasing the number from the colleges and schools, will have more to do in shaping the educational, social, political, and religious future of the country than the other 275,000,000 combined. They will be the teachers in the schools, the editors of the newspapers, the natural and recognized leaders in every department. No effort should be spared to direct them to Christ as the Way, the Truth, and the Life.

This great student class is the most hopeful class in India. If the ranks of organized Hinduism are to be broken in this generation, here is the vulnerable point. This great class is accessible. Bring the bright, aggressive young Christian manhood of the West into daily heart contact with the young manhood of India, and there is bound to be an outcome. What a magnificent opportunity for the Church of Christ! It thrills one to think of the possibility of capturing this host for Christ.

THE NEW ERA IN CHINA.

In China the opening is equally marvelous. The Emperor has issued a royal edict calling upon the governors of the provinces to protect the missionaries against misrepresentation and violence, and declaring that the object of Christian teaching is to make men better. Through the mighty power of God, the seemingly impregnable wall of Chinese indifference is at last being broken down. The Emperor is himself greatly interested in Christian books, of which he has recently bought a large collection. The palace is favorable to Christian thought, so that it is reported the Emperor will not do work on Sunday, but suggests a service day similar to those he reads of in the Bible. The Christian magazines and papers are being everywhere read with intelligent interest, and are a power with the more intelligent men.

The provisional governments have begun to plant State institutions on the basis of Western learning. China is bound to have the new education and with it the new civilization. Shall it be a godless education and a godless civilization? To this the tireless force of missionaries answer " No."

At the present time all the great schools and colleges of China are led by missionary teachers. The students in these colleges will become the teachers in the new government schools. If the large body of students in the mission colleges can be won to Christ and enlisted in the Christianization of their native land, they will become the generals of the Christian army of New China.

THE OUTLOOK IN JAPAN.

In Japan as well the outlook is most encouraging. Dr. DeForest, a well-known missionary, writes: "These great nations of the East are now for the first time in real contact with Christian nations and Christian civilization. God, in his providence, in this fulness of time, is swinging these millions toward monotheism, and away from idolatry and paganism. There was never seen on God's earth such a rapid extension of Christian thought as is seen here among the 40,000,000 of Japan.

"I don't want to go home. My wife and children are there, but to be here, seeing this vision of God's great plan, and knowing I'm working with him in it, is infinitely better than being in our own New England, whose 'rocks and rills,' whose 'woods and templed hills,' I do not cease to love."

DELAY IS DANGEROUS.

In all parts of the mission field it is either time to sow or time to reap, and in some cases the field invites both sower and reaper at once, for there are some who need the saving message, and others who have heard and are ready for further teaching and in-gathering. If ever, in human history, delay meant danger, nay, certain disaster, it is now. If we do not sow the wide and open fields of the world with good seed, Satan will sow them with tares.

THE MEANS AVAILABLE.

God never opens a door until it is possible for his people to enter it. At the very hour when the world is open we find sufficient means placed within the hands of the Church for its evangelization. Great missionary organizations are ready to *send.* Thousands of young men and women, prepared in the universities, are being raised up by the providence of God, ready to *go. The present need is for consecrated stewardship and clearer realization of personal responsibility.*

THE NEXT STEP.

A great advance in the future may be looked for along the line of a closer tie between the workers abroad and the supporters at home. In this advance the Church Missionary Society of Great Britain, the strongest Protestant missionary society in the world, leads the way. Two years ago, when facing a deficit, they decided, instead of making a reduction in the work, to invite the society's friends to contribute special subscriptions toward the sending out of the new missionaries for the next three years. They further decided to appoint all suitable candidates, and place the responsibility for their going or remaining upon the churches. Within two weeks of the time the offer was made to churches and individuals to have their own missionaries, the support of seventy-seven missionaries was pledged.

This movement created such wide-spread interest that special booklets on the subject were prepared, and one and a quarter million copies distributed. This movement goes on with increasing momentum until the present time.

"THE FORWARD MOVEMENT."

In this country a number of the leading boards, the American Board, the Presbyterian Board, the Baptist Board, the Reformed Board, and others have adopted a similar policy, which has come to be called "The Forward Movement." Under this plan individuals, churches, Christian Endeavor societies, or groups of societies, can have their own representative on the foreign field. This method possesses marked advantages to the *supporter*, to the *missionary*, and to the *Mission Board.* To the supporter it makes the work more vivid. It is easier to follow the work of one man than a thousand. It assures the missionary of definite prayer in his behalf, and of the earnest advocacy of his work at home. The wide adoption of this method will assure the boards of a reliable financial backing.

RESULTS ACHIEVED.

In the Presbyterian Board, the salaries of 500 out of 716 missionaries are now being provided by this method. The recently appointed secretary for "The Forward Movement" of this board has during the past six months been securing salaries of individual missionaries at the rate of one a week.

In the Baptist Board the support of all the outgoing missionaries is being provided in this way. It is found that this method results in a large increase of interest, gifts, and prayers. For example, a Young People's society, which last year raised $16 for the general fund with a great effort, this year raised $300 toward the support of their own missionary and found it a much easier task. Another Young People's society which last year gave only $11.73, this year gave $524 for their own missionary, and for the new year they have pledged $1,200, the salary of two missionaries.

The secretary of one Young People's association writes: "We have found it a joy and a blessed privilege to give of our substance, that we may have a missionary and his wife who stand as our representatives preaching Christ to lost men. We find that all other departments of our work are feeling the impulse of this effort and are moving forward with greater zeal."

Quiet Hour Meeting. Gospel Tabernacle.

THE MOVEMENT IN THE COLLEGES.

The great advance in the giving of students in the higher educational institutions of this country has been made by means of this method. Twelve years ago the colleges and seminaries of this country were giving about $5,000 a year to foreign missions. Last year they gave nearly $40,000. Over one hundred institutions now support a missionary either entirely or in large part. In many cases this giving means real sacrifice. For example: forty young men in Pine Hill College, Halifax, have pledged $800 toward the support of one of their number as a missionary. Many of these students are dependent for their support upon what they earn during their vacations. The following pledge is being circulated in one institution: —

PLEDGE OF THE HEROIC MOVEMENT FOR THE SUPPORT OF MISSIONARY WORK.

I hereby declare my intention to live on the same scale that I would have to live on were I a missionary (i. e., as economically as possible, consistently with my health and usefulness), and to devote all my surplus income to the Lord's work as he may direct.

INDIVIDUALS SUPPORTING SUBSTITUTES.

The time is drawing near when many individuals will taste the joy of supporting each his own substitute in the foreign field. Even those with small means may enjoy this privilege. I know a lady who is too poor to keep a servant, but she is so rich that she is supporting one home and two foreign missionaries. A school-teacher from her salary of a thousand dollars sustains her substitute in China with five hundred. A widow in Boston, living in one room of a tenement-house, gave eight hundred dollars in the foreign-mission collection. When her pastor called and asked her how she could give so much, she said, "Here I am comfortable, and have enough, living upon two hundred dollars a year; but I do not know how I could go to meet my Lord if I lived upon the eight hundred dollars, and gave him only two hundred." A stenographer who works all day long in an office began some years ago to save her small earnings and quietly to send them out to the foreign field, until to-day, through God's blessing on her gifts, more than a thousand souls in India can look up into the face of the heavenly Father and rejoice in the possession of eternal life through Jesus Christ.

SOCIETIES SUPPORTING REPRESENTATIVES.

There must be thousands of Endeavor societies in this country which might have the joy of supporting their own representatives upon the foreign field, and upon the home field, too, for that matter. When an individual society has not sufficient strength, a group of societies could unite together for this end. Why should a society be satisfied with giving $25 if it has it in its power to give or collect $500, and so have its own missionary?

A CALL FOR COLLECTORS.

Endeavorers have a work to do not only as *givers* but as *collectors*. How is it that the average giving of Christians to the foreign mission cause is only forty cents a year per church-member? The reason for this is that while a few give largely the great majority do not give at all. It has been stated that one-third of the members of Christian churches know nothing and care nothing about missions; another third know little and care little; the remaining third know much and care much. Those who belong to this last third must not think that they have discharged their whole responsibility when they have given all the money they can give. They have further responsibility in interesting others and leading them to give. I know a lady who has little means of her own, but who has interested a large number of friends and annually collects from them $1,000, the support of two missionaries. I know a servant-girl who has interested the servants in the houses round about and annually collects from them $50.

FIELD CAMPAIGN WORK.

Young people are just beginning to realize the great possibilities within their reach as collectors. A number of students from the Arts and Medical Colleges of one denomination in Canada devoted their summer vacation last year to deputation work among the Young People's societies of that denomination throughout the Provinces. Six hundred churches or societies were visited; 60,000 people listened to the missionary appeal of these students; about twenty districts as a result have entered on systematic giving; approximately $15,000 were pledged for the board of that denomination, and the indications are that a score of missionaries will be supported on the field through the board as a result of this summer's work. These results were not achieved *without toil and sacrifice* on the part of the workers.

What was done by these students could, by God's help, be reproduced throughout the country if earnest Endeavorers who love the cause would devote themselves to the task of awakening in their churches, communities, and the societies round about them a realizing sense of the present opportunity and the responsibility of Christians with regard to it.

GOD CALLS FOR SACRIFICE.

With the world open and a thousand million of heathen and Mohammedans easily accessible, with thousands of villages actually asking for teachers and preachers, with a great company of educated and consecrated young men and women willing to go, is not God calling on his people for unusual giving and sacrifice? Heathen lands will not be evangelized in this generation if the Church continues to be so engrossed with the things of the world. Our style of living in this country is always rising. We decorate our lives till further decoration seems impossible. Our expenditure on ourselves is enormous. And over and above all expenditures for comforts and luxuries, Christians in this country are "laying up" annually nearly one hundred times the amount they give to foreign missions.

We pray God to give the means to send forth laborers. Has he not given us the means? Have we not the means to send forth missionaries? Have not our friends the means? And when we pray God to give the means should we not *pray him to consume the selfishness which expends our means upon ourselves?*

Can it be satisfactory to him when the women in the churches spend ten times as much for jewelry as they give for missions, and when the men in the churches spend ten times as much on tobacco as they give for missions? One church spends more for its printed programmes than it gives for missions; another spends twenty times as much for its choir as for missions. I know a church in New York State the members of which give $400 a year for foreign missions, but the men of that church spend $4,000 a year for tobacco. I know a church in Massachusetts the members of which give $500 a year for foreign missions, but the Sunday-school superintendent, a resident banker, told me that the members of that church spent last year on theatres, dancing and card parties, liquor, and tobacco not less than $10,000, the support of twenty missionaries.

Is there not danger that when we see the Lord Jesus we shall be "ashamed before him at his coming"? Did he die that we might live a life of self-pleasing? He died and rose again that "they which live might not henceforth live unto themselves, but unto him."

> "The Son of God goes forth to war,
>   A kingly crown to gain.
> His blood-red banner streams afar ;
>   Who follows in his train?
> Who best can drink his cup of woe,
>   Triumphant over pain,
> Who patient bears the cross below,
>   He follows in his train.

> "A noble army, men and boys,
> The matron and the maid,
> Around the throne of Christ rejoice,
> In robes of light arrayed.
> They climbed the steep ascent of heaven
> Through peril, toil, and pain;
> O God, to us may grace be given
> To follow in their train."

Dr. McCrory's masterly challenge to Endeavorers, "Prove Your Pledge," was a twelve-stroke. He was glad that it rained, so that his audience could not run away, but none could have torn themselves away after his brilliant opening sally. It rained hard, bracing common sense and flashed brightest wit inside while it poured down torrents of water and shot forked lightning without.

Presently it not only poured down, but poured through. Umbrellas had to be hoisted and seats shifted; but when Dr. McCrory asked whether his time had expired, the audience cried, "Go on!" And go on he did, and up, until every one went away with "Prove Your Pledge" ringing in his ears. And Endeavorers *will* prove their pledge, as he exhorted, in business, in citizenship, in politics, in office, in trial, in triumph.

Address by Rev. James T. McCrory, D.D.,
Pittsburg, Penn.

PROVE YOUR PLEDGE.

This subject is not of my own choosing, but I like it none the less. It means business. It rings out like a trumpet-call. Prove your pledge, Endeavorers. Every individual of you, every man and woman of you, every boy and girl, every company, regiment, battalion, and the whole mighty host organized on behalf of "Christ and the Church," prove your pledge. There is something manful, stirring, energetic, aggressive, in that. It has the ring of a call to men and women who have been set to do something in the world. It might almost seem that the bronze lips of the silent horseman yonder, our hero of New Orleans, had been moved to utterance by some mighty spirit of patriotism to inspire to martial glory and heroic achievement our armies of the closing years of this century as he did those of its first decades. Prove your pledge! Might not that be an echo, indeed, still ringing through the mountains of this glorious Southland from the martial call of some brave leader to his embattled host of the "blue" or the "gray"? Aye, it might be a living voice out from the nation's capitol, from the commander-in-chief of our armies and navies, to our noble sons and brothers on land and sea, in camp and field and walking the decks of our matchless men-of-war, as they go forth under the old starry flag to battle in humanity's name on behalf of the helpless and the oppressed. Oh, might we not take it as a thrilling trumpet message from the throne, from that One whose unflinching faithfulness to his engagement on our behalf brought him to the Cross ere it could bring him to the Throne, to be loyal to our promise to him that we may make manifest by our character and conduct the power of a pledged and consecrated Christian life to produce the most perfect and exalted type of character possible to humanity at the close of these nineteen Christian centuries!

But how may I best secure your attention to this theme, and bring out the lesson it is desired to set forth? May I not urge and encourage you to prove your pledge by setting before you the splendid results and outcome of a pledged career? About the time it was proposed to me to discuss this subject the whole world was saddened by the announcement of the death, at Hawarden Castle, of England's greatest public character, except her Queen. Victoria is first in the hearts of every loyal Britisher, and deserves to be. The woman is worthy of the Queen. She is a queenly woman and a womanly Queen. Long may she live! But taken all in all, William Ewart Gladstone was one of the finest specimens of Christian statesmanship matured in the garden of Christendom. May heaven speedily favor all the nations of the earth with an abundant harvest after this kind. But as I thought of Gladstone I was reminded of another and, if our British friends will permit me to say so, a greater public and political character than even the "grand old man," and one by whose life I will undertake to illustrate my discussion this evening. This greater character came into public notice a long time ago, centuries, indeed, before the Saviour was born into the world, and for a period of more than seventy years he stood in the blaze of that white light that beats about a throne without the discovery of a single flaw in his splendid character. And as we look back across two and a half millenniums he stands alone, sublime, above all the mighty peaks that rise between, as snow-crowned Rainier towers above the mighty summits of the cascades, or as Pike's Peak looms high over all the giants of the Rockies. That man was Belteshazzar as the politicians knew him, but his plain Anglo-Saxon name, given him by his good mother, was Daniel. And, now, whether "Father Endeavor Clark" and Portland will concede it or not, Babylon was the place, and Daniel was the founder, of the first "Simon-pure" Christian Endeavor society. For when Daniel purposed in his heart that he would not defile himself with the king's meat nor the wine which the king drank, he meant that "trusting in Jehovah for strength he would strive to do whatever the God of his fathers would like to have him do;" and his three companions said, "We are with you, Daniel," or words to that effect, and that society was in working order. We find them, also, going directly to the Bible to learn what God would have them do, and depending implicitly on the divine guidance in every matter that came up for settlement. In a word, I assume that the purpose Daniel and his three friends formed and proceeded to carry out meant for them, as consecrated Hebrews, precisely what the Endeavor pledge means for us as sincere Christians. They meant that they would frame their whole lives according to what appeared to them to be the mind of God, and that they would be diligent in the use of the means necessary to enable them to live up to their ideals. That, as I understand it, is the meaning of the Christian Endeavor pledge. It is a solemn purpose put into words, on the part of a Christian, to live as nearly in harmony with the revealed will of Jehovah as it is possible for him to live, while the things specified in the pledge as things he will do are necessary adjuncts, he believes, to the carrying out of his solemn purpose.

Now as to proving the pledge: Daniel's pledge was tested in every way conceivable and never was man more faithful to his promise or results more satisfactory and glorious. Your pledge will do for you, Endeavorer, precisely what Daniel's did for him. Shall I call attention to some of these effects and results? They are not difficult to discover; indeed they lie out so plainly on the surface of his life-story that no thoughtful reader can miss them, and it seems almost like repeating commonplaces to mention them. But here they are; make the most of them.

I. Your pledge promises and will produce the very highest type of Christian manhood and womanhood. That was a thrilling, supreme moment for Daniel and his three fellows, as well as for the Church of God, when they stood before the king at the end of their three years' college course to be examined by the high and mighty monarch, Nebuchadnezzar. Personally, the king is not acquainted with a single one of them perhaps.

The examination has not proceeded far, however, until these four young fellows command his special notice. Fine-looking young fellows he sees they are. Fresh and fair, clean-cut and self-controlled, looking the sovereign squarely in the eye and answering his questions of philosophy, history, science, politics, poetry, and whatever he was pleased to put to them, with a readiness and clearness that made him fairly wonder. Nothing like these boys had ever graduated in his schools before to his knowledge—first-honor men, every last one of them, and there were no seconds; ten times better in all matters of wisdom that the king inquired of them than all the magicians and astrologers in all his realms. The Ph. Ds., LL. Ds., S. T. Ds., and all the rest of them could not hold a candle to these young men in straightforward common-sense questions and answers. And that was the result of the pledge they had *taken* and *kept*. Christian Endeavor, as you are aware, was not organized primarily to assist in the physical and intellectual development of young men and young women. There is no hazard, however, in the assertion that the pledge faithfully kept during a college course will mightily assist in putting a student at the head of his classes and sending him out into the world, into the battle of life, equipped in both body and mind to reach the highest position his God-given endowments fit him to occupy and adorn. And there is great danger to-day, as there was in Daniel's day, from eating and drinking and over-indulgence in our colleges, and no young man is safe or is assured that he will be prepared to stand "before kings" unless he takes a very firm grip on Jesus Christ and is constantly guided by the word and spirit of the Lord. Things have developed during the past year in connection with college and university life to call for a ringing emphasis to be put on this point. And what the Christian Endeavor pledge will do for the student it will do also for the boy and girl entering any of the walks and callings of life. Prove your pledge, young people, and it will prove the most certain and satisfactory assistant to a successful and worthy career.

II. It prepares one to be true to God and to stand firmly by his honest convictions everywhere. A boy reading the account of Daniel's elevation to the first place in the cabinet of Darius the king got it this way : " Then this Daniel was preferred above the presidents and princes because an excellent *spine* was in him." The boy was right if the reading was not. A first-class spine, what we commonly call backbone, was very necessary to men who would be tempted to save their lives by yielding just a little. I look into the blazing furnace and then listen to the calm, resolute reply of these three brave young Hebrews as they stand there alone against the world, firmly refusing to yield the slightest recognition of the false religion and deny their God, although they know that refusal will hurl them into that seething hell of fire, and I say, Thank God for the conviction of righteousness that will hold men true to him under such tremendous provocation to turn aside. Such conduct deserves the applause of the universe. Angels cannot show anything to surpass that. Nothing can surpass that. And then see Daniel long years afterward, when he had risen to the very pinnacle of political and social influence, calmly bending his knees in prayer three times a day with his windows open toward Jerusalem, knowing all the time that for his conduct he would be thrown to the hungry lions — that is sublime. And how did these men come to that firmness of character, that purpose and courage? By taking a pledge to do whatever they believed the Almighty would like to have them do and *keeping it*. Your tests, Endeavorers, may not come in the same form, still there are just as hot furnaces and as hungry lions waiting for you; but once you learn to respond promptly and unflinchingly to the voice that speaks in the soul you will not count your life dear to you any more than Daniel or Shadrach or Paul counted theirs, that you may do his will, whatever he would like to have you do.

I read sometime ago an incident of the Civil War related by a Confederate veteran at a camp-fire, recounting the bravest deed that came under his notice during his army experience. It was a scorching July day. The Confederates were in rifle-pits. The sharp-shooters of the Federal army were watching them like hawks, and picking off every fellow that dared to lift his head above the trench. All about them in the front lay Federal soldiers wounded, who had charged right up to these rifle-pits and fallen there. Only a few steps away lay a Federal officer suffering the most awful thirst, as he lay there dying and pleading most piteously for water. In the rifle-pit near the one who related the incident was an ungainly, raw, red-headed boy. He had only recently joined the regiment, was green as grass, and little attention had been paid to him, only it had been noticed that he was a reliable fighter. He was not yet callous to the sufferings of others. At last, with tears flooding his grimy face, he cried out, "I can't stand it no longer, boys; I'm going to take that poor fellow my canteen." For answer to this foolhardy speech one of the men stuck a cap on a ramrod and hoisted it above the pit. It was instantly pierced by a dozen bullets. To venture outside a step would be the maddest suicide. But all the while the dying officer's moans could be heard pleading for water: "Water! Water! Just one drop, for God's sake, somebody! Only one drop." Then the tender-hearted boy could endure it no longer, and against every remonstrance he flung himself, after several desperate efforts, over the embankment amid a storm of bullets. He crawled toward the dying man, broke off a sumac-bush, tied his canteen to it, and succeeded in landing it in the hands of the sufferer. Such gratitude as that dying man gave expression to! He wanted to tie his gold watch to the stick and give it to the boy. But the brave fellow refused to take it and crawled back and flung himself into the trench again without a single scratch. Every soldier congratulated and praised him. They said it was the bravest deed any of them had witnessed during the war. He made no answer. His eyes had a soft, musing look. "How could you do it?" asked his comrade in a whisper, when the crack of the rifles ceased for a moment. "It was something I thought of," said the boy, simply. "Something my mother used to say to me — 'I was thirsty and ye gave me drink.' She read it to me out of the Bible and she taught it to me till I never could forget it. When I heard that man crying for water I remembered it. The words stood still in my head; I couldn't get rid of 'em. So I thought they meant me — and I went. That's all." That's all; yes, that's all, but it reveals the source of the finest, noblest deeds that are done under heaven. It is precisely this letting the word of Jesus Christ get such a grip on one that it seems to stand still in one's head, and speaks so directly, personally, and definitely that it means "me," and when his will requires something to be done or not done it must be obeyed. That is what makes the real Christian heroes. Dare to be a Daniel; dare to stand alone. And having done all, to stand.

III. It will compel recognition from the opposers of your religion. The royal edict of the Chaldean king proclaimed the supremacy of Daniel's God and the superiority of his religion over all others throughout the whole earth. That was the result of Daniel's character and faithfulness. As a matter of fact, Christian Endeavor has overcome the prejudice that at first confronted it in congregations, communities, and churches by the character of its members. They know you by your daily walk. You are not like the little Christian Scientist maiden who was hesitating about going down-town because of a bad "Billy" goat that infested the way. Of course real Christian Science is a sufficient protection against anything so material and vulgar as a billy-goat, as well as everything else. So the mother remonstrated with her little daughter about her unworthy fears, and said, "You know, daughter, you need not fear a billy-goat, because you are a Christian Scientist." "Yes, I know, mother," assented the child; "I know I am a Christian Scientist; but the billy-goat doesn't know it." Well, the hungry lions somehow knew that Daniel was not their meat. The flames somehow knew they were not to consume the three Hebrew children when there was in the furnace with them one like unto the Son of God. The Sanhedrim somehow knew that Peter and John had been with Jesus. And if we but give our pledge half a chance it will produce such character and conduct as will inevitably persuade the world of the truth of our religion. And I do not know of anything the world needs just now more than such a testimony. I plead with you, Endeavorers, let us give it.

IV. It wipes out the false distinction between religious and secular, and renders the whole life devotional — an acceptable service to God. Darius spoke of Daniel as one who served his God *continually*, and yet we do not hear any complaint from him that Daniel neglected his duties to earthly sovereign. He was the chief of the three presidents who were over the cabinet of one hundred and twenty princes, with all the responsibilities of that important trust on his hands, and yet he served God *continually*. That was only possible because every duty he performed, whatever its apparent end or character, was a service to his God. Praying, presiding at council, attending to matters great or small connected with the government, — everything was service to Jehovah.

This is what the Church needs to learn, and this is one of the supremely important lessons a faithful keeping of the pledge will enable us to teach and exemplify. We are for Christ and the Church not alone on the Lord's Day and in the Lord's house, but every day and everywhere. In the home, the school, the counting-house, the social circle; at the caucus, at the ballot-box, in the court-room, the halls of legislation, in the President's chair, — we are the Lord's and are to render him acceptable service. This is one of the lessons of Christian life we are to put emphasis on to-day. God calls for this from our organization.

V. It awakens one to the consciousness of his higher relationships and destiny. How vulgar and earthly most of our lives are! Even we Christians are not more than half conscious of our spiritual relationships. That we are a part of the spiritual universe is more a dream than a reality. It was not thus with Daniel. His feet were on the earth, but his head was above the clouds. Babylon and its throne and sovereigns were great indeed, but they bore no comparison to the cities and thrones and sovereignties he was constantly associated with. The throne of the universe, the hierarchies of the heavens, and the invisible hosts and armies of the eternities were as real to him as the world about him — more real, indeed. And then he was a part of the glorious enterprises he saw going forward in that spiritual world. He gazed with open eyes upon the sublime unfolding purposes of Jehovah, talked as a familiar with angels and archangels, and felt in his own soul the thrill of the eternal, irresistible forces which make for righteousness and were to finally overthrow all opposition and set up on this earth the kingdom of the heavens. Yes, thank God, man need not grovel. He may aspire. He may arise and live a life worthy the child of a King, as he is. While he is immersed in the plain, practical, every-day duties of this earthly life he may be thrilled and glorified by the consciousness of the life divine. Try it, young people. Give your pledge a chance and it will do this for you. O brethren, the world needs a generation of seers; men and women who really see things that are not visible to the natural eye. And such things there are to be seen. Thrilling, inspiring, glorious things are within the range of our spiritual vision, and are to be seen and *must be seen* by those who would enter hopefully, enthusiastically, all-conqueringly, into the work for "Christ and the Church." May heaven open our blind eyes and awaken our dull aspirations and fill us all with a vivid consciousness of spiritual things! And, believe me, faithfulness to our pledge will assist mightily toward attaining this desire.

VI. It fills him with the consciousness of the divine presence and of coming exaltation and reward. What a thrilling, cheering sentence that with which the book of Daniel concludes: "Go thou thy way till the end; for thou shalt rest and stand in thy lot at the end of the days." And there was still ringing in his ears, remember, the precious assurance, "And they that be wise shall shine as the brightness of the firmament; and they that turn many to righteousness as the stars for ever and ever." And so there is lifted up before the eyes of this faithful servant a fadeless, flashing crown. Down into his soul came the sweet assurance of rest and reward. God means that his servants, while toiling amid the difficulties and uncertainties of time, shall be cheered by foretastes of heaven and the certainties of victory and eternal reward. "Doth Job serve God for nought?" I am aware that Satan by that inquiry intended an infamous falsehood, a black and devilish lie and slander of the grand old patriarch of Uz. But at the same time he suggested a cheering and glorious truth. Job was not serving God for nought. No man ever did, ever does. For there, amid the wreck of fortune, the sorrows of unparalleled bereavements, the physical affliction that rent every ounce of his flesh with agony and made every nerve-centre a nest of fire, "stung to grief and shame and desperation almost beyond endurance of mortal mind by miserable comforters," with every earthly prospect blighted, with the last star of hope fading from the darkening heavens, but true to Jehovah through it all, — into that crushed but trusting heart there came the heaven-born confidence which rings forth in that thrilling sentence, "I know that my Redeemer liveth; and that I shall see him."

Look at Paul. Listen to his account of the sufferings and trials of his devoted life, and then read his life-story and mark the sweet cheerfulness and hopefulness that shines out on every page of his history and ask yourself, How is this? And there is another proof that the soul that is true to its promises to Christ is sustained by the presence of the Son of God, as were the three Hebrews in the midst of the burning, fiery furnace, and has foretastes of heaven that sweeten the bitterest cup and fill with light and glory the darkest earthly night. Young men and women, let me plead with you to prove your pledge and see what it will do for you and for the world. It will insure for you the highest type of character; it will make you true to God; compel recognition of the superiority of your religion; wipe out the false distinction between the religious and secular in life; awaken in you the consciousness of spiritual relationships; fill you with a sweet abiding sense of the divine indwelling that will glorify your earthly existence. Prove your pledge.

The Daily Quiet Hour in the Gospel Tabernacle,

Conducted by Rev. J. Wilbur Chapman, D.D.,

Philadelphia, Penn.

The Union Gospel Tabernacle is a noble structure, with a noble and wonderful history. During the convention week it added to that history a chapter full of spiritual splendor. Day after day the influence of those blessed meetings deepened. At the very first session the key-note of heart-searching was struck. Elisha's prayer was the theme: "Let a double portion of thy spirit be upon me." "I wonder," said Dr. Chapman, "how many of you would seek power if you knew that you would be stoned to death for it when you got home. Why, we ought to testify in such a way that we should win hundreds to Christ, or else our lives should be so lived before wicked men that they will want to stone us to death. Oh, for the end of these miserable lives of compromise!"

It is our sins that keep us from power, but "the cure is not to attack individual sins; the cure is the exaltation of Jesus Christ in the life. When once a man or woman has got a vision of Christ, there's no more trouble about the card-table or the dance."

It was a solemn moment when the speaker asked those to rise and quietly to sit down again who, above everything else in the world, wanted God to fill them. While all heads were bowed in silent prayer, Mr. Estey sung the heart-stirring consecration hymn, "I'll go where you want me to go, Lord; I'll be what you want me to be."

"And now," came the invitation, "if it is your earnest desire that God shall give you a double portion of his Spirit, say, softly, 'Yes, God.'" The low pleading arose from all parts of the Tabernacle. "And, now, if before God you would be willing to let him between this and to-morrow morning search your heart and see if there be any wicked way in you,— I do not ask you if you will give it up,— just say again, 'Yes, Lord.'" And again they murmured the two words, a great whispered prayer. And very softly, with heads still bowed, they closed this first Quiet Hour with singing, "My Jesus, I love thee."

The key-note of the second Quiet Hour was the angel's wrestling with Jacob. "My friend," pleaded Dr. Chapman, "if your life is shorn of power, it is simply because you have not taken hold of God's word and applied it to your own soul." It was such Bible truth that was pressed home during this blessed hour. "Mr. Moody says that no man ever takes a step up till he takes a step down, by which he means that no man ever comes to God till he has come to the end of himself. There is no man here but may have victory over himself if he will simply link himself to God. It is not a question as to whether I can keep from sin and failure myself; it is a question as to whether the Lord Jesus Christ can keep me if I surrender myself to him. As with Jacob, there may be between you and God something as small as a sinew. God must touch it, and it must wither away before you can have power."

No brief synopsis can give any idea of those five wonderful Quiet Hours. Every one will be glad that Dr. Chapman is to write out his searching, masterful addresses for the United Society to put into a book. The themes led on from day to day up to the height of glad consecration, and hundreds, yes, thousands, followed them up the mountain, and found at the top a shining peace. To our knowledge, many a life was transformed by those pentecostal moments. Many a preacher gained there a new vision and a truer purpose. Many a sin was cast off forever. Many a soul went forth from that tent of meeting to walk henceforward step by step with the Master. Praise God for the Quiet Hours at Nashville!

SATURDAY MORNING.

Union Gospel Tabernacle.

Annual Junior Rally.

The Convention thought it had been having the best music of all its sessions, and it was not mistaken; but when, after Bishop B. W. Arnett's opening prayer, the army of white-robed children, with its centre occupying the platform and its right and left wings in the front galleries on each side, arose and poured from hundreds of musical throats their opening chorus, the most generous meed of applause yet granted was vouchsafed right heartily. Every one of the audience who had elbowed one another for places in the Tabernacle, even those who had never taken the pledge, subscribed to it with all hearts, hands, and faces when the Juniors had so sweetly and melodiously chanted their pledge in unison.

If any addition was needed to the welcoming smiles of the children, it was their welcome song, which Mr. Foster helped them to render in such jubilant strains.

One lesson was taught in Mr. Shaw's trenchant style: that in this age of great trusts the greatest of trusts is the boys and girls. The church-members who allow Junior societies to disband because the superintendent moves away should have heard themselves arraigned for betraying a trust which in magnitude and importance to the nation makes the coal, steel, sugar, and all the other colossal combinations of capital, shrink into insignificance.

Address by Treasurer William Shaw.

OUR TRUST: THE BOYS AND GIRLS.

The larger part of this morning's programme is by and for the boys and girls. But I am to speak for a few minutes more particularly to the older people. A company of ministers were discussing the meaning of Matthew 18:6. After nearly all had expressed their opinion as to what the Saviour meant by those words, they turned to an old man, the Nestor of the club, a man of great ability, who had been silently listening to the discussion, and appealed to him for his opinion. He said, "Read the passage." They read, "But whoso shall offend one of these little ones which believe in me, it were better for him that a millstone were hanged about his neck, and that he were drowned in the depth of the sea." "That's what it means," thundered the old man, and those young men received a lesson in the interpretation of Scripture that they never forgot.

And, friends, it means just that to-day — nothing more, nothing less. But I want to remind you that you can offend by neglect as well as by active hostility. The time was, and that not many years ago, when the churches as a rule did not welcome the children to their membership. They acted as if the wilderness were a better place for the lambs of the flock than the fold. They were so fearful lest a little wolf in lamb's clothing should come in that they left the lambs out among the wolves. And then, when the wolf-nature was sufficiently well developed in the lamb so that he could have a striking experience when converted, they would go out after him and try to bring him in. But, alas for the Church, the vast majority preferred to stay with the wolves! Foolish and short-sighted have we been not to realize that there is an experience for a child that is as real, and a conversion that is as vital, as that of Peter or Paul — different, but no less genuine. The appeal to the child is the appeal to love; and if the teaching and the example set before the children were what they ought to be, children would love Jesus as naturally, and obey him as readily, as they do their mothers. Mr. Spurgeon said that he had received scores of children into his church, and never had to discipline one of them, a statement he could not make concerning the adult members.

The children are *our trust*. A trust involves responsibility. There is a day of accounting for every trustee. How shall we meet it? In my long experience in Junior work, I cannot recall a single instance where a society died because there were no children to attend the meeting. Yet I can point you to the graves of hundreds of societies, and on the stone is written, "Dead, because the superintendent moved away, and there was no one to take her place." Churches with a membership of one hundred, three hundred, five hundred, and not one person with enough love for the children and consecration to Christ to give one hour in the week to lead them to the Saviour, and train them in his service! Oh, the neglect of those who find time for everything else but no time for God's little ones! If Christians would take as much time to learn how to lead a Junior society as they do to learn how to ride a wheel, if some were as persistent in learning how to teach as they are in learning how to play whist, and if they would give one-quarter as much time to the Juniors as they do to these amusements, we should have a flourishing society in every church before our next convention.

"Woe unto the world because of offences! for it must needs be that offences come; but woe to that man by whom the offence cometh!" Woe unto the mothers, and fathers, too, who are so careful about the bodies of their children and so careless of their souls; who cultivate grace of manner, but tell them nothing about the grace of God; who are so fearful lest they shall unduly influence their children to accept Jesus Christ before they understand fully what such a step means that they will not let them go to the Junior meetings; who, if they let their children go, do absolutely nothing to help them or their superintendent in their work! Woe unto these fathers and mothers, who some day in the anguish of their spirit will cry, "Oh, if I only had!"

Woe unto the churches that are so careful of their reputation that they dare not receive the little ones into their membership lest perchance some may fall away and disgrace the Church! Woe unto the churches that are so busy with other things that they cannot fold and foster the little ones of the flock!

Woe unto the societies of Christian Endeavor who are so selfish in the enjoyment of their own privileges that they have no thought for the Juniors! They shall prove the truth of Christ's words, "Whosoever will save his life shall lose it."

Woe unto the pastor whose library shelves are so attractive that he has no time to read the message of God written in the fresh young lives about him! He, too, when he comes to himself and realizes how far he has removed himself from the actual life of the young people, will cry out in bitterness of soul, "Oh, if I only had!"

Let us to-day, if never before, accept the trust God has placed in our hands, consecrating ourselves to the service of the children, in the name of Him who when he was on earth took the little ones in his arms, and blessed them, and said, "Of such is the kingdom of heaven."

A remarkably pretty feature of the Convention and one forcibly illustrating our international fellowship was the chain of greetings that brightened the Junior rally with messages from Juniors in almost every State of the Union and almost every country in the world except Russia. Very interesting to see were the originals of many of these

যীশুর প্রতি দৃষ্টি রাখিয়া

Looking Unto Jesus.

A LINK FROM THE JUNIOR CHAIN.

messages, and the polyglot character of the chain is shown by some of the links here reproduced.

Even Turkey was represented by several messages, although saying, "We are not allowed in this country to take the name of Christian Endeavor, but we have the thing itself." And the children of Harpoot expressed delight at being represented in the great gathering. From an orphanage at Van came the appropriate and pathetic passage, "Who shall separate us from the love of Christ? Shall tribulation, or distress, or famine, or nakedness, or peril, or sword?" Bardezag sent a reminder to "remember them that are in bonds as bound with them," and the Intermediate society of Euphrates College, Harpoot, gave the charge, "Be thou faithful unto death, and I will give thee a crown of life."

Even the sword does not sever the ties of Christian love, and every Spanish Junior society was represented. The superintendent wrote, "I suppose the Spanish flag will not be a welcome sight even to all Christian Endeavorers, yet we hope that the sight of it at such a time may arouse feelings of Christian sympathy and love, for Spain needs the elevating influence of Christian Endeavor more than ever before." From the girls' society at Santander came, "We wish for you health, joy, and great success."

Distant Johannesburg wrote, "The Lord be with you as with us." From India and Burmah came many voices. One was, "Salaam. We like Christian Endeavor."

Another was: —

"Jesus loves our pilgrim band;
He will lead us by the hand,
Lead us to the better land.
Happy home on high."

A society in Assam pleaded, "Brethren, pray for us." "The Little Flock of Guides" at Hoshangabad testified, "Thy word is a lamp unto my feet and a light unto my path." Lahore wished for the "brother and sister Endeavorers in America more power in the Lord's work of winning souls for him."

From China's societies with picturesque names, such as "Pure Heart Hall," "Hill of Protected Happiness," came words equally pleasing: "With joy we constantly chorus your songs of melody." "It is diffi-

যীশু খ্রীষ্ট কল্য অদ্য ও যুগে যুগে
সেই আছেন - ইব্রীয় ১৩-৮-

Jesus Christ the same yesterday and today & forever – Hebrews 13.8.

JUNIOR LINKS FROM THE HINDU GIRLS' SCHOOL AT BARISAL.

cult for us to fly across to the great Convention, but we hope the Spirit's grace will be given to you and yours." "Formerly we children did not know the truth, but now God has shown us the right way."

The boys of the Union Church, Kobe, Japan, sent, "Watch ye, stand fast in the faith, quit you like men, be strong;" and the girls, "I can do all things through Christ which strengtheneth me."

The wide-awake Australian Juniors of Yarra Street, Geelong, sent a reminder that

"Though sundered far, by faith we meet
Around one common mercy-seat,"

and the society in Albany, Australia, gave as its motto for the year, "All for Jesus."

From the islands of the sea, too, the greetings were echoed, and Honolulu Juniors added to their "Aloha," "We are trying to serve the Master."

A number of links came from our neighbors in Mexico, among them this from Chihuahua:

"The children are gathering from near and from far,
The trumpet is sounding the call for the war,
The conflict is raging, 't will be fearful and long,
Then gird on your armor and be marching along."

The English cousins sent many loving messages like that from Chester, —

"Children of Columbia's land,
May God's blessing on you rest;
Guided by our Father's hand
We shall meet in heaven at last."

The London Juniors assembled in their annual convention at the Metropolitan Tabernacle said, "Keep to the right, walk in the light." From Leicestershire came the wish, "As C. E. is in the middle of Lei-CEster, and Leicester is in the middle of England, so may the Christian endeavors of our Juniors be at the heart and centre of all the young life of our nation." Bristol's message was full of meaning, — "What the boys and girls are to-day the world will become to-morrow. Let us get all the boys and girls to love Jesus to-day; then the whole world will love him to-morrow."

Saturday Morning.

CHINESE LINK FROM THE JUNIOR CHAIN.

Great Britain's was the place of honor. A boy and a girl, in costumes made in the national colors, stepped to the front, bearing the chain links of colored paper with the Union Jack, while Dr. Clark read the message. These are a sample of all. Syria, Spain, the Marshall Islands, Jamaica, Australia, South America, Mexico, Canada, followed with unique and striking costumes; and, as the representatives of each retired, the chains they held were linked together, forming one continuous chain circling the platform, and the messages were pinned to the large Christian Endeavor monogram standing on a table in the centre of the platform, around which the costumed children were grouped, and around which they marched to music.

It did not dampen the delight of the audience when Dr. Clark reminded them that all they had witnessed and enjoyed, and all for which it stood, would be in vain unless the Junior society brought the children to Christ.

When Secretary Baer mounted the circular press-table and faced the Juniors, his theme had been told in these words. His heart was charged with that one message, and with the thrilling illustration of a lad who gave himself to save his brother he sent it home where it will tell in young lives given to Jesus.

Junior Rally Notes.

Next to that of our own country, the message from Spain elicited the loudest and most spontaneous applause. The little Spanish maiden, with her yellow robe and black lace mantilla over her head, was a picturesque figure.

The Chinese Juniors' message was written on the back of a yellow triangular Chinese flag.

Hawaiian annexation demonstrated its popularity by the climax of applause which greeted Dr. Clark's introduction of the representatives of "Hawaii, U. S."

Dr. Clark said, "We have no representatives this year from Cuba or the Philippines; but come to Detroit next year, and you will see them there."

A wide sombrero was the distinguishing feature of the Mexican costume. Dr. Clark announced that the Mexican national convention was then in session at Toluca, and had sent a telegram of greeting.

The youthful representatives wearing the Stars and Stripes received an ovation. The audience arose *en masse* and shouted their tribute to their native land.

No more sincere applause made the air vibrate than that which rung out in grateful acknowledgment of the services of the originators of the rally, Mrs. F. E. Clark, Mrs. J. L. Hill, and Mrs. G. W. Coleman, of Boston, and Miss Coleman, of Nashville.

Canada and America stood side by side when the flashlight was touched off.

SATURDAY AFTERNOON.

Auditorium Endeavor.

PATRIOTISM was forced to the front all through the Convention by the fact that this was the first International Convention on Southern soil. If we were forced constantly to remember this, it was not because there was anything but the heartiest cordiality among the Endeavorers of all sections. It was because the "you all's" and the soft, beautiful Southern speech and the courteous Southern manner reminded us of it everywhere.

Not since the war, we venture to say, has so significant a patriotic meeting been held as that red-hot, shining-eyed hour of enthusiasm when General Evans and Bishop Fitzgerald, from the South, and General Howard and General Morgan, from the North, shook hands over the precious relic of the original Old Glory, first christened at Nashville. "The Convention of Brotherly Love"— it was a Southern man, Dr. Vance, who baptized the gathering into that name. It was deserved by the splendid fraternal addresses of the generals. It was deserved when white and black joined hands in the persons of Bishops Arnett and Fitzgerald. Most of all was it deserved by the vigorous applause given to every reference to our Christian Endeavor brothers and sisters in Spain.

Percy S. Foster set the wave of patriotism rolling when he announced "America." "You only cracked the roof on that verse," he said, by way of stimulating the audience ; " now tear it to tatters this time."

Dr. Clark's reminder that it would be fitting to open such a service with prayers for the Endeavorers in the army and the navy was followed by an allusion to Meilstrup, Jencks, and Rushworth, the three heroes of the *Maine*, pictures of two of whom he displayed. The silent prayer and the invocation voiced by Dr. John Henry Barrows made a deeply impressive opening.

When Dr. Clark spoke of the special significance of the afternoon and alluded to the presence on the platform of veteran generals of both sides in the late war, the highest enthusiasm was aroused. When he introduced first Gen. O. O. Howard, a veteran of the Union army, it became evident in a moment that the Convention had been holding a full-blown Chautauqua salute for him up its sleeve, and out it came with the audience on its feet.

Address by Gen. O. O. Howard,
Burlington, Vt.
A NEW BAPTISM OF PATRIOTISM.

Mr. President, Young Ladies, Young Gentlemen, and Veterans of Both Armies (for they are here): — I thank you very heartily for this cordial greeting. I have been treated to a warm reception — I do not refer to the weather — ever since I started toward the South: at Mobile, at Tampa, at Atlanta, at Chickamauga, at Ft. Alger, or Camp Alger, and now, to cap it all, I am again welcomed here at Nashville. I have been wondering why it was that the press of the country was so taken up with stories of the war, and gave so little space to this wonderful combination, this collection of young people from all parts of the country, here at Nashville. However, you have had your day. When forty thousand came together in New York City,— when I tried for two hours to get into the building itself, and finally had to be carried in by force there were so many there and when I got in there were so many people that they could n't possibly hear a single word, only about a third of them could hear the sound of my voice,— I remember that I made a short speech. I was invited to speak by the Hon. Mr. Wanamaker, of Philadelphia, and I got up and said, "Welcome to New York," and I sat down again; and everybody insisted that I should speak again, just as you wanted to hear the Jubilee Singers again, and so I said once more, "A Christian welcome to New York," and then I sat down, and that was the extent of my speech. You are here in this beautiful city of Nashville, and I want to congratulate you upon it. It is a great deal cooler city than St. Paul, or Chicago, or Cedar Rapids, or New York City.

I am aware that I am not talking upon the subject for which I am advertised; that is, "A New Baptism of Patriotism," and baptism is a very delicate subject upon which to speak. I wrote it in a letter and your secretary brought it out, but still I will venture to say a word or two upon baptism. All Christians agree that baptism is by water and by the Holy Spirit, and that baptism by water as a general rule, you know, with some few high church exceptions, is a sign. We may have a store where the sign outside is, "West India Goods and Groceries," and we go inside and we find not an iota of West India goods and groceries. The sign is not always enough, you know; you must have the thing signified inside. But the baptism of the Spirit, that is the achievement, that is the accomplishment; and if you have the baptism of the Spirit and the baptism by water — then you are all right.

But that is not exactly the baptism I am to speak of, that is the new baptism of patriotism. Everybody knows that patriotism is love of our country, and love of our country should, when we get broad enough and big enough, like our friend who has travelled around the world, and who spoke last night, Dr. Barrows, be as wide as the world and the brotherhood of mankind will be complete. But for a while we want to confine ourselves to the patriotism which is the love of our country, that is the patriotic spirit. Some people seem to think that this patriotism is something we should not have, that it narrows one. Well, it may, but it may enlarge one. Properly speaking, patriotism is the stepping-stone to a larger life, to love of one's kind, to love of one's neighbor, and the neighbor anybody on the face of the earth to whom we may minister.

Now this patriotism of ours manifested itself especially in our Revolution, on the field of battle. You all remember that little poem that was attributed to General Warren at Bunker Hill, beginning,

"Stand, the ground's your own, my braves."

THE JUNIOR RALLY. GOSPEL TABERNACLE.

I believe that is the first one I learned and recited in the school-room. I think it shaped my feelings; I have not been half as kind toward Great Britain, perhaps, as I would have been if I had n't learned that.

While in convention over the Declaration of Independence, what did we do? Why we quarrelled over it a great deal, but we read it on the Fourth of July.

Declaration of Independence of what? Well, of dynasty, an individual declaration that the people had a right to a voice in the government that is over them. We have that sunk down deep into our souls, and there is not a young man in the country who does not feel the pulsations of it in his heart. This is one reason that the flag goes floating from here to Cuba, and along to Porto Rico, and somehow bubbles up a little in Manila. Oh, how wonderful, wonderful, wonderful! One of our authors says (you know he represents a poor farmer with his daughter brought all the way from Russia), "Margaret, look, look, all the waves are rising, wonderful, wonderful,"—and I say, wonderful, wonderful, that our forefathers could have had the foresight to have established a constitution like that of ours. True, we differed, North and South, and had to fight over it, General Evans and I, awhile as to our interpretation of the Constitution, and we each adhered to our own view of it and spilled our blood for it.

Educated at West Point, I fought for the Union. I imagine sometimes that I have probably the proper patriotism in me, but I can conceive of a young man from South Carolina who would meet me on the street, and if I should tell him that South Carolina was not bigger than the United States he would knock me down.

Patriotism like this is intense. Oh, I never had as great a loyalty for the United States as he had for South Carolina and as General Lee had for the commonwealth of Virginia. You may believe as you please, those are the simple facts, and the war knocked them all out of us and put us all together on a new basis.

Oh, the literature, how much there is of it! Before the great war came on it really modified my feelings, the old literature; the history of the Revolution was as sacred to me as the Bible. I had to learn after awhile that Washington's battles were not so large, because we had larger ones; that his struggles were not beyond description, for I had seen greater struggles. Now the manifestation of this patriotism has recently had what I call a revival, I don't know how you look at it. I came before a Boston audience not long ago, and most of them were clergymen; there were about a thousand of them, they called it a club, and somebody came up and whispered to me and said, "General Howard, more than half, yes, two-thirds of them are against you; they don't believe as you do." One dear friend came up and whispered to me, "I can't see that this war is right, I can't see it;" and another one who had just come from Washington said, "General Howard, those representatives down there, they are all wrong, they are merely politicians, it is all humbug, there is no genuineness or sincerity among them." I replied, "Doctor, doctor,—he is an old friend of mine,—if you have just come from Washington you have n't interpreted them rightly." "I have been all over the country; I have travelled from the East to the West, and I tell you that the people are behind and are urging on our congressmen."

Well now, what was the matter? Some people said it was the *Maine*, " Remember the *Maine*; remember the *Maine*," and the two hundred and sixty-six of our good people belonging to the navy, our marines, that were drowned in the harbor of Havana.

Well, then they said, "Why do you say, 'Remember the *Maine*;' does n't that indicate revenge? A spirit of revenge should not be entertained in a Christian's heart." That is not the right spirit with which to look at this matter, and I began by saying to my friends over in Boston, "Look at Armenia, where forty thousand people were killed, murdered by the Turks in cold blood— then we blamed England, why did n't England, great England, intervene?" We repeated that all over the country. All the press of the North and of the country began to express itself in that way. It has been brought right home to us now. Right here at our borders there has been extortion upon extortion for years and years, there has been murder and assassination upon assassination. What has been accomplished by the Captain-General? He has sent away these poor creatures into perpetual bondage beyond the seas, into the penal colonies, and he has taken away the rights of the people. Again, by the Weyler process of the Trocha, coralling the people up and driving them away from their homes, the incompetents, the old men and women and children, two hundred thousand of them, have thus been murdered by slow starvation. Yes, I say, remember that, remember the iniquity, remember the sin. We have borne long with them. McKinley wanted to delay a little longer with the hope of peace, wanted to expend a little more money if he could to prevent war.

We would have waited longer and longer if there had been any hope; but, my friends, I believe myself, and I believe it as solemnly as that I stand here, that in the providence of God the measure of iniquity was full and it was time for us to say, "Remember the *Maine*," because the Spaniards had sent our soldiers to the bottom of the sea. Remember the iniquity of the people, because they have destroyed their own people, thousands of them. Remember also that those people in Cuba were as honest and as earnest as our fathers, and they had worked hard and long, and held out against numbers six times as great as themselves, and nothing but the providence of God could have sustained and kept them. I advocated years ago granting them belligerent rights, and then I suggested giving them their independence. To-day McKinley is trying to give Cuba an independent government, and though my own sons are in the conflict, and my friends are baptising that soil with their blood, yet I say I believe it is from God, and that the work will go on.

Senator Hoar says, "The life and glory of a nation does not depend on its army, nor on its navy, nor on its exercise of power, nor on its commercial transactions, nor on its conquests, but upon the character of the individual citizens of the nation." If that be true, my friend, what ought to be the character of the citizens?

A gentleman asked me here in Nashville, "General Howard, what would you do; how are you going to solve these problems?" I remember one of our greatest statesmen said that when the time shall come that there will be no problems for this nation to settle, then this nation's work will be done on the earth. I want to say this, that I have met the Anglo-Saxon people frequently in extremities and I have found them, by God's help, equal to the emergency, and I believe that when the problems come up, one after another, that they will be settled wisely and truly in the love of man and the fear of God. Do you ask me what I would propose, what I proposed to this gentleman? I proposed to him just simply this: raise the standard of citizenship. Raise the standard of citizenship all of you who belong to the Christian Endeavor society. How is that to be done? Oh, it seems to me that all you have to do is to do that which many of you have been doing, take your place as Christian citizens, citizens with vital Christianity, with purity written in your foreheads and uprightness in your hearts. Oh, when you get the majority,— and you will get the majority if you will keep at it,— when you get the majority of citizens brought within this influence, you will never be troubled. A great many people are in great distress about the superiority of Tom, Dick, Harry, and Bill. That is all nonsense. The Christian's duty is so plain and so straight that any thinking man can meet it. What is it? To remember that God wants you to do all that you can for your neighbor, to love your neighbor as yourself, to love your heavenly Father with all your heart, and the one who comes within reach of the influence of your mind and heart.

Now, my friends, you have other speeches to hear this afternoon and I only want to give you this as a sort of epitome of what I would like to say to you if I had time. Can you believe me? May the Lord keep you, and may the Lord help you to carry on this work here in America until you have a vast majority who love God and his son Jesus Christ.

Mr. Excell's new patriotic solo, "Song of a Thousand Years," with a chorus by the audience that swelled to the dome, was a superb afterclap. Never did his massive chest and resonant voice project richer and more rolling tones into any auditorium.

Dr. Clark, having referred to General Howard as "the hero of Gettysburg," which designation always provokes from the modest old soldier the explanation that there were 200,000 heroes of Gettysburg, said that he supposed that if General Evans should now be introduced as "the hero of Appomattox," he would affirm that there were hundreds of thousands of such.

A specially happy circumstance of the moment was the exhibition by Dr. Clark of a piece of the original "Old Glory," which had been owed by a Nashville Unionist, who kept it sewed up in his coverlet during the war, and brought it out to wave over the capital when the Union forces entered it. He presented this memento to General Evans, who received it with emotion.

"In all the charges I have made against this flag," solemnly declared the general, "I have never seen it floating before me on crested ridge or parapet with resentment toward it in my heart."

Proceeding to his theme, he paid a delicate tribute to beautiful Tennessee by quoting from Governor Taylor the declaration that Tennessee's mountains " rose from fertile vales which limpid rivers watered every hour, and, aspiring to make known in heaven the resources of the State, pushed their peaks beyond the clouds and called the attention of the celestials to the better land in Tennessee by tickling the feet of the angels."

Address by Gen. Clement A. Evans, D.D.,
Atlanta, Ga.
OUR UNITED COUNTRY.

This scene excites our patriotism into the ardors of a glowing faith that liberty, humanity, and religion are in the safe keeping of our united country. Coming into the present enjoyment of your councils, I bring to this hour, to this occasion, and to *you* from the South Atlantic border of our mighty land the blessings of a generous people on every movement that bears our country and the world into the unity of the spirit and in the bonds of peace.

I count myself most happy in speaking in this fair city and noble State whose people touch all sections with radiating sympathies, and draw unto themselves the admiration of all States by their magnetic patriotism. Tennessee well deserves the eulogies of its present inimitably genial governor, who never tires in telling the world of its glories. They say he once declared before a vast audience in brilliant sentences which ascended like Jacob's ladder to a climax among the stars, that "Tennessee's mountains, rising from fertile vales, whose limpid rivers watered every hour, and aspiring to make known in heaven the resources of the State, pushed their peaks beyond the clouds and called the attention of the celestials to the better land in Tennessee by tickling the feet of the angels."

The happy conditions of such an hour and such a place invite me to a short, concise survey of some national triumphs won by the people of the United States in using the agencies of peace.

On the indented shore line of the Atlantic as seen in the early days of America, from the borders of Maine to that lovely isle off Georgia's coast where Light-Horse Harry Lee now sleeps, the gleam of settlement lights that trembled upon the ocean tides signalled eastward that unto Christian civilization a new hope was born, and unto free humanity a new continent was given; and then the angels, seeing higher and broader liberties for the human race, sang, "Glory to God in the highest, peace on earth and good will to men."

The currents of population starting from all European sources were bearing mixed masses across the great sea, debouching them upon a new forest world which confronted all high purpose with forbidding aspect, and threatened every great endeavor with disaster. Yet these physical barriers which aided the hostilities of savage occupants of the soil were not such obstacles to the victories which the new populations were ordained to win as were the various conflicting prejudices which were brought from the old world, — as germs of fever sometimes come in ships. The languages of the Dane and Dutch, of English and French, of Spanish and Portuguese, betrayed in speech the various views, passions, and prejudices of the nations they represented. The conflicting schemes of monarchs and lords, of great grantees of lands and smaller speculators, of Cavalier and Puritan, of Protestant and Catholic, made strifes that first bubbled in little circles, then widened into national wars. Ambitious explorers marching under inimical flags intersected each other's paths and fought for territory of which there was already enough for the world to occupy in peace.

Looking upon this scene of conflict in new America among the children of Japhet, looking upon the turbulence of early colonial times, upon vast America which for three centuries after discovery remained formless and void, while darkness sat upon the boisterous political deep, who could logically foresee the people of this same great land brought into national brotherhood, speaking one language, possessing one patriotism, serving one great constitutional government, and bannered by one flag? Four centuries after Columbus announced to Europe that a new world was found, four centuries after the mightiest struggles of conflicting policies, our eyes behold a great people pledged by every principle of gratitude to Divine Providence to hand down to posterity the blessings of free government to all people on earth. The fourth century of occupation, now at its close, presents to the world the happy aspect of seventy-five millions of free Americans moving together in one mighty Christian endeavor to demonstrate that nations may grow to greatness without forfeiture of personal freedom.

I. The earliest conspicuously peaceful triumph of our colonial ancestors was manifested in their surrender of local ambitions for colonial aggrandizement to the greater glory of one constitutional government of the United States. This voluntary abdication of these independent colonial thrones which had been erected under grants from kings, and secured by colonial struggles against the oppressions of kingdoms in Europe, was by no means a minor event in the history of great human actions. New England had much to boast of in patriotic traditions peculiar to itself, and possessed advantages which allowed many of its people to prefer a New England republic to a nation of States. New York colony, won from the Dutch, had a seaport city with imperial territory at its back, sufficient to support a nation, and a harbor in its front ample to invite the commerce of a world. Virginia, the matronly sponsor for American institutions, sat superbly invested with a royalty in domain extensive enough to make it evident that Virginia, if she so wished, could become the ruling power on the continent. The Carolinas and Georgia were almost equally endowed with all resources for great nationality, and in fact all except the smallest of the colonies saw by survey of the situation that there could be several great nations formed, each with an Atlantic front, and each with domain greater than that of many powerful European nations.

Within this grand scope where temptation pointed out the field of colonial glory there also lay reasons for separate colony government which were based on varieties of material interests, of political views, of religious creeds, of social customs, and of inherited European antagonisms. Personal ambitions also intruded into the councils of patriots, and sectional prejudice injected its distrust of any unity where there was so much diversity.

For twenty years the vastly important question of colonial community in a union of sovereign States was discussed in all its phases. Every selfish view was presented, every fear was aroused, every doubt was considered, until at length a popular patriotism won the sublime victory over all passions, prejudices, and selfishness, in the adoption by States of the wonderful Constitution of the United States. Virginia donated her empire without losing it, winning her foremost place forever as Mother of States, and statesmen. New England gave up her opposition without forfeiture of her ancient traditions. The other States, one by one, moved into their respective places on the Union field, over which the star-spangled banner waved, without being shorn of a single ray, and Washington, who had been first in war, won the title, "first in peace, and first in the hearts of his countrymen."

II. I notice next that our American people won in peaceful convention of their delegates a victory over the attractive form of monarchy, entrenched though it was in the usages of nations, supported by the dogma of the "divine right of kings," fostered by order of the nobility and defended by standing armies. With deliberate judgment they discarded the rule of a king and established a republic — electing a president and congress from among themselves. When we review this period of our national history, which came on after the achievement of independence by the valor of the army amidst the disordered conditions of the first Confederation, with the influences of the old monarchies still exerted to transfer "the trade of kings" to the new government in the new world, with all the glitter of its aristocracy; when we consider the power of the great American leaders, both civil and military, and the temptation common among men to acquire personal aggrandizement, we will perceive the moral greatness which they won, led by Washington, Adams, Jefferson, and Hancock. I say this was a triumph over the fascinations of monarchy. From the days of King Saul until even now people fancied that monarchy, with all its glamour of crown and throne, and hereditary title is the only strong form of government. Thus thought some of our great patriotic statesmen of the colonies who, seeing danger of disorganization, suggested a modified monarchy for America, while monarchists in Europe at the same time predicted a failure of the resort to sovereignty in the people. Yet over the fears at home and the jeers abroad, and over the common pride in a great and glittering government our patriotic fathers gained a victory for themselves and humanity by establishing the doctrine that government exists by the just consent of the governed.

This century has justified their judgment. The strength of the republic of States has been shown in every war with kings, from the date of the American Revolution to this present hour, when the Stars and Stripes float over a powerful nation of people loving peace, liberty, honor, and humanity, and are able to bring to the same conditions of peace and benevolence that arrogant monarchy whose name in America stands for oppression of its colonies abroad and neglect of its poor people at home.

But, while achieving this victory over the monarchial habit of the world, our fathers were not beguiled into the alluring and illusive dream that government of a great country can exist by the unrestrained will of every man in it. Self-government they knew to be another name for self-restraint. The one-man power of monarchy was, according to their judgment, not more vicious than the fierce power of the unbridled multitude. With these and kindred axioms of true civics firmly set in their minds and luminous with the great light of their experience, the wise patriots of the past builded even better than they knew, — a republic of States, a fabric of constitutional representative democracy founded on the eternal rock of this one great principle, that the liberty, equality, and happiness of universal mankind shall be the chief end of all nations, and is the demand of God upon the ruling of the people.

It is true that they wrought with the sword in one hand and the trowel in the other, as the wall-builders toiled in the times of Nehemiah, but the beneficent government which we enjoy was not dictated by a Cæsar at the close of a bloody conquest; it was born in fraternal debate, the child of patriotism; fathered by reason, and hallowed by prayer, and then, laid in the lap of a great faith in God and humanity, it has grown sinewy by the struggles of a country strong in the confidence of its people, and competent to become the leader of all nations in fulfilling the vast designs of the one almighty Ruler of men.

III. You will heartily appreciate even a brief mention of the fact that all civil glory would have been lost to our country if the founders of it had not broken away from the chains of religious intolerance. No less glorious than the noble victories of the American people over the seductions of false civics is their most laudable and complete overthrow, first by law, and next by common public opinion, of the fell, fierce, intolerant spirit of religious bigotry. It will sometime hence seem to be one of the exaggerations of history, or a lurid fable congenial to Dante's "Inferno," that the religionists of the world one while lit up the path to heaven with the fires of hell. Buddhist, Brahman, and Turk among the religious illusions, Jew and Christian from the ranks of true faith, are alike in the fearful condemnation of implacable bigotry. Christianity is craped in memory of her children slain at the altar of holy worship by the sword of believer and unbeliever. The laws of councils, parliaments, and legislatures, the proclamation of kings, and the dicta of judges tell a shortened story of sectarian unreason and inhumanity. The religious wars of that old world were, in some of their aspects of intolerance, reproduced in the policies of the new. Persecuted sects flying from Europe to the American wilderness shut the gate of heaven upon their persecutors. Civil interests imperiously called for an exclusive form of worship in colonial states. Commercial greed made one sort of piety the standard in trade. Many men of many minds were resolutely bent on bringing to pass the saying that "the kingdom of heaven suffereth violence, and the violent take it by force." Argument on all adverse sides seemed to the antagonists to be conclusive, and when exhausted the last resort was arms. Yet upon and amidst these rampant waves there came One, breasting the storm of contrary winds, walking the waves in the radiant majesty of supreme authority, who, stepping aboard the American ship, said to religious passion and prejudice, " Peace, be still; " and, thank God, we who are here in this place are the grateful beholders of a great calm! We are surrounded also by a vast and brilliant cloud of witnesses unseen to mortal sight, whose coming reminds me again that the aspirant peaks of Tennessee mountains, pressing their electrified tops between the stars above us, so tickled afresh the feet of the angels when this American victory was won that they came dancing like David before the ark of religious freedom, and laid it with celestial rejoicing upon the bosom of the Constitution in the Temple of the Union.

IV. I could enlarge on our victories over illiteracy won in arousing the people from the neglect of general education, which had stupefied the masses of other countries, and warn you against the danger to liberty even under constitutional free government if the people's children grow up in ignorance. I could show the steady advance which we have made without the flash of the sword or the firing of a gun against the resistance of avarice, jealousy, parental apathy, popular poverty, mistake, and error, until redemption from illiteracy draweth so nigh that another generation will witness a whole people educated to perform the sacred duties of citizenship. I would also speak of our battles against all the attacks on the family institution, — among our victories being a final and utter overthrow of that dangerous foe of humanity called Mormonism; and also among our moral triumphs the protection of the marriage-altar against the lewdness of free love ; and among our victories waiting yet to be won is that of the defeat of the free statutory divorce — but with this bare mention let us pass to a topic which in times past caused great concern.

V. In the bloody quadrennium of fraternal strife, a generation ago, some results were certainly produced by war. For once peace counsels had failed and the sword determined the end. Dauntless courage stood through tha struggle against resistless onset, until weight bore down weakness. Happily for this country and the world the Federal Constitution withstood the storm, the star-spangled banner marched out of the mist of fire, and standing over and among the lately contending camp, rallied all sections to its ægis. Once more millions of people living in 1865, gazing like the Southern poet through the haze of dawning era, burst out afresh in the words of his great song, —

"O say, can you see by the dawn's early light
. . . .
'T is the star-spangled banner ; oh, long may it wave
O'er the land of the free and the home of the brave."

The victories fought for in this Union after Appomattox had hushed the cannon's roar and sheathed the Southern soldier's sword were won, as far as they have been won, in the councils of peace. The great general who received the surrender of Lee matched his military immortality with an equal immortality as a patriot when he gave the watchword to his people in words as much of command as suggestion, "Let us have peace." Lee, the magnificent ideal of martial and civic manhood, and lustrous in his character with virtues which exalt American character in every country of the civilized world, counselled his people to return to the vocations of peace. The answering South took up its harp to utter the requiem of its Confederation, swept its strings until all were broken, then hung that harp on its country's wall, hoping amid its fears that the "war-power" would be directed to the power of peace, saving the people's liberties in an indissoluble constitutional union.

No sight on earth ever equalled the majesty of the dissolving armies which fought through those four years. On the Union side there was the *eclat* of success, with a magnificent parade of victors through the streets of the nation's capital, and then the dismissal of the volunteers homeward. On the Southern side, behold the unarmed thousands marching without organization from the fields where they had fought and the camps where they had been paroled across the unprotected Southern States in groups and squads, committing no outrages, and reaching their homes to take up at once the habits and occupations of civil life. Was there ever such a dismissal of an army before, and ever such a triumph over the lawlessness engendered by war? Consider the temptation of the discharged army to commit acts of disorder; consider the unchanged convictions of these defeated soldiers, and credit these thousands of Southern soldiers with a moral victory over themselves, more brilliant than their victories at Manassas and Fredericksburg.

Four decades are passing away in which the leaven of the great moral and popular spirit of patriotism has worked in those three measures of meal called the executive, the legislative, and the judicial departments of our government, slowly bringing each toward a just administration of a renovated country. Commerce, travel, inter-marriage, all interposed their offices to restore fraternal feeling. Time, moving on, cooled the passions of many, and meanwhile a better understanding was reached where the two sections of our country could see that disparagement of either lowered the other, and dishonoring one degraded both. Still it must be admitted that the victory is not yet complete; still are the problems of our unique form of government involved with some remains of the carnal sectional mind; still it is required that heroic Christian endeavor shall pursue the path of Godlike conquest until all members of the Union shall be knit together in a living national body.

VI. Our united country has achieved greatness in war and in peace. Our territory has expanded from ocean to ocean by grant, cession, or purchase, and never by conquest. No foreign colonies have been brought to distress by the floating of the American flag over their homes. French, Spanish, and Mexicans have in their turn been brought under our jurisdiction, and in each instance their political conditions have been improved. Our armies have marched to relieve the oppressed and to give them good government. Steadily, without endangering our own liberty, we have helped all America to freedom except the adjacent isles of the sea, whose appeals are being answered by Dewey in the Philippines and Wheeler in the Antilles.

Our united country is evidently destined to grow immensely greater. The era now upon us will disclose an uprising of forces which will uplift the nation into a most conspicuous position among the powers of the earth. The same laws of national increase which made other peoples powerful are working in the elements of our national body, producing a similar result. The new century so near at hand beckons us to its bosom with promises of a greatness which no other nation ever reached.

What, then, is to be our greatest national triumph? What our greatest victory, not in war, but in peace? It is to demonstrate that nations can attain great power with many millions of people occupying vast territory and yet preserve their liberties unimpaired. I do not hesitate to say that our form of government is adapted to that end, and that there are no reasons in civics nor in ethics why a nation should fall because it had been blessed with greatness.

I commit to you then, in concluding, the injunction not to despair of our republic because you see it defending its seamen who were slain by treachery, and rescuing the isles of the adjacent ocean from oppression. Let not distrust of the coherency of sovereign States in a constitutional Union cause you to fear the fall of your country. Steady as is the firmament when telescopes reveal additional stars moving in the spaces beyond will be our union of many republics as its power increases by multiples of present population and wealth. Guided by Almighty God in his wisdom, and governed by the suffrage of the people who love both " God and native land," we will triumph gloriously over the temptations that beset grandeur, and lead the world in the ways of righteousness and peace.

No sooner had General Evans sat down amidst a storm of applause than from a corner of the chorus platform the strains of " Dixie " burst forth from a band of lady singers whom Mr. Estey led in this compliment to the old Confederate hero. The audience quickly caught up the chorus, and made it ring.

Secretary Baer read a telegram which came from farther up on the map, Mayor Maybury, of Detroit, assuring the Convention of the city's deepest sense of appreciation for selecting Detroit. "Nothing that Detroit has promised will be forgotten, and many things not promised will be remembered at that time."

Rev. Chas. B. Newnan, of Detroit, was called to the front, and read a second telegram, which came too late to be presented to the trustees. It was this: " Characteristic July weather here. Average temperature, 67. Bring the '99 Convention to enjoy the refreshing breezes from our inland seas."

Remarks by Rev. Chas. B. Newnan,
Detroit, Mich.

Mr. President and Brethren in Christian Endeavor: — Our people at home entrusted their committee with two commissions: —

First, to use all right influence to induce the Board of Trustees to locate the next International Convention in our beautiful city. The issue of that you know.

Second, in case our city should be chosen, we were then to present you with an urgent invitation to accept our hospitality and share our fellowship in '99. We wish you to come. We long to look into your faces and to take you by the hand. Some years ago, your throng, with song and shout, with banners waving and flags flying, swept by us on your way to Montreal and Boston. We waved our greetings as you passed. Again, returning tides swept by us, whose faces were set toward the Golden Gate; again we waved you greeting. Now we wish to welcome you in our own homes; and the tides of life from East and West, from North and South, are to meet and mingle on our shores. We wish our Canadian brethren also to come. With them already we celebrate the birthday of the

Queen, and fly the flag on the Fourth of July. From far-off lands and from the islands of the sea, we wish you to come. Our pines will wave you welcome from afar. Our fields will smile upon you. Our lakes, blue as the skies above them, will ripple into laughter at your coming. Our homes are open. Our hearts are high with hope and filled with delightful anticipation. We wish you to come for the information, the enthusiasm, the inspiration, which you will bring. Many burdens will you lift, many tasks make lighter, much help give, if you come. Come to Detroit in '99!

It seemed as if the climax had been reached when Mr. Foster led in "The Star-Spangled Banner," the singers suiting the action to the word as they sung, "Long may it wave."

But the mountain-peak was not to be reached yet. Bishop Fitzgerald, of the Southern Methodist Church, had to be reckoned with. Bishop Fitzgerald repeated his short creed: "I love everybody in the world; some better than others. That includes Spain. I love her so well that I want her well spanked, so that she will behave herself hereafter." It reminded him of a colored preacher who had told his hearers that there was one place where they could always find sympathy, — in the dictionary. He feared that if Spain wanted sympathy she would have to go to the dictionary.

Speaking of the South's wanting no more fratricidal war, he said it reminded him of a boy eating buckwheat cakes. He said he had never had enough. So he ate and ate until he began to be troubled. His sister, noticing his distress, asked him teasingly whether he did n't want some more cakes, and he answered, amidst groans and grimaces, "I don't want what I've had already." That was the way with the South.

Alluding to the nations of Europe who wanted to help Spain, he said it reminded him of a colored brother who, in the anti-bellum days, ran away and went to New York in search of freedom and happiness. He soon came to suffering for food and shelter, and begged alms. Several whom he approached asked him whether he had had a good master. He answered, "Yes." "Then you were a fool for not staying there." "Gentlemen," he replied, "what you say must be true; but, if any of you want the job, the situation is still open." So it was open to the would-be helpers of Spain.

The bishop said that he had a special engagement to be in Havana next Christmas. By the co-operation of General Shafter and certain generals with Spanish names he expected to be able to keep the engagement. He had visited Havana four years ago, and talked with many stalwart young Cubans, every one of whom had said to him, "We shall be free, or there will be none of us left."

The bishop had invited Booth-Tucker to spend Christmas with him in Havana, and the latter had accepted. He now extended a special invitation to General Howard, the sight of whose empty sleeve moistened his eyes, and whom he loved, and to his brunette brother, Bishop Arnett, to join the party.

General Howard had left, but Bishop Arnett accepted the invitation. In introducing the next speaker, Dr. Clark said, "We shall hear from

Gen. John T. Morgan, D.D., LL.D., on 'The New Republic and Its Duties.' It is surely very remarkable that these generals of war are also generals of peace. General Howard is president of the Congregational Home Missionary Society. General Morgan is the secretary of the Baptist Home Missionary Society. They are still in the vanguard, you see. General Morgan, who commanded the Union forces in the battle of Nashville, and knows more about it than any other man, perhaps, on one side, at least, will now speak to us."

Address by General John T. Morgan, D.D., LL.D.,
New York City.
THE NEW REPUBLIC AND ITS DUTIES.

We have entered upon a new and strange era in the development of our national life, and have embodied in actual reality the ideals of the Republic more fully than at any former period of our history. Some of the changes have been of slow growth, while others have been sudden and startling. Let us look for a moment at a few of those characteristics which separate us as a new republic from our own past history.

First. We are now a nation of free men. So long as African slavery existed, sanctioned by law and protected by the courts, it was recognized as an element of weakness in the national life. The Declaration of Independence boldly proclaimed the doctrine of human equality, and the whole theory of our republican government was built up on this cardinal doctrine. Our theory was correct; our practice was wrong: the one was in violent contradiction to the other. After decades of discussion we seemed as far removed as ever from any practical solution of this antagonistic dualism. In the strange providence of God a civil war waged on the one hand for the establishment of an independent confederacy, and on the other for the preservation of the national integrity, resulted in the utter destruction of slavery on the continent. We emerged from the smoke of battle a nation of free men. Our Constitution was amended to conform to the fundamental doctrine of the Declaration of Independence. The old nation had gone down in the midst of blood and carnage; the new nation arose out of the conflict. That the new is better than the old none are now so hardy as to deny. Liberty is better than bondage.

Second. We are a united nation. For many years before the outbreak of hostilities between the North and the South the two sections had been slowly but surely growing apart. We were literally a "house divided against itself." Slavery constituted a chasm between the two sections, which grew wider and wider until it was filled up with human bodies, and cemented with human blood. The political estrangement engendered by slavery was greatly intensified by the bitterness born of war. The presence in the South of a vast body of people formerly slaves, suddenly elevated to citizenship and entrusted with the suffrage, and finding naturally perhaps their political alliances with parties regarded as unfriendly to the South, retarded the healing process of peace, and perpetuated the animosities and estrangements of the past. Happily, this has largely passed away. Men who were prominent as officers in the Confederate army, recognized everywhere through the South for their courage and devotion to the Southern cause, are to-day in command of troops in the United States army, and are fighting as bravely and loyally under the Stars and Stripes as they ever fought under the Stars and Bars. We are once again a united nation. Mason and Dixon's line has apparently disappeared forever. Old issues have passed away, and new issues confront us. Old ideals have vanished, and new ideals have taken their places.

Third. We are essentially a homogeneous people. Notwithstanding the fact that there have come to our shores within the last fifty years, from all the nations under the heavens, a host of at least twenty millions of foreigners; and notwithstanding the fact that eight millions of our people are Africans or their descendants, and despite the separative influences of race, language, and religion, it is not too much to claim that this is essentially an Anglo-Saxon Republic. Everywhere we speak the English language — the language of Milton, Shakespeare, and of the English Bible; we cherish English ideals of personal liberty. Every man's home is his castle. The public-school system is slowly but surely doing its wholesome work of breaking down artificial barriers and uniting all of our people upon a common basis of manhood and civil and religious liberty. While it is true that we are "the heir of all the ages," and have incorporated into our national life elements of good from the civilizations of the Jews and the Greeks, not neglecting what was admirable in that of the "barbarians;" and while it is true that we have developed an American life and civilization in some respects unlike that of any other, it yet remains true that we are essentially Anglo-Saxon. This oneness of national life is a tremendous factor, more characteristic perhaps of us to-day as a new republic than any other that could be mentioned.

Fourth. We are a nation of great power. Beginning on the Atlantic coast in the early part of the seventeenth century we have been clearing the forests, bridging the rivers, tunnelling the mountains, cultivating the plains, opening the mines, until we have brought under subjection a vast region of country stretching from ocean to ocean, and from the Lakes to the Gulf. Our physical resources are practically without limit, and our wealth adequate for all purposes. Our population of seventy millions, animated by lofty patriotism, stimulated by an unconquerable love of liberty, inured to hardship, educated as no people has ever been educated, efficient in all varied human industries and pursuits, pre-eminent in the arts of peace, and unexcelled as soldiers and as sailors, makes of us one of the great nations of the earth.

Our Constitution, which it was feared might not be able to withstand the strain of civil war, or to hold together a vast population made up of peoples with interests so diverse as those of the East and West, the North and South, has thus far proven adequate to every test. With the present facilities of intercourse and communication, which annihilate time and reduce space to a span, the difficulties that once menaced the Republic have disappeared. Numbers of people and vastness of territory, once regarded as elements of weakness, are now clearly recognized to be constituents of our might. There is no element of national power wanting.

Fifth. We have taken a new position among the nations of the earth. With almost startling suddenness we find ourselves recognized by the nations of the old world as a new world power which must be reckoned with in the settlement of any great international problems. Hitherto we have been to a large extent an insular people, occupied with our own internal affairs, following loyally the teachings of Washington in his farewell address; avoiding all entangling alliances with foreign powers and contenting ourselves with the thought that our national obligations were limited principally by our national boundaries.

After witnessing patiently the enormities of Spanish despotism and the cruelties of military rule in Cuba, we were forced by our sympathy with the suffering Cubans to recognize that we were under moral obligation to come to their aid in the time of their dire necessity. With no greed of gold, lust of power or conquest, but simply impelled by keen moral sense of obligation, we said to Spain that, as it had become plainly evident that she could not suppress the rebellion, she must abandon the effort, evacuate Cuba, and allow the inhabitants of that beautiful island to establish a government of their own. This brought on the war. By a singular and apparently providential circumstance, a magnificent stroke of seamanship made by the incomparable Dewey, we found ourselves on the first of May in practical possession of the Philippine Islands, with a population of nine millions of people who had endured, if possible, worse treatment at the hands of Spain than even the Cubans. To-day our flag, the symbol of humanity, the emblem of human freedom, the ensign of national majesty and power, the pledge of national fidelity to duty, floats over the Gem of the Antilles and over the capital of the Philippines.

Surely we are a new republic indeed! Almost in the twinkling of an eye we have dropped our insularity, our isolation, and, spanning half the globe with our fleets and our armies, we stand alongside of our Mother, England, as the promoter of civilization, the friend of the downtrodden, the staunch defender of human freedom.

Turning now from this contemplation of ourselves as a new republic we may well ask with all seriousness, What are our new duties? This question possibly cannot be answered conclusively and finally at the present time. We are in the midst of a current of events that is sweeping on resistlessly, changing national relations, and no man can predict with any degree of certainty what the outcome of a twelvemonth may be. But so far as human foresight can predict, it seems inevitable that before the present war is ended we shall find ourselves in full control of the Spanish colonies in the West Indies and in the Philippines. Nearly two millions of people in the Atlantic Ocean, and possibly ten millions in the Pacific Ocean, freed from three hundred years of Spanish rule and wrong, will be under the protection of our flag, and look to us for stable government, for justice, and for guidance. What shall we do with these people?

Shall we restore them to Spain? To ask this question is to answer it. Such a course would be manifestly absurd. Why should we wrest these colonies from Spain at all, if only to give them back? It is true that we began the war in the interest of the Cubans, with no ultimate aim at securing possession of the Philippines; nevertheless, inasmuch as the course of the war has thrown the Philippines into our possession, we become morally accountable for their final disposition. While we would have been slow to undertake to wrest them from Spain, however strong the appeal of humanity, now that we have them in our power it would be as unjustifiable in us to restore them as it would be for us to institute a government over them as remorseless and cruel as that hitherto exercised by Spain herself. Shall we surrender the Philippine Islands to any other nation? No nation has any claim on them, so that we are not called upon to recognize ourselves as under any possible obligation to give them up to any other people. We have no right to sell them, for they are not ours to sell; we are not dealing in people; we are not authorized to establish an auction-block for the sale of colonies. The only possible reason that could be urged why we should surrender them to Great Britain, or Germany, or Russia, would be that the inhabitants of the islands would be better cared for by some other power than by us. This we are not prepared to admit. There is nothing in our Constitution, nothing in our history, nothing in the genius of our institutions, to indicate any lack of ability on our part as a nation to safeguard the rights of the inhabitants of the Philippine Islands as sacredly, and to promote their prosperity and progress in the lines of civilization as thoroughly, as can be done for them by any nation under the sun. On the other hand, our whole history as a people has been apparently in the line of preparation for the exercise of the sort of guardianship which we seem called upon to furnish both in the West Indies and the Philippines.

Under the protection of our flag there may be established both in the West Indies and the Philippines some form of local government which shall be at once free and stable, modeled after our own, under which the people may enjoy the advantages of civil and religious liberty, and be sharers in the products of their own toil. On the restoration of peace and the re-establishment of law and order there should be inaugurated such reforms as will lead eventually to the political, industrial, intellectual, and religious revolution of the people. These radical changes do not come hastily,—nearly three centuries have elapsed since the Pilgrims landed at Plymouth,— but they will in time. It is our high privilege to inaugurate these reforms and supply the conditions of their progress. Three hundred years of Spanish rule have witnessed little or no progress among the subject peoples. Spain has no love for liberty, and no genius for colonization. It is our privilege and our most solemn obligation to replace Spanish despotism with American liberty: to substitute for Spanish mediævalism the Christian civilization of the twentieth century.

This, then, is the new republic as I conceive it: seventy millions of free men, firmly planted on a continent of exhaustless wealth, rich in material resources and mighty in its institutions; a polyglot people rendered homogeneous by language, liberty, law, and loyalty; nurtured and disciplined by Providence for its lofty mission of embodying in its Constitution and laws the highest ideal yet attained of democracy. Its new duty, that which lies at its doors, which it cannot shirk without weakness or neglect without shame, is to throw its strong, protecting arms around the West India Islands in the East and the Philippine Islands in the West, until the providence of God shall make clear to us that our mission for this people is ended. We are to extend the zone of human liberty, and to take our place along with Great Britain as the agents of civilization, the harbingers of peace.

A stirring moment was that following the close of General Morgan's address. Bishop Fitzgerald said that Dr. Clark had made one mistake. He had announced that both sides in the late war would be heard, but all that had been said had been on one side.

Dr. Clark happily retorted, "Because there is but one side any more."

Bishop Fitzgerald then stated that his purpose in rising was to propose that the bishop of the African Methodist Episcopal Church be presented to the Convention. Amidst the most impressive expectation Bishop Arnett arose, and, taking Bishop Fitzgerald's hand, said, "Not only have the blue and the gray stood side by side; but now the black and the white shake hands across the chasm, and it is all done!"

It was an instant for which decades have waited. It was a foretaste, indeed, of that "new republic" in which all but the love of God's children for one another shall be forgotten.

True were the words of Chairman Landrith: "It is hard for us who have been born since the war to believe that there ever was a war. And, if there had been such Christian Endeavor Conventions held North and South prior to 1860 there never would have been a war."

The glorious meeting was then dismissed by Rev. Dr. Curry, of Birmingham, Ala.

SUNDAY.

A Sabbath of God's Power.

NOT since that pentecostal Convention Sabbath in Boston have we had one like it. Nashville had been described by several citizens as "a Sunday-place," it being as difficult to bring out its people to a mid-week religious meeting as it is easy to gather them on Sunday. That day, then, was the time on which the Convention might have been expected to place its strongest impress on the locality.

And this expectation was not disappointed. Of course, a detailed account, even the most meagre, of the more than one hundred services conducted by the visiting Endeavorers is impossible. The delightful weather was an inspiration, the unparalleled scenes of the past few days another inspiration; the crowded churches, the throngs of fresh young faces, the eager receptivity, the hearty appreciation, all moved upon the preachers; and, even though they had won national and international reputation by many a noble sermon, they surpassed themselves on this occasion.

The day was not permitted to pass without one stupendous exhibition of divine power. This came at the morning Quiet Hour, when, at the call of Dr. Chapman for a definite consecration to God, a wholehearted surrender, a giving themselves up to complete obedience, a promise to be written down in the Bible and confessed openly before men, at least one thousand souls, with tears and sobs and glad rejoicings, took the great step. They crowded the space along the platform, falling on their knees. The aisles from front to back were filled with kneeling penitents. It was the hour of God's right hand. Hundreds of ministers found at that moment a new baptism of power. Some of the most famous of them, men gloriously blessed of God, yet testified that that hour was the turning-point of their lives.

Two deeds of brotherly service carried out by the Endeavorers deserve to be ranked even with this superb event. One was the meeting in the car-shed with the street-car men and motor-men, inspired and conducted by that warm-hearted Californian, E. C. Gilbert. Among the speakers was Dr. Clark. As a result of the meeting, a Christian Endeavor society is to be formed among the street-car men of Nashville.

The other service was in the penitentiary. The Endeavorers crowded into the chapel until many had to be turned away. Mr. Wallis, the noble Kentucky laborer for prison Endeavor, led a magnificent and powerful service, as the result of which one more is to be placed on the glorious roll of prison Endeavor societies.

If it bore no other fruit than this Sabbath brought forth, the Convention must be counted a spiritual triumph.

SUNDAY AFTERNOON.

Meeting for Men Only.

Conducted by John Willis Baer.

NO gay-tinted, gauzy, summery female attire, brightened by colored ribbons and tropical-hued hat-plumes; only a sea of black waistcoats, or drab or crash, with now and then a white vest displayed and a warm-hued necktie, lightened the monotonous sombreness of the physical side of the men's meeting. But there was spiritual warmth on the expectant faces and in the singing of the rich baritone and bass voices, which, under Mr. Estey's leadership, rolled out a volume of song that filled the building.

One fruit of the meeting plucked early was the following announcement which was sent up: "God willing, when I get home Thursday night, I will summon all the pastors of my little city, with their working members, and make a prayerful effort to carry the spirit of this meeting into my entire town."

By this time every one was familiar with the consecrated voices of the Convention musical leaders and soloists, — Foster, Excell, Yarnelle, and Estey; but there remained the rare good fortune of hearing these four sweet singers joined in a superb quartette. Try to imagine the rapturous silence with which "Does It Pay?" and "Come Back, My Boy," were listened to, and the irrepressible encore which was clapped from hands that were wet while they clapped with moisture from tear-blurred eyes. But words fail. It was simply wonderful.

Before Dr. J. Wilbur Chapman had spoken a word, "Hallelujah," "Amen," and "Glory to God!" were heard all over the room.

Dr. Chapman said that under such circumstances it did not seem necessary to preach. And he did not preach, in the usually accepted sense of the word. He told them about the conversion of Elijah P. Brown, the former infidel, who founded *The Ram's Horn*, and of Colonel Atkinson at the Bowery Mission; and the pathos in these wonderful revelations of the love of God just melted the audience, until tears and sobs and hallelujahs mingled all over the room.

It was a meeting to be remembered along with that memorable men's meeting in Tent Williston at Washington and the mountain-top scenes in some of Dr. Chapman's noon-day meetings at San Francisco. No, not alongside of them, but ahead of them in the deep, mighty power of the Spirit of God, whose throbbings could be felt all through the assembly.

And when Dr. Chapman closed with the question, "What does God ask in return for his love?" and answered it by the story of a deaf and dumb girl who, in the absence of her loving father in Europe, had been taught to speak in an asylum for mutes, and, when he arrived home, utterly overcame his fatherly feelings by exclaiming, "Papa, I love you!" it seemed as if the message had gone to the very bottom of every heart and broken up its fountains.

Hundreds of hands went up in request for special prayers, and hundreds arose in silent emphasis of that request.

First Presbyterian Church.

Honoring God's Day.

It would not be a Christian Endeavor Convention without a Sabbath-observance rally. During the Tennessee Centennial the exposition-grounds were closed on the Lord's Day, and of course that was the rule of our Convention. The ordinarily thronged street-cars were deserted, the Sunday issues of the papers were ignored, and Nashville's many stately churches were crowded with throngs of reverent young folks.

The Sabbath-observance meeting was held in the afternoon, at the First Presbyterian Church, under Treasurer Shaw's skilful direction. Three strong addresses constituted a powerful battery.

The singing was led by Mr. Excell, and Rev. W. F. McCauley, of Ohio, conducted the devotional exercises.

The first speaker was Rev. Mr. Perry, of California.

Address by Rev. Barton W. Perry, Ph. D.,
San Leandro, Cal.

The Sabbath and Christian Evangelism.

The first step in developing Christian growth is to march in accord with evangelical doctrines. And a most important doctrine is Sabbath Observance. This law of God is written in his Book and upon our physical natures. It is necessary that we have this sacred time in order that we may be able to feed the spiritual life. We need this time as individuals, in order to influence and mould the community. Health, morals, and spiritual life demand it. When God gave the Sabbath law, he attached a penalty. That penalty was nothing less than death. Does that punishment follow to-day? We have a picture of a Garden of Eden where the beasts of the field were at peace with man. All nature was at peace. Man disobeyed God, and all nature began a warfare against him. This conflict continues until this day.

On the plains in 1849 the men and horses that rested on Sunday reached the land of gold in advance of those who travelled every day. The Jew has a thousand generations of Sabbath-keeping ancestors back of him, and he will be about his little "bishness" some ten years after the average American is dead. The physical part of man runs down unless this "seventh day of rest" is accepted to restore the exhaustion after six days of labor. This is a recognized law of science to-day, but it appeared in the Law of Moses and had the same penalty as the ultimate result.

From the physical we turn to the moral. It has been well said that if a child's body grows and its mind does not, it will be an idiot; if the body and mind grow and the morals do not, it will be a criminal. This law needs to be emphasized. Every Christian Endeavor society ought to be and is, if true to the pledge, a training-school in good morals. We must arouse ourselves, and all the good people of the country, to the fact that immorality is dangerous to the State. The great Blackstone said, "To profane the Sabbath will corrupt the morals." The old-fashioned American Sunday was the Gibraltar of this nation. The first act of our fathers, as they landed on the bleak New England coast, was to kneel in prayer. Then they went out to build a church, before building houses in which to live.

We are proud of the fact that we are a great nation, but we cannot hold up the truth too often that a holiday Sunday will bring us to our ruin. Look at the people of Southern Europe; they are not altogether bad, but they have no proper idea of God's law of the Sabbath. It is a mild statement to say that those people have degenerated. Even in the matter of the Sunday holiday it has come to pass that it is only for the rich. The tailor is not out with his children at the merry-go-round. No! He is working away at the bench for dear life. The mason is not eating his picnic lunch on the banks of some beautiful river. No! He is handling the trowel on the boulevards of Paris. That is the picture of the poor man and Sunday in Southern Europe.

The infidel, the saloon, and the Sunday paper are doing a work that, unless checked, will drag our poor people down to the same level. Satan has combined his forces to entice the laboring man to cut down the tree that has given him shelter and rest since the foundation of this government. These forces of hell are united to destroy the Sabbath day. If the divinely ordained day of rest is destroyed the Church will soon go. With the Sabbath and the Church gone, we must bid good-by to our American liberty.

Let us in a word contrast the people of Scotland with those of Southern Europe. In Scotland, on Saturday afternoon the preparation for the Sabbath is made. The house is thoroughly cleaned, including the stone front doorstep. On Sunday, all places of business, restaurants, and saloons are closed. The people throng the streets with hymn-book and Bible in hand, going to church. Scotch character and religion has stamped itself upon every civilized spot in the world. And we may add that the stock at home is as good as when the transplanting began.

We can see that a holiday Sunday will bring to the laboring man the husks of the prodigal son. We as the Church of the living God have a most difficult work to do. We are not discouraged; and we believe that it is according to the spirit of the words of our Lord Jesus that all Christians should stand foursquare against the attempt of the saloon-keepers, the Sunday press, and criminals generally, to transform our Sabbath day of rest into the holiday of Southern Europe. Bull-fights will follow as the next step after our present Sunday ball-games, bicycle-races, and open beer-gardens. With this will come the illiterate degeneration of Spain.

Our American liberty came in at the same door and at the same time with what has been known as the American Sabbath. Not only civilization, but the Christian religion will halt and fall back if the Sabbath day of rest is lost out of our homes and communities. The nations that have stamped characters and civilization upon the world are the God-fearing, the Sabbath-keeping, the Protestant lands of England, Scotland, and America. In the natural course of events, which is the providence of God, these three nations are one in aim, one in purpose, one in destiny.

Dr. Hathaway, general secretary of the American Sabbath Union, "hath a way," as Mr. Shaw said, of illuminating the Sabbath question. He speaks with extreme force and vigor; he is a Sabbath-defence Gattling-gun.

Address by Rev. I. W. Hathaway, D.D.,
New York City.

THE AMERICAN SABBATH: SACRED OR SECULAR?

Mr. Chairman and Fellow Christian Endeavorers:—What shall be the character of the American Sabbath in the opening years of the twentieth century?

No institution can be of permanent benefit to the human race except it be rooted to the eternal truth, and developed in obedience to the law of its purpose.

The Sabbath is an institution co-extensive with time, and inhering in eternity; an institution of marvellous history, and one of infinite benefaction to man, and vital to every interest of the human race, both present and future.

We must know its nature and be obedient to its purpose if we would enjoy its benefactions.

Every flower must grow in obedience to the design of its being if it would reach the goal of beauty or fragrance. So every tree and every institution must be obedient to its purpose if it would bear fruit good for man.

The question of the Sabbath which now confronts the American people is, Shall this day be a holiday or a holy day?

THE IMPORTANCE OF THIS QUESTION.

The importance of this question is but little appreciated by the American people.

There is no question that can be propounded to an American audience of greater moment than this one, no one upon the answer of which more vital issues depend.

If I may be instrumental in arousing one soul in this great audience to a new realization of what the Sabbath means to the people of this country, to its overshadowing importance, and its vital relation to every American institution and interest, I shall not have travelled two thousand miles in vain.

The one great need to-day in the American Church and in the American public is that they shall be awakened and educated to the nature and value of the Sabbath day as a day to be kept sacred to rest and worship.

There are tens of thousands of young people growing up in this country without conviction or knowledge of the true nature and purpose of the Sabbath, and many of those who do know are either indifferent or careless as to how it shall be used.

The question for each one of us to answer is, Shall the American Sabbath be a day for rest and worship, or shall it be a day given over to secular pursuits, amusements, pleasure, games, sports, excursions, and with these an ever-increasing amount of business transactions? Shall it be a day of communion with God, a day of spiritual quickening, a day for the healing of the soul, or a day wherein God is forgotten, his book closed, his house forsaken, and his name dishonored? Shall it be a day of quiet and peace, or shall it be a day of noise and confusion? Shall we have the church bell, or shall we have the clash of brazen instruments heading the procession and enlivening the excursion?

Some of us who have reached mid-life can remember the Sabbath mornings of our youth, when it seemed to us that the very air was redolent with the perfumes of the heavenly gardens and that the angels were hovering over, dispensing their richest benedictions in gifts of peace and joy and love in the home, in the community, and in the church; when it was a calm, sweet day of communion with God and our earthly friends, a day of rest of the body and the soul, a day of refreshing and recuperation of both physical and spiritual life.

Shall the American Sabbath of the twentieth century be such a day, or shall it be a day of sports, gaming, boat-racing, bicycle-riding, ball-playing, horse-racing, and all secular amusements and business?

The pressing and immediate demand of this question is but dimly comprehended either by the Church or the State.

There are to-day a thousand questions which are given the precedence to this by our moral and religious teachers; a thousand things that occupy the attention of our people, all of which are subordinate and should be subordinated to this greater question of saving our American Christian Sabbath.

There are many questions that claim the attention of our scientists, philosophers, statesmen, and business men, questions that will revolutionize our business and social relation, that may change the geography of the world, or pull down or build up empires, not one of which are as pregnant with the weal or woe of our people, with the strength or weakness, the glory or the shame, of this nation, as this one — What shall be the character of the American Sabbath?

For this reason, that a secularized Sabbath will produce heart-failure in all American institutions.

Whether this nation shall go forward to its ultimate, legitimate destiny does not depend upon the issue of the present war, or of other wars that yet may be, but the character of her Sabbath shall determine whether her future shall be one of advance or decline.

I would bring this Sabbath question to the front, which its importance demands. God forbid that it shall longer be treated with indifference and contempt. God forbid that it shall longer be trodden under foot and relegated to the rear by those who love their country and who are seeking the welfare of their fellow men.

Why should this question be further neglected? Why should it longer be subordinated to a thousand questions less important?

THE FUTILITY OF CHRISTIAN WORK WITHOUT A SACRED SABBATH DAY.

We do not seem to realize that all Christian endeavor, all church work, all ministrations of the gospel, all ethical teaching, in short, all efforts of the Christian or the statesman for the defence of the American home, the American Church, or the American State, without a sacred day, is love's labor lost, for a profaned Sabbath will quench the fires of a Christian civilization faster than we can kindle them. The American Church is sending out hundreds of missionaries to convert the heathen world to a religion whose citadel is being captured by an enemy at home. Our armies are carving out empires among the islands of the seas, while the citadel of both civil and religious liberty at home is being destroyed.

The lamp of the "Goddess of Liberty enlightening the world" is in imminent danger of extinction by a secularized Sabbath.

The entire American people need to give special attention to the conservation of the American Christian Sabbath, for it is the palladium of both the Church and the State.

THE DUTY OF THE CHURCH.

That the Church should be aroused to the defence of the sacred character of the Sabbath goes without saying. If the Church does not defend the sacred character of the day, no one will. If the American Christian Sabbath is lost to this nation, it will be lost because of the lethargy and indifference of the American Church. If it is saved, it will be saved by the awakened interest, the quickened conscience, and the renewed fidelity of the Church. Upon her rests this great responsibility. In her hands has been placed the oracle of God; at her hands it will be required.

THE NECESSITY OF SABBATH LEGISLATION.

That there should be civil law to protect and safeguard the Sabbath day is a principle too well established to require in this day any defence. The claims of the Sabbath require the enactment of civil statutes for the peace and good order of society, the same as any other part of the moral law requires attention of our civil authorities—not for any prescribed form of Sabbath observance, nor for the enforcement of any religious obligation of faith or worship, but wholly in the interest of morality and the protection of the inalienable rights of the individual to a day of rest and the opportunity of worship.

REASONS WHY THE SABBATH SHOULD BE KEPT SACRED.

Let us now briefly look at some further reasons why the Sabbath should be kept as a day sacred to rest and worship, a day for religious exercise and spiritual culture.

We are often told that we should not endeavor to promote Sabbath observance upon religious grounds to those who are not professed Christians, or who do not accept our religion or Bible.

But we cannot ignore the fact that man is a religious creature; and more, that he is a child of God, and in connection with this fact that the Sabbath is a divine institution, given of God to meet the innate demands of man's nature, as he, too, came from God. The Sabbath and man are cognate, as are the air and the human lungs, or the light and the human eye. If man shall shut his eye and refuse the light, we cannot teach him any other use for this organ. If man shall reject God and turn from the truth, it will not change his nature nor his needs — man needs God, and because of this the Sabbath was given. Man's need of God is not changed by man's rejection of God, nor can the purpose and nature of the Sabbath be changed to meet the conditions of his unbelief.

THE PRIMAL PURPOSE OF THE SABBATH.

The primal purpose of the Sabbath was and is that man shall know God, may become acquainted with his nature, may be able to recognize his own relation to God, his need of the Divine Presence, and the infusion of the Divine Life into his own.

The Sabbath was given that one day in seven the demands of the world should halt, that man may learn that he has a soul, and that he is something more than an animal.

To this end, the Sabbath was made the first memorial of creation, a contemplation of which is calculated to inspire adoration, worship, and faith, while the Christian Sabbath is memorial of both creation and redemption, and especially so of the crowning miracle and witness; namely, the resurrection. The Christian Sabbath is not only memorial but prophetic of all that lies within the hope of the Christian soul. The Christian Sabbath is the divine searchlight, revealing to the eye of Christian faith the blessedness and glory of the Eternal City and Life.

Can this statement be controverted, that the Sabbath was given for religious uses to meet the religious demands of human nature? If not, any and all secular use of the day is a desecration.

It is true that man's body needs the Sabbath because man is a unit in his being, and the needs of his body are in harmony with the needs of the soul. *The body must rest in order that the soul may worship.*

There is no meaning in the word "Sabbath" nor the day so designated apart from the fact that man is the child of God. The so-called civil Sabbath is but a superstructure resting upon this foundation. No Sabbath can long be maintained apart from its divine authority and sacred character. A secularized Sabbath perverts its purpose, and therefore becomes a curse rather than a blessing to man and the world. Every blessing of this life, abused and perverted, becomes a curse. Every evil in this world is the product of a perverted blessing. A secularized Sabbath becomes a positive source of evil. God is less honored and Satan better served on a secularized Sabbath than on any other day of the week.

There is little, if any, physical rest in a secular Sabbath. Nearly every method of spending the day, aside from that of rest and worship, is a weariness to the flesh as it is a disturber of the peace. A body, to be rested, must have the co-operation of a healthy mind and a clear conscience. Monday morning does not find the laborer recuperated for his task either in brawn or brain who has spent the Sabbath forgetful of his spiritual need, even though he may have refrained from all positive excess, save that of laziness, during the day.

A secular Sabbath robs man of his rest, and opens the door to temptation and indulgence to that which enervates and weakens the moral and physical man.

Those who have to do with laboring men will tell you that Monday morning they never expect a full force to be ready for work, because many have not recovered from the excesses and profanation of the Sabbath. The same is true of all classes who secularize the day. They are exhausted rather than recuperated.

Blackstone affirms, and experience confirms his word, that a profaned Sabbath is usually followed by a flood of immorality, and Emerson speaks truly when he emphasizes the contagion of the immoral.

The evils therefore of a secularized Sabbath are not simply negative, but positive. Voltaire justly remarked that Christianity could not be overthrown until the Christian Sabbath was first destroyed. He might have justly added that with the destruction of the Christian Sabbath not only would Christianity be overthrown, but with it would go public morality, national virtue, and all civil and religious liberty. Fast upon the heels of a profaned Sabbath will come the grasping avarice and competitive greed of business, that shall enslave both body and soul of the employees.

THE SIGNS OF THE TIMES.

It requires no profound study to discover that the drift is setting strongly toward a secular Sabbath in these United States of America, and that the secular current is being augmented year by year by a thousand rivulets, so that to-day it is swollen into what threatens to be an irresistible flood.

Time forbids us to undertake to enumerate or catalogue the many forces, social, political, and commercial, that are to-day combining to sweep away our distinctively American Christian Sabbath.

But the greatest danger lies in the fact that those who should be actively engaged in its defence are standing idly by, or perhaps for lack of conviction or knowledge are by their influence and example giving aid or comfort to the forces of the enemy.

THE EXAMPLE AND TEACHING OF JESUS CHRIST.

Many persons endeavor to believe that Jesus abrogated the law of the Sabbath as expressed in the decalogue, and in its place has given us a Sabbath of liberty, wherein each man shall be a law unto himself. This they do because he corrected the false interpretation and the traditional teaching of the Pharisees. There is not a shadow of evidence that he, by word or act, lessened the binding obligation of the Sabbath law. First, he tells us distinctly that he came not to destroy but to fulfil the law. In his native town of Nazareth, we read that he went into the synagogue as was his wont on the Sabbath day. I will call your attention briefly to three allusions to the Sabbath made by him, all of which were in defence of the Sabbath, and his interpretation of the same.

First. He said," The Sabbath was made for man, and not man for the Sabbath." In this he pronounced the Sabbath co-extensive with the human race, that man always had and always would need the Sabbath. It was made for man of the nineteenth and twentieth centuries no less and perhaps more than during any previous period of man's history. Again, to get the true and full force of this remark, we must try and understand his estimate of man, what he means by man. We must remember that it was the man whom he had come to save.

The trouble with us is that we take our estimate of man and try to fit the Sabbath to such a man. To those whose highest estimate of a man is found in a prize-ring the Sabbath would be made for prize-fighting. But the man in the estimate of the Lord Jesus Christ is the immortal man, made in the image of God. For him the Sabbath was made.

Second. He said, "The Son of man is Lord also of the Sabbath." What other part of the decalogue did he thus dignify? And he certainly could not have announced himself Lord of that which he had or was about to destroy. He is not the Lord of the dead, but of the living.

Third. Jesus said in defence of himself when the Pharisees were about to slay him because he had healed the impotent man at the pool of Bethesda on the Sabbath day, "My Father worketh hitherto, and I work." This was in defence of his Sabbath work. What did this mean other than that his Father worked on the Sabbath to save man as he had done?

It is generally conceded that the days of creation were millenniums, in the last of which man was created. After the ages of creation succeeded the age of rest, or the Sabbatic age. God rested from creation and turned to the work of redemption, which is the Sabbath occupation of both God and man.

The Sabbath is rest from worldly occupation that we may work for and with God for the saving of men.

This is the plain interpretation of the words of our Master when he said, in his own defence, "My Father worketh hitherto, and I work."

HOW SHALL THE AMERICAN SABBATH BE SAVED?

What this land needs more than all else to-day is a revival of Sabbath observance. What the Church needs is a new conversion and a strong conviction on this subject.

The public conscience needs a new quickening concerning this matter.

But above all, we must depend upon the young people of America, members of the Christian Endeavor society and all similar organizations of our Christian young people. If they inform themselves on this subject and interest themselves in this cause, with the enthusiasm and zeal which characterizes all of their work, our American Sabbath may yet be saved.

In New Jersey we have a Sabbath Observance Department of the State Union, with a superintendent who is securing the appointment of superintendents in each County Union, securing Sabbath Observance committees in each local or church society. Some of these are using pledges, pledging their members to abstain from certain popular and flagrant methods of Sabbath desecration. But with or without the pledge, they are, by both precept and example, creating a healthier tone, and, by the distribution of Sabbath literature, promoting education on this subject and creating a new interest in regard to the command of God, which says, "Remember the Sabbath day to keep it holy."

The American Sabbath in the opening years of the twentieth century will be what the young people of America to-day shall make it.

The answer to this great question is with you. May the Spirit of God awaken you to its infinite importance, and may your inestimable privilege be realized, and your golden opportunity improved, and may the reward which shall be commensurate with the divine approbation be yours.

"A craftsman," said Mr. Shaw, "is a man that has something to do and knows how to do it. This man Crafts has something to do, and knows how to do it." And the honored head of the Reform Bureau proved by his vigorous address that this was no empty eulogy.

Address by Rev. Wilbur F. Crafts, Ph.D.,
Washington, D. C.

THE SABBATH IN THE TWENTIETH CENTURY.

We are told that "the complicated civilization of our times requires that Sabbath observance and Sabbath laws shall be relaxed." Nay; this is a new reason why they should be maintained and strengthened. Did Adam, to whom the Sabbath law of work and rest was given before the fall — did he, who knew nothing of "cut-throat competition," and "soulless corporations," and "hard masters," and wearying "tricks of trade," need a Sabbath law more than we do to-day, when sin has put its curse into the Edenic blessing of labor? At Sinai, where the Sabbath law was re-proclaimed, did those Hebrew herders, moving on at three miles an hour, need a law to protect them against the overstrain more than the engineers of to-day, who drive their iron dragons a mile a minute with hand on the throttle, eye on the track, every power alert? Did those dozen farmers from whose plowing-bee Elisha was called to be a prophet,— I have seen in that region a modern plowing-bee of eighteen,— did those farmers, gossiping together as they kept step with their slow oxen, need a Sabbath law more than the lumberman of our Northwest, who saws out a hundred thousand feet of lumber a day, and must watch the swift-moving circular-saw with intensest gaze lest in a moment of inattention it should mistake him for a log? Did the farm of Boaz, where the friendly co-operation of capital and labor left nothing to be desired — did that and other such places of that age require a Sabbath law for protection of servants more than it is required by the millions of employees to-day whose master is "neither man nor woman, neither brute nor human," but the ghoul without a soul we call a corporation? Did Dorcas, sitting out in the sunlight beside her cottage, distaff in hand, leisurely spinning and weaving the coats and garments for the little orphans that played at her feet — did she require the protection of a Sabbath law more than the young girl of fourteen in a modern mill, working in the close air and clanging noise, under a hard master?

Turning to the more recent times, when the foundations of this republic were laid on the Bible, the Sabbath being the tap-root of American institutions, did our fathers, when they lived half a mile apart, and worked in the forest and field in the open air, every man his own master or with his father or his neighbor for his master, and came in at dark to sleep undisturbed by the bells and whistles, curtained with the soft velvet of silence, need a day of protected quiet more than their sons in the tenement of to-day, where the going to bed at night is often like the "charge of the light brigade"—noises in the flat above, noises in the flat at the right, noises in the flat at the left, noises in the flat below; the high fiddle-diddle of a midnight dance on the floor overhead; the crash of a family jar just beyond the wall on the right; a piano through the wall on the left, making love on that side and hate on this side at midnight; while the flat below does its share in the torture by an early start on a fishing-excursion to murder sleep in the morning.

When nearly all the work was in the open air, in forest and field, was there more need to protect the toilers' right to one day's release from labor than now, when many thousands work day and night in the mine, and thousands more in stifling shops? Is there more excuse for keeping thousands toiling on the Sunday mail now, when a letter is carried from New York to San Francisco in five days, than in our fathers' days, when such a journey took five months? Was there less excuse for our fathers to issue Sunday papers when news crossed the Atlantic in two months than there is for us, when the news of Europe reaches us by telegraph the day before it happens?

Every change in the world since the Sabbath was instituted has been a new reason why God's Sabbath laws and ours should not be changed. They came to the kingdom for such a time as this. More than ever before we should see to it that neither ourselves nor others cause any Sunday work except of necessity or mercy.

A quartette of male voices from the Jubilee Singers sang in an exquisite manner, "Remember Thy Creator," and Dr. Vance pronounced the benediction.

First Cumberland Presbyterian Church.

The Women's Meeting.

Woman's Work for Children.

The First Cumberland Presbyterian Church was packed. It would not be a bull to say that this meeting was manned throughout by women. Mrs. F. E. Clark led. Mrs. J. L. Hill conducted devotions. The exercises then took the form of an open parliament.

It was found that about one-third of those present were mothers, one-half were Junior superintendents, and nearly all of them Sunday-school teachers.

The first part of the hour was devoted to mothers. Some had never heard of mothers' meetings. Others knew of such meetings, but had never attended them; but all agreed that they must be a good thing. A few promised to go home and try to organize them in their own churches. Thirty-seven women took part in this parliament, and Mrs. J. L. Hill, of Salem, Mass., made an address.

The second part of the time was devoted to Junior Endeavorers. The parliament brought out objections to the term "associate member," because too many were satisfied to remain in that relation. "Trial member" met with objections on opposite grounds. It was agreed to substitute the term " preparatory member," and strive to fulfil its meaning.

In the third, or missionary part of the meeting, Miss Margaret W. Leitch, of Ceylon, made an address.

The women spent an hour and a quarter, and then, singularly enough finding that the last word had not been spoken, resolved to adjourn to meet again at Detroit, '99.

MONDAY MORNING.

First Cumberland Presbyterian Church.

Junior Workers' Conference.
A MINE FOR JUNIOR WORKERS.

That is just what the Junior school of methods was. It crowded the spacious First Cumberland Presbyterian Church, and even the standing-room was filled. Mrs. J. L. Hill, of Salem, Mass., presided most gracefully, wittily, and wisely.

That wide-awake Junior worker, Mr. C. J. Atkinson, of Toronto, had "a live subject;" namely, a genuine boy, whose pockets he dared to investigate, hauling out a baseball, a whistle, a string, *The Youth's Companion*, a paper of stamps, an old Sunday-school lesson leaf. He came to the conclusion that the average boy is devoted, 50 per cent of him to sport, 15 per cent to fun, 10 per cent to noise, 10 per cent to hobbies, 5 per cent to religion, and 10 per cent to asking questions. The point he made was that the worker with boys must consider their natural inclinations if he would win and hold them. His own Junior society, starting with four boys and seventeen girls, now has an average attendance of one hundred boys and twenty-five or forty girls. The reason? In connection with the society is a baseball club and a football club, each champions for two seasons, a bugle band, an orchestra, and a "hobby club."

Miss Elsie L. Travis, one of Boston's best Junior workers, gave an inspiring set of illustrations of what Junior societies are actually accomplishing. Mr. W. T. Ellis, of Philadelphia, followed with an account of the workings of Intermediate societies so clear and attractive that it elicited a regular bombardment of questions from the interested audience.

The Canadian Junior, Master Charles E. Eggett, captured the audience with his violin medley of patriotic airs. And, by the way, Juniors never sang better than that choir of more than one hundred beautiful Nashville Juniors.

Mrs. F. E. Clark wanted to beg off from the crowded programme, but the audience as one voice said, "No." She graphically described the great pile of methods such a conference heaps up, each labelled, "Take one," and added another label, "Don't take one;" that is, don't take them to litter the streets with them, as some of the Convention "samples" are thrown away, but take only what you need and are sure you can put to use. Then, premising that she was a "camera fiend," she gave a delightful series of snap-shots at some Junior societies in foreign lands, each with a practical lesson.

Mrs. Hill said that a snow-storm was not expected from Nashville, but nevertheless Mr. Thomas Wainwright, of Chicago, who opened the question-box, was fairly snowed under with questions. However, he was equal to the surprise. The most valuable point brought out was how to get the boys into the society. Eight of the superintendents had more boys than girls in their societies, and they told how they did it. "I invite them to my home every night in the week," said one, "and talk over with them all their affairs." Said another, "The young man who is my assistant is a boy with the boys." Mr. Wainwright urged that always a man and a woman should work together in each Junior society.

One of the most earnest Endeavorers in the Southland is Miss Rebel Withers, of Florida, whose beautiful talk on "Junior Light-bearers," with its story of what was accomplished by a single brave little prayer by a Junior, led all to see the value of the prayer drill in our Junior work. "All Southerners are orators," said Dr. James L. Hill, "from Miss Withers down to the governor." As to that whirlwind of wisdom, Dr. Hill's open parliament that followed, there's no use trying to summarize it here.

After the Bible exercise on kindness to animals so brightly presented by Nashville Juniors, Mr. Baer talked about some "ideas to be kept to the front," — the missionary idea; the prayer-meeting, which must be more than a splendid phonograph; and evangelistic work with children.

"I fear there's something wrong with a man's life," said Rev. Ira Landrith, in the last of this splendid series of addresses, "if he doesn't love little children; and if a woman doesn't love them, I *know* her life is wrong." His talk was an earnest plea, to be summed up in the words, "The time to save little souls is before they are lost."

Mrs. Hill gave for our year's motto, "They brought young children to him," and many hundreds present took upon them the vow, "I will try to bring one young child to Christ," a blessed promise carried by Dr. Francis E. Clark's closing prayer up to the very throne of the child-loving Christ.

Committee Conferences in the Various Churches.

Good-Literature Committee Conference.
By Judge Anson S. Taylor, Washington, D. C.

The meeting of this committee was held in the Sunday-school room of the First Baptist Church.

In the absence of the leader, Judge Anson S. Taylor, of Washington, D. C., acted as chairman. A very interesting and helpful conference was held, made more so by the active part taken by almost all present. Miss Zue H. Brockett, chairman of the District of Columbia Christian Endeavor Union, furnished the conference with a number of copies of their methods of work and suggestions. Under her direction five members of the District of Columbia Union had prepared short articles on

1. Necessity for the Good-Literature Committee.
2. The Good-Literature Committee at work:
    (*a*). Along educational lines.
    (*b*). Collecting and distributing literature.
    (*c*). In the society. (Helping other committees.)
3. The work of the Union Good-Literature Committee.

These articles were distributed to, and read by, persons present, and were well received. Special stress was laid upon our duty to look after bad literature, even while we are circulating the good. Reports were made of active work in assisting the army and navy Young Men's Christian Association.

City Union Officers' Conference.
By Mr. A. E. MacDonald, Chicago, Ill.

The City Union Officers' Conference held in the Young Men's Christian Association Building was well attended, nearly fifty being present. After an opening prayer by Mr. R. N. Stewart, president of the Hyde Park Division of the Chicago Christian Endeavor Union, Mr. A. E. MacDonald, chairman of the conference, presented the following outline of topics and asked that all express their opinions and experience on them freely and promptly.

Topics for Discussion.

1. Union Meetings.
    a — Frequency of.
    b — Nature of.
    c — How to make more helpful.
    d — How to get better attendance on the part of Endeavorers.
2. Pastors' Relation to Union.
    a — Attitude toward.

    b — Attendance at union meetings.
    c — Desirability of a Pastors' Advisory Board.
    d — Pastors as union officers.
3. FINANCIAL SUPPORT OF UNION WORK.
    a — Assess members.
    b — Voluntary contributions.
    c — Collect at union meetings.
    d — Excursions or entertainments.
    e — Legitimate expenses of union.
4. DEPARTMENTS OF UNION WORK ADVISABLE TO UNDERTAKE.
    a — Missionary.
    b — Christian citizenship.
    c — Evangelistic, etc.

The general opinion expressed was that union meetings ought not to be held too frequently, not often enough to in any way interfere with the local church work. The thought was also brought out that it was best to have speakers at the union rallies who understand Christian Endeavor principles and are in thorough sympathy with the workings of Christian Endeavor; that it is most desirable to have a Pastors' Advisory Board to be called together when necessary by the president of the union, and consulted, but that it is best to have laymen rather than busy pastors for union officers.

All present agreed that as little money as possible be asked for from the societies for the union work, and that the function of the union is not the undertaking of any sort of work of an evangelistic, missionary, or such like nature, as a union, but is to instruct as to what Christian Endeavor means, to inspire all Endeavorers to renewed consecration and effort in Christian work, and to extend the bond of fellowship.

Our conference was honored by the presence of Dr. Clark, Secretary Baer, and Treasurer Shaw, and the first two named gentlemen took part in the conference. Dr. Clark suggested in the form of an interrogation the advisability of arranging uniform topics for the use of unions in their rallies, and the conference selected Mr. William T. Ellis, president Philadelphia Union; Mr. A. E. MacDonald, president Chicago Union; Mr. E. C. Gilbert, superintendent of railroad men's work, San Francisco; Mr. H. A. Kinports, president New York City Union; Mr. H. L. Brown, president Memphis Union, as a committee to arrange in conjunction with the officers of the United Society a suggestive list of union meeting topics for the coming year.

The general expression was to the effect that the conference was interesting and helpful.

Lookout Committee Conference.
By Mr. W. S. Leslie, Montreal.

The Lookout Committee Conference was largely attended, and was marked by a free and helpful discussion of this important work. The different divisions of the subject were opened by Mrs. Allan, of Nashville; Rev. J. S. Conning, of Caledonia, Ont.; Mr. G. W. Loggie, of Somerville, Mass.; and Miss Cameron, of St. Louis. Among the suggestions drawn up were the following:—

SECURING NEW MEMBERS.— Always announce the Christian Endeavor meetings on the church leaflet, and at times distribute printed invitations at the church door; have non-members attend several meetings before urging them to join the society; invite the officers of the society, the pastor and church officers, and the Prayer-Meeting Committee, to meet with your committee at times; use socials as a means of interesting possible members, and specially invite them; get all the society to help the Lookout Committee, but don't remove the responsibility from the committee; after each semi-annual election of officers have a conference of all the committees, at which names will be suggested for the Lookout Committee to work on. A teacher of a large Sunday-school class of boys from fourteen to sixteen years old got them interested, first by attending a local union meeting, then by asking them to her own society, and secured nearly every one as an active Christian worker. Above all we must be right ourselves before we can draw others A Philadelphia society ceased for one year any special efforts for new members, but sought to raise the spiritual life of the members, with the result that a number of young people came and asked to be admitted as members.

REACHING YOUNG MEN. — Have a Brotherhood Committee or a separate chapter of the Brotherhood of Andrew and Philip; — an after-meeting on Sunday evening after service, for men only, resulted in fifteen conversions and fifty young men added to the roll of a California society; don't lower the standard if you want the respect of young men; — the Young Men's Christian Association in some places tries to place all its new members in some Endeavor society. Set young men to reach young men.

DEALING WITH UNFAITHFUL ACTIVE MEMBERS. — Meet every two weeks, remembering especially the negligent ones; study their needs, surroundings, and difficulties; think deeply of them; feel deeply for them, especially the timid ones; love them deeply, and show it; pray deeply and definitely for them, and remember the responsibility your prayer places on yourself. Keep a record of the participation of each member, and let them see it at intervals; but use much tact in this. Have each one spoken to by the one best able to. approach him, even if not a member of the committee.

WINNING ASSOCIATE MEMBERS. — You must have a consistent life yourself, love for them, realization of the value of a human soul, faith in God's power to save, a working knowledge of the Bible, power in prayer, and the baptism of the Holy Spirit. Improve your opportunities; choose wisely those with whom to work, usually one of your own sex and about the same age and position in life. Invite all the older Sunday-school scholars to your meetings, and show a personal interest in them there and outside. Ask associate members to go with you on your Christian work, and get them interested in it; we have evangelistic meetings in the church once a week, and the Lookout Committee are scattered through the meeting for personal work. A Virginia pastor had the town divided into twenty districts, and twenty boys of his church who acted as scouts bringing word of new families and their church preferences, and doing errands for him. Six of them have recently joined the church. Make the meetings so spiritual that they must see there is something real in our religion

Corresponding Secretaries' Conference.
By Miss Jennie T. Masson, Indianapolis, Ind.

The conference began exactly on time. The leader distributed printed slips containing twenty-eight themes for conference relating to "The Corresponding Secretary in Local Society Work," in State work, and in United Society work.

The following are some of the points given by various delegates: —

1. Select for corresponding secretary the best worker, even if she has to hold an additional office.

2. One reason of failure in duty in this office is that people who organize societies do not instruct the corresponding secretary in her duties; therefore, before attempting to organize a new society, appoint a committee to learn how to organize.

3. The pastor can help the corresponding secretary by keeping her office in mind, and by informing her of those expecting to leave the city, that she may communicate with the corresponding committee of the State.

4. Presidents can assist by conferring as to what announcements or other communications should be read in the society, and by insisting that the secretary make the announcements. (Being the best worker, of course she can do this.)

5. All committees can assist by keeping their records in good shape so the corresponding secretary can glean from them the information desired by State and United Society officers.

6. Supply the corresponding secretary with stationery and postage funds.

7. Make the corresponding secretary chairman of the Information Committee. Invite her to the committee meetings. Make her a permanent member of the Missionary Committee.

8. Protect the society from advertising schemes, by holding the list of members sacred.

9. Have the corresponding secretary report in business meeting, and read messages from absent members in the consecration meeting.

10. Let the corresponding secretary occasionally visit other societies with a message from her own, and write to other societies for messages.

11. Supply the corresponding secretary with all literature helpful to her work.

12. Hope for the time to come when corresponding secretaries can report to the county, county to district, district to State, State to general secretary. In the meantime, corresponding secretary will have to report to each of these officers, newly organized, disbanded, or re-organized societies.

13. For failure in duty, admonish, rather than scold the corresponding secretary.

14. Suggest to officers that they send out only *one* statistic blank a year, making it do for all convention reports.

15. The Corresponding secretary should take *The Christian Endeavor World*, and induce all other members to do likewise.

16. Remove inefficient corresponding secretaries by incorporating in constitution a clause that continued failure of any officer to do his work is equivalent to his offering his resignation.

Treasurer William Shaw, of Boston, was present, and urged the secretaries to prevail upon their societies to take up work with the Christian Commission among the soldiers. The conference was energetically opposed to the sale of liquor in the canteens.

The conference is not expected to end this year, as the secretaries took dozens of the printed slips home to distribute to county and district secretaries, and to their own members for study.

One secretary said, "I have found in this conference that I don't know anything,"—a great discovery when coupled with the resolution to hereafter find out all possible.

Sunday-School Committee Conference.
By Mr. Thomas Jones, Kansas City, Mo.

The Sunday-school Committee Conference on Monday morning at the First Baptist Church was full of interest and practical suggestions as to the best methods of work. Among some of the questions asked were the following:—

1. What is the best way of getting the Sunday-school scholars interested in the Endeavor society?

2. Is the Sunday-school Committee subject to the orders of the superintendent?

3. Do you think it advisable to place on the Sunday-school Committee one who is not *especially* interested in children for the purpose of developing an interest in them?

4. Is it necessary always that the Sunday-school teacher be a Christian if they teach?

5. What is the best method of conducting a quarterly review?

Among the answers and suggestions offered were these—as to the work of the Sunday-school Committee:—

The committee, as a rule, should have about five members, who are especially interested in children and young people, and they should endeavor to ascertain how many of the Sunday-school scholars there are who do not attend or belong to the Christian Endeavor society, and *vice versa*, how many of the Christian Endeavor society there are who do not attend the Sunday-school, and then labor with those. The Sunday-school Committee can do much in the line of looking after the absent ones, by visiting them and through personal work. The testimony of one person present was that Sunday-school classes always went to pieces under a teacher who was not a Christian, and the consensus of opinion was that we should always try to have out-and-out church-members and Christians for teachers, though there were instances where that could not always be realized. It was suggested that the Sunday-school Committee could be very helpful in furnishing substitute teachers; also that a conference of the Sunday-school superintendent and his officers and the Christian Endeavor society officers should be held occasionally, and thus the mutual interests of the two organizations could be advanced, for there is so much in common between them. It was also said that the committee could do much to promote the work of the Home Department, and that the end should be always kept in view; viz., that the primary aim and object of this committee was the *saving* of our boys and girls in the Sunday-school, and of bringing the Christian Endeavor society in close touch and harmony with its twin sister, the Sunday-school, and thereby increasing the usefulness and efficiency of each.

Lord's Day Committee Conference.
By Rev. Wilbur F. Crafts, Ph. D., Washington, D. C.

Rev. Dr. Crafts, of Washington, D. C., conducted the conference on Lord's Day Committees. He opened the exercises not with a gavel, but with a saw from Nazareth, such as Christ used when he toiled on earth as a working man; a saw such as he gladly laid aside on the eve before the weekly Sabbath, saying, "The Sabbath was made for man."

"Surely," said Dr. Crafts, "the Church that was founded by a carpenter ought to be in close sympathy with the real rights of working men, chief of which is the right to the weekly rest day. But, in fact, the churches are doing but little in defence of the Sabbath, which was never so much attacked and never so little defended as now. From the very nature of the case little can be done to stay the tide of Sabbath desecration by churches acting singly. In this matter a federation of the churches of each city is a manifest prerequisite of effective work, and yet such federations are few indeed. Every Young People's society should have a Lord's Day Committee or a Christian Citizenship Committee, with Sabbath defence as a part of its work; and these committees of all denominations in each town should unite in a Union Lord's Day Committee, to which may well be added some or all of the pastors, the secretary of the Y. M. C. A., the Sabbath observance superintendent of the W. C. T. U., and others interested, including some of the labor leaders. Nothing less than this is adequate to the great work.

"This Sabbath Defence Federation, as it might be called, should hold a series of carefully prepared public meetings to plow the public mind, then sow it with literature carried from door to door by young people going two and two, and by the use of the daily press through a committee of ready writers, after which the harvesting should be done by committees on voluntary closing, on police gazettes and bill-boards and slot machines, not forgetting to appoint a committee to wait on the city and county officers to express and request co-operation. All this ought to be considered the A. B. C. endeavoring. It clearly ought to be done everywhere, but I have not heard of it being done anywhere except years ago at St. Paul, where such a campaign of house-to-house visitation by Endeavorers helped to break a 'ring' which had long enslaved the city. If I were to take a text for what I am seeking to do among the Young People's societies, it would be, 'As the eagle stirreth up her nest.' When the eaglets are old enough the mother bird in seeming severity, but real love, stirs up the nest and pushes her young birds out over the cliff, that they may learn to fly toward the sun. I feel that too many Endeavorers are lingering in the nest, content to go to happy meetings with each other. Let me chide you out by reminding you that going to meetings is only to meals — not 'divine service,' but only preparation for it. Imagine an idling servant talking of serving his master faithfully because he is always on hand at meals and 'takes some part.' Such a one complained, 'It's working between meals that's killing me.' Some Young People's societies are not dying that way. They think they are endeavoring when they are only eating. Let us not only come to Christ, but go forth in some aggressive service.

"The best convention I ever heard of was one where a meeting that would naturally have had an hour and a half of talk was cut down to half an hour and the other hour devoted to systematic work by the five hundred present going two and two from block to block, by card assignments, to bring others to a subsequent meeting and to Christ. Why not so turn out Sabbath-schools, prayer-meetings, Endeavor meetings, for distribution of Sabbath reform literature, in one hour over a whole city? Carry for your shield the completest statement of God's law of the Sabbath, Isa. 58: 13, 14, which ought to be repeated from memory every Sabbath in these times at breakfast, or in some meeting. It presents the three uses of the Sabbath to provide for worship, for rest, and most of all to wean us from selfishness, for which purpose selfish pleasure as well as selfish work is forbidden, the lower 'pleasure' to give place to higher 'delight' in doing good; the stopping of selfish work to increase, not lessen, our prosperity, for it is the Sabbath-keeping nations that ride upon the high places of the earth. The nations that devote seven days a week to selfishness are the poorest physically, mentally, morally, financially, politically; dying nations like China and Turkey, France and Spain. Let us not forget that to-day our most serious foes are not Spanish soldiers but Spanish Sundays."

Following this address there were questions and brief addresses on practical methods of work.

California was the only State reporting any large number of Lord's Day Committees, but the questions showed an earnest desire to go back and undertake definite, united work for Sabbath defence. The conductor urged that Dr. Clark's watchword, "more fruit," be so given practical application.

Rev. Barton W. Perry, Ph. D., of California, greatly helped the conference by his wise suggestions.

Floating Society Workers' Conference.

By Miss Antoinette P. Jones, Falmouth, Mass.

A small but enthusiastic gathering of Floating Christian Endeavor workers and friends met in the chapel of the First Cumberland Presbyterian Church. Miss Antoinette P. Jones, of Falmouth, Mass., was chairman of the conference.

Mr. Miles M. Shand, of Washington, D. C., led the devotional exercises, relating personal experiences on shipboard during a recent six-weeks' voyage on a government errand to South America, referring to his acquaintance with our brother, Carlton H. Jencks, who "went home" from the battleship *Maine*.

The chairman gave a concise account of the Floating Christian Endeavor work, — its beginning, extent, late incidents, and future plans, — with a history of the Christian Endeavor Home for Seamen, Nagasaki, Japan. An extract from a letter from the *Olympia* Endeavorers when at Hong Kong was read by Miss Kellogg. Questions were asked and answered.

Portland, Maine, was represented by C. H. Moseley, who gave an earnest talk on the methods and results of the work in Portland and Saco, Maine.

Miss Lulu Phillips, secretary of the Virginia Union, spoke on the work at Norfolk, Va., and interest aroused at the State Convention by a ship-service for delegates.

William Moore told of the sailor work in that city, and shipboard services.

Miss Elsie D. Kellogg, of Grand Rapids, Mich., newly appointed to Floating Christian Endeavor work for Michigan, told of her desire to engage in the work and welcomed us to Detroit in 1899.

Dr. J. L. Hill, of Salem, Mass., noted the deepened interest of every one in the work of the sailors just now since our navy had been called into prominence, adding responsibility to the work of Floating Christian Endeavor, which was advancing into as yet unexplored regions for Christian Endeavor.

"Sing unto the Lord a new song, and his praise to the end of the earth, ye that go down to the sea, and all that is therein."

Missionary Committee Conference.

By Miss M. Josephine Petrie, New York City.

The Missionary Conference was held in McKendree M. E. Church, and was exceedingly helpful to all present. The following questions and suggestions were offered by the chairman, bringing forth prompt and helpful responses from the audience: Define the distinctive work of the Missionary Committee. What is a successful committee? (Bringing out the need of an enthusiastic chairman as of first importance.) How often should meetings be held? How can you *get* and *keep* members? The best kind of programmes. Best way of giving. Tenth Legion. Best division of $100 given for missionary purposes. Mission study classes, libraries, and other literature. What is your denomination doing toward helping your young people in missionary working and giving? Where to send for supplies for work.

Necessarily the answers were brief, but many denominations were represented, and many new thoughts and plans of work presented which will bear fruit during this coming year.

State Officers' Conference.

(From the Christian Endeavor World.)

President F. M. Gardner, of Massachusetts, had his large gathering of State workers well in hand, and such a team as it was! Among the State presidents were Brett, of New Jersey; McCrory, of Pennsylvania; Sweet, of Iowa; Harlan, of Kansas; Miller, of Ohio; Schumacher, of Maryland; Grotthouse, of Texas; with Miss Masson, Miss Catlin, and other elect women.

The multiplicity of conventions was a question that caused brows to knit. No general conclusion could be reached. Some localities need district conventions because they can be reached by the State officers in no other way.

Most of the State officers testified that they had found it impossible to affiliate with other young people's organizations.

The mission of the State and local unions was the vital theme. The temptation sometimes is to take up with new fads instead of placing the emphasis on greater loyalty to the local church and efficiency in it. The discussion waxed exceedingly interesting on the question whether a union should do specific good-citizenship, evangelistic, missionary, or benevolent work, as a union, or in the main confine itself to re-affirming the fundamental principles of Christian Endeavor and intensifying the life of the local society.

State secretaries' duties were succinctly stated by Secretary McDonald, of Pennsylvania. He keeps record of societies, distributes literature, encourages local societies to report fields where new societies could be organized, co-operates with the presidents and superintendents of departments in sending out circulars regarding conventions, finance, etc.

President Schumacher, of Maryland, suggested that each State, at its convention, emphasize the Quiet Hour.

NOTE.— It is greatly regretted reports of the other splendid conference, the Prayer-meeting, did not arrive in time to be included in this report.— *Scribe.*

MONDAY AFTERNOON.

Auditorium Endeavor.

MISSIONS TO THE FRONT.

Important greetings by telegraph, cable, and letter were announced by Secretary Baer at the beginning of the session from the Paris Chris-

Exterior Auditorium Endeavor, and Parthenon (State Headquarters).

tian Endeavor Union, the Victorian and Australasian Unions, the Japanese Christian Endeavor Union, the National Council of Congregational Churches in session at Portland, Ore., the Californian State Epworth League, the Mexican National Convention in session at Toluca, the Lone Star Christian Endeavor Society of Central America, and from the Spanish Y. P. S. C. E. at Biarritz, France, formerly of San Sebastian, Spain, the Hon. William C. Maybury, Mayor of Detroit, Mich.. the Christian Endeavor Society of the First Presbyterian Church, Hoboken, N. J., and the Endeavorers in South Africa.

The devotional exercises were conducted by Rev. W. S. Danley, Owensboro, Ky., and Rev. B. Wrenn Webb, Maysfield, Ky. Rev. W. J. Darby, of Evansville, Ind., trustee for the Cumberland Presbyterian Church, presided, and " Common-Sense Missionary Methods " was the theme. All the addresses were of unusual power, and were enthusiastically received by the large audience present.

Address by Rev. Arthur Vale Casselman,
Columbiana, O.

MORE GENEROUS GIVING.

It has not been very many years since the insanity of missionary methods was a very popular subject for discussion, even in religious circles. Not so very long ago the sending of Christian missionaries into the far East was characterized by the officials of the East India Company as "the maddest, most expensive, most unwarranted project ever proposed by a lunatic enthusiast." To-day we are gathered not as "lunatic enthusiasts," but as consecrated Endeavorers, to consider not the insanity, but the common sense of missionary methods. Not least among these is " more generous giving."

A wonderful thing is this Christianity of ours. There is nothing like it. They used to say in apostolic times that it "turned the world upside down." It is at the same business to-day. Especially is this true of the world of money. The religion of Jesus Christ takes money, the prolific root of so much of the pride, and covetousness, and selfishness, and sensuality of the world, and completely transforms it into a mighty power for the service and glory of God. It takes the coin of this world, purifies it on the altar of love, and presents it at the great treasury of God, where it is re-coined, receives the stamp of the mint of heaven, the image and superscription of Jesus Christ, and is returned legal tender for all heavenly blessings.

But what are the methods by which such results are effected? Some years ago, at a meeting of one of the mission congregations of Jamaica, a collection was to be taken for missionary purposes. One of the brethren was appointed to preside. and the following resolutions were adopted: "*Resolved.* first, That we will all give. *Resolved*, secondly, That we will give as the Lord has prospered us. *Resolved*, thirdly, That we will all give cheerfully."

Let this incident be our outline and, as Christian Endeavorers in pursuance of a method by which more generous giving to the cause of missions can be secured, let us resolve, in the first place, that we will all give. If there is one fact which is pressing in on the life of the Church for recognition to-day it is this: that the money for the extension of God's kingdom on earth is not to be raised by the spasmodic giving of the few, but by the systematic giving of everybody. The time was, not long since, when our mission boards endeavored to carry on this work almost exclusively by large donations from individuals. But that time is rapidly passing away. Last winter a prominent New York pastor was preparing a paper on the subject of giving, to be read at the Sixth Conference of the Foreign Mission Boards of the United States and Canada. He took one of his most devout members into his confidence and asked him what he would say if he were permitted to speak. "Tell them," said this man of very moderate income, "that in their zeal to secure vast gifts from the few they have forgotten the little gifts of the multitude." Let us learn a lesson from the government. A great war is in progress. One million dollars a day is needed for its support. How is it to be raised? By soliciting great gifts from patriotic millionaires? No. By taxing great corporations thousands of dollars a day? No. How, then? By little insignificant two-cent stamps in the hands of the great mass of citizens. But there is a greater, holier war than that with Spain. There is a greater Leader than Wm. McKinley, who honors himself to enlist as a private under him. The heat of the battle in this conflict is also in foreign lands. Revenue must be raised. How is it to be done? By great donations and legacies from the rich? No; but by the little revenue stamps of God's great tithing system placed upon everything of value that passes through the hands of any loyal citizen of the kingdom of God. Remember that "the mites of the poor become the might of the Church."

Let us resolve, in the second place, that we will give as the Lord has prospered us. The great, yes, the awful, need of more money for God's work, the awful disproportion in the comparison of what God's people spend for themselves and what they spend for God, is appalling. The pleading cry of many of God's servants who labor for the lost in heathendom is heart-piercing. With work waiting to be done in Burmah, yet utterly destitute of funds, Adoniram Judson, in agony of heart, wrote thus of his fellow-Christians in the United States: "I thought they loved me, but they would scarce have known it if I had died. I thought they were praying for us, but they never once have thought of us." Can we blame him when we Christian Endeavorers spend more in a year for collars than we do for the evangelization of the world for Jesus Christ? Can we blame him when one-third of a cent a day from every Christian would evangelize the world in this generation, and we refuse to give it? Yet, as in this world, so in the kingdom of heaven, a man is judged by his money. The standard of judgment, however, differs mightily. The world thinks of money-getting; Christ, of money-giving. The world asks, What does a man give? Christ asks, How does he give? The world asks the amount; Christ, the motive. The world asks, What does he own? Christ asks, How does he use it? The world asks, What does he give? Christ asks, What does he keep?

In the third place, let us resolve that we will give cheerfully. Cheerful, generous giving — and cheerful giving will always be generous — is the inevitable result of consecration, and the secret of such giving in the Christian Endeavor society is the consecration meeting. What is consecration? According to its etymology, it is a making sacred with, a devotion to holy use. It is a practical surrender to the ownership of God, with whom alone we can be made sacred. There were, perhaps, no more cheerful givers in apostolic times than the Macedonians. And what was the secret of their joy and liberality? "Moreover, brethren," says Paul, "we make known to you the grace of God which hath been given in the churches of Macedonia; how that in much proof of affliction, the abundance of their joy and their deep poverty abounded unto the riches of their liberality. For according to their power, I bear witness, yea, and even beyond their power, they gave of their own accord; but first they gave their own selves to the Lord." There is the secret. As soon as we are consecrated, our property is consecrated. The two go together. We cannot consecrate our person without our purses. We can never raise the needed money till we have the consecrated Endeavorers. Remember the consecration meeting and the abundance of our joy will abound unto the riches of our liberality.

Let us return to the Jamaica missionary meeting. After the adoption of these resolutions, each member came forward according to custom, and deposited his offering on the communion-table under the eye of the presiding officer. One of the most well-to-do members hesitated until he began to be noticed. When he finally deposited a small gift, the brother at the table remarked, "That is according to the first resolution but not according to the second." The member retired angrily to his seat; but conscience kept on working, and soon he came forward and doubled his contribution, saying, "Take that, then." "That may be according to the first and second resolutions, but it is n't according to the third," said the brother at the table. The giver, after a little, accepted the rebuke and came up a third time with a still larger gift and a good-natured face. "That," said the presiding brother, " is according to all the resolutions."

But notice another offering. It, too, is being collected in a far-off country. The building, however, is not the little missionary church at Jamaica, but rises resplendent and magnificent amidst the beauties of Judea's hills. The collection-box is here also, near the altar, and "over against" it sits the Son of God, watching and weighing the gifts cast into the treasury. Silver and gold rattle and ring as the rich pass by. "All these have of their abundance cast in unto the offerings of God," mused the heavenly spectator. "And there came a poor widow, who cast in two mites, which was a farthing. Of a truth, I say unto you, that this poor widow hath cast in more than they all," is the remark of the divine observer.

And yet another offering let us notice. It is being lifted in Maine, in California, in Mississippi, in Michigan. The cause is foreign missions. The members are youthful and on the wall hangs a pledge. As the collection-plate is passed around, if you will look closely you will see beside it the same form that sat over against the treasury, engaged in the same occupation of watching and weighing the gifts of men. And if you listen, as some daintily-gloved hand gracefully smuggles a dirty little brown penny from its soft palm into the plate, you may hear Him say, "That is according to the first resolution, but not according to the second." And as some one casts in a larger sum than he wants to because some one sitting beside him has done so, you may hear the divine visitor remark, "That is according to the first and second resolutions, but not according to the third." But as some Endeavorer whose eyes have been on the wall, whose heart has taken in the full significance of the words, "Trusting in the Lord Jesus Christ for strength, I promise him that I will strive to do whatever he would like to have me do" — as that Endeavorer's gift drops into the plate, hard and heavy, you may hear the Master beside the plate say "That is according to all the resolutions."

Next came an address by Rev. Mr. Johnson, of North Carolina.

Address by Rev. T. M. Johnson,
Greensboro, N. C.

More Earnest Study.

More earnest study; more zealous work. How can they accomplish anything except they be zealous? How can they be zealous except they be interested? How can they be interested in that of which they know nothing? How can they know except they study? Some one has said the great missionary facts constitute the fuel; the Holy Spirit, the fire. Bring these together in one soul, and you have a missionary fire — a soul on fire for missions; or, as Paul would express it, "Fervent in spirit." The Psalmist would call it, " The zeal of thine house ; " that is, zeal for the cause.

Our English word "zeal" is derived from the same Greek word that is translated "fervent" in Paul's exhortation to the Romans to be "fervent in spirit." It means to be hot, to boil. About the same idea is in the word translated "zeal" in the declaration of the Psalmist, "The zeal of thine house hath eaten me up." It means to be red, red-hot. Now where there is heat, where there is boiling, there is energy. The scientist discusses how many units of *energy* it requires to raise the temperature of a gallon of water to the boiling-point. The steam-engine is dependent upon its boiler and its boiling for its energy. Without this it is powerless. The engine can get along and do good work without some of its parts, — can do without a whistle, without a bell, without the ornamental parts, — but it cannot do without a boiler or without boiling.

Zeal, then, for God's cause, especially for that part of the cause we call missions, is the result of more earnest study. The honest looking into any worthy cause must, in the very nature of things, enlist the interest of the investigator. Get the people to studying missions earnestly and you will get them interested in missions deeply. You will then have the "fervent in spirit" kind and the "zeal of thine house" kind. Boiling hot, bubbling over with energy, is what it means. We would then have more generous giving and more spirited meetings.

I like to see one full of zeal for his work. We find men so in business; sometimes young people are so in pursuit of pleasure. I like in this connection to think of David as he came bounding into the presence of his father, brothers, and the prophet Samuel, who was there for the purpose of anointing one of Jesse's sons king. His ruddy face, which was especially noticeable as his lifeblood tingled in his veins, reminds us of the idea with which we started out, and, no doubt, was an indication of the zeal that filled his being. This is the same David who killed the lion and the bear that would destroy the sheep, and that slew Goliath, who would have destroyed Israel. Such a one with such courage and such energy would do for the king of Israel. And Paul, who had so much zeal for what he thought to be God's cause as to breathe out threatenings and slaughter against supposed enemies, such a person with such zeal would be worth saving to the true cause, even by a stroke from heaven.

This zeal comes by the more earnest study of which we talk. A band of young students, whom I knew personally, had a somewhat indifferent interest in missions. They began the study of the subject. It was not long before those young men were standing before the missionary board of their Church and before God saying, "Here am I, send me." They found that before that time they had been saying, as Mr. Moody puts it, "Here am I, send somebody else." It was the study of missions that changed it all. A man in a town in my native State began an earnest study of missions. It was not long before his interest and enthusiasm induced his members to study. He preached missions; he prayed for missions; he talked missions; and I believe it is said that he seemed to walk missions. The interest of the people of whom he was pastor deepened; they prayed for missions, and talked missions, and gave to missions until they, though not a large congregation and not very strong financially, supported a missionary at a cost of $800 to $1,000.

The great thrilling facts will stir almost any soul if you give them a chance. We need to know the sore need of the heathen world. We need to realize more fully God's readiness and power to save them. We need to learn that the heathen is our brother and that God is our Father.

Induce the young people to read the lives of missionaries, instead of yellow-back novels, and they will be thrilled. Let them read of the condition of the heathen, especially of the women, and they will be stirred. The Missionary Committee can do no better than start a missionary library and encourage the young people to read. Put in this library not mere books of travel, but books crowded with missionary fact and thought. Encourage and stimulate the study by holding an occasional missionary meeting. Use stereopticon views if practicable. In arranging the programme, appoint some one to give a review of some one of the most interesting books. When I am at home, I pass almost every day by a part of the railroad where they rub up the engines, oil them, and fire them ready for the run. There are usually standing there three or four or more of the great locomotives of the Southern system. The engines rubbed, oiled, water in the boiler, fire in the furnace, are ready for tremendous use. If those engines were missionaries, I would say they are, while standing there, engaged in "more earnest study." When they are ready for service, they are literally boiling and hissing out with energy. Let us take a lesson from the locomotive. Bring fuel into the soul in the form of facts, then be filled with the Spirit. Result: boiling with energy for missions. God give us enough interest to begin the study! After that, the interest will take care of itself if we will keep up the study.

"More Spirited Meetings" was the next topic upon the programme.

Address by Rev. Ernest Bourner Allen,
Lansing, Mich.

MORE SPIRITED MEETINGS.

A famous missionary sojourning for a time in this country said recently, "Of our church-members, one-third know nothing about missions and do nothing for them; another third know a little and do a little; the other third know much and do much." The public meeting is one of the most potent factors in reaching the two-thirds who know and therefore do little. The inference from our theme is that a spirited meeting will accomplish more than a spiritless meeting. Few are attracted and inspired by a lagging zeal. We do well, however, in demanding a more spirited meeting, to remind ourselves that in the ultimate analysis spirited and spiritual are synonymous. A meeting's life consisteth not in the abundance of noise it maketh. People, like things, are sometimes "spirited away" to an unknown realm by quiet, unseen, and yet controlling forces. Power and noise are not co-ordinate.

What kills our missionary meetings? Diagnosis must precede prescription. You must be frank with yourselves in acknowledging your faults. First, the very announcement kills some meetings. Better not announce them at all unless you can do it with real spirit and not in a mournful. apologetic manner. Second, abnormally presented, old, half-digested facts will kill a meeting. For example, I confess I begin to groan when I hear told how many people have died across the sea while the speaker was talking. I think I could add one more to the number nearer home! I should feel better and find my pulse throb quicker to be told how one poor soul *lived* for Christ over there, in the face of dirt, degradation, desertion, and death! Third, the long meeting you hold to-day kills the next meeting you announce. Let me charge you to see to it that you do not allow the next missionary meeting to run over time. Try having more speakers and shorter addresses. Make these speakers do the work of preparation. Do not feed them with a spoon out of some missionary magazine or scrap-book. Compel them to a healthful originality.

It becomes expedient, betimes, not to ask for a talk from that dear old saint who is "so interested in missions" that she does not know when to stop! And do not ask the missionary crank. His name is legion and his force is ever destructive. Give him rest, *rest*. Do not allow any geographical fiend to kill your meeting. He has a place. After a while we shall be more interested in the products of Timbuctoo and the number of square miles in Inhambane, but it will be after we are more interested in the poor souls there. Do not try to sing "From Greenland's Icy Mountains" and "Ye Christian Heralds, Go Proclaim" at every meeting. (Some modern congregations, let me say parenthetically, seem to think that these are new hymns which have crept into our hymnals.)

There are two open secrets of a spirited, successful meeting: first, *the leader had a plan;* second, *he pushed it.* Whatever may enforce the axiom that the prepared man has the chance fortifies the assertion that the prepared meeting has the chance. And the leader who, under the permission of his strategic board,—the Missionary Committee,—goes to battle with old, illy-constructed, dissimilar weapons deserves the defeat he courts so wantonly. In a day of rifles a man cannot fight with flint-locks. Every soldier needs to be equipped with modern guns and to be master of the drill. Missionary workers must have fresh facts, well-digested, closely related, logically presented. No man ignores or undervalues the Civil War because he is conversant with the present struggle and gets his timely illustrations from it. No worker forgets the historic acts of the apostles because he emphasizes the noble acts of to-day. But the difference in range is sometimes tremendous. Yesterday is far away. To-day presses close upon us. (*a*) Plan your meeting. (*b*) Push your plan. (*c*) Use modern facts.

That was a wise train-boy who, passing through his car, gave to each passenger a single peanut. When they had a taste they wanted more. You must give your constituency a taste of the inspiring facts of modern missions. "Where there is no wood the fire goeth out." Facts are the fuel for your fire. Tell them of those twenty-eight Armenian preachers who sealed their last sermons with their own life-blood, and see if some of your young people do not raise the question, "What does my religion cost *me*?" Tell them that foreign missions pay financially, socially, spiritually. Every year our trade with Hawaii through the one port of San Francisco exceeds in amount the entire cost of missions which undeniably created the country in over seventy years of American missionary work. From Micronesia the United States receives annually $40 for every dollar spent in missions there. Fifty years of missionary work have made Fiji a land of safety and Christianity instead of a place of barbarity and cannibalism.

Tell them that our own land affords illustration of the power of the Christ, and that this Southland has a hero in black. He was a poor carpenter in a southern city, who felt that his people needed intelligent preaching, and who lived on five cents a day while he got his education. A loaf of bread thrice divided with pure water was his bill of fare. His course completed, he was sent to one of the hardest fields, where all that seemed to be left was a church quarrel. The church house burned, and for five months he gave his entire princely salary of $10 per month for the new building. With ragged clothes he went into the building for which his own hands had toiled, and prayed the God of the prophets to send him something to wear. A little later the barrel came from the North, and he took it into the little chapel that he might open it. And when his hammer struck the head of the barrel he shouted, "Glory Hallelujah! The God of the prophets is *my* God!" Tell them that, and see whether giving does not increase.

Finally, remember that the secret of missionary interest and of a spirited meeting lies in the spiritual life. The better the Christian the better the meeting he plans and pushes. To deepen the spiritual life is to create vigorous missionary enthusiasm. This personal element is absolutely essential. "If my hand slacked," said Antonio Stradivarius, "I should rob God, for while God is fullest good he cannot make Antonio Stradivarius violins without Antonio." Spirited meetings come from spirited people whose hearts are afire with the love of Jesus Christ.

Then came the splendid address by Dr. Manton, of Texas.

Address by Rev. Chas. Manton, D. D.,
Paris, Texas.

PARTNERSHIP WITH GOD.

Who would not be a living epistle, sanctified and surrendered for God's use? We are engaged in a sublime mission, the work of reconciliation in winning a world to God, and united in a grand endeavor to bring alienated souls into friendship with him. Every believer is a divinely commissioned soul, God working with him and giving efficacy to his work, incarnating his truth into his personality, and saying, "Lo, I am with you alway, even unto the end." God knowing infinitely the needs, necessities, and capabilities of the human heart, within his grasp the instrumentalities, for the past Sinai, for the present Calvary, the seed of truth in fertility great and good enough to redeem the world, redeemed humanity, the sowers.

No life is too purposeless, or missionless; God given, each life is to be so wrought into his, that harvests of spiritual grain shall be garnered for the Lord. God carries on his work of redemption by the energy of the individual, as into their hearts he pours the power of his Spirit, and upon their heads he lays his hand in consecration.

A swift glance at the history of the world will reveal to us in the names of Abraham, Moses, Samuel, David, Elijah, and Paul, such partnerships with God that the world was saved from its ruin, as each one with a happier heart and in happier times told his message of God's love to men. Faith in eternal promises of God led men into such a partnership with him that a few rugged souls, planting their feet on Plymouth Rock, made it the corner-stone of a mighty kingdom, that to-day brings fear to the hearts of nations that in their inhumanity to men forget God.

This partnership is for every redeemed man and woman, because every one can live in the secret guidance of God's instruction, to be taught of him, to win souls, and to shine as the stars in the firmament. We are often tempted, that because our lives are small, because our circumstances are limited, therefore we cannot be brought into such a relationship as workers together with God. It is from such surroundings, such obscurity, that God leads men step by step into the larger life of partnership, until the beauty of the relationship bursts upon them, and they see themselves a part of God's husbandry. Our lives are small, and from a human conception of them we may doubt whether they belong to the thought of God at all, or whether he can use them at all for the accomplishment of his divine purpose.

Partnership with God is not measured by any stock in trade we may possess, nor dependent upon any capital, small or great, which we may bring to him. The mother whose name is unknown outside the circle that lisps it with hallowed affection, or who is unheard of beyond the melody of her own voice, as she sings the old lullabys, is living in partnership with God, as her life goes down into the life of her babes, as truly as when the children go out to touch the world with the power of consecrated lives.

That teacher who in some almost nameless place is quietly and humbly letting her life down into the lives of her pupils is in just as intimate partnership with God as when those same children have grown into the strength of years, and face the winds that blow from every direction, and help carry the burdens of a nation's destiny.

Partnership with God is not to be measured by the importance it occupies in the thoughts of men. It is one of the wonders of grace, not only how God has bound himself to humanity, but how he has bound humanity to himself. A miner's son sings in the streets for his bread; but after awhile he leads the Reformation, and unlocks the Bible for the world. A tinker in Bedford jail is so transformed by the power of divine truth and the fellowship of God that he writes the story of " Pilgrim's Progress," that by the power of its influence ranks next to the Word of God. Four country boys under a haystack are praying, and in the providence of God American missions are born. Aspirations that come of the divine heart become our own, and we fall into the place of working out God's purposes in a holy partnership.

From the day when God called Abraham to leave home and country, from the time when Moses stood in the presence of the burning bush, down to the present hour, God has been calling men into partnership, working in and through them. The history of modern missions is the history of men in partnership with God, separated by the Holy Ghost to the work — God opening the door of access to nations, and then opening the door of human hearts to faith in his word; God ever working with them.

Illustrious examples there are, not a few. William Carey pegging away at his bench, his mind on a people far away and far from God, is chosen by him to open up India to the gospel. In a time when there was no missionary atmosphere, when the Church denied her responsibility, and when bitter sarcasm and indifference was supreme, this unlettered man, under the tutelage of God, kindled on church altars fires that have burned ever since for the evangelization of the world. In 1792 twelve obscure Baptists consecrate an offering for the redemption of the heathen, and organize the first missionary society, and William Carey, God's working partner, leads the van by giving himself to India as God's representative.

Christian F. Schwartz, apostolic in character and in life, in co-partnership with God, walked among the people of India, winning men of all estates as few have ever done in the history of the Church.

David Livingston, inspired of God to walk with him in the development of a divine purpose in Africa, travels thirty thousand miles, studies the flora and fauna of a continent, searches into the geology of the land, opens up her highways to missionary organization and Bible translation, watches the most trifling incidents that shape character and destiny, his spiritual vision continually bright with "In all thy ways acknowledge him and he shall direct thy paths;" Moses-like, counting all the honors that a grateful people would shower upon him as nothing, that he might lift, as God's co-laborer, the shadow of night from darkest Africa.

God's call to partnership has received but scant recognition; finite partners are always in demand; the need for such is seen in the Macedonian cry, that has multiplied until it is the voice of many waters. Yea, it is the voice of the Son of man, speaking in behalf of humanity at home and abroad. He stands before the eyes of this generation, calling, commanding, seeking to touch all alike with his personal power. Have you the faith to see him as he appeals to God's husbandry? to hear him as he pleads for co-laborers? No difficulties are insurmountable when we once see that it is God working in us, and that God and we are working together under the guarantee that nothing can prevail against us.

Listen; God is calling the youth of this generation to a new consecration, a new separation, a new mission. Volunteers are needed to be partners with him in a twentieth-century movement, to awaken the multitudes from the slumber of indifference, to kindle burning aspirations, to purify and make possible a Christian citizenship, to make the press nobler and less venal, to deepen the aims of society, to make homes purer, life more simple, to trample upon the base power and influence of gold, to plant the banner of Emmanuel upon every hill-top, that every valley may rejoice and the nations shout. "Christ for the world." Will you respond? Dare you be God's men, partners with him in the coming redemption?

The heart of the matter was laid wide open in Miss Margaret W. Leitch's address on the "Tenth Legion." She told how the simple native Christians of Ceylon gave every tenth bushel of rice and the fruit of every tenth tree. They have also a thank-offering after every harvest, when the people bring as free-will offerings sheep, goats, fowls, grain, vegetables, etc., a sale of which is made for the Lord's work.

Miss Leitch's closing suggestion was a practical and hopeful one,— that each one of the ten thousand enrolled tithe-givers try during the year to secure ten others, so as to bring the enrolment up to one hundred thousand.

Address by Miss Margaret W. Leitch,
Ceylon.

THE TENTH LEGION; FORWARD MARCH.

We have come to this Convention to seek for a blessing. We desire a blessing in our own hearts, and we desire to carry back a blessing to our societies and homes.

The Lord Jesus has told us how to get a blessing. He has said, "He that hath my commandments and keepeth them, he it is that loveth me; and he that loveth me shall be loved of my Father, and I will love him and will manifest myself to him" (John 14: 21). This greatest of all blessings, the abiding presence of the Blessed One in our hearts, is conditioned upon the keeping of his commandments. If we fulfil the conditions, he will fulfil the promise.

Shall we not lift up our hearts in prayer to him, and continue to lift them up all through this session, asking that by his Spirit he will reveal to us his will, and enable us to surrender our wills in glad obedience?

GOD'S CLAIM.

The topic before us is *Tithe-Giving*. In considering this important subject, let us remind ourselves that all we have belongs to God. He is the absolute owner, and he has never conveyed away his ownership. " Behold the heaven and the heaven of heavens is the Lord's, and the earth also, with all that therein is " (Deut. 10 : 14). " The earth is the Lord's and the fulness thereof; the world and they that dwell therein " (Ps. 24 : 1). " Every beast of the forest is mine and the cattle upon a thousand hills " (Hag. 2 : 8). As the Creator, he must have absolute ownership in all his creatures; and if an absolute claim could be strengthened, it would be by the fact that he who gave us life sustains it and with his own life redeemed it. " Ye are not your own; for ye are bought with a price " (1 Cor. 6 : 19, 20).

If God has absolute ownership in us we can have absolute ownership in nothing whatever. Those houses and lands and corner lots, those shops and mines and bank-accounts, are not ours at all. We are not proprietors apportioning our own. We are all of us only " tenants at will " of the Almighty. We are told to " occupy." We are stewards; we are to be reckoned with; we must give account.

Does not the owner expect from his tenant some sort of tribute or acknowledgment? Surely he does, and he is not content to take a few hollow and empty words of " Thank you."

In order that we may constantly remember the fact that all we have belongs to God, he has taught us in his Word that, while all should be used in the way that will best honor him, one-tenth should be set aside for his direct service. " The tenth is the Lord's; it is holy unto the Lord " (Lev. 27 : 30).

EXAMPLES FROM SCRIPTURE.

Abraham paid tithes of all to the priest of the Most High God, Melchizedek (Gen. 14 : 20). Jacob vowed, " Of all that thou shalt give me I will surely give a tenth unto thee " (Gen. 28 : 22). In many places in the Old Testament the giving of the tenth and of free-will offerings is most clearly enjoined. God asked those gifts from his people because he wished to bless them by lifting them up out of a life of selfishness into a life of communion with himself. Had the Jews, through tithes and thank-offerings, "kept the Lord always before them," they would not have committed the sins which brought punishment upon them and upon their land.

The Levitical order of the priesthood with its sacrifices was done away by the Great Sacrifice; but we who are under a new and better priesthood, that of Him who was " made a priest forever after the order of Melchizedek " are not thereby freed from the obligation of tithe-giving. Tithes were paid to this order of priesthood centuries before the Levitical order was proclaimed.

In no place in the New Testament do we read that Christ disannulled the law of tithes. On the contrary, he expressly commended tithe-giving in Matthew 23 : 23, " Ye pay tithes . . . These ought ye to have done and not to leave the other undone."

If it was incumbent upon the Jews to pay tithes, is it not more incumbent upon us? Greater obligations are resting upon us than rested upon the Jews. Under the old dispensation the Jews were only required to care for their own nation, but under the new dispensation the command is, " Go ye into all the world and preach the gospel to every creature." In view of the larger work entrusted to us, it seems that a tenth is the very least that a disciple of Christ should give, and that over and above that he should give as God has prospered him.

THE PRACTICE OF THE EARLY CHRISTIANS.

It is a matter of history that the early Christians paid tithes, and that they continued to do this centuries after the resurrection of our Lord. Grotius says, " From the most ancient ages a tenth has been regarded as the portion due to

God according to both Greek and Latin historians." Ambrose says, "Whosoever fails to pay his tithes fears not God, and knows not what true repentance and confession mean."

Augustine says, "Tithes are required as a debt. Pay tithes and out of the nine parts give alms." Many of the councils of the early Church proclaimed to Christians the obligation of paying tithes, resting the duty not on the authority of ecclesiastical law, but on the sure basis of the Word of God. This is the unanimous judgment of the fathers and the voice of the Church uncontradicted for more than a thousand years.

The rapid spread of Christianity during the first centuries is doubtless due, in no small measure, to the fact that the Christians devoted a tenth of their income to the extension of Christ's kingdom.

GOD A GOOD MASTER.

To our short-sighted view it may perhaps seem severe that a working woman, whose income is only a dollar a day, should be required to give ten cents of that, or that a widow with little children should be asked to give a tenth of her small earnings for the extension of Christ's kingdom. But the Master met this very condition in the third request in the Lord's Prayer, "Give us this day our daily bread." "Leave thy fatherless children with me, and I will preserve them alive; and let thy widows trust in me." "I will never leave thee nor forsake thee." "Give, and it shall be given unto you."

In the Master's first sermon he referred to the widow of Zarephath. She had only a handful of meal in a barrel and a little oil in a cruse, yet out of that small quantity she was bidden first to make a little cake for the prophet. To this obedient widow was given the high honor of sustaining God's prophet, and in return God sustained her and her son throughout the whole period of famine.

THE GIVING OF NATIVE CONVERTS.

Will giving the tenth impoverish? I can testify from ten years of missionary experience that even among the poorest native converts the giving of the tenth does not impoverish.

In Ceylon, as in most Eastern countries, the great majority of the people are poor. The ordinary wage of a working man there is only a sum equal to eight cents a day. But although the majority of the native Christians are poor, they are not so poor that they cannot give for the support of the gospel. When they read in the Bible that a tenth is the Lord's, they just believe it. They are simple-hearted children in the Christian religion, and they have never been taught that they should not believe what they read in the Bible. Believing, they begin to give accordingly. Those who are employed in government or mission service give a tenth of their salaries. The farmers are accustomed to give every tenth bushel of rice.

Those who have gardens give the fruit of each tenth tree. They give the tenth before they begin to use any part for themselves. They find that giving in this way brings them a spiritual blessing. They also find by experience that nine-tenths with God's blessing goes as far as ten-tenths used to go.

The Christian community is rapidly increasing. It is the best educated, the most respected, and the most prosperous community in the island.

FREE-WILL OFFERINGS.

Although the native Christians begin by giving a tenth, they do not always stop there. When a convert from heathenism is received into the Christian Church he takes the tenth as a starting-point and says, "Less than this I will not give." He does not say that he will not give more. Many of the native Christians as they grow in grace begin to give more than the tenth. Every year, after harvest-time, a thank-offering meeting is held in each church, when the people bring as free-will offerings sheep, goats, fowls, fruit, grain, vegetables, and other things. Such meetings are held on a week-day. After a joyful praise-service in the church a little sale is held outside under the wide-spreading trees, and the proceeds go to help carry on God's work. As a result of such giving the majority of the native churches are self-supporting, and the remainder are fast becoming so. In addition the native Christians give toward the support of Christian schools, toward the work of the Bible society, and their native missionary society.

I merely speak of Ceylon as one instance. The self-sacrifice shown by the native converts in many mission fields is such as to put Christians in this land to shame.

DAILY GIVING.

The Christian women in Ceylon have a method of their own for giving to foreign missions. The Christian mother in each home, as she measures out the rice for the evening meal, takes out each day a handful or more and puts it into a little box called "The Lord's box." At the end of each month the treasurer of each church visits the Christian homes, collects the rice from these boxes, sells it, and the money goes to aid the native missionary society in supporting native Christians as missionaries in distant villages.

These poor native Christians in Ceylon cannot afford such luxuries as I see on every hand in America. Their tables are not loaded with dainties. Many of them have only one meal a day. They cannot afford to worship in magnificent churches with stained-glass windows, highly-paid choirs, and church debts. But they are enjoying one luxury. They are sending out and supporting native workers in the "Regions Beyond." Why could not every church in this country enjoy such a luxury? They could if their members were to join the "Tenth Legion."

MORE THAN MONEY.

The native Christians in Ceylon are giving more than money; they are giving their sons and daughters to Christ's work. Many of the young men educated in the higher educational mission schools have gone as Christian workers to other parts of the island; to India, Burmah, Singapore, the Straits Settlement, Penang, and Bornea. They are now employed in connection with twelve different missionary societies. These young men are cheerfully accepting, in mission service, one-sixth or one-eighth of the salary which they might have secured in government service. Their question is not "Where can I make the most money?" but "Where does God want me?" And at his call they are, like brave soldiers, leaving home and friends and going to the front, where the battle is the hardest.

THE REWARD.

These sons do not need to hear a great many missionary sermons to induce them to become missionaries. They had seen the father setting aside the tenth for the Lord's service, a giving that often entailed real sacrifice. They had seen the mother putting aside the daily handful of rice with a daily lifting of the face to Christ and a daily prayer that his kingdom may come. He who said, "Bring ye all the tithes into the storehouse that there may be meat in mine house, and prove me now herewith, saith the Lord of Hosts, if I will not open you the windows of heaven, and pour you out a blessing, that there shall not be room enough to receive it," has made good his promise, granting to those parents the unspeakable blessing of seeing their children consecrated to the service of God.

Sometimes in a palatial home in this country a mother will say to me, "I feel very sad and anxious about my children; my sons are prospering in business, my daughters are devoted to society; but they do not care for the things of God." And I say to such a mother, "What have you been seeking for your children? Have you been seeking first the kingdom of God?"

If when God calls we answer, then when we call "the Lord will answer." When we cry he will say, "Here I am."

OUR OWN NEED.

We need to give for our own safety.
Christ speaks of but one power in the universe as likely to become a dangerous rival for that throne in man's heart and life which belongs to God himself. That subtle power, that dangerous rival, against which he warns us, is Mammon, the love of money. He tells that between the pursuit of gain and the service of the living God every man must choose. "Ye cannot serve God and mammon."

THE WORLD'S NEED.

We need to give for the sake of others.
Never before were the fields so white for the harvest or the calls for laborers so loud as now. Mission fields are open. The world is the field. All fences are down. "The Christian Church stands to-day face to face with its answered prayers."

THE NEED IN CHINA.

Look, for example, at the marvelous changes which have taken place in China within the last few years.
Formerly the literati of China, who practically hold all the offices and are the real rulers of the Empire, were Christianity's strongest opponents; but since the China-Japan war, the Chinese government leaders have become convinced that the Empire must change front. It had been facing toward the past. Not wishing to confide in the ambassadors of any of the nations, under the circumstances, it is a fact that they sought counsel from Christian missionaries. After frequent interviews, high government officials requested the missionary leaders, who were in their confidence, to put in writing their suggestions for the reform of China, and this was done. The immediate result was a special order to the provinces making it emphatic that missionaries are not only to be tolerated, but protected. Rev. Timothy Richards, one of the leaders of this movement, who has been for twenty-seven years in China, says, "When I think of the importance of this movement, I feel appalled by its magnitude. The leaders of four hundred millions of people turning to the Christian Church for light and leading! Take time to realize what that means. And now that they have come to you, I hope that you will not allow them to go astray for lack of a sympathizing hand to lead them into the way of righteousness."
The missionary force in China should be increased without delay.

THE NEED IN INDIA.

India presents a crisis equally as great as that in China. As a result of the kindness shown and help given by the missionaries to the famine-stricken people during the last famine, a remarkable mass movement is taking place toward Christianity, and many thousands are forsaking idolatry and openly avowing themselves the disciples of Christ. To instruct these multitudes of inquirers more missionaries are needed, and should be sent to India at once.

THE NEED IN AFRICA.

An equally remarkable transformation is taking place in Africa. That dark continent, for centuries the home of terrible oppression and indescribable misery, is rapidly being opened up to civilization and the gospel. Look at the transformation in a single district — Uganda: "Ten thousand souls brought into contact with the gospel, half of them able to read for themselves; two hundred church buildings erected by native Christians; two hundred native evangelists and teachers entirely supported by the native Church; ten thousand copies of the New Testament in circulation; six thousand souls under daily instruction; the number of converts doubling yearly for the last six years; the power of God shown by changed lives; and all this in what was once the centre of the thickest darkness in the world." Truly

"We are living, we are dwelling, in a grand and awful time,
In an age on ages telling. To be living is sublime."

WORKERS READY.

Not only has God opened the long-closed doors, but he has raised up an army of workers eager to enter them.

More than five thousand young men and women, many of them the brightest students from the colleges and seminaries of this country, have signed the Student Volunteer Declaration, saying, "It is my purpose, God permitting, to become a foreign missionary."

Over eleven hundred of these have already been sent out by their respective mission boards, and more than four thousand are either in course of preparation or are waiting for an opportunity to go.

On one hand is the loud call for reinforcements, and on the other a great company of young volunteers. What hinders the advance? Nothing but the lack of funds.

A FORWARD MOVEMENT.

Who can make a forward movement possible? The 3,000,000 members of the Young People's Society of Christian Endeavor can do it. I bless God that now, in the fulness of time, he has called into existence this mighty organization and has put it into the hearts of its leaders to enroll a Tenth Legion. This Tenth Legion is now over ten thousand strong. I pray God that it may number 100,000 at the next annual meeting, and that it may keep on growing until the principle of tithe-giving shall permeate the whole of Christendom. When that day comes it will be the morning, so to speak, of the new creation. There will then be abundant means to carry on God's work at home and abroad, and "twenty years should not pass till the story of the Cross should be uttered in the ears of every living man." The Master, who has given us our great life-work, the evangelization of the world, has provided ample financial resources for the carrying on of that work. He has given us a system of Biblical finance which needs no revision, and which, if followed out, will furnish ample revenues for his kingdom. The annual income of the forty millions of Protestant church-members is estimated at fifteen billions of dollars — a tenth of that would be 1,500 millions. Supposing that four-sixths of that tithe was given to the support of the home churches and local charities, and the remaining two-sixths was divided equally between home and foreign missions, the foreign mission cause would then receive not merely fourteen millions as at present, but 240 millions; and instead of having, as now, one missionary and four native workers for every 95,000 heathen, the Church could have one missionary and four native workers for every 5,625 heathen. In other words, if Christians were to give one-tenth of their income to God's work and one-sixth of that tenth to foreign missions the gospel could be preached to the whole world in one generation.

For the advancement of an object so dear to the heart of our Risen Lord, shall we not every one of us resolve that, God helping us, we will do our part? Let us lift our faces and our hearts to him "whom having not seen, we love," and say to him, "Lord Jesus, it may be only a little that I can do to show my love to thee, but by thy grace it will be my best, my uttermost. By thy grace I will do it at once."

If we will enroll our names in the Tenth Legion, and make it henceforth a part of our life-work to promote the practice of tithe-giving in our churches, societies, and among our friends, our lives will not have been lived in vain. Perhaps in no other way could we do so much to promote the coming of Christ's kingdom.

LITERATURE.

May I suggest that, to this end, we would do well to secure *the wide distribution* of such booklets as "The Tenth Legion," by Amos R. Wells; "The Opportunity of the Hour," by Eddie; "God's Tithe," by A. J. Gordon; "Christian Missions and the Highest Use of Wealth," by President Gates; and "Money and the Kingdom," by Dr. Josiah Strong. (The circulation of this last booklet brought in $40,000 to the Congregational Home Missionary Society.) These booklets can be secured through the United Society.

We can also help the cause by preparing striking charts and maps, by arranging meetings on the subject of the Tenth Legion and by circulating enrolment-blanks at such meetings, and by enclosing them in letters to friends.

HAVE A DEFINITE AIM.

If each one of the 10,000 tithe-givers would make an earnest effort to secure, by God's help, the enrolment of twelve others within the next twelve months, and if the secretary could announce at the next annual meeting, "Over 100,000 names enrolled in the Tenth Legion" all the churches and all the benevolent societies would begin to feel the blessed influences of a mighty forward movement.

Brothers, sisters, let us make this effort to the glory of God. He who has promised to use "the weak things of the world to confound the mighty" can use even us, if we will but yield ourselves utterly to the doing of his good, acceptable, and perfect will.

The Convention got its blood-cells well shaken up when the only and original Mr. Puddefoot began his address on home missions.

Address by Rev. W. G. Puddefoot,
South Framingham, Mass.

OUR COUNTRY FOR CHRIST.

The thirteenth verse of the ninth chapter of the prophecy of Amos reads as follows: "Behold, the days come, saith the Lord, that the plowman shall overtake the reaper, and the treader of grapes him that draweth forth, and the mountains shall drop new wine, and all the hills shall melt."

A shepherd on the Syrian plains, guarding his flock with club and staff, fighting the lion and the bear, and sleeping under the wondrous sky of the Orient, Amos lived when men plowed the stony ground with a sharpened stick, when the weapons of war had to be carried with the peaceful implements of agriculture, when famine came oftener than good crops, where the robbers hid in the little hills, and when all men were Ishmaelites. In spite of all this, and the far-off rumors of oppression in the cities, the luxuries of the rich and the needs of the poor, this man had a glorious vision.

Last June I stood high up on the Alleghanies at sunrise. I watched the first flush on the highest point, and saw it spread from peak to peak; the bosky glades grew rosy with the dawn, the deep gray valleys turned purple; the hidden farmhouses were brought to view, and nature's best and cheapest diamonds glistened by the million. The news came that day that far off on the Gulf Coast the first ripe sheaves were falling before the reaper, a tiny point at the extreme south; and I had a vision: I saw the point expand as the sun rose, — it widened out a thousand miles — two thousand — and then across the continent; in billowy waves of gold it swept northward; its crest broke against and over the Sierras and the Rockies. I saw its flush suffusing the vales of Utah, Idaho, and Wyoming, and sweeping over the great prairies of Montana, among the cascades of Washington, and at last, nearly four months after the first sheaves were stooked in Texas, I saw the harvest home in the far Northwest lit up with merry dances of the aurora borealis. But long before this the plow had gone into the mellow soil of the Southland. The plowman had overtaken the reaper; the second crop was harvested as the first was finished. The husbandman of the South sat under the shade of the oleanders, the new sweet wine was running, the mountains melted, and the prophet's vision was fulfilled.

And we are happy? Yes, very happy. Because of the fulfilment of the prophecy? No, but because it has failed elsewhere. Alas, and is it so that our happiness and prosperity depend on some other's adversity? That a good harvest the world over means trouble for us? That we are glad not because of bountiful harvest, but because food is scarce and we shall have more money?

The farmer is to be enriched, and so we shall have good times. Not that there will be any more money, but it will change hands; a vast number of poor people will pay more for bread. Wheat is getting dear. Think of that, friends. What joy; the greatest necessity of man is going up! Think of that, ye toiler of the tenements. Thy poor brother, the farmer, is really going to be rich. What rapture! The poor farmer out yonder on the prairie, he has nothing but a house to live in, a hundred acres of land, often free, a few chickens, a cow, a pig, a span of horses, some vegetables, fuel—and nothing more. What desolation! Well may thy heart rejoice, my brother of the city, as thy beautiful cerulean blue milk at eight cents a quart enriches the delicious coffee sweetened by sugar from the tropics. See, it is brought to thy door and thy fuel can be put in a closet, thy meat carried thousands of miles by rail and laid down in thy kitchen for double the price the poor farmer gets for it.

Is it not high time to drop the saying, "poor farmers"? True, the first few years are trying times, but see that young man (one of millions), his wife and two or three children. If in the forests of Michigan he takes them in his log-house, if on the prairie his little shack, or sod-house—humble little places in either case, but they are homes. Around them nature in all its pristine beauty; flowers, lakes, woods. Take this one of a thousand. The young husband is returning from his work; near the house the good wife is milking the patient cow. The wee ones run to meet father; he stoops, picks them up, and one on each shoulder he marches on, tired but happy; he stoops to let them down, and kisses his wife as she rises from milking; they have no money, yet are they rich. Another year, and a calf is added; the lonesome little pig of last year has a portly look, and is followed by a whole colony of little grunters, while broods of chickens are everywhere. The vegetables from his garden are fresh, such as few taste who have to buy. Their sleep is such as only tired labor knows when breathing the free air of the boundless West. What exultant feelings swell the breast of the young man as he looks out upon his own! A few years pass, of sober, steady plodding, and he goes to town in a top buggy. His family fill a whole pew in church. He saw the little gray speck at the corners grow from a store to a town; and his children are reading books taken from the public library. His eldest son is in college. The others are helping in various ways, and he lives to see in one generation the wilderness blossom as a rose, the plowman overtake the reaper. Millions starting as poor as he have seen the same over and over again, and yet we still cry "the poor farmer!"

His father sold corn at five cents a bushel and had to carry his grist to mill over one hundred miles. His grandfather gave over eighty bushels of wheat for a pair of stogy boots, and his great-grandfather had to eat turkey-breasts for bread with his buffalo-meat and guard his home and crops with his rifle. The grandchildren don't know what hard times are. The farmer now rides his plow, has a market at his door, and is still grumbling; and yet the poorest farmer in the land is rich compared with the city poor; and compared with the starving millions of the Orient he is a prince. The very States in which we hear so much about the poor farmer are the States that show the most astounding progress that the world has ever seen, and during the last two years have paid hundreds of millions off their mortgages. Those who have tilled their ground have plenty of bread; others have followed vain persons and have property enough. "A faithful man shall abound with blessings, but he that maketh haste to be rich shall not be innocent;" and here lies the great trouble,—haste to be rich—not to get the comforts of life, but to get rich. Men fear, as Carlyle puts it so forcibly, "the hell of not getting on." The farm is too slow. The young man can make more, so he thinks, by buying wheat that was never grown than by selling what he can raise. He wants to overtake the reaper by a short cut, and he is often cut short. No real blessing can come to a man or a people by the mere overtaking the reaper. Man doth not live by bread alone.

When the Pilgrim Fathers landed in America they had an abundance of spiritual food and a short allowance of corn. To read Governor Bradford's history of Plymouth colony and then turn to Mr. Atkinson's distribution of products is like going into a new world. The Pilgrims had starvation staring them in the face; their descendants are so full of the world's goods as not to know what to do with them. To see the poor men living on clams because the corn was exhausted, often too weak to resist when attacked by the Indians, and then to read that the work of seven men now produces enough bread to feed a thousand people is like a page from the "Arabian Nights." To see how painfully they cleared the land, how slow their progress, turn to Dr. Strong's book on the city of the twentieth century, and realize if you can that for forty years the wilderness was changed into farms at a rate of 16,000 acres a day, that a ton of the produce is carried a mile for so small a sum that we must go to China to find a coin small enough to represent it, and yet in spite of this the poor man pays for his loaf at the rate of $18 for a barrel of flour made from ninety-cent wheat. To know that in the midst of this abundance crime has increased out of all proportion to the population, that strikes and lockouts follow each other with swift certainty, that thousands of hungry tramps travel all over the land, while thousands of honest men lack food for their families, is enough to make us pause and ask the cause of all the trouble.

I think without doubt the real trouble is what Kossuth prophesied, "If shipwreck should ever befall your country, the rock on which it will split will be your devotion to your private interests at the expense of your duty to the State;" and Dr. Strong remarks that for more than a generation since then our course has been laid directly toward that rock.

Now there will be no devotion to the State at the expense of self-interest until men have grown to an altruism which is not found outside Christianity. The gifts of Christians to the cause of Christ have increased when compared with the past, larger in the aggregate, larger *per capita*, but not so large when compared to the increase of wealth. It is the one alarming symptom of the times, this enormous growth of material riches compared with the spiritual results. I do not forget the millions spent for benevolent objects, such as old people's homes, hospitals, fresh-air funds, colleges, etc. Call the amount $30,000,000 annually, and you have about the increase of wealth that is added to the nation in seven days, or less than two per cent of that increase used for benevolent purposes for home and foreign missions.

There is nothing new in all this. It has ever been so. Great material prosperity has always dwarfed spiritual life. The Israelite of old brought the maimed, the blind, and diseased cattle as their gifts to God. The Pilgrim Fathers brought wampum that would not pass in the market. So that the old prophet's question has always been in order, "Will a man rob God?" "Yet ye have robbed me." Wherein have we robbed thee? In tithes and offerings. "Ye are cursed with a curse, for ye have robbed me even this whole nation."

These are awful words — are they true of us? I am afraid so. The cost of crime alone in our country for one year would keep ten thousand workers in the dark places of our land for a century, while Christian Europe has spent a thousand million dollars a year for the last twenty-five years for war. Crime of the worst kinds has grown so in the past ten years that the *North American Review* employed a scientific expert to tell us the reasons, and Professor Lombroso tells us it is due to climate, mixture of races, environment, and heredity, and we feel quite comforted in finding out it was not us at all, but this wretched quartette. Of course climate has a great deal to do with it. It will cause the cows on the Falkland Islands to change into various colors, dwarf the imported horses in a few generations to Shetland ponies, put feathers on a bird's legs, etc.; but stop a moment, Palestine had a bad climate, mixed races, for the Jews were mixed until the Ghetto produced a type; poor environments and heredity at work too, and yet Greece never produced men of such moral fibre as the great prophets — and Jesus and the apostles were from there, too. Paul had all these to contend with, mixture of races at Pentecost, and Rome, and everywhere, and as for heredity, he belonged to the tribe of Benjamin, and Jacob said Benjamin "shall raven as a wolf," and he did, till wives and children were gone and Benjamin had to steal new wives from the daughters of Shiloh when they came out to dance; yet in spite of heredity and mixed races and a Roman prisoner in Nero's Rome — he wrote with the music of his clanking chain, "The saints of Cæsar's household salute you." So then there is something stronger than climate, heredity, and all the rest? Yes, the grace of God that bringeth salvation nigh. That can overcome crime, cleanse municipal corruption, bring lasting peace to men and nations, make wars cease to the ends of the earth, feed the hungry, clothe the naked, and make this a delightsome land; and all nations will not only call us blessed, but will be blessed through us.

In order that this state of things may be brought about, we must be more systematic in our gifts, and, what is vastly more important, we must give more. Just consider for a moment what the young people of the Society could do. They could put a thousand men and women at work in the dark places of the earth at a cost of five cents a week per member, and pay the entire salaries; as half the support comes from the field, they could keep two thousand at work, and all for the price of a glass of soda once a week. It would be quite easy for the Christian young people to raise ten million dollars a year for Christ's work. It need not be all applied to preaching, but could be used for actual Christian work. They could endow hospitals. They could have model homes for men and women in the city and fresh-air farms in the country for the sick and the children. In short, they could do anything they willed to do. What an object-lesson would the Y. P. S. C. E. model home for working girls be! "It's love that makes the world go round;" yes, but you must have dollar wheels, and cents make dollars. Count the church-members at 20,000,000 only, — let them give one cent a day for benevolent purposes, and we have $73,000,000 a year. What a fund to work righteousness with!

I know it pleased God by the foolishness of preaching to convert them that believe; but it pleased God by Christian living to convert them who do not believe. I know there are many people who think the Church has nothing to do but to look after men's souls. Well, their souls are inside their bodies. True, a clean shirt does not give a man a clean heart; nevertheless, if all men could have clean environments both bodies and souls would have a better chance, and what the world is waiting for to-day is an organized Christianity that will go into God's work in fighting sin as the world's people fight one another. There is not a city to-day that could withstand the onslaught of the united efforts of the young people if they were organized for work. When James Fisk was pushing the Erie Railroad he said, "When we were in a State that was Democratic we were Democrats, when in a Republican State we were Republicans; but we were for Erie all the time." So our young Christians, dropping the slavish chains of party, must be for Christ all the time. If we are for Christ, and "The World for Christ" our motto, the Church won't know herself in five years, and the time will soon come when in the Lord's harvest-fields the plowman will also overtake the reaper, and it will come just as soon as you are ready for it.

The son of a missionary, there are no speakers on the broad theme of the world's conquest who overtop Dr. Barrows. After travelling over Asia, he is satisfied that there are more morality, virtue, and honesty in New York or Pennsylvania or New Jersey than in the whole Asiatic continent. Sometimes naval officers and globe-trotters declare there is no good in foreign missionaries, but he quoted Lord Cromer, who said that the best work done in Egypt was done by the Christian missionaries, and a non-Christian Madras paper to the effect that the noblest characters in the world must be searched for among the Christian missionaries. The slanderous statements usually come from European residents whose impure lives are rebuked by the very presence of the missionaries.

Address by Rev. John Henry Barrows, D.D.,
Chicago, Ill.
THE CONQUEST OF THE WORLD.

The Christian religion is inherently expansive, and the idea of a world-wide conquest entered its heart and brain from the very beginning. The strongest argument for the truth of Christianity which I could bring to bear upon many Hindus' minds was this: its essential universality, not only because of its adaptation to all men, and its claims upon all, but from its present world-wide extension,—an argument which Christian missions of the nineteenth century have put into their hands. I have returned home from a voyage around the world with a new and deeper sense of the gospel's universal efficacy, after hearing the old Christian hymns sung in Arabic and Marathi, in Hindi and Kanarese, in Tamil and Bengali, and in the languages of China and Japan. Many times in the early morning hours the voices of little children carrying old tunes in strange tongues have floated to our ears across the Mission Compond of some city in the Punjab, or by the spicy and surf-beaten shores of Ceylon, and my heart beat faster as I realized the oneness of Christian hope and faith and love in the breasts of all disciples, and as I felt anew the sweet glory of that gospel which it is your work and mine to carry to all those whom God loves, and for whom the Saviour died.

A few years ago there came to me, in the providence of God, a deep, invincible feeling that it was my mission to preach Christ not only in America, but also in the far East. It was the larger Christ which I was moved and inspired to preach, the Christ who has not forgotten nor forsaken any part of the world, the Christ who has illumined in some measure all hearts, but who blazes forth in redemptive disclosure from Bethlehem's cradle, from the Galilean Mount of Teaching, from the Tree of Life on Calvary, from the opening heavens, from the eternal throne, and from the Pentecostal fires of the Holy Spirit which gleam and flash wherever the historic Christ is faithfully and lovingly presented. And now that I have finished the work to which I was commissioned, and now that I have been permitted to carry the Christian message to the schools of India and Japan, I shall be glad if any word of mine shall help, however slightly, that sure and swift-coming revival of enthusiasm in America for the missionary cause, which, in its origin, character, and purpose, Dr. Wayland rightly deemed the sublimest that ever awakened the hopes and called forth the moral energies of mankind.

I find, and you also find, among some people in our own country a scepticism, with regard to the wisdom and success of all Christian efforts in Asia, an unbelief springing sometimes out of a lack of knowledge of the real results of Christian missions, and occasionally from the feeling that Christianity has nothing supremely important to give to the followers of Buddha and Confucius, and to those who, it is supposed, have been trained in the great philosophies of India. It is very common for travellers and naval officers to circulate the report that they have found nothing to praise and much to condemn in the work of the missionaries. Such critics might learn something from the testimonies of great British statesmen in India, one of whom, Sir Alexander McKenzie, governor-general of Bengal, a strong friend of missions, said to me that he looked forward to the time when there would be a national turning of the people of India to the gospel of Christ, when the work already begun should go forward rapidly under the leadership of native Christian prophets. These critics of missions might learn much from Colonel Denby, for twelve years our efficient minister at Peking, or from Consul-General Jernigan, of Shanghai, or even from the *Indian Social Reformer*, a non-Christian paper, published in Madras, which had recently said that "if you wish to find examples of the noblest benevolence, you must go to Christianity and not to Hinduism," and has also expressed the opinion that "the highest types of Christian character yet evolved from our race were found among some of the Christian missionaries of India."

It might be well, however, to put to these critics a few questions. Will you give us the names of a score out of the thousands of the Christian missionaries in the Orient whom you came to know personally, and to know so well that you could form an accurate judgment of them and of their work? And then since missionaries are doing such a vast variety of things to help the bodies and souls of men, will you tell us what work you found ineffective or harmful? Do you disapprove of the translation of the Bible, the writing of Christian literature, the teaching of children in schools, of young men in colleges, the preaching on the streets, the visiting of women in their homes, the work of the dispensary, or the work of the hospital? If you know not one missionary personally, if you have never studied the various forms of work with your own eyes, where did you get your opinions? Did you get them from the not overmoral European populations in the corrupt port-towns of Japan, China, and India? Are you reflecting the hostility of unworthy representatives of Christianity in the Orient? Is it becoming in any one to endeavor to break down the work of men and women who, leaving their own country from love of Christ and love of humanity, are at any rate striving to enlighten, uplift, and save their fellow-men? Those who mislead American travellers in the Orient would be equally out of sympathy with earnest and aggressive Christian work carried on here in our American cities.

I have seen enough of Christian evangelism in Asia to fill me with joyful hope. I never met a missionary in India or Japan who was doubtful about the final result. And I have seen enough of the practical workings of Hinduism, Buddhism, and Islam to crystallize into adamantine firmness my previous strong conviction of their futility to give the soul peace with God, to remove the weight of guilt and grief, to lay the foundations of a vigorous individual and national morality, and to brighten earth with the light of a blessed immortality. The notion that Asia does not need the gospel of Christ because of the refined and lofty moral sentiments in the religious books of the East, or because Oriental speakers trained in Christian schools and shaped by Christian environments are able to make an agreeable impression expounding their faiths on American platforms, is born of ignorance. The famous apostle of Hinduism to America, who, according to recent reports, is doing very much to break down Hinduism in India, and who has been driven from a Hindu temple because he had polluted it by his presence, a man of great eloquence and plausibility, was graduated from a Presbyterian college in Calcutta, and infuses into his so-called Hinduism many of the truths and sentiments of the Christian gospel.

My observations and labors were largely given to India. It was a lectureship in connection with the University of Chicago, founded by a devoted member of a church in Michigan City, Mrs. Caroline E. Haskell, which led me to the Orient; and the brightest visions which met my eyes in the dark continent of Asia and elsewhere were the mission stations at which your gifts and efforts have kindled points of celestial light. The lectureship was fortunate in having an American origin, and fortunate also in its connection with a movement of religious fraternity and conciliation which touched the heart of a proud people. It has been our hope that this foundation would prove not only a useful factor in the evangelization of India, but also a bond of brotherhood and loving interest between East and West. It is plain that Christian education must be a main factor in the evangelization of a land where the very foundations of rational theistic and Christian faith are yet to be laid. I look upon the Christian colleges of India as important elements in the national regeneration, even though comparatively few of their students are brave enough to defy disinheritance, family persecution, and relentless social ostracism in order to declare, in the face of the cruel intolerance that prevails, the faith of Christianity which thousands of them are secretly cherishing. The lectureship is intended to supplement the work of Christian literature and the Christian colleges.

It was my mission, in speaking to the educated classes, to lodge as firmly as possible in the Hindu mind our conviction that Christianity is essentially a universal religion; to show that it must not be identified with any Western nation, or with the faults and vices of any one people. Flattered by the praises of European scholars who unearthed for him his own sacred literature, the philosophic Hindu began to think that Hinduism reformed and purified was good enough for his people, and indeed possessed a glory which did not belong to the Christian gospel. It was my effort, therefore, to show that Christianity, judged by any tests which bring out its true nature, is essentially universal. It has the appearance, which belongs to no other faith, of compassing the globe, molding more and more the peoples who make the modern world. Its fruits, whether in individual or social life, whether among the barbarous or civilized peoples, in past times or in the present, dwarf and eclipse the best results which other faiths, working over limited areas, can possibly produce. The literature of Christianity, its Sacred Book, judged by its form or contents, has universal characteristics not discoverable elsewhere. Its doctrine of God is so perfect and so adapted to human need that enlightened men, living in a world of suffering and sin, can never permanently be contented with the agnosticism of Buddha, the pantheism of the Hindu, or the stern monotheism of Islam. Furthermore, Christianity presents an absolutely unique phenomenon in the historic Christ, essentially universal in his nature and teaching, Son of God, Son of Man, living for human example, dying for human redemption, rising and ever living to be the inspiration of human hope,— a Christ who, from the very beginning, lodged in his followers the ineradicable conviction that his religion was meant for all, was adapted to all, and would yet be accepted everywhere. This earnest proclamation of the essential universality of the Christian faith was, of course, startling and not altogether acceptable to the proud and isolated Hindu spirit.

It has been the habit of that mind in recent years to claim for Hinduism every excellence which other religions bring to his attention. My persistent advocacy of Christ's universal claims, my insistence that Christianity is a missionary religion, seeking after the whole world with its message of love and salvation, stirred up not a little antagonism, and at the close of one of my lectures in Poona, a young Brahman, representing the omnivorousness of his nation, which has swallowed almost everything in the world of the spirit, came to me and said, "Dr. Barrows, you are right in saying that Hinduism has not been a missionary religion, but it is going to be"! Of course there is nothing more preposterous than this bit of airy vanity. The currents of four thousand years are not to be turned in precisely the opposite directions. The swamp is not to transform itself into a fountain, nor the Dead Sea into the Amazon. The all-credulous Hindu mind may believe that a few lectures on Hindu philosophy visiting western lands have reversed or will reverse the spirit and attitude of circles of centuries, but it still remains true that Hinduism is a national religion, and that to enter its circle is a question of geography as well as of race. The Brahman priest in the temple of Parbati to whom I put the question, "How can I become a Hindu?" answered correctly, "It is impossible. To be a Hindu, one must be born a Hindu." How difficult it is in some cases to lodge in the Brahman mind the notion that there is a universal religion which deserves acceptance by the Indus and the Ganges, as well as by the Hudson and the Thames, was illustrated by the chairman of my lecture in one of the cities of Southern India. I had finished my address, whereinto I had put every ounce and atom of my earnest conviction in regard to the sovereign claims of Christianity over every human mind and conscience, when the chairman, after the usual complimentary remarks, said to his Hindu hearers, "You see how thoroughly the lecturer believes his religion. His whole heart is in it. His earnestness has made him strong. What lesson may we learn from him? It is this: that we should be as earnest and devoted to our religion as he is to his!"

In setting forth the claims of Christianity, it was my duty to use the comparative method. The comparative method is certainly the fairest. It seeks for truth, and endeavors to determine where, at each point of the comparison, the greater, the purer, the completer, the more effective truth is found. Now I wish to say, with the greatest possible emphasis, that my conviction, arising out of perhaps a unique experience, in meeting large numbers of non-Christian hearers, Hindu, Moslem, and Buddhist, is clear and strong that the comparative method when faithfully applied by the Christian to other religions is not

Address by Rev. John Henry Barrows, D.D.

only the fairest, but is also the most enlightening, humiliating, and even exasperating method. Comparisons are not always agreeable, even when they serve to bring out the truth. Christian missionaries may set forth the gospel of Christ in what I may call the usual method, that prevailing in Christian lands, and awaken often only a sluggish interest and arouse a little antagonism. I might have followed the usual method, and probably would not have called forth so many columns of hostile criticisms as those with which the native Indian press abounded. I must testify, however, to the general spirit of courtesy which prevailed even in the criticisms, and I must also say that the constant kindness which I received and the patient and respectful hearing given to the lectures were remarkable. Missionaries informed me that they would scarcely have ventured before such audiences of educated men to have spoken with such frankness and fulness of conviction. I believe there was no lack on my part of appreciation of what is best in other religions. There was general testimony that my lectures contained no abuse of Hinduism, but at every point of comparison I indicated the immense superiority of Christianity. While Hinduism is national, Christianity is universal. While the effects of Hinduism are so mixed of good and evil as to condemn it, when judged by a lofty standard and seen through long periods of time, the results of Christianity demand a favorable verdict for the gospel of Christ.

While the polytheistic and pantheistic elements have led to degrading worship or produced moral paralysis, the holy, loving, redeeming God of Christian theism has awakened and confirmed the best possibilities of human nature. The superiority of the Christian over the Hindu scriptures is dazzlingly evident at every point of comparison, while to rank Crishna with Christ is to put ones self out of the domain of scholarship as well as out of the precincts of morality. Furthermore, the philosophy which the Hindu revivalists exploit as something more certain and permanent than the New Testament history is, after all, a jumble of fantastic speculations. One set of opinions is ridiculed by the holders of rival theories, and while the influence of their philosophies is revealed in the acute minds and distorted and untrustworthy moral character of the Brahmans, they have not benefited the Hindu millions with their so-called sublime abstractions. What has affected popular Hinduism has been the legendary history, if I may so call it, of the Ramayana and Mahabarata, which seems like a barbarous, grotesque caricature of the true supernaturalism of the gospel.

I did not expect to find the work of Christian missions so varied, wise, faithful, and effective as I discovered it to be. This discovery came in part from the unusual opportunities enjoyed of seeing the work of many societies, European and American; of seeing the work in all parts of India; of seeing all kinds of work in schools, colleges, hospitals, bazaar-preaching, tract and Bible distribution in villages and cities; and of seeing all this world under the eyes and with the explanations of those Christians, native and foreign, whose lives are most closely identified with it. The study of missions was not with me something subordinate and secondary. It was not put off until after I had seen the tombs, the temples, the streets, and the shops, the monuments and the palaces. It was a chief business of my hours not devoted to public speaking. I learned of missions from those who knew most about them, who knew their failures and their successes; from those who had been benefited by them; from those who opposed them. Most of all I relied on my own observations; constant, careful, repeated, daily observations. If men wish to learn of the trade of a country, or of its colleges, or of its politics, they confer with traders, college-men, politicians. They study on the spot and under the guidance of experts. After three months in India and nearly one month in Japan, wherein amplest opportunities were mine for seeing and knowing the labors of Christian propagandists in the Orient, I record the deep conviction that Christian missions in the East are more wonderful, more admirable, and better worth studying than any other feature of the life of Asia.

I am grateful that in the work of a score of missionary societies I could see so many evidences of the fruitfulness, hopefulness, and beneficent power of Christian evangelism. Certainly the bishop of Tinnevelly who, between a year ago last November and the following March, was permitted to confirm more than two thousand native converts, does not despair of the evangelization of India. Having conversed with Brahman-Christian preachers, and professors in colleges, having seen a Brahman in the bazaars of Benares proclaiming Christ amid the hideous idolatries of that city, having seen whole rows of Brahman converts in Christian churches, I not only repudiate the mendacious story that no true Aryan is ever converted, but I cherish a hope that in time to come multitudes of the twice-born classes will be born again by the Spirit of God.

Let one visit one hundred Christian schools in which I have seen gathered the dark-eyed boys and girls of Arcot, Bengal, and the Punjab; let him see the native congregations of Christians in Lucknow and Palamcotta, in Ahmednager and Madras, and contrast their homes with the conditions out of which they came; let him visit the hospital work in Amritsar and Indore; let him study the various forms of organized labor by which the Church Missionary Society reaches the ignorant, the benighted, the blind, the deaf, the dumb, and the poor in Palamcotta; let him see what the Pundita Ramabai is doing in Poona for the relief and instruction of Hindu high-caste widows; let him mark the biblical, literary, and scientific instruction given to the eighteen hundred boys and young men in the Christian College, Madras, and to the hundreds in Duff College, Calcutta; Forman College, Lahore; Reid College, Lucknow; Wilson College, Bombay; Wesley College, Bangalore; St. John's College, Agra; St. Stephen's College, Delhi; let him follow the Bible women in their diligent teaching of the Scriptures; let him hear the reports of the great army of Christian ladies who are carrying light and cheer, comfort and hope, into darkened zenanas; let him note how millions of printed Christian pages are spreading all abroad the mighty gospel of redemption; let him study such huge turnings to Christ as have followed the preaching of the Baptists among the Telugus and the Methodists in northern India; let him renew his acquaintance with the monstrous usages which prevailed eighty years ago, and which Christian civilization in India has swept away; let him read the reports already published, which show that the last year has been the most fruitful and glorious year in the whole of the history of Indian missions; let him note the hundred signs that the old Hinduism is decadent and doomed; let him study the reformatory movements which the presence and power of Christianity have started into life; let him remember that with all the forces which keep people back from open confession, the membership of native churches in India has increased more rapidly during the last twenty years than has the population;— and he will be convinced that, though only a good beginning has been made, and generations of Christian effort are yet required to do for the Empire of India what the gospel wrought for the regeneration of Ancient Rome, still he has seen and learned enough to dispel the error contained in the oft-quoted remark that Christian missions in India are a failure.

One morning in a village six miles from Ahmednager, I was permitted by Dr. Robert A. Hume to baptize and receive into the Church two young men, recent converts to Christ. It was a very humble place where the villagers assembled, but I was never before so deeply moved by such a service. Sitting and standing on the floor of earth were true confessors of the old faith which I had heard chanted in stately cathedrals by the Tiber and on the Rhine. Here were believers in that Name before which emperors have bowed, and my hand trembled as I touched their dusky foreheads with the baptismal waters. It seemed to me that he who stooped to the lowliness of Bethlehem and Nazareth was almost sensibly present in the little meeting-house, which the dark hands of humble people had decorated with fruits and wild flowers out of regard to one of Christ's ministers who had come to them from the other side of the sea.

A single glimpse of a congregation of Hindu Christians is a better argument for missions than any eloquence can elaborate. Things seen are greater than things heard, and yet things heard by the heart of faith and good-will and by minds of keen and sympathetic intelligence ought to awaken such an interest as to sweep Christian America into the very vanguard of the missionary battle.

It is almost an impertinence for me or any one else to eulogize the spirit of wisdom and courage and self-denying devotion which has marked the lives of your missionaries, those now living and those who have entered into brighter spheres. The stars of the Southern Cross look down through the palm-trees of India upon the graves of many American Christians, graves as sacred as any in Plymouth or Princeton, in Greenwood or Gettysburg, at Havana or Santiago, and the voice which comes from these heroic sepulchres is such an appeal to the Christian heart of America that, mingled with the plaintive voices of Asia's dying millions, it will not permit you to take one step backward.

A rich treat awaited the audience at the close of this great double programme, in the shape of a half-hour's concert by the Fisk Jubilee Singers, who had remained, some of them at considerable financial sacrifice, to enliven the Convention by their sweet songs. Others had travelled a considerable distance to return to it.

MONDAY NIGHT.

Closing Meeting — Auditorium Endeavor.

THE CONVENTION'S LOOKOUT MOUNTAIN.

With what songs and rejoicing, sunny faces and expectant hearts, the tribes came up to the Convention's hill of privilege! The great hall was laid out in beautiful garden-plots of delegates. It was a singing throng — and how could it help it? — long before Dr. Clark called the consecration meeting to order.

Mr. Excell and Mr. Foster led an inspiring song service, after which Rev. Ralph W. Brokaw, of Utica, N. Y., and Rev. Preston Taylor, of Nashville, led in prayer.

Then occurred one of the pleasant incidents of the Convention. Mr. F. A. Wallis, of Kentucky, arose and presented Dr. Clark with a beautiful gavel, which had been carved and inlaid by the converted Christian Endeavor prisoners in the Kentucky prison at Frankfort. Dr. Clark received it amid a shower of applause, and used it during the rest of the meeting.

The trustees' hearty resolutions of thanks to Nashville, cordially emphasized by the applause of the Convention, were fittingly followed by the presentation to the audience of the Committee of '98, headed by "that little man," Ira Landrith. Speaking for his two thousand helpers on the local committee, their chairman said, "We have no regrets and no apologies, because we have done our little best; and, if we had a chance, we'd do it again."

Resolutions from the Board of Trustees of the United Society of Christian Endeavor.

Since a Christian Endeavor Convention has no legislative power, but, in harmony with a cardinal principle of the movement, recognizes the entire subordination of each society to its own church, your committee on resolutions confines its report to expressions of gratification and of gratitude concerning this very happy and successful Convention now closing.

First of all we desire to render devoutest thanksgiving to God, who has brought us together from many lands into this Seventeenth International Convention, and has so graciously and abundantly blessed us throughout all our meetings. This Convention will take its place in the annals of Christian Endeavor as a convention conspicuously characterized by brotherly love, by Christian patriotism, and by spiritual quickening and spiritual power. For all these, we devoutly thank our heavenly Father.

Our thanks are due and most gladly given to the chairman of the Committee of '98, Rev. Ira Landrith, to each member of the committee itself, and to every sub-committee and every agency, for the clearness of foresight with which they have anticipated every want of the Convention, the wisdom with which they have planned to meet these wants, and the effective and self-sacrificing energy with which they have so completely provided for every convenience and comfort of delegates and visitors to this delightful Convention. The simple fact that all this manifold service, down to the smallest detail of its drudgery, has been rendered as a loving service to our common Lord enriches the service itself and deepens our grateful appreciation of it.

We desire to record our grateful appreciation of the cordial co-operation of the Epworth Leagues, the Luther Leagues, and the Baptist Young People's Union, of this city and vicinity, with our societies of Christian Endeavor in receiving and caring for this Convention, which has been so happily christened "The convention of brotherly love." This fellowship in preparing for the Convention has permeated the Convention itself, and has been one of its most pleasing features — not to us only, but we believe to our unseen Lord as well.

To all the churches which have not only opened wide their doors to receive us, but have placed their pulpits at our disposal and have so generously stood ready to render any service within their power, we wish to extend assurances of grateful appreciation. Within these sanctuaries many of us have entered into a fuller knowledge of the secret of the Lord and from them we will carry with us precious and helpful memories of the fellowship of his saints.

To the citizens of this beautiful city, — this typical city of the Southland, — who have with proverbial Southern hospitality received us so cordially into their homes and so freely made us welcome to their very best; who have, by so many tokens, assured us of their esteem and friendship, we desire to return our assurances of Christian affection, of grateful appreciation, and of fond and enduring remembrance of all their kindness to us. Although we have been but brief sojourners here, the citizens of Nashville have not permitted any of us to feel as strangers within the gates of their goodly city.

The railroads, which brought us into the city without accident of any kind, deserve our thanks not only for granting us reduced rates, but for efficient and courteous service rendered while *en route*.

The newspapers of this city have rendered our cause a most conspicuous and valuable service by their full and accurate reports of the addresses, the conferences, and all the proceedings of this Convention, thus multiplying its power for good by reaching multitudes who otherwise would have been beyond its reach and influence.

For all these favors we desire to make most sincere and grateful acknowledgments.

Dr. Sweeney, of Virginia, who preached the first of the Convention sermons, is one of the great preachers among the Disciples of Christ.

He is a tall man with Websterian eyes and vehement utterance. His splendid theme was the royalty of service.

Sermon by Rev. Z. T. Sweeney, D.D.,
Richmond, Va.
THE ROYALTY OF SERVICE.

As we leave this transfiguration convention, let us bear away a lesson upon the greatness of service. Man has always had his gauges of greatness, but they have been continually changing, and this is well, for it indicates that he is a progressive being. Were the standards by which we measure things changeless, it would indicate the death-lock of human advancement. In primary ages, the athlete was the great one; later on came the patriarch; then the sheik; and last of all the warrior and diplomat. Europe is overburdened to-day with monuments to warriors. One could almost desire it to be smitten with a monumental cyclone, that for a time, at least, we might forget the pugnacity of our ancestry.

What do the nations of Europe call greatness? Take Russia. Her Czar rules one-sixth of the landed globe, and a hundred millions of people tremble when he frowns. But is he satisfied? No. He is reaching out one hand for Corea, and with the other grasping at the fairest portions of the Celestial Empire. He is looking down from his Pamir plateau over the Himalayas to see if India be worth wresting from England by a bloody struggle. He hovers over the "sick man of Europe" like the vulture of the desert over the dying camel, ready at the opportune moment to pluck the crown from his brow and set it sparkling in the diadem of Peter the Great.

Germany is one great military camp. The brass helmets of her two millions of soldiers flash back the reflection of the setting sun-rays, as they wait the command of "Vorwart" to cross the Rhine, tread down the purple clusters of French vineyards, and water their horses in the Seine and Rhone.

France has a similar army bristling with revenge and hatred, waiting to repel the invaders, while Austria, Italy, and Spain follow this great lead as closely as they are able.

In England we find a better condition. Her civilization is no longer upon a war basis. She has outgrown war, and all her interests are for peace. Some people worry about an Anglo-American war in the future. Such people know neither of these great countries. They can never have another war for the reason there is too much of the Man Christ Jesus in the hearts of the great English-speaking nations. But England has her false idea of greatness. The curse of England is caste. There are a million men in England to-day who would give, if they had it, a million pounds sterling if they could trace their genealogy back to William the Conqueror, the illiterate and illegitimate son of a tanner's daughter. Tennyson tried to teach them that "kind hearts are more than coronets, and simple faith than Norman blood;" but his failure is found in the fact that they dubbed him knight before they laid him to rest in their great mausoleum.

America tried to import a little of this. Our Virginia cavaliers brought it over, and their children cling to it yet, but it is held only as a sentiment.

John the Baptist was the original Democrat. Addressing the first families of Judea (F. F. J.'s), that looked on with complacency at his excoriation of the common people, he said, "Say not within yourselves that we have Abraham to our father. God is able of these very stones to raise up children unto Abraham." Every tree that bringeth not forth good fruit is hewn down, no matter what nursery brand it may bear. The time has gone by in America when a man is honored simply for what his parents have been. 'If a man desires to be honored he must be honorable; respected, he must be respectable; loved, he must be worthy. The latest degenerate is the Anglomaniac. Oh, it is pitiful to see the grandson or grand-daughter of a Knickerbocker searching the records of foreign heraldry to find a lineage! I am not a believer in evolution, but when I see the ease with which some people lapse back into monkeydom, it seems possible for a monkey to make at least an Anglomaniac out of himself, if not a man.

While America has largely been freed from caste, she has her false standard of greatness. We as a nation worship at the shrine of the almighty dollar. The man who can pile up a large fortune, regardless of the widows' tears and the orphans' cries for bread, is the American aristocrat. It has eaten the vitality out of politics, and we can no longer have a candidate unless he has a "bar'l." The preacher must be selected with a view to large collections, and marriage is conducted strictly upon the principles laid down by Dunn and Bradstreet.

CHRIST'S STANDARD.

Right across the face of all this comes the young man of Nazareth, with hands hard from the carpenter-shop, and says, "If you will be great, serve; if you will be aristocratic, minister." He took on himself the form of a servant, and it was this that made him the brightness of the Father's glory, the express image of his person.

The highest conception that I have of the Almighty is that he is the great servant of every created thing.

As the chief glory of the coronet that decks the brow of the Prince of Wales is found in the words, "Ich Dien"—"I serve"—on its forefront, so on the zoneless brow of the uncreated Godhood may be written in immortal symbols, "I serve."

Jesus was pre-eminently a servant of men. His biography has been condensed into the four words "went about doing good." This was the law of his life from the cradle to the grave. Every great religious teacher in the history of the world agrees with him that the service of man is the end of all philosophy and religion. Humboldt, representing science, says, "All the world is but a scaffold on which to erect a manhood."

As the Aloe plant toils patiently for ninety-nine years that on the hundredth it may burst into a shower of beauty and glory, "and thus the energies sublime of a century burst full-blossomed from the thorny stem of time," so the long train of ancient earth-life dragged its way through the slime and detritus of primeval ages that it might find its flower and fruit in man,—the masterpiece in the gallery of God's handiwork.

Granting the truth of what I have said, what is the irresistible conclusion to which we must come? Simply this: the service of man is the grandest service to which man can give himself. To aid you in making this practical, let us separate this general principle into details of application:—

First. Every trade or profession is to be viewed in the light of its ministry to manhood. See to it that you choose no life-work that does not in some way serve mankind. The mere piling up of dollars has no moral signification above piling up bricks or stones, unless those dollars are to be made the servants of humanity.

I would rather be the humblest school teacher in the backwoods of the wild West than the greatest millionaire in New York who lives in a golden spider-web. Break the alabaster box of your life only on the feet of him for whom Christ died.

Second. The true end of government is to be found in the fact that it serves the citizen. We often hear it said that "we are the greatest nation on the earth." That is true,—true in a far higher sense than many a spread-eagle orator means when he utters it. But it is not true in all senses. As a military people we are not great. As a naval power we are raw and crude. In art, and science, and literature we are infants, and so in many ways that the world calls greatness we are not great. But after all, I repeat it as a most deliberate conviction that we are the greatest people on the globe—great in the fact that everything in the government is made for the citizen. Our great free schools, whose playgrounds are the greatest levellers in the world, stimulate the young mind to free thinking. Our vast printing-presses, without censorship or dictatorship except an enlightened public opinion, stimulate the free-thinking citizen to freely express his thoughts. Our ballot-box gives that citizen the right not only to think and speak, but to act as well. Over all, the starry flag of freedom guaranteeing all these rights by the power of a great people.

TRIBUTE TO OLD GLORY.

It is the sweetest flag that ever kissed the sunlight of God in the breezes of heaven. It enjoys the greatest heritage and history of human rights of any banner on earth. Under the guidance of the young eaglet whose talons were just sprouting, it drove the British Lion from off our shores never again to set dominant foot upon them. It sailed under the frowning cliffs of Algiers and taught the haughty Sultan of Morocco, and with that half-savage potentate all kings of Christendom, that the rights of American free men must be respected. It led our fathers over the Sierra Madres of Mexico and waved in triumph over the halls of the Montezumas. It pioneered the pathway of the pathfinder over the Rockies and gave us the Eldorado land of California. It flaps its broken shreds in the North to-night nearer the pole than any flag on land or deep. Under it our fathers and mothers courted and married; under it we were born. And when the awful chasm opened in the forum of our national life that would not close until into it had been poured the purity, patriotism, and chivalry of our nation, and though it brought sorrow into every home in the North and made my own Southland billowy as the ocean with the graves of her sons, thank God, the price was not too great, for the old flag waves to-night over the homes and schools of a great, free, and undivided people. And though it has been sleeping in peace for a third of a century, it is unfurled again to the shock of battle and comes forth as a bridegroom from his chamber and rejoicing as a strong man to run a race. It led the brave son of the Green Mountain State into Manila's harbor and witnessed the sinking of Spanish hulks to the bottom of the sea. Hardly had the applause of the nation died away when brave young Hobson of Alabama set it one notch higher in the skies than ever before by his heroism in the mouth of Santiago harbor. While we do not boast of our prowess in war, yet there is vigor enough in that banner, if the service of humanity demands it, to strew the high seas of God with the wreckage of every navy of oppression.

Third. This law of service also decides the question of the true Church. The Church of the twentieth century will not be known by its doctrines, by its rituals, nor by the amount of motion, emotion, nor commotion it can raise. It will be known and honored in the nation that it goes about, like its Master, doing good.

If I may be permitted to use an illustration, I would say that all the prosperity and popularity that God has bestowed upon Methodism is owing to the fact that Methodism has made itself the servant of humanity.

When Methodism gets proud and seeks for the rich and great ones, God will write "Ichabod" over the doors of her neglected chapels, for her glory will have departed.

What is true of Methodism is true of every other Church in Christendom. Especially will it become true of the Endeavor movement.

Fourth. This spirit of service to others will destroy the evil spirit of sectarianism that seems so hard for the Church of God to exorcise. Sectarianism was begotten and born in selfishness; it has thrived and prospered in selfishness; and it holds its power to-day because of the selfishness of humanity.

Every great movement against the Church of God may be traced to self-seeking men. Every great movement against our Endeavor work may be traced to the same source. Our glorious movement was born in the desire to serve humanity, and there is room upon its broad platform for all who love God and man to stand side by side. But there is not room for two sectarians! We meet upon one great question; namely, "What think ye of the Christ? whose son is he?" If we can get men right upon Jesus Christ, we can trust him to get them right upon everything else. As the new sap in the springtime forces off all the old dead leaves that have clung through the winter-time, so the life of Christ in us will cause us to slough off all doctrinal and ecclesiastical excrescences, and leave only the new life in Christ.

The world will soon forget its masters, but will cling with loving remembrance to its servants. I used to live within twenty miles of the old dusty and neglected grave of Hannibal, the haughty son of Hamilcar that drove back the proud Romans to the very gates of the Eternal City, but I never had time or interest to go and look at it. But I used frequently to go out in my caique upon the rippling waters of the Golden Horn to see the last rays of the setting sun kiss the windows of an old armory building in Scutari good-night. As I gazed upon the blazing windows of the rough yellow-washed building it seemed to me the glory of God shone round about it, and that it was the house of God and the gate to heaven; for through those long aisles once walked sweet Florence Nightingale with her Christlike helpers, breathing a prayer here, writing a letter there, and moistening the lips of a poor Russian, Turk, Englishman, Frenchman. The names of Florence Nightingale, Elizabeth Fry, Dorothea Dix, John Frederick Oberlin, William Wilberforce, William Lloyd Garrison, and John Brown will grow green in the memory of men while the names of the Hannibals, Cæsars, and Napoleons shall rot in oblivion.

Dr. MacArthur, of New York, of Canada, of Scotland, the second Convention preacher, appropriately represented in his own person the international character of this Convention.

Sermon by Rev. R. S. MacArthur, D.D.,
New York City.

CHRIST, AND HIM CRUCIFIED.

For I am determined not to know anything among you save Jesus Christ, and him crucified.— 1 Cor. 2: 2.

It is said that leading to an Austrian city there is a bridge in the parapets of which there are twelve statues of Christ. One statue represents him as the Sower, another as the Shepherd, another as the Carpenter, and another as the Physician; others represent him as the Pilot, Prophet, Priest, and King; and still others represent him in yet other characters. The simple-minded country people coming into the city in the early morning with their produce for the market pause and pray before Christ the Sower. A little later, the artisan on his way to his workshop worships Christ the Carpenter. Later still, when the sun has scattered the mists of the morning and has flooded the earth with his supernal splendors, the invalid, creeping from the city to breathe the fresh air of the country, presents his morning prayers to Christ the Physician. Doubtless there is much of superstition in this worship, but there is in it also a great truth. Each worships the Christ who is nearest to himself — the Christ who best interprets his own thoughts and best supplies his peculiar wants.

It is the glory of Christ that he can be everything to everybody the world over. To-day I lift before you Christ, and him crucified. This is the view of Christ which gives significance and glory to all other representations; it is the one which so engaged the whole being of the apostle, which captivated his imagination, controlled his intellect, and constrained his heart. In all the history of the race there was not to Paul such a life as Christ's, and in all the life of Christ there was no such glory as that which gathered round his cross.

Sadly Paul leaves Athens, goes forty-five miles and comes to Corinth. This famous Grecian city was situated on the isthmus which joins Peloponnesus to the mainland of Greece. Horace calls it " bimaris " — on two seas. Corinth was the natural portage from the Ionian Sea on the west to the Ægean on the east. Both the Greeks and the Romans attempted to join the two seas by cutting a canal across the isthmus, but owing to the rocky character of the country the effort was not successful. By an ingenious contrivance galleys were carried across on trucks. Corinth had two harbors, Lechæum on the west and Cenchreæ on the east. It thus became the mart of Asia and Europe. Its ships whitened the seas. Foreigners crowded its streets. Near the city the Isthmian games were celebrated. These games attracted strangers from all parts of the world. The religion of Corinth was debasing. Venus was the principal diety, as Diana at Ephesus and Minerva at Athens. " It is not for every one to go to Corinth " became a proverb which merchants well understood as referring to the debasing worship of Venus. Old Corinth became subject to the Romans 146 B. C. For nearly one hundred years the city lay waste. But Julius Cæsar sent thither a colony of freedmen from Rome, and soon the wealth, splendor, and vices of ancient Corinth reappeared in the new city. It was to this new city that Paul came. Corinth has been called the " Paris of antiquity." Wealth abounded. Luxury held constant carnival. Vice triumphed. In the name of the holiest instincts of the soul the foulest sins of the body were committed.

To such a city as this Paul came. Here he preached. Here a church was formed — a church to which or from which Paul's most famous epistles were written. The gospel that could win in Corinth can win anywhere. After Paul had left Corinth, and while at Ephesus, intelligence came to him concerning the Corinthian church from the household of the pious Chloe, and also from an epistle which the Corinthians had addressed to him. The painful condition of things thus communicated to him led him to write this epistle. In this letter he opens to us his heart. He is a hard-hearted man who can read these words without emotion. As we study them we can feel across the continents and the centuries the throb of that great heart which beat in the bosom of the greatest apostle. Our theme this hour is Paul's determination at Corinth.

CHARACTERISTICS OF PAUL'S DETERMINATION.

1. Let us, in the first place, notice some of its characteristics. It was a deliberate determination. Some have supposed that Paul was disappointed alike with the methods and with the results of his work at Athens. But others claim that his sermon there was an admirable illustration of his own principle of being all things to all men that he might win some to Christ. The latter would make his determination at Corinth refer rather to his purpose to discard all mere rhetorical finish and oratorical art. It is also to be borne in mind that his sermon at Athens was never completed. He had just begun to speak of the resurrection and the judgment when the interruption came. To say that he made a mistake at Athens involves difficult questions of inspiration. No one is warranted in making that statement. Nevertheless, it seems to me that there is in the text an undertone which suggests a decided contrast between the method pursued at Athens and that now determined upon at Corinth. The word used here implies that his determination was reached after much reflection. Paul was not a man who would rashly come to a conclusion. Neither was he the man who would be likely to abandon a position which he had deliberately taken. That resolution was not accidental. In that great and sinful city of Corinth he deliberately determined to know and to preach only a crucified Saviour.

It was also a courageous determination. Paul well knew the fondness of the Greeks for a finished rhetoric and a graceful elocution; he also knew their love for philosophical speculations. He gives us in some of his epistles indications of his own natural fondness for abstruse and metaphysical discussions. He well knew that such discussions would attract the attention and awaken the enthusiasm of his audience. On the other hand, he knew that his chosen theme would expose him to the contempt and derision of his critical and captious hearers. Still, he had the courage of his convictions. Addressing poets, orators, and philosophers, he discoursed not of poetry or oratory or philosophy. It is true that it was Athens which was called "the eye of Greece, mother of arts and eloquence," and that Corinth was especially noted as a great mercantile city. Still, Cicero calls Corinth, because of her intellectual attainments, "the light of all Greece." Paul knew how a Jew would be despised by the Greeks. Physically and mentally they were Pharisees; they despised all others as barbarians. They were the favored sons of sunny Greece; and Paul comes to speak to them of a Jew who was crucified by his countrymen as a felon. I tell you, friends, that was grit, that was grace, that was pluck, that was piety.

We still speak of the offence of the cross; but we oftener speak of its glory. How its meaning has changed since Paul preached at Corinth! Then it was to his hearers what the gibbet or the gallows would be to an audience to-day. Behold the transformation! Poetry with unfading garlands now decks the cross; sculpture honors it; architecture, in noblest cathedral, copies its form; painting sits before it until its heavenly light illumines the canvas; genius, in every department of thought and activity, has found its highest glory in placing the diadem on the brow of the Crucified. To-day many of you bear the image of Christ and him crucified in your deepest souls. You have just sung

"In the cross of Christ I glory,
Towering o'er the wrecks of time."

That song expresses the deepest joy and the highest glory of millions on earth and in heaven. At this very hour, I doubt not, some of you would rise from these seats, walk to that street, and lay your head upon the block rather than deny him who once hung on that cross. O brave Paul! Our hearts catch the enthusiasm of thy courageous determination. How men in our day ought to blush who are ashamed of Jesus! A man who is ashamed of his Christian principles is a man of whom his Christian principles have cause to be ashamed. Oh for the lofty courage of Paul's noble determination!

But it was also an intelligent determination. Paul was a student of history. He was not a narrow man. If he was a man of one idea, as some have said, it was an idea so broad that it included all true and noble ideas. He was a cosmopolitan man. The truth that flashed upon him as he journeyed toward Damascus enabled him to interpret the Old Testament in the light of the cross. He saw that all the ways of God's revelation converged toward and met in the cross. He saw that if you take it away the Old Testament is meaningless. He saw that the cross is the centre of the Bible. It is more, and thoughtful men in our day are beginning to recognize the fact: it is the pivotal point around which all the events of the world's history revolve. "All the light of" secular as well as "sacred story gathers round its head sublime." All the centuries before Christ's coming prepared for that coming; all the centuries since expand and illustrate the significance of his advent. Christ is King. All events of history previous to his death converged toward the cross; all events since have diverged from it. The cross stood at the confluence of three streams of civilization. The superscription on it was written in three languages: Hebrew, the language of religion; Greek, the language of culture; Latin, the language of law. A marvelous blending of these three varieties of national life prepared for the spread of Christ's kingdom. Are you a student of history? You must "build your studio on Calvary." Nations flourish and decay, kingdoms rise and fall, but amid all changes the student will see "Jesus only." As well might a man attempt to write a text-book on astronomy and refuse to recognize the sun, as write a history of this world and leave out Jesus Christ. Christ is the Sun of the moral universe, and around him all events revolve. The disciple of truth will find Christ everywhere. Perhaps Hugh Miller went too far when he claimed that he found the cross in the hoary rocks. But we are sure that the true student of history will see it as the crowning glory of every century. He will see along the track of the ages the footprints of the Son of God. Paul thus saw the glory of Jesus. To see it was the master-passion of his master-mind.

Well might Paul determine as he did. His decision heightens our admiration for the clearness of his intellect as well as for the tenderness of his heart. I ask no favors for him. Judge him in the clear light of this nineteenth century. His determination will bear the test. He was a man of brains; he had that most uncommon kind of sense which we call common sense; he was true as brave and brave as true. Come on, ye philosophers of history, will ye measure swords with this man? We may say of the noble Paul what Dr. Schaff says of the great Neander: He was "a child in spirit, a man in intellect, a giant in learning, and a saint in piety." How the great God who sitteth in the heavens must laugh at the weakness and wickedness of men in denying his presence and opposing his power in the world he has made!

Men have thought they could hew down his cross and dethrone the Lord of glory. They have thought they could overturn the Rock of Ages. They shall learn that "the grass" of sceptical philosophy "withereth, and the flower" of infidel oratory "fadeth," but the word of our God shall stand forever. We commend Paul's deliberate, courageous, and intelligent determination to know only Christ, and him crucified.

THE MEANING OF PAUL'S DETERMINATION.

2. Notice, in the second place, the meaning of Paul's determination. Can we get the sweet kernel out of his stirring words? Christ's matchless Person and redemptive work were Paul's theme as here expressed. Let us look more closely.

He preached the humanity of Christ. By the mystery of the incarnation Jesus Christ became the Son of man. He had to assume the nature which he came to redeem. He said of himself, "a body hast thou prepared me." He took upon himself the form of a servant; he literally emptied himself. He came not to be ministered unto, but to minister, and to give his life a ransom for many. We stand by the cradle in Bethlehem and remember that he whose arm upholds the universe was once himself borne upon a woman's arm. He was a true man. Christ did not lay hold of the nature of angels. He came to save men, and if he would lift our poor fallen nature he must put himself beneath it. We need a living, loving, divine-human Redeemer. The heart cries out for a Saviour so near us as to win our tenderest love, and yet a Saviour so far above us as to command our highest reverence. The soul needs just such a Saviour as was Jesus. It can know no true rest until it can repose on his bosom. Christ was more than *a* man — he was *Man*. He was the head of a new race. All the virtues of woman and all the nobilities of man are in him. I stop not to prove, in any formal way, the humanity of Christ. We all accept it as true.

But we need to make more of this truth. We have often put Christ too far away from us. Never until I was in my last year in the theological seminary did I fully feel the uplifting power of Christ's divine-human sympathy. The foundations seemed to be slipping from beneath me; I cried with an intensity of desire, born of an awful fear, and an arm mighty as God's was put about me; and it lifted me to a heart tender as a mother's. Some enemies of the truth have done good by calling attention to Christ's humanity. His life has been vividly written. Renan, and others of his class, can be cleavers of wood and drawers of water for Christ's servants. The places Jesus visited have been graphically described. He has been called out of the shadows of time and distance, and made to appear in a vivid historic reality. Writers of this class have done, perhaps unintentionally, great good. "The man Christ Jesus" touches our hearts with tenderness and inspires them with hope. The proper presentation of this truth is the only antidote to some errors which have grown out of its suppression. How shall you prevent the mariolatry of the Romanist? That he does worship Mary cannot be denied. In Rome to-day she is placed far above Jesus Christ. Shall you denounce her and her worship? You will by so doing only multiply her champions and worshippers; and you will also be false to fact, for she was a true and noble woman. Shall you summon to your aid reason and Scripture? Yes, and you can readily show that there is not a passage in the Bible which can fairly be quoted as favoring her worship. But the devout Romanist will still continue his worship. What shall you do? This: preach Christ in all the fulness and glory of his divinity and humanity. Where Christ is not so preached Mary embodies a tender thought and supplies a real want in the human soul. In heathenism physical power was everything; moral purity was nothing. Christ introduced a new thought. He taught that purity is power, meekness might, and gentleness greatness. These were womanly virtues. Mary came to represent them. Mary came in process of time to be worshipped. We must show that all that is purest in woman and noblest in man is found in Jesus; that he meets every want of every soul.

We must learn that the best way to preach down error is to preach up truth. Never raise Satan unless you are sure you can lay him. Never throw down the gauntlet to him unless you know that you can give him a deadly lunge. The best way to keep out the plants of error is to fill every spot of the soil of the heart with the good seed of the kingdom. To keep chaff out of the measure fill it with wheat; then let the wind blow the chaff as it pleases. The great mass of church-going people have learned from Christian ministers almost all that they know of Darwin, Huxley, and others of their class. If the theories of these men are demonstrated to be true, we shall have neither need nor right to oppose them. So long as they are only theories what is the use of directly opposing them? God is One; truth is one. God cannot contradict himself. Why waste time on theories? The pulpit has something better to do than to advertise the devil's nostrums. To cure error, liberate truth. Christ not only proposed to give Lazarus life, but liberty also. The truth must be loosed. To be fair with an opponent, you must state him clearly. Often the statement, being largely in his language, is clear and strong; often the refutation is obscure and weak. The statement is remembered, the refutation is forgotten. The valiant knight of truth often succeeds only in giving prominence and dignity to a hitherto unseen and perhaps unknown foe. We have paid the devil too much respect; we owe him nothing but contempt and disobedience. As preachers we cannot know everything about everything; but we ought thoroughly to know God's word. Let us fully, fearlessly, and kindly declare it, and victory over every error will be on the side of God's truth.

Oh how precious it is to think of the manhood of Christ! He was the only person ever born into the world who had his choice as to how he should come, and he chose to come as a babe and in poverty. He trod the lower walks of life, and poverty was dignified. He became a babe, and babyhood was glorified. He lived as a boy, and boyhood was forever honored. All the conditions of life into which he entered he exalted and sanctified. On the cross he gave a young man's life for the world's sin. On the throne to-day he sits with the dew of immortal youth and the glory of eternal manhood. Once he suffered; now he forever will sympathize. The whole race is ennobled by the thought that humanity with Divinity sits at the right hand of the Majesty on high.

Paul preached Christ's divinity also. A man cannot save his fellow. However exalted Christ might be as a man, he would still be helpless to save a soul from death. A man cannot find a ransom; a man cannot meet the claims of God's law; a man cannot stand in the holy place; a man hath not clean hands and a pure heart. The Saviour must be God as well as man. Man may sympathize; God alone can save. We need both the humanity and the divinity of Jesus Christ. If you deny either, you contradict Isaiah when he speaks of Christ as "a child born, a son given," and at the same time as " the mighty God, the everlasting Father, the Prince of Peace." John distinctly tells us that the " Word was God," and also that the " Word was made flesh." But I am not undertaking to prove to you, brethren, his divinity. This is not necessary. I am simply showing how in harmony with this view are the trend and spirit of Scripture. Some men say Christ was good, was the best man the world has ever seen, but he was not divine. Out of their own mouths such men shall be convicted of inconsistency and stupidity. Christ was either divine or he was not a good man; he was God, or — can we say it with reverence? — he was an unpardonable egotist or a hopeless lunatic. He claimed to be divine; he was put to death because of that claim. John says he was full of grace and of truth; but if not divine, he was full of falsehood. From the first majestic words of Genesis to the last love-note of Revelation the uniform testimony of

ELECTRIC WELCOME.

HEADQUARTERS COMMITTEE OF '98.   TULANE HOTEL.

every devout heart concerning Christ is, in substance, "My Lord and my God." This truth fired the heart of Paul. How grandly he bursts forth with his magnificent doxology: "Now unto the king eternal, immortal, invisible, the only wise God, be honor and glory forever and ever. Amen." And let all the people say, amen and amen. A symmetrical Christ, perfect man and perfect God, is the need and is the hope of the world.

But Paul preached Jesus Christ, and him crucified; he recognized the expiatory character of Christ's atonement. This glorious doctrine is the very pith and marrow, the warp and woof, the very heart, of the whole Bible. This doctrine has always been an offence to some opposers; to the Jews it was "a stumbling-block;" to the Greeks it was "foolishness." Both Jew and Greek have their representatives still. There are in our day those who regard the atonement, considered as a propitiatory sacrifice, with the utmost disfavor. They deny that his death had any reference to the satisfaction of divine justice; that he was in any sense the sinner's substitute; that he did anything to satisfy the claims of God's justice. His death, they claim, was due to man's wrath, and its effect is simply in its moral influence over us by his self-sacrificing example.

That Christ's death exercises such a power we joyfully admit. It has its manhood side, but that because of its Godward side. It must not be forgotten that while God is a loving Father he is also a righteous Judge. God must be just; if unjust he must vacate his throne. What is the testimony of the Scriptures? They affirm that "it pleased the Lord to bruise him;" "he was wounded for our transgressions;" that "he hath made him to be sin for us who knew no sin," and that "Christ suffered for sins, the just for the unjust." All God's revelations, in symbol, type, and prophecy, declare with trumpet-tongue that "without shedding of blood there is no remission;" and the glory of Jesus, of which the redeemed shall ever sing, is that he "bare our sins in his own body on the tree." The man who will deny that these scriptures teach the vicariousness of Christ's death could not be convinced by any amount of scriptural authority. The true view gives to Christ's self-sacrificing example all the power which the moral influence theory does, and it also satisfies both reason and faith by giving us an expiating Saviour, who meets the claims of God's law, and thus wins the homage of man's love. To preach Christ and him crucified, then, will include all the marvellous mystery of his august person, the great facts respecting his spotless life, the efficacy of his atoning death, his triumphant resurrection, his glorious ascension, and his prevailing intercession; it includes our pardon and peace by the blood of his cross, our complete salvation in him here, and our blessed home in heaven hereafter. Here is enough to excite the joy and exhaust the skill of the highest angel.

THE MOTIVE OF PAUL'S DETERMINATION.

3. Let us look, in the last place, at the controlling motives of the apostle's determination.

This was the only preaching which could harmonize the facts of Christ's life. Some tell us that Christ grew sullen and morose, toward the end of his earthly life; that those severe denunciations near the close, contrasting in so marked a way with the Sermon on the Mount, show how bitter was his spirit and how keen was his disappointment. These men forget that Christ's conversation with Nicodemus took place some months before the Sermon on the Mount. In that conversation he distinctly described the manner of his death; he distinctly foretold that as Moses lifted up the serpent even so must he be lifted up. In that conversation he gave us the fullest statement of the means of salvation which ever came from his lips. Nowhere else in the gospels, and nowhere in the epistles, can you find so clear a description of the work of each person in the blessed Trinity in human redemption. It is true that until a little time before his death Christ did not in public discourse plainly allude to that death, and there were reasons for this omission. But in this conversation with Nicodemus the allusion is explicit. Christ's baptism was also a symbol and prophecy of his death and resurrection. The cross, gloomy and grand, ever lifted itself before his mind; that he should die on that cross was one of the ends for which he came into the world. Now Paul saw this. He always meant to be true to the Christ. My soul has ached for him when I have seen how he sinned through ignorance of the true Messiah. But on that Damascus highway what blessed light flashed upon the Old Testament teachings of the Christ! What a new world of thought and feeling was revealed to him! Now he sees the symmetry, the harmony, the glory, of the truth. He sees how the Sufferer is still the King; he sees that the way to the throne is by the cross; he sees that he who would reign must serve; that to conquer it is necessary to stoop; that lowliness is loftiness. He sees that Christ is the world's Prophet, Priest, and King, because once he died as a sacrifice for the world's sin. The cross was his throne — blessed revelation! Now to Paul, Christ's life is a sublime harmony. So Paul gloried in the cross. He would have no other glory. On earth he caught the first notes of the song which ever since his exaltation he has been singing in heaven, "Worthy is the Lamb which was slain."

This, we remark again, was the only preaching which could harmonize the tributes of God. How shall we reconcile the apparently contradictory attributes of God? He describes himself as exercising loving kindness, and at the same time as inflicting judgment. He is at once a merciful Father and a righteous judge; a just God, and yet a saviour; abounding in mercy, and at the same time hating iniquity. This is the true character of God as made known in Scripture. Men have erred when they have taken one-sided views of God. Some regard him as too merciful to punish sin; others, going to the other extreme, regard him as too just to forgive sin. The result is that while one class presumptuously approach him, the other class sink hopelessly into despair. These are important considerations. In the administration of human justice no question is more perplexing than that of granting pardon. If never granted, government may become tyranny; if granted often, law becomes only advice. A law without a penalty is not law; it is only advice. Mercy and justice cannot always meet in the human judge. The human judge may have to condemn his own son. But in God there is a union of all perfections. Only as he is seen in the face of Jesus Christ can he be rightly known; only in the sacrifice on the cross can the mercy and justice of God be seen in blessed union. In the cross, God shows himself to be eminently a merciful Saviour; there he shows his hatred of sin; there, too, he shows how it may be forgiven. It is the glory of God that he can be just, and at the same time be the Justifier of the believer in Jesus. He can preserve the honor of his law, and yet extend pardon to the penitent. The harmony of these seemingly inconsistent attributes gives glory to the cross of Jesus. It lifts God's plan of redemption above all human conception, makes it a constant marvel to the angels, and gives the redeemed in glory a theme for eternal praise. At the cross the beautiful words of the Psalmist have their sublime illustration:

> " Mercy and truth are met together,
> Righteousness and peace have kissed each other."

Standing beneath the cross, we remember that God spared not his own Son, but freely gave him up for us all; there we see the boundless mercy of God. Still standing beneath the cross, we remember that it pleased the Lord to bruise that beloved Son, and to make the iniquities of us all to meet upon him when he took the sinner's place—there we see the inflexible justice of God. In the cross, these glorious attributes meet. Here is the atonement—the "at onement," as Bishop Hall and other English writers once wrote it. Around the cross these glorious truths meet in eternal harmony. Here let us stand, and with angels and glorified spirits sing, "Oh, the depth of the riches both of the wisdom and knowledge of God!"

Futhermore, Paul knew that this was the only preaching which could save men. This truth had saved him. He had the testimony of personal experience. The lion had been changed into the lamb; the bitter persecutor into the loving disciple. It is impossible to account for that change if the power of this truth and the grace of God be denied. Almighty grace came to his soul; like the walls of Jericho, its ramparts fell before the power of God. The power that could tame him could subdue the hardest heart.

With undaunted heart we stand beside the cross to-day. In this sign we shall conquer the world. An uplifted Christ is still the mightiest magnet to attract the hearts of men. That cross is still the power and the wisdom of God. Some men affirm that the old gospel is losing its power; that "modern thought" demands a modern gospel. They have denied that the gospel is a finality; they have invented other gospels. But what is new in these inventions is not true, and what is true is not new. They have tried spiritualism, and it has proved itself to be a vulgar cheat, a contemptible fraud. They have tried materialism, and it has proved itself to be what Carlyle, in his coarse way, called it, "a gospel of dirt." They have tried various shades of liberalism, but negatives are poor food for hungry souls. They have tried science. To a true science, religion has no objections to urge. What God says in his works must agree with what he says in his Word. Genesis and geology, when each is rightly interpreted, must harmonize. A true science will lay its crown at Jesus' feet. Men have tried atheism. They would dethrone God, and they would degrade men; but God refuses to be pushed out of the world which he has made. One scarcely knows whether most to pity or to despise these false teachers. They certainly excite our pity; they almost justify our contempt. They are blind in the gleaming light of the nineteenth century. Once Thomas Paine boasted in the Broadway Hotel, in New York, that in five years there would not be a Bible in America. How we smile at his folly! The day will come when the defiant predictions of another blatant and blasphemous infidel will excite corresponding pity and contempt. The pulpit losing its power! The Bible becoming obsolete! The pulpit never was so mighty a power as it is at this hour. The Bible was never so triumphant as it is to-day. I tell you that as a Christian man I walk with my head among the stars. The highest point of human greatness men ever reach is when they bow at the feet of Jesus Christ and take him for their Lord and God. Away with the devil's nostrums! I respectfully decline to be orphaned in my Father's world. We want the old, old gospel,—old as eternity, and new as the last sunbeam which has kissed your cheek. Nothing but the bread of heaven can feed the hungry soul. Nothing but the balm of Gilead can heal the heart's sorrow. Blessed be God! His gospel will never lose its power until Satan is crushed beneath our feet, and Christ is worshipped as Lord of all.

What Paul preached we should believe — unconverted men and women, you should believe it. It is your only hope. Before you I uplift the Crucified One. Here behold the grandest display alike of God's justice and love. Look and live. "Behold the Lamb of God, which taketh away the sin of the world." Ministers of Christ, you should believe it. You will be shorn of your power if you do not. Uplift that cross. Display that blood-stained banner. Teach the old doctrines. Do not apologize for God; declare him. The best evidence of Christianity is Christianity. The cross is its own witness. The Christian minister who uses his position to betray his Lord had better have his arm paralyzed at his side; had better have his tongue cleave to the roof of his mouth. In proportion as the spirit of the cross controls every thought and feeling of our lives, glistens in the eye, trembles in the voice, and is felt in the affectionate grasp of the hand, shall we be successful. Here in the presence of God and his people, let us determine to be loyal to Christ's gospel until our work is done and our reward is won. Christ and him crucified, our theme in life, our watchword in death, our song in heaven.

What we believe we should propagate. Any truth that is worth holding is worth propagating by the printed page and the living voice. No argument is needed to convince you of the power of the press. The old Homeric heroes are represented as standing on the hill-tops of Greece and sending out their voices into its clear air to brother heroes seven miles away. The press is the hero of the nineteenth century, who stands by the mighty Atlantic and sends his voice across a continent to the mightier Pacific; sends it around the world. The devil shall not have the best of everything. The discoveries of our day are for Jesus. When good Dr. Warren saw a ship leaving the dock at New York, with a group of missionaries on her deck, he said, "That is what ships are made for." He was right. Steamships and railroads, the press, the telegraph, the telephone, are all for Jesus. "Thine, O Lord, is the greatness, and the power, and the glory, and the victory, and the majesty; for all that is in the heaven and the earth is thine. Thine is the kingdom, O Lord, and thou art exalted as head above all." Let the Assyrian boast of the number that he cut off. What was the Assyrian? This: "The rod of God's anger, and the staff of his indignation." Let Cyrus boast of the mighty work that he accomplished. How did he do it? Thus: "I girded thee," God says, "though thou didst not know me." "The Lord reigneth; let the earth rejoice; let the multitude of isles be glad thereof." Jesus is King. He is laying his hand on the discoveries of the hour; the inventive genius even of his enemies shall contribute to his glory. Man, horse, and steamships shall carry his truth; telegraphs shall girdle the world with his glory, and telephones shall make the world "a whispering-gallery" with his praise. When the pierced hand of Jesus Christ shall be laid on the press of the world the first rays of the sun of millennial day shall color the sky with its crimson and gold. We need the living voice of the living preacher; nothing can surpass that instrumentality. We need also the printed page sent out as leaves for the healing of the nations.

We must feel a personal responsibility for the preaching of the gospel. You cannot do effective work for Christ at long ranges. A Roman youth complained to his father that his sword was too short. "Add a step to it," said the father. The Bible is the "sword of the spirit." To use it well, you must come into close quarters. "The Autocrat of the Breakfast Table" says, "We are the Romans of the modern world—the great assimilation people. And so we come to their style of weapon. Our army sword is the short, stiff, pointed *gladius* of the Romans." And he adds, "The race that shortens its weapons lengthens its boundaries. It was the Polish lance that left Poland at last with nothing of her own to bound." He then asks, "What business had Sarmatia to be fighting for liberty with a fifteen-foot pool between her and the breasts of her enemies?" It will not do for us to fight our Lord's enemies in this fashion. We must come to close quarters. This Christ did. The warm heart of the living prophet touched the cold heart of the dead boy. You rejoice in the glorious gospel of the crucified Christ which Paul preached; let others share your joy. I appeal to you as men and as Christians, as you love Christ and glory in his cross give money to send the men who shall carry the good news to the perishing, so that the dumb may sing with joy, and the desert may blossom as the rose. May the theme of "the matchless Paul" at Corinth—Christ, and him crucified—be our glory in life, our hope in death, and our song in heaven! God grant it, for his name's sake. Amen.

A most beautiful passage closed the sermon. Dr. MacArthur told about the sweet Hawaiian salutation, "Aloha!" which means "Love!" "You may as well learn it, because, you know, you will soon need it. 'Aloha!' it is the salutation of this Convention. 'Aloha!' it is the salutation the North gives the South to-night, and the South sends it thunderingly and deafeningly back to the North. 'Aloha!' it is the salutation that the Sandwich Islands send to America. 'Aloha!' it is the salutation that the imperial American people send across the Atlantic to their glorious British mother. 'Aloha!' it is the salutation that Britain sends over her vast empire, and the Himalayas send it thundering down through India to Adam's Peak in Ceylon, and that 'Aloha' shall break down all the castes in India,—not the 'Aloha' of man, but the 'Aloha' of God; for God so loved the world that he gave his Son."

From this thrilling sermon it was easy to respond to the solemn touch of Mr. Tomkins's words, as, with tender, heart-searching pleading he led all hearts close to the throne.

Remarks by Rev. Floyd W. Tomkins, Jr.,
Providence, R. I.

As we come to these sacred closing moments, are there not emotions within us which are not easily expressed? We feel, but we cannot speak. Such, I think, will be the first great experiences in the other world when we first see God. "There will be silence in heaven."

But this emotion of ours to-night must be lasting. I wish to sum it up in three words: God, ourselves, life.

1. God. Oh, how dear it is to know him, and to know that he loves us! He is our father, our saviour, our guide; near us, within us, never leaving us or forgetting us, finding joy for himself when we return his love. *Never forget God.*

2. Ourselves. Not much to be proud of, and yet having such privileges! For we are sons of God. God has breathed his breath into us. Even our bodies are temples of the Holy Ghost. We are the last and best of God's creatures, destined for a glorious eternity. Poor are we, yet our poverty is hidden in the riches of Christ. Unknown, perhaps, yet *well-known* of God. Sinful, yet redeemed and washed. "But ye are redeemed, but ye are sanctified, but ye are glorified." Hence the struggle to become more and more like Jesus.

3. Life. We are placed here to do something for our God. Like Christ, or rather *with* Christ, we are to redeem the world. We live to bring salvation. It may be a cup of cold water to a thirsty one; it may be a word of kindness; it may be a leading, a pointing to God of some doubting one. It may be some great work of public reformation. But whatever we do must be for good. May God give us grace, as we go from this week spent in God's near presence, to know him better, to give ourselves more absolutely to him, to serve him better than we ever have before.

In opening the last and crowning portion of the session, the great brotherhood roll-call, Dr. Clark urged us all to make our consecrations definite and individual, though we spoke in a crowd. "God is here!" we were bidden to say softly to ourselves. "God is here! and God sees us!"

Illinois, the banner delegation, outside of Tennessee, was the first to respond to the roll-call,— a great, compact, eager body.

President Gardner voiced the purpose of the delegates from Massachusetts: "We seek for culture that we may have character, and would model our character after Jesus Christ, and follow Christ to the conquest of the world."

Connecticut's delegation was notable for the number of its young men. Mr. Estey led Pennsylvania's fine body of youth in their consecration song of "Loyalty to Christ." New York was crucified with Christ, Christ living in her.

Ohio's testimony was striking: "Loved, therefore loving; sought, therefore seeking; saved, therefore serving."

Mr. Baer here led us all in a most tender and earnest prayer for the dear ones that could not be with us, and especially for the associate members.

Indiana's magnificent representation showed the result of the hard work done in that State in behalf of the Convention. "Our homes for Christ" was the motto; "our State for Christ; our country for Christ; the world for Christ." A cornet led them in their jubilant State hymn.

California's delegation spoke from a distant gallery, and was followed by the tall folks from Texas, led by President Grotthouse, with their noble "Lone Star" hymn, "Texas for Christ."

The earnest-faced Endeavorers from the Dominion looked forward to the time when His dominion should be from sea to sea, and from the river to the ends of the earth.

Florida's testimony was a noble one: "There is yet much land to be possessed. We can do all things through Christ who strengtheneth us. We will go up and possess the land."

It was at this point that the lights went out, and did not return till near the close of the wonderful meeting. The peaceful audience once more broke out with "There's Sunshine in My Soul," lamps were brought, and we went serenely on, the following responses sounding weirdly out from the darkness of the great hall.

Kentucky's lovely version of "My Old Kentucky Home," and Maryland's of "Maryland, my Maryland," were enjoyed, as they always are. Indian Territory was not represented. Utah and Wyoming were heard from. Many States gave beautiful Scripture quotations. Some of the State delegations had been obliged to leave earlier in the evening, but left their messages for us.

Our three delegates from the extremes of India spoke for her fifteen thousand Endeavorers. . Mr. Wallis spoke for the prison Endeavorers, and Mr. Ellis gave the message left by our soldier Endeavorers before they returned to camp. Then Dr. Chapman prayed touchingly for these our brothers on sea, in camp, and behind the bars.

England, Japan, the lovely consecration hymn of the Jubilee Singers, Tennessee's grand chorus, "Where He leads me, I will follow," with Mr. Landrith's warm words of appreciation for the members of Epworth Leagues, Baptist Young People's Unions, and Luther Leagues that have worked so heartily for the Convention,— why, how crowded with blessed incidents was that hour!

And then at length came the moment when we stood together with uplifted hands, first the Endeavorers, then all members of young people's societies, then all in the room that loved the Lord and were willing to stand with us,— and solemnly and joyously we repeated after Dr. Clark our consecration vow: —

> "Lord, here's a hand!
> Oh, take this hand and lead me at thy side,
> For I would never ask another guide.
> I lift it, Lord, withdrawn from other hands,
> For thee to grasp and lead in thy commands.
> Lord, take this hand!"

Bishop Whipple says that man cannot reach a hand up to God without reaching a hand down to other men. That was the thought with which we lowered the hands we so sincerely raised. That was the thought with which we joined in Dr. Clark's closing prayer, in Mizpah, in " God be with you till we meet again," and went forth into the world to spread everywhere, God willing, the joy and inspiration of

NASHVILLE, '98.

The Daily Chalk-Talks in Hall Williston,
By Rev. Robert F. Y. Pierce, Scranton, Penn.

CHALK THAT MADE ITS MARK.

"I'm getting sermons out of this that I'll preach all winter," said one listener to Mr. Pierce's chalk-talks. And they were sermons that could n't be forgotten. "We are living in a visual age," declared Mr. Pierce; and he showed us how to utilize the modern passion for pictures.

For instance, he printed swiftly on his sheet of paper:

Jesus
Owns
You

Read the initials. Understand that fact, and you have the secret of the Christian's joy. "It is not necessary," said he, "to have a pretty picture in order to teach a truth."

John 3:16 he summarized thus:—

God's
Only
Son
Purchased
Eternal
Life.

It is the entire *gospel*, you see, in a nutshell.

Christ came to bring   Life,
to fill men with   hOpe,
he came to   saVe,
and to lead us to heaven, our   homE.

In those five words you have his life summed up. What is the fifth word? It runs through all the rest: *love*.

Mr. Pierce then went on to show how simple a picture could set forth a great truth. There appeared a cross with a horizontal line leading to it from a perpendicular. It is easy to draw a child to Jesus. Lines were made to extend from the cross to points on the perpendicular successively lower and lower as the child went on down the years, and each line was steeper, indicating how much harder it is to convert a man as he grows older.

On another day the superintendent was shown how last quarter's lessons might have been reviewed by drawing a book, a heart, a road connecting them, and twelve telegraph-poles along the road, to stand for the twelve Sundays through which the truth is conveyed to the heart. A letter on each pole helps to spell the theme: "Jesus Saves."

Mr. Pierce told of a lady who goes to the seashore for the summer, gathers up the clam-shells that the waves wash up, and paints delicate little landscapes in them, selling them as souvenirs to the summer visitors. So the teacher may take a few simple, crude pictures, and through them send home priceless truths. These daily chalk-talks were remarkably well attended, and proved one of the most popular and enjoyable features of the Convention.

The Early Morning Prayer Meetings.

Ready at the morning call for prayer, the cool early hours saw hundreds of Christian soldiers fall into line at the seven sunrise prayer-meetings.

The working men of Nashville, with their dinner-buckets on their arms, found the first street-cars filling with bright-faced Endeavorers going with glad faces to the place of privilege.

On the first morning the usual number went astray, who, bewildered by the squares and circles on the map, had to ask questions and light their candle of common sense and hunt diligently until they found.

The leaders were from the ranks of successful State and local workers, and the practical themes drew out the best that was in the participants.

While the red-nosed early toper was knocking with nerveless hand at the side door of the saloon for his fiery stimulant, these clear-eyed, clear-headed, earnest, joyful disciples were drinking from a fount of inspiration that flows with blessing for the world.

Who can tell how much of the lofty spiritual tone of the splendid larger meetings, and, indeed, of the grand things which Christian Endeavor must achieve during the coming year, is due to these Bethels of prayer!

The Street Panorama.

There were no boarding-houses in Nashville; they were "Christian Endeavor Homes," with as big a "Welcome" within as that displayed in bunting without.

The Chamber of Commerce had erected a brilliant incandescent display over one of the main streets of the city, the flashing lights of which spelled out the word "Welcome."

Even the flowers were given voice, and the beautiful medallions and monograms in bloom and foliage on the Capitol and private grounds spoke an eloquent welcome.

The old, colored "mammy" with her red bandana about her brow and a basket or bundle on her head was a frequent and picturesque street figure.

No one could pass the Tulane Hotel without being attracted by the showy windows of the headquarters of the '98 Committee. The committee also had a room in the Parthenon.

Nashville's fine store windows were most tastefully decorated in honor of the Convention.

Lunch in the "gourd arbor" in the Centennial Park was a novel Convention experience.

The remaining exhibits of the Tennessee Centennial attracted many visitors and gave some idea of how excellent an exhibition it must have been when n its prime.

Even though none needed the kindly ministry of the fully equipped emergency hospital in Centennial Park, what a piece of thoughtful enterprise it was!

New Board of Trustees of the United Society of Christian Endeavor.

FOUR YEARS.

Rev. Wayland Hoyt, D.D., Philadelphia, Penn.
Rev. Francis E. Clark, D.D., Boston, Mass.
Rev. J. Z. Tyler, D.D., Cleveland, O.
Rev. David James Burrell, D.D., New York City.
Rev. John Henry Barrows, D.D., Chicago, Ill.
Mr. William Shaw, Boston, Mass.
Rev. Howard B. Grose, Boston, Mass.
Rev. John T. Beckley, D.D., New York City.
Rev. N. Boynton, D.D., Detroit, Mich.
Rev. James L. Hill, D.D., Salem, Mass.
Rev. F. D. Power, D.D., Washington, D. C.
Rev. George B. Stewart, D.D., Harrisburg, Penn.
Rev. Wm. Patterson, Toronto, Ont.
Rev. Teunis S. Hamlin, D.D., Washington, D. C.
Rev. M. Rhodes, D.D., St. Louis, Mo.

THREE YEARS.

Bishop B. W. Arnett, D.D., Wilberforce, O.
Rev. Ralph W. Brokaw, Utica, N. Y.
Rev. W. J. Darby, D.D., Evansville, Ind.
Bishop Samuel Fallows, D.D., LL.D., Chicago, Ill.
Rev. Rufus W. Miller, Reading, Penn.
Mr. W. J. Van Patten, Burlington, Vt.
Rev. W. H. McMillan, D.D., Allegheny City, Penn.
Rev. P. S. Henson, D.D., Chicago, Ill.
Bishop Alexander Walters, D.D., Jersey City, N. J.
Rev. J. H. Garrison, D.D., St. Louis, Mo.
Prof. James Lewis Howe, Lexington, Va.
Rev. H. F. Shupe, Dayton, O.
Rev. J. M. Lowden, Olneyville, R. I.
Rev. M. M. Binford, Brooklyn, N. Y.
Rev. Canon J. B. Richardson, London, Ont.

TWO YEARS.

Rev. Gilby C. Kelly, D.D., Birmingham, Ala.
Rev. H. K. Carroll, D.D., New York, N. Y.
Rev. J. Clement French, D.D., Newark, N. J.
Rev. Floyd W. Tomkins, Jr., Providence, R. I.
Rev. W. H. Vogler, Indianapolis, Ind.
Rev. Wilton Merle Smith, D.D., New York City.
Rev. U. F. Swengel, York, Penn.
Mr. W. H. Pennell, Washington, D. C.
Mr. George A. Chace, Fall River, Mass.
Rev. Allan B. Philputt, D.D., Indianapolis, Ind.
Rev. Chas. A. Dickinson, D.D., Boston, Mass.
Rev. Maltbie D. Babcock, D.D., Baltimore, Md.

ONE YEAR.

Rev. C. I. Brown, Mount Joy, Penn.
Prof. H. L. Willett, Chicago, Ill.
Rev. Samuel McNaugher, Boston, Mass.
Rev. A. C. Crews, Toronto, Ont.
Rev. Hugh K. Walker, D.D., Los Angeles, Cal.
Rev. J. Wilbur Chapman, D.D., Philadelphia, Penn.
Rev. George E. McManiman, Steubenville, O.

Presidents of State, Territorial, and Provincial Christian Endeavor Unions.

One Year.

ALABAMA. — Rev. J. R. Crawford, Huntsville.
ARKANSAS. — Mr. W. W. McLaughlin, Little Rock.
CALIFORNIA. — Mr. George P. Lowell, San Francisco.
COLORADO. — Mr. W. E. Sweet, Denver.
CONNECTICUT. — Rev. Asher Anderson, D.D., Meriden.
DELAWARE. — Rev. W. L. S. Murray, Ph.D., Wilmington.
DISTRICT OF COLUMBIA. — Mr. Grant Leet, Washington.
FLORIDA. — Mr. C. Arthur Lincoln, Auburndale.
GEORGIA. — Mr. William H. George, Atlanta.
IDAHO. — Rev. E. N. Murphy, Boise.
ILLINOIS. — Dr. S. A. Wilson, Chicago.
INDIANA. — Rev. Jacob W. Kapp, D.D., Richmond.
IOWA. — Rev. C. W. Sweet, Des Moines.
KANSAS. — Rev. M. E. Harlan, Topeka.
KENTUCKY. — Judge John D. Ellis, Newport.
LOUISIANA. — Mr. F. F. Morse, Jennings.
MAINE. — Rev. E. R. Purdy, Portland.
MARYLAND. — Mr. W. A. Schumacher, Baltimore.
MASSACHUSETTS. — Rev. Frederick M. Gardner, East Boston.
MICHIGAN. — Rev. W. K. Spencer, D.D., Adrian.
MINNESOTA. — Mr. Charles N. Hunt, Minneapolis.
MISSISSIPPI. — Mr. John A. Stinson, Columbus.
MISSOURI. — Rev. E. W. Clippinger, Warrensburg.
MONTANA. — Mr. E. H. Talcott, Livingston.
NEBRASKA. — Mr. F. F. Tucker, Lincoln.
NEW HAMPSHIRE. — Rev. W. H. Getchell, Lakeport.
NEW JERSEY. — Rev. Cornelius Brett, D.D., Jersey City.
NEW MEXICO. — Mr. J. E. Wood, Santa Fe.
NEW YORK. — Rev. John H. Elliott, Rochester.
NORTH CAROLINA. — Rev. A. D. Thaeler, Winston.
NORTH DAKOTA. — Mr. C. H. Phillips, Jamestown.
OHIO. — Rev. J. H. Bomberger, Tiffin.
OKLAHOMA. — Rev. Joel Harper, Oklahoma City.
OREGON. — Mr. C. G. Le Masters, Dallas.
PENNSYLVANIA. — Rev. J. T. McCrory, D.D., Pittsburg.
RHODE ISLAND. — Mr. Edward P. Metcalf, Providence.
SOUTH CAROLINA. — Mr. F. F. Whilden, Charleston.
SOUTH DAKOTA. — Mr. W. H. Mullins, Hetland.
TENNESSEE. — Mr. W. L. Noell, Huntingdon.
TEXAS. — Mr. H. H. Grotthouse, Dallas.
UTAH. — Mr. Harry N. Tolles, Salt Lake City.
VERMONT. — Col. E. G. Osgood, Bellows Falls.
VIRGINIA. — Mr. William R. Kennedy, Lexington.
WASHINGTON. — Mr. H. J. Fries, Tacoma.
WEST VIRGINIA. — Mr. H. G. Boughner, Clarksburg.
WISCONSIN. — Mr. Alton G. Leffingwell, Appleton.
WYOMING. — Mr. Robert Lawson, Cheyenne.
BRITISH COLUMBIA. — Mr. J. S. Gordon, Vancouver.
MANITOBA. — Mr. W. H. Thomson, Winnipeg.
NEW BRUNSWICK. — Rev. George M. Young, Chatham.
NORTHWEST TERRITORIES. — Mr. A. H. Smith, Moosomin.
NOVA SCOTIA. — Rev. A. L. Geggie, Truro.
ONTARIO. — Rev. William Johnson, South Zorra.
PRINCE EDWARD ISLAND. — Rev. W. J. Kirby, Charlottetown.
QUEBEC. — Mr. W. L. Shurtleff, Coaticook.
CANADIAN COUNCIL. — Mr. G. Tower Fergusson, Toronto.

NUMBER OF SOCIETIES REPORTED JULY 1, 1898.

UNITED STATES.

	Young People's.	Junior.	Intermediate.	Mothers.'	Senior.	Parent.	Total.
Alabama	142	45	4				191
Alaska Territory	7						7
Arizona	19	3					22
Arkansas	128	36	5				161
California	716	552	92		3		1,363
Colorado	202	120	7	1			330
Connecticut	535	217	13		2		767
Delaware	75	33	3				111
District of Columbia	84	60	8				152
Florida	146	54	1				201
Georgia	179	33	3				215
Idaho	54	21	1				76
Illinois	2,072	1,046	56	33	1		3,208
Indiana	1,414	590	39				2,043
Indian Territory	44	17	1				62
Iowa	1,358	552	29	1	1		1,941
Kansas	998	397	15	11	1		1,422
Kentucky	355	109	7	1			472
Louisiana	61	12					73
Maine	655	203	11				869
Maryland	389	138	5	1	1		534
Massachusetts	948	525	36	1		1	1,511
Michigan	1,072	489	36				1,597
Minnesota	556	285	22		1		864
Mississippi	67	22			1		90
Missouri	904	482	17		1		1,404
Montana	53	29	1				83
Nebraska	592	245	18	2	1		858
Nevada	11	6					17
New Hampshire	320	122	4		3		449
New Jersey	828	447	18	3			1,296
New Mexico Territory	26	7	1				34
New York	3,117	1,391	49		2		4,559
North Carolina	258	66	6				330
North Dakota	119	41	1				161
Ohio	2,450	992	63	4	1		3,510
Oklahoma Territory	175	27					202
Oregon	300	137	8		1		446
Pennsylvania	3,679	1,535	86	9	4		5,313
Rhode Island	149	76	7		1		233
South Carolina	84	11	1				96
South Dakota	213	78	4	1			296
Tennessee	366	160	9				535
Texas	465	239	24				728
Utah	40	27	2				69
Vermont	352	140	4	1	1		498
Virginia	242	41	3				286
Washington	274	101	7				382
West Virginia	237	54	2				293
Wisconsin	548	263	14	1			826
Wyoming	21	6	1				28
	28,099	12,282	744	70	26	1	41,222

CANADA.

	Young People's.	Junior.	Intermediate.	Mothers.'	Parent.	Total.
Alberta	12	2				14
Assiniboia	48	8				56
British Columbia	48	7				55
Manitoba	120	24				144
New Brunswick	216	33				249
Newfoundland	6					6
Nova Scotia	409	66	1			476
Ontario	1,795	301	8	1		2,105
Prince Edward Island	68	4				72
Quebec	200	71	1		2	274
Saskatchewan	5					5
	2,927	516	10	1	2	3,456

FOREIGN.

	Young People's.	Junior.	Intermediate.	Mothers.'	Senior.	Total.
Africa	89	9			12	110
Australia	2,056	224			4	2,284
Austria	2					2
Belgium	1					1
Bermuda	7					7
Brazil	2	1				3
British Guiana	10					10
Burmah	15					15
Chili	6					6
Colombia	1					1
China	123	16				139
Denmark	2					2
Egypt	3	1				4
England	4,037	597	5	6	2	4,647
France	68					68
Germany	69					69
Guatemala	1					1
Hawaiian Islands	9	5				14
Holland	1					1
Hungary	2					2
India	382	50			1	433
Ireland	195	18				213
Italy	3					3
Japan	63	4				67
Labrador	1					1
Laos	10					10
Madagascar	93					93
Marshall Islands	6					6
Mexico	72	28				100
Norway	4					4
Persia	3	1				4
Samoa	10					10
Scotland	481	54				535
Siam	1					1
South Sea Islands	2					2
Spain	8	5				13
Sweden	34					34
Switzerland	8					8
Syria	3	1				4
Turkey	35	16				51
Upper Hebrides	1					1
Wales	327	4				331
West Indies	73	11				84
	8,284	1,045	5	6	19	9,359

RECAPITULATION.

	Young People's.	Junior.	Intermediate.	Mothers.'	Senior.	Parent	Total.
United States	28,099	12,282	744	70	26	1	41,222
Canada	2,927	516	10	1		2	3 456
Foreign	8,319	1,045	5	6	19		9,394
Floating Societies							119
	39,310	13,843	759	77	45	3	54,191

COMPLETE INDEX OF THE REPORT.

Topics of Services. — Themes of Addresses, Sermons, Etc. — Conferences, Rallies, Studies, and Special Meetings. — Illustrative Anecdotes. — Greetings, Resolutions, Presentations, Etc. — Some Convention Incidents. — Reports and Statistics. — Personnel.

TOPICS OF SERVICES.

Better Work	123
Christian Endeavor Reaching Out	107
Christian Endeavor Unions	116
Closing Hours	229
Enduement with Power	5-48
For the Church	100
Missionary Methods, Common Sense	192-215
Our United Country	159
Sabbath Observance	176

THEMES OF ADDRESSES, SERMONS, ETC., WITH SUB-TOPICS.

Advisory Board of Pastors	115
American Sabbath: Sacred or Secular	177
Anglo-Saxon Alliance	67, 92
Best Things Accomplished During Past Year	61
Better Committee Work	124
Better Prayer-Meetings	126
Better Socials	123
Blessed Life, The	77
Brotherhood of Nations	135
Charge to the Republic	81
Christian Citizenship	66, 74, 76
Christ and Him Crucified	220
Christian Endeavor Reaching Out : —	
To Sailors and Soldiers	107
To Railroad Men and Street-Car Men	108
To Commercial Travellers	109
To Prisoners	114
Christian Heroism	140
Christian Union	134
Christian Endeavor Unions : —	
Advisory Board of Pastors	115
Practical Topics	116
Limitations	117
Possibilities	118
Christian Endeavor Bugbear	120
Church, More Fruit for the	65
Commercial Travellers	109
Committee Work, Better	124
Common Sense Missionary Methods	193
Conquest of the World	210
Consecration Appeal	229
Daily Quiet Hour	152
Detroit's Welcome	168
Detroit Announced as Next Year's Meeting-Place	58
Drink Problem	132
Enduement of Power	41
Forward Movement in Missions	142
Graduate Department	64
Graduate Endeavor	101
God's Hand in the Nation's Conflict	85
Heart of the Whole Matter	31
Holy Spirit, The Work of	5-48
Honoring God's Day	176
Intellectual Conditions for the Enduement of the Spirit	43
Junior Chain	155
Junior Light-Bearers	185
Junior Question-Box	185
Local Union Limitations	117
Mid-Week Prayer-Meeting, The	103
Missions	192-215
Missions, Advanced Movement in	68
Missions, Contributions to	60
Missionary Libraries	196
Missionary Problem	133
Meeting for Men Only	175
Mine for Junior Workers	185
More Earnest Study	195
More Fruit	62
More Generous Giving	193
More Spirited Meetings	197
Mutual Dependence of the Races	69
Nation, More Fruit for the	66
New Baptism of Patriotism	160
New Republic and Its Duties	170
Only Way to the Throne of Power	35
Our Country for Christ	206
Our Enemy — the Saloon	72
Our Trust — the Boys and Girls	154
Our United Country	163
Partnership with God	198
Pastors' Cabinet, The	100
Patriotism	160
Place and Fruit of the Spirit	45
Pledge, Proved	147
Poem, The Convention	81
Possibilities of Local Unions	118

Practical Topics for Union Meetings . . 116
Prayer-Meetings, Better 126
Present-Day Problems 131
Prison, Christian Endeavor in . . . 49
Prisoners, Messages from 114
Promise of the Father 13
Prove Your Pledge 147
Question-Box 105
Quiet Hour 60, 174
Quiet Hour, Daily 152
Race Problem 131
Railroad and Street-Car Men . . . 108
Reaching the Masses 134
Relation of the Holy Spirit to Character 9
Roll-Call 229
Royalty of Service 217
Sabbath, the American 177
Sabbath and Christian Evangelism . . 176
Sabbath of God's Power, A 174
Sabbath in the Twentieth Century . . 182
Sailors and Soldiers 107
Saloon, Our Enemy, The 72
Socials, Better 123
Social Problem 131
Some Hindrances to Spiritual Enduement 14
Source of Power 19
Spiritual Life — Its Manifestations and Development 42
Spiritual Power — Its Source and Effects . 28
Strength and Power 22
Sunday-Evening Service, The . . . 104
Surrender of the Will as the Condition of Receiving the Holy Spirit 5
Temperance Address 72
Temperance Problem 132
Tenth Legion 200
Ten Questions Answered 105
Tithe-Giving 200
Woman's Meeting, The 183
Woman's Work for Children . . . 183
World, More Fruit for the 67
Why Should We Desire Enduement with Power? 20

CONFERENCES, RALLIES, STUDIES, AND SPECIAL MEETINGS.

Bible Study Conference 68
Chalk-Talks, Daily 231
Committee Conferences: —
    Good-Literature Committee . . 186
    Lookout Committee 187
    Sunday-School Committee . . 189
    Lord's Day Committee . . . 190
    Floating Societies Workers . . 191
    Missionary Committee . . . 192
Christian Citizenship Conference . . 129
Denominational Rallies 95
    African M. E. 96
    Baptist 97
    Christian 98
    Congregational 95
    Cumberland Presbyterian . . . 95
    Disciples of Christ 95
    Free Baptist 97
    Lutheran 96
    Methodist Episcopal 95
    Methodist Protestant 96
    Moravian 98
    Northern Presbyterian and Canadian Presbyterian 98
    Protestant Episcopal 100
    Reformed Church 98
    Southern Presbyterian . . . 95
    United Brethren 98
    United Evangelical 96
    United Presbyterian 95
Early Morning Prayer-Meetings . . 232
Evangelistic Meeting 175
Junior Rally 154
Junior Workers' Conference . . . 185
Meeting for Men Only 175
Officers' Conferences: —
    City Union Officers 186
    State Officers 192
    Corresponding Secretaries . . 188
Pastors in Conference 128
Sunday Services 174
Women's Meeting, The 183

ILLUSTRATIVE ANECDOTES.

Illustrative Anecdotes . 11, 18, 25, 28, 32, 34, 36, 37, 38, 40, 47, 55, 56, 72, 74, 75, 77, 78, 79, 80, 89, 91, 108, 109, 118, 120, 125, 126, 127, 133, 135, 140, 145, 148, 149, 150, 154, 169, 193, 194, 195, 196, 197, 198, 199, 200, 202, 203, 206, 207, 209, 214, 217, 218, 219, 220, 224, 228.

GREETINGS, RESOLUTIONS, PRESENTATIONS, ETC.

Addresses of Welcome: —
    From Committee of '98 . . . 51
    From City Pastors 53
    From Governor 55
Greetings from All Around the World 192, 193
Greetings from the Y. P. S. C. E. of
    Eddyville Prison 114
    Kentucky Penitentiary 115
Presentation of Banners: —
    Christian Citizenship . . . 71
    Increase in Societies 130
    Increase in Junior Societies 130
    Proportionate Increase in Societies . 130
    Proportionate Increase in Junior Societies 130
Presentation of Gavels . . . 49, 215
President McKinley's Message to the Convention 50
Responses to Addresses of Welcome: —
    From the East 57
    From the North 58
    From the South 58

Index. 241

Resolutions of Thanks and Appreciation from the Board of Trustees of the United Society of Christian Endeavor . 216
Resolutions Adopted by the Southern Presbyterians 95
Resolutions Passed at the Rally of the Northern and Canadian Presbyterians 98

SOME CONVENTION INCIDENTS.

"Convention of Brotherly Love" . . 159
"Heroes of the *Maine*" 159
"Lights Out" 69
"Lights Out Again" 230
"Old Glory" 163
Presentation of Gavel Made by a Kentucky Prison Endeavorer 49
Presentation of Gavel Made by Frankfort Prison Endeavorers 215
Street Panorama 232
"The Blue and the Gray, the Black and the White" 173
War of the Elements 130

REPORTS AND STATISTICS.

Annual Address of President Clark . . . 62
Annual Report of Secretary Baer . 59
By-Laws of the United Society, Changes in 60, 61
Presidents of State, Territorial, and Provincial Christian Endeavor Unions . . 234
Societies in Foreign Lands 236
Statistics of All Kinds 59
Statistics of the Y. P. S. C. E. in the World . 235
Trustees, List of New 233, 234

PERSONNEL.

Alexander, Mr. B. G. 52
Allen, Rev. Ernest Bourner . . 197
Allan, Mrs. 187
Arnett, Bishop Benjamin W. 22, 96, 154, 173
Arrick, Rev. A. J. 101
Atkinson, Mr. C. J. 185
Atkinson, Rev. D. B. 98
Baer, Mr. John Willis 59, 99, 158, 168, 175, 185, 187, 192, 229.
Barrows, Rev. John Henry . 99, 135, 159, 210
Beckley, Rev. John T. . . . 97, 100
Binkley, Rev. G. W. 97
Blanton, Mr. J. D. 52
Bomberger, Rev. J. H. . . 98, 100
Bond, Rev. James 129
Bookman, Mr. Bertram . . 96
Boone, Rev. A. U. 97
Booth-Tucker, Com. F. DeL. 140
Brett, Rev. Cornelius . 124, 192
Brockett, Miss Zue H. . . . 186
Brokaw, Rev. Ralph W. . . 19, 215
Brooks, Rev. Jesse W. . . . 98
Brown, Rev. C. A. . . . 98

Brown, Mr. H. L. 187
Burns, Rev. George J. 108
Burrell, Rev. David James . . 72
Caldwell, Private 108
Cameron, Miss 187
Casselman, Rev. Arthur Vale 193
Catlin, Miss 192
Chamberlin, Rev. W. I. 5, 130
Chapman, Rev. J. Wilbur . 100, 152, 175, 230
Cheek, Mr. Joel O. 52
Clark, Rev. Francis E. . . 49, 62, 69, 115, 128, 129, 158, 159, 163, 173, 174, 186, 187, 215, 229, 230.
Clark, Mrs. F. E. 159, 183, 185
Clinton, Bishop B. W. 68
Clippinger, Rev. E. W. 123
Coleman, Mrs. Geo. W. 159
Coleman, Miss 159
Conning, Rev. J. S. 187
Cowan, Rev. J. F. 68, 96
Cox, Rev. J. E. 97
Crafts, Rev. Wilbur F. . . 99, 182, 190
Curtis, Rev. J. E. 98
Curry, Rev. Dr. 173
Danley, Rev. W. S. 193
Darby, Rev. W. J. 193
Defur, Rev. Clarence 98
Dixon, Rev. A. C. 77
Dorris, Mrs. M. C. 52
Doyle, Rev. Sherman H. . . 126
Du Bose, Rev. H. M. . . . 140
Edinburn, Rev. J. S. . . . 99
Eggett, Master Charles E. . . . 185
Eller, Rev. J. G. 96
Elliott, Rev. John H. . . . 31
Ellis, Mr. Wm. T. . 99, 115, 185, 187, 230
Estey, Mr. C. L. . . 49, 98, 152, 168, 175
Evans, Gen. Clement A. 163
Excell, Mr. E. O. . 49, 77, 95, 115, 129, 130, 163, 175, 176, 215.
Fallows, Rt. Rev. Samuel 43
Fergusson, Mr. G. Tower . . 58
Fisk Jubilee Singers . 49, 57, 94, 119, 139, 183, 215, 230.
Fitzgerald, Bishop . . . 169, 173
Foster, Mr. P. S. . 49, 69, 97, 100, 139, 154, 159, 169, 175, 215.
Funkhouser, Rev. A. P. . . . 98
Gardner, Rev. Frederick M. . . 97, 192
Garrison, Rev. J. H. . . . 14
Gilbert, Mr. E. C. . . 110, 174, 187
Grotthouse, Mr. H. H. . 58, 192, 230
Hamlin, Rev. Teunis S. . . 5
Hathaway, Rev. I. W. . . . 177
Hill, Rev. Jas. L. . 95, 107, 185, 191
Hill, Mrs. James L. . 159, 183, 185
Howard, Gen. O. O. 160
Huffer, Rev. V. E. 97
Johnson, Rev. T. M. . . 96, 195
Johnston, Rev. Howard Agnew 35, 98, 129

Jones, Miss Antoinette P.	191	Power, Rev. F. D.	131
Jones, Mr. Edgar	52	Puddefoot, Rev. W. G.	206
Jones, Mr. Thomas	72, 189	Reed, Mr. Erskine	52
Kapp, Rev. Jacob W.	118	Regennas, Mr. Eugene G.	98
Kellogg, Miss Elsie D.	191	Reynolds, Mr. T. A.	52
Kinports, Mr. H. A.	187	Rhodes, Rev. M.	9
Landrith, Rev. Ira	51, 52, 186, 215, 230	Richardson, Canon J. B.	96, 100
Lathrop, Mr. H. N.	97	Robertson, Mr. Peyton	52
Leitch, Miss Margaret W.	142, 184, 200	Rust, Rev. J. O.	97
Leslie, Mr. W. S.	187	Rust, Mr. J. N.	52
Loggie, Mr. G. W.	187	Shand, Mr. Miles M.	97, 116, 191
MacArthur, Rev. R. S.	85, 97, 220	Shaw, Mr. William	105, 129, 154, 176, 187, 189
McAulay, Rev. N. A.	100	Shupe, Rev. H. F.	98
McCash, Rev. I. N.	45	Shurtleff, Rev. Ernest Warburton	81
McCauley, Rev. W. F.	128, 176	Spencer, Rev. I. J.	38
McCord, Rev. James	97	Starr, Sergeant	108
McCrory, Rev. James T.	115, 130, 147, 192	Stephan, Rev. C. A.	96
McFadden, Mr. E. S.	52	Sterns, Mr. W. D.	98
MacDonald, Mr. A. E.	186, 187	Steward, Mr. R. N.	186
McManiman, Rev. George	96	Sweeney, Rev. Z. T.	217
Manton, Rev. Chas.	13, 198	Sweet, Rev. C. W.	69, 192
Masson, Miss Jennie T.	188, 192	Swengel, Rev. U. F.	96
Maybury, Hon. Wm. C.	193	Swengel, Mrs. U. F.	96
Metcalf, Mr. E. P.	57, 97	Taylor, Judge Anson S.	129, 186
Miller, Rev. Rufus W.	98	Taylor, Rev. Preston	215
Moall, Miss Mary	97	Taylor, Gov. Robert L.	55
Moore, Rev. George W.	115	Tomkins, Jr., Rev. Floyd W.	41, 96, 100, 229
Moore, Mr. William	191	Travis, Miss Elsie L.	97, 185
Morgan, Gen. John T.	97, 170	Troxell, Rev. M. F.	96
Mosely, Mr. C. H.	191	Tyler, Rev. J. Z.	20, 140
Myers, Mr. H. S.	97	Vail, Rev. S. N.	49
Newnan, Rev. Charles B.	77, 168	Vance, Rev. James I.	53
Noell, Mr. W. L.	52	Vogler, Rev. W. H.	98
Palmer, Rev. C. J.	100	Wainwright, Mr. Thomas	185
Palmer, Prof. O. L.	97	Wallis, Mr. Frederick A.	114, 174, 215, 230
Patterson, Rev. William	42, 99	Walters, Bishop Alexander	28
Pence, Rev. E. H.	103	Washington, Pres. Booker T.	69
Pendelton, Rev. Philip Y.	71	Webb, Rev. B. Wrenn	193
Penfield, Rev. Thornton B.	117	Wells, Prof. Amos R.	120, 129
Perry, Rev. Barton W.	176, 191	Wheatley, Prof. Mrs. Ella C.	97
Petrie, Miss M. Josephine	99, 192	Willis, Mrs. F. I.	98
Phillips, Miss Lulu	191	Withers, Miss Rebel	185
Pierce, Rev. Robert F. Y.	231	Zartman, Rev. Parley E.	104
Pilcher, Mr. M. B.	52	Zirckel, Mrs. J. W.	97

www.ingramcontent.com/pod-product-compliance
Lightning Source LLC
Chambersburg PA
CBHW022355040426
42450CB00005B/187